SERIES ENDORSEMENTS

"There are so many fine commentaries available today, but it's great to have a reliable author you can turn to for solid Reformed reflections on Scripture. In this case, there are sixteen of them—friends and fellow shepherds who have given me great insight into God's Word over the years. I'm looking forward eagerly to each one of these sermonic commentaries!"

Michael S. Horton
J. Gresham Machen Professor of Apologetics and Systematic Theology at Westminster Seminary California
Host of the *White Horse Inn* Radio Show
Editor-in-Chief of *Modern Reformation* magazine

"Those of us who have promoted and practiced *lectio continua* expository preaching through the years eagerly await the volumes announced in The Lectio Continua Expository Commentary on the New Testament. We are equally eager to read such a series written by pastors who have practiced the method in their churches. The international and interdenominational character of the series will only add to the richness of its insights."

T. David Gordon
Professor of Religion and Greek at Grove City College
Author of *Why Johnny Can't Preach*

"As the history of preaching is unfolded, it becomes clear how important the orderly, systematic preaching through the Scriptures has been, and why it has been a favorite homiletic approach over the centuries. One is surprised to discover how many of history's great preachers made a regular practice of preaching through one book of the Bible after another. Origen, the first Christian preacher from whom we have any sizable collection of sermons, preached most of his sermons on the *lectio continua*. We find the same with John Chrysostom, who is usually referred to as the greatest Christian preacher. We find the same true of Augustine as well. At the time of the Protestant Reformation, Zwingli, Calvin, Bucer, and Knox followed this system regularly, and they passed it on to the Puritans. Today, we see a real revival of *lectio continua* preaching. The Lectio Continua Expository Commentary on the New Testament represents a wonderful opportunity for the church to recover a truly expository pulpit."

Hughes Oliphant Old
Formerly John H. Leith Professor of Reformed Theology and Worship at Erskine Theological Seminary
Author of *The Reading and Preaching of the Scriptures in the Worship of the Christian Church*

"The concept behind this series is a fascinating one and, given the list of authors, I am confident that the final product will not disappoint. This promises to be a great resource for churches seeking to know the Word of God more fully."

Carl R. Trueman
Professor of Biblical and Religious Studies at Grove City College

Romans

THE LECTIO CONTINUA
EXPOSITORY COMMENTARY ON THE NEW TESTAMENT

Series Editors

Joel R. Beeke | Jon D. Payne

Other available books in this series:

First Corinthians — Kim Riddlebarger
Galatians — J. V. Fesko
Ephesians — Ian Hamilton
Hebrews — David B. McWilliams
Revelation — Joel R. Beeke

Romans

J. V. Fesko

REFORMATION HERITAGE BOOKS
Grand Rapids, Michigan

Romans

Reformation Heritage Books
2965 Leonard St. NE
Grand Rapids, MI 49525
616-977-0889
orders@heritagebooks.org
www.heritagebooks.org

Printed in the United States of America
18 19 20 21 22 23/10 9 8 7 6 5 4 3 2 1

Library of Congress Cataloging-in-Publication Data

Names: Fesko, J. V., 1970- author.
Title: Romans / J.V. Fesko.
Description: Grand Rapids, Michigan : Reformation Heritage Books, 2018. | Series: The Lectio Continua expository commentary on the New Testament | Includes bibliographical references.
Identifiers: LCCN 2018012035 (print) | LCCN 2018020655 (ebook) | ISBN 9781601786203 (epub) | ISBN 9781601786197 (hardcover : alk. paper)
Subjects: LCSH: Bible. Romans—Commentaries.
Classification: LCC BS2665.53 (ebook) | LCC BS2665.53 .F47 2018 (print) | DDC 227/.1077—dc23
LC record available at https://lccn.loc.gov/2018012035

For additional Reformed literature, request a free book list from Reformation Heritage Books at the above regular or e-mail address.

Contents

seemingly new approach. But Zwingli explained that the *lectio continua* method of preaching was not new at all. On the contrary, important figures such as Augustine (d. 430), Chrysostom (d. 407), and Bernard of Clairvaux (d. 1153) all employed this homiletical approach. Zwingli is quoted by his successor, Heinrich Bullinger (d. 1575), as saying that "no friend of evangelical truth could have any reason to complain" about such a method.[4]

Zwingli rightly believed that the quickest way to restore biblical Christianity to the church was to preach the whole counsel of God verse by verse, chapter by chapter, book by book, Lord's Day after Lord's Day, year after year. Other Reformers agreed and followed his pattern. In the city of Strasbourg, just ninety miles north of Zurich, preachers such as Martin Bucer (d. 1551), Wolfgang Capito (d. 1570), and Kaspar Hedio (d. 1552) practiced *lectio continua* preaching. Johannes Oecolampadius (d. 1531) boldly preached the *lectio continua* in Basel. And let us not forget John Calvin (d. 1564); between 1549 and 1564, the Genevan Reformer preached sequentially through no fewer than twenty-five books of the Bible (over two thousand sermons), which he was able to do because he also preached regularly for weekday services.[5]

The example of these Reformers has been emulated by preachers throughout the centuries, from the post-Reformation age down to the present. In the last half of the twentieth century, Donald Grey Barnhouse (1895–1960), Martyn Lloyd-Jones (d. 1981), William Still (d. 1997), James Montgomery Boice (d. 2000), and John MacArthur all boldly preached straight through books of the Bible from their pulpits. But why? Surely we have acquired better, more

4. It is interesting to note that the year before Zwingli began preaching sequentially through books of the Bible, he had received a new edition of Chrysostom's *lectio continua* sermons on Matthew's gospel. See Hughes Oliphant Old, *The Patristic Roots of Reformed Worship* (Black Mountain, N.C.: Worship Press, 2004), 195. Cf. Hughes Oliphant Old, *The Reading and Preaching of the Scriptures in the Worship of the Christian Church,* vol. 4: *The Age of the Reformation* (Grand Rapids: Eerdmans, 2002), and Timothy George, *Reading Scripture with the Reformers* (Downers Grove, Ill.: IVP Academic, 2011), 228–53.

5. T. H. L. Parker, *Calvin's Preaching* (Edinburgh: T&T Clark, 1992), 159.

contemporary methods of preaching? Is the *lectio continua* relevant in our twenty-first-century context? In a day when biblical preaching is being increasingly undermined and marginalized by media/story/therapy/personality-driven sermons, even among the avowedly Reformed, these are important questions to consider.

Shortly before the apostle Paul was martyred in Rome by Emperor Nero, he penned 2 Timothy. In what proved to be some of his final words to his young disciple, he wrote, "I charge thee therefore before God and the Lord Jesus Christ...*preach the word;* be instant in season, out of season; reprove, rebuke, exhort with all longsuffering and doctrine" (2 Tim. 4:1–2 KJV). This directive was not meant only for Timothy. It is the duty of every Christian minister (and church) to heed these timeless words; according to God's divine blueprint for ministry, it is chiefly through the faithful proclamation of the Word that Christ saves, sanctifies, and comforts the beloved church for which He died.[6] In other words, the preaching of the gospel and the right administration of the sacraments are the divinely sanctioned and efficacious means by which Christ and all His benefits of redemption are communicated to the elect. For this reason alone the *lectio continua* method of preaching is a helpful practice in our churches, providing a steady diet of law and gospel from the entirety of God's Word.

Some may ask, "Why another expository commentary series?" First, because in every generation it is highly valuable to provide fresh and reliable expositions of God's Word. Every age possesses its own set of theological, ecclesiastical, and cultural challenges. Thus, it is beneficial for both current and rising ministers in every generation to have trustworthy contemporary models of biblical preaching. Second, these volumes uniquely feature the expositions of an array of pastors from a variety of Reformed and confessional traditions. Consequently, this series brings a wealth of exegetical, confessional,

6. See Matthew 28:18–20; Romans 10:14–17; 1 Corinthians 1:18–21; 1 Peter 1:22–25; Westminster Shorter Catechism, Q. 89.

experiential, and practical insight, and furnishes the reader with an instructive and stimulating selection of *lectio continua* sermons.

This series is not meant to be an academic or highly technical commentary. There are many helpful exegetical commentaries written for that purpose. Rather, the aim is to provide *lectio continua* sermons, originally delivered to Reformed congregations, which clearly and faithfully communicate the context, meaning, gravity, and application of God's inerrant Word. Each volume of expositions aspires to be redemptive-historical, covenantal, Reformed and confessional, Trinitarian, Christ-centered, and teeming with spiritual and practical application. Therefore, we pray that the series will be a profound blessing to every Christian believer who longs to "grow in the grace and knowledge of our Lord and Savior Jesus Christ" (2 Peter 3:18).

We are pleased to announce that this series of commentaries is now being published by Reformation Heritage Books, which graciously agreed to take over this large task from Tolle Lege Press. We thank Tolle Lege for printing the first three volumes (*First Corinthians* by Kim Riddlebarger, *Galatians* by J. V. Fesko, and *Hebrews* by David B. McWilliams). We, Joel Beeke and Jon Payne, look forward to coediting the remainder of the series for Reformation Heritage Books. The goal is to publish two volumes per year in the King James or New King James Version, according to the choice of each author.

In addition to thanking Reformation Heritage Books and its faithful team for producing this series, we wish to thank our churches, Christ Church Presbyterian, Charleston, South Carolina, and the Heritage Reformed Congregation, Grand Rapids, Michigan, for warmly encouraging us as ministers to work on projects such as this one that impact the wider church. Furthermore, we thank our dear wives, Mary Beeke and Marla Payne, and our precious children for their heartwarming support, which makes editing a series like this one possible. We both feel that God has greatly blessed us with God-fearing wives and children who mean more to us than words can express.

Finally, and most importantly, thanks and praise must be given to our blessed triune God, the eternal Fountain of all grace and truth. By His sovereign love and mercy, and through faith in the crucified, resurrected, and ascended Christ, we have been "born again, not of corruptible seed, but of incorruptible, by the word of God, which liveth and abideth for ever. For all flesh is as grass, and all the glory of man as the flower of grass. The grass withereth, and the flower thereof falleth away: but the word of the Lord endureth for ever. And this is the word which by the gospel is preached unto you" (1 Peter 1:23–25 KJV).

—Joel R. Beeke and Jon D. Payne, Series Editors

Acknowledgments

I want to thank Jon Payne and Joel Beeke, editors of the Lectio Continua series, for inviting me to contribute to this wonderful project by writing the installment on Romans. When I first received their e-mail I enthusiastically told my wife, Anneke, about this wonderful opportunity. But I was filled with excitement and angst at the thought of the honor and responsibility to write on what is probably Paul's most famous letter, if not the most famous letter in all of history. Nevertheless, I am humbled and grateful and pray that my modest contribution will both meet the high standards of the Lectio Continua series and in some small way help the church obtain a clearer and firmer understanding of Paul's majestic epistle.

I want to thank a number of people who read through early drafts of the book when it was in manuscript form, including David Winslow, Clif Daniel, Jonathan Cruse, and my faculty colleague, Dennis Johnson, who read portions of the manuscript. I am also grateful for the encouragement and love that my family gives me. Thank you, Anneke, for continuing to cheer me in my writing. And thank you, Val, Rob, and Carmen, for helping me stay grounded and remember that God has been kind to us in many ways, not only in the redemption we have through Christ but even in the small things in life.

I dedicate this book to my daughter, Carmen Penelope, who was born while I was in the midst of working on it. My wife was in labor, and in no pain, I should add, because of the wonders of modern medicine. Hence, the epidural freed me to do a little writing while we awaited your birth (I assure you that when it was time, I put my computer away—regardless of what your mother tells you). I was working on Romans 8 as I sat in the corner of the delivery room. As I thought about the riches of that passage I could not help but pray and hope that you, my daughter, will embrace the glorious gospel of Christ, and that you will never know a day apart from God's love in Christ—that neither height, nor depth, nor anything in the entire creation, death nor life, angels nor rulers, things present nor things to come, will ever separate you from the love of God in Christ Jesus our Lord. This, my precious little girl, was and is my hope and prayer for you.

Preface

I need to offer a few brief comments regarding the length and division of the material that follows. First, at times I have a slightly unorthodox approach to the way that I divide the text (I know, writing the word *unorthodox* in the same sentence as Romans might raise the hair on the back of your neck. Fear not!). I am aware of the amount of time that some pastors have taken to preach through Romans. Most famously, Martyn Lloyd Jones (1899–1981) preached through Romans over a period of thirteen years (1955–1968) in 366 sermons.[1] By comparison, my own sermon series, the basis for this expository commentary, lasted about one year and originally consumed fewer than fifty sermons. This was a brute fact of which I was keenly aware. I can remember watching the 1988 vice presidential debate between Senator Lloyd Bentsen and Dan Quayle in which the latter stated that he had more experience (in terms of years served) than John F. Kennedy. Bentsen famously responded, "Senator, I served with Jack Kennedy. I knew Jack Kennedy. Jack Kennedy was a friend of mine. Senator, you're no Jack Kennedy." I was fearful that people would wonder why I did not take things slowly, methodically, and deliberately. Why was I sprinting through Romans at breakneck speed? I could hear people mutter to themselves, "This young Turk is no Martyn Lloyd Jones...." But there was, and still is, a method to my homiletical madness.

1. Martyn Lloyd Jones, *An Exposition of Romans,* 13 vols. (Edinburgh: Banner of Truth, 2003).

I understand that there might be great benefit to savoring each individual textual morsel within Paul's magisterial letter, but pressing in the back of my mind was the truth that Romans would have been read in one sitting. When the church at Rome received the letter, they would have corporately gathered on the Lord's Day and had someone read it in its entirety. This truth encouraged me to take much larger portions of Romans at a time. Lloyd Jones, for example, has more than nine sermons on Romans 1:1–4, whereas I have one. When I preached through this book, I did not want my congregation to lose the forest for the trees. If one of the points of preaching *lectio continua* is to give the church a sense for the whole of the book, then I wanted my congregation to keep the big picture in view. I knew that my church could, if they wanted, delve more deeply into the particulars by reading, for example, Lloyd Jones's published sermons on Romans.

Second, this brings me to the way that I have divided the text. There are some sections in which I reflect on a few short verses, such as Romans 12:1–2. Yet there are other portions, such as Romans 7, that I take in one fell swoop. I believe that sometimes a close examination of a few verses is best, and other times, given the flow of Paul's argument, a much larger survey of his text is warranted so as not to lose his main point. I hope and trust that readers will be able to benefit from what I have written regardless of where their text-division convictions lie.

One last reflection comes to mind regarding this book. I suspect that some will sigh with disbelief, "Oh no, not another commentary on Romans." Well, if they have pressed past their commentary fatigue enough to read this far into the book, my hope is that they will consider the following. True, Romans is perhaps one of the most discussed books in the Bible. Ministers undoubtedly have shelves full of Romans commentaries. But as my grandfather used to say, "You can't give away what you don't own." In other words, I firmly believe that each and every generation must take possession of the truth. We cannot assume that if our fathers embraced these truths that their faith and admiration for Paul's letter will suffice.

I hope that each and every generation will continue to exegete, reflect, preach, and teach Paul's letter to the Romans so that they own it. And once they own it, they can pass its glorious truths on to the next generation. Indeed, Romans sets forth the glorious gospel of Christ, the power of God unto salvation. Each generation, therefore, must pursue this truth. Just as Jacob wrestled in the wilderness with the preincarnate Christ, we must grapple with the truths in Paul's epistle and refuse to let go until Christ blesses us. And even then, like Jacob's lifelong limp, our prayer should be that Paul's epistle would mark us for the rest of our lives.

Introduction

Paul's epistle to the Romans is perhaps one of the best-known books in the Bible and likely the most famous letter in all of history. Throughout church history this letter has influenced numerous significant and notable theologians. Saint Augustine (354–430), who is perhaps the greatest theologian in the history of the church, recounts in his autobiography, *Confessions*, that he was converted by reading Romans. He heard a voice say, "Tolle et lege [Take up and read]," and his eyes fell on Romans 13:13–14, "Let us walk properly, as in the day, not in revelry and drunkenness, not in lewdness and lust, not in strife and envy. But put on the Lord Jesus Christ, and make no provision for the flesh, to fulfill its lusts." These words shattered Augustine's stony heart and caused him to embrace Christ by faith. Augustine writes: "I neither wished nor needed to read further. At once, with the last words of the sentence, it was as if a light of relief from all anxiety flooded into my heart. All the shadows of doubt were dispelled."[1] Romans played a key role in the sixteenth-century Protestant Reformation. Martin Luther's (1483–1546) reflections on Romans 1:17, "For in it the righteousness of God is revealed from faith to faith; as it is written, 'The just shall live by faith,'" caused him to break with the common understanding of salvation promoted by the church, and he eventually embrace the gospel of free justification by faith alone. Luther reflects on his Romans meditations when he writes:

1. Augustine, *Confessions*, trans. Henry Chadwick (Oxford: Oxford University Press, 1991), 8.12.29 (pp. 152–53).

> Night and day I pondered until I saw the connection between the justice of God and the statement that "the just shall live by his faith." Then I grasped that the justice of God is that righteousness by which through grace and sheer mercy God justifies us through faith. Thereupon I felt myself to be reborn and to have gone through the open doors into paradise. The whole of Scripture took on a new meaning, and whereas before the "justice of God" had filled me with hate, now it became to me inexpressibly sweet in greater love. This passage of Paul became to me a gate to heaven.[2]

During the sixteenth century there was an explosion of new biblical commentaries due to the renewed interest in exegesis of the biblical text. Seventy commentaries on Romans led the way, with fourteen of them appearing in the decade between 1532 and 1542 alone.[3] Among the many theologians to write on Romans, John Calvin (1509–1564) noted that this one epistle was the key to unlocking the treasures of Scripture.[4]

Later, in the eighteenth century, Romans continued to leave an indelible impression on the lives of its readers, most notably in the heart of John Wesley (1703–1791). Wesley reluctantly attended a meeting on Aldersgate Street in the heart of London in which someone read the preface to Luther's commentary on Romans, and at that moment he famously testifies, "I felt my heart strangely warmed. I felt I did trust in Christ, Christ alone, for salvation; and an assurance was given me that He had taken away my sins, even mine, and saved me from the law of sin and death."[5] Nearly two centuries later in the wake of the devastating destruction of World

---

2. Roland H. Bainton, *Here I Stand: A Life of Martin Luther* (New York: Abingdon, 1950), 65.

3. T. H. L. Parker, *Commentaries on Romans, 1532–42* (Edinburgh: Bloomsbury T&T Clark, 2001), vii–viii; and David Steinmetz, ed., *The Bible in the Sixteenth Century* (Durham, N.C.: Duke University Press, 1990), 1.

4. John Calvin, *Romans and Thessalonians*, Calvin's New Testament Commentaries (1960; repr., Grand Rapids: Eerdmans, 1996), 5.

5. John Wesley, *The Works of the Rev. John Wesley* (London: The Conference Office, 1809), 1:280.

War I (1914–1918), another theologian turned to Romans. He surveyed the conflict that killed millions and left the fields of Western Europe charred and soaked with blood. He was naturally overwhelmed by the inhumanity and carnage he saw but also dismayed that his liberal theology professors had endorsed the policies of Kaiser Wilhelm II (1859–1941) that led to the calamitous war. Karl Barth (1886–1968) turned to Scripture and penned a commentary on Paul's famous epistle. To say the least, Barth's commentary on Romans was like an artillery shell dropped onto the theologians' playground. Barth famously wrote, "The Gospel is not a religious message to inform mankind of their divinity or to tell them how they may become divine. The Gospel proclaims a God utterly distinct from men. Salvation comes to them from Him, because they… have no right to claim anything from Him."[6]

While there are undoubtedly disagreements among the different theologians who have commented, preached, and exegeted Paul's famous letter, this much is certain—the epistle has left a deep and lasting impression on the life and theology of the church. Christians who willingly ignore this epistle, therefore, do so to the impoverishment and detriment of their faith.

Author, Date, Audience, and Occasion

There is no serious disagreement that the apostle Paul wrote this epistle, as the opening statement clearly indicates: "Paul, a bondservant of Jesus Christ, called to be an apostle, separated to the gospel of God" (Rom. 1:1).[7] Precisely when Paul wrote Romans is in question, but a likely time frame is somewhere between AD 55 and 58. And he likely wrote the letter from Corinth given that he entrusted the letter to Phoebe (Rom. 16:1–2), who was from the church in Cenchreae, one of the port cities of Corinth. Specifically why Paul

---

6. Karl Barth, *The Epistle to the Romans*, 6th ed., trans. Edwyn C. Hoskyns (1918; repr., Oxford: Oxford University Press, 1968), 28.

7. For introductory matters pertaining to Romans, see Thomas R. Schreiner, *Romans*, Baker Exegetical Commentary on the New Testament (Grand Rapids: Baker, 1998), 1–27.

wrote the letter is also clouded in a mild degree of uncertainty. Paul did not, for example, plant the church at Rome, as best as we can tell. Unlike the Galatian church, which he planted and was therefore concerned about their doctrinal drift from the gospel (Gal. 1:6–9), Paul wrote to the Roman church without having a personal history with them. The precise origins of the church are unknown, but it appears from what Paul writes in Romans 9–11, and to a certain extent in 14–15, that the Roman church consisted of Jews and Gentiles (cf. Acts 2:10; 18:1–3; Rom. 16:3–4). Given the diverse cultural backgrounds among the various Gentile people groups, and especially in comparison with Jewish practices and beliefs, there was tension between the two parties. It also appears that since Jews were expelled from Rome in AD 49 and Paul directs most of his pastoral counsel at Gentiles (e.g., Rom. 11:28–32), that Gentiles constituted the majority of the church at Rome. But what motivated Paul to write to Roman believers?

Some have suggested that Romans embodies a summary of Paul's theology given that Paul does not offer a specific conflict or occasion for writing the letter as he does in Galatians or 1 Corinthians. Since Paul states that his ministry was almost complete (Rom. 15:19), others have suggested that Romans constitutes a last will and testament of sorts. Another possibility is that Paul wrote the epistle to address the Jewish-Gentile tensions in the congregation. Apart from any explicit statements by Paul, the specific reason for the letter is anyone's guess, but at the same time we may safely assume that Paul had a number of reasons for writing, which included the desire to address the Jewish-Gentile tensions (likely common in many of the churches Paul knew) and to apply the gospel in its fullest sense to the church at Rome. Paul's desire was to see Roman believers unified by the gospel of Christ; hence, he sets forth his most systematic presentation of it. From beginning to end, Paul applied the gospel both to the glory of God and for the obedience of faith (Rom. 1:5; 16:26).

Key Themes

Given the expansive nature of Paul's epistle, there is a sense in which the apostle offers a panoramic view of the breadth, height, and depth of the gospel. Many of the passages in Romans are jack-in-the-boxes that suddenly open to reveal a massive amount of theological content. Nevertheless, Paul addresses subjects such as general and special revelation, the universal sinfulness of all humanity, justification by faith alone, union with Christ, sanctification, freedom from the law, adoption, prayer, the order of salvation, suffering, election, preaching, and the Christian life in its sundry relations within and without the church. While Paul addresses many subjects, Romans is not a comprehensive systematic theology, though his epistle is sweeping in its treatment of the nature of the gospel, and the power of God unto salvation: first for the Jew, then for the Greek (Rom. 1:16). But we should not think that Paul's letter is a dusty tome filled with theological conundrums and ethereal abstractions. We must recall that Paul first and foremost had the heart of a pastor and wrote to bring about the obedience of faith among his recipients.

Redemptive-Historical Context

One of the important aspects of Paul's letter to the Romans—indeed, for the entire New Testament corpus—is understanding the redemptive-historical context from which he writes. Many who come to the New Testament have a certain assumption about the nature of eschatology, or last things. They assume that the last days immediately anticipate the last sliver of history before the return of Christ and that the new heavens and earth do not begin until after Christ returns. By way of contrast, when New Testament authors talk about the last days and in-breaking of the new creation, they maintain that the last days begin with the first advent of Christ in His incarnation and that He inaugurates the new creation through the outpouring of the Spirit at Pentecost (cf. 1 Cor. 15:45; cf. Acts 2, esp. vv. 22–35). The following illustration shows the differences between the common misunderstanding and the biblical view:[8]

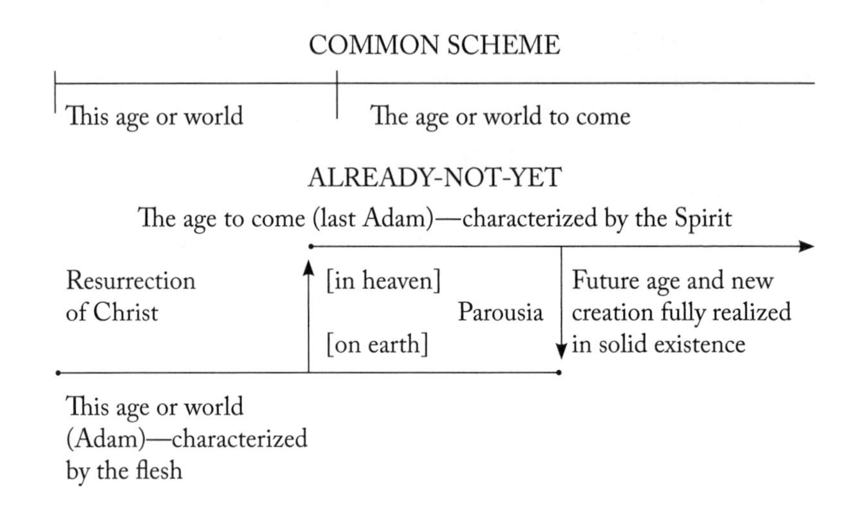

When Paul, for example, talks about the flesh-Spirit antithesis (e.g., Rom. 8:4–19; Gal. 3:3; 5:16–17; 6:8), he does not contrast the material and nonmaterial—that is, our supposedly sinful bodies versus an inherently superior disembodied spirit. Rather, Paul contrasts two overlapping periods of time that are each characterized by different things: the flesh (sin) for the present evil age, and the Spirit (holiness) for the age to come. Once Christ returns, however, the present evil age will be closed, and only the new creation will remain.

The structure of redemptive history, therefore, helps us understand both the big picture of Paul's letters and also key passages in his writings. As we will see in Romans 1:1–4, when Paul says Christ was descended from David "according to the flesh" and was "declared to be the Son of God with power according to the Spirit of holiness," he has in view this two-age structure, or what the New

8. This diagram is adapted from Geerhardus Vos, *The Pauline Eschatology* (Phillipsburg, N.J.: Presbyterian and Reformed, 1979), 38n45.

Testament calls this "present evil age" and the "age to come" (Matt. 12:32; 1 Cor. 1:20; 2:6–8; Gal. 1:4; Eph. 1:21; 1 Tim. 6:17; Heb. 9:9). Moreover, when Paul discusses many present redemptive realities, we can genuinely say that the new creation is here and that the last days, the eschaton, have dawned. But we do not want to mistakenly say that the present evil age in which we currently live has been totally eliminated. The present age will not pass away until Christ's return. This means, for example, that though we are presently raised and seated with Christ in the heavenly places (the already), we are nevertheless still subject to the temporal authorities of this present age until Christ's return (the not-yet) (cf. Eph. 2:6; Rom. 13:1–7). Hence, when references appear to this present evil age, the age to come, the inaugurated new creation, or the already-not-yet, readers should be familiar with the structure of redemptive history.

Basic Structure of Romans

While there are certainly more detailed outlines of Romans, readers should be aware of the following basic structure of Paul's epistle:

I. Introduction (1:1–15)
II. Thesis statement (1:16–17)
III. The universal sinfulness of humanity (1:18–3:20)
   a. Gentiles (1:18–32)
   b. Jews (2:1–3:8)
   c. Humanity (3:9–20)
IV. God's righteousness in justification (3:21–5:21)
   a. Received by faith alone in Christ alone (3:21–31)
   b. Old Testament evidence of Abraham (4)
   c. Peace with God (5:1–11)
   d. The consequences of the representative (dis)obedience of the first and last Adams (5:12–21)
V. The implications of justification (6–7)
   a. Justified from sin (6)
   b. Justified from the law (7)
VI. Life in the Spirit (8)
   a. Justification and the Spirit-led life (8:1–4)

- b. Life in the Spirit (8:5–13)
- c. Adoption (8:14–17)
- d. Suffering (8:18–25)
- e. Prayer (8:26–27)
- f. The order of salvation (8:28–30)
- g. The love of God (8:31–39)

VII. Election, proclamation, and God's faithfulness
- a. Election (9)
- b. Preaching the gospel (10)
- c. God's faithfulness to Israel (11)

VIII. Life as a living sacrifice (12:1–15:13)
- a. In the church (12:1–21)
- b. The civil government (13:1–7)
- c. The world (13:8–14)
- d. The weak and the strong (14:1–15:13)

IX. Paul's plans and final words (15:14–16:27)

Conclusion

While all of Scripture is a mine studded with precious gems and stones at every turn, the particular shaft that we call Romans is exceptionally adorned. My hope and prayer is that everyone who comes to Paul's famous letter would fall in love with Christ and be grateful for the life-changing message of His gospel. So, like Augustine, *tolle et lege*. Take up and read!

1

The King's Ambassador

ROMANS 1:1–7

Paul, a bondservant of Jesus Christ, called to be an apostle, separated to the gospel of God which He promised before through His prophets in the Holy Scriptures, concerning His Son Jesus Christ our Lord, who was born of the seed of David according to the flesh, and declared to be the Son of God with power according to the Spirit of holiness, by the resurrection from the dead. Through Him we have received grace and apostleship for obedience to the faith among all nations for His name, among whom you also are the called of Jesus Christ; To all who are in Rome, beloved of God, called to be saints: Grace to you and peace from God our Father and the Lord Jesus Christ.

Criminals do not have royal ambassadors. The authorities lock them up, punish them, and strip them of their rights for their crimes. People look down on them because of the shame that they bear. This is true in our own day as much as it was in the first-century Roman Empire. But this was even more so for crucified criminals. For those brigands who were arrested and hung on a cross, people would pass by and not look on them because of their criminal status and because of the gruesome sight. Death by crucifixion was a horrible way to die—painful, drawn out, and gory. So why would a former Hebrew of Hebrews, a Pharisee, and one who fastidiously obeyed the law identify himself as the ambassador of a crucified criminal (Phil. 3:9)? Paul provides the answer to this question by showing that the man the leaders of Israel and Roman authorities once crucified is indeed the King of kings, that Paul is His royal ambassador to the nations, and that Paul has been summoned to bring about the obedience of the nations.

The Inaugurated King

Like many other writers in the first century, the apostle Paul begins his own letter by identifying himself as the author. However, more important is the person that Paul serves. In this case, the significance of Paul's identity is directly proportional to the person whom he represents, Christ Jesus. That Paul lists the title *Christ* first (in the Greek text) is likely indicative of his desire to highlight immediately the identity of the person he serves (Rom. 1:1). Paul invokes the title of *Christ*, which is the transliterated Greek term that translates the Hebrew term *Messiah*. For any first-century Jew, the title of messiah would bring to mind a host of ideas and concepts. If, for example, a presidential candidate were to invoke the name of George Washington, American political history and ideas would come to people's minds. For the average first-century Jew, the Messiah was the one who was supposed to restore Israel's place of preeminence among the nations. The Messiah would run off Israel's oppressive Roman overlords. But for the person in tune with the Old Testament Scriptures, a different set of ideas would come to mind.

The Messiah was the One who would restore God's rule and authority to a fallen and rebellious creation—He would bring the raging and plotting nations under subjection to His authority (Psalm 2). The Messiah was the One who would sit at the right hand of God and rule in the midst of His enemies—indeed, He was equal to Yahweh (Psalm 110). The Lord's servant would be anointed to bring the good news to the poor, bind up the brokenhearted, and herald freedom to those imprisoned in captivity (Isa. 61:1). Paul identifies Jesus as *the* Christ, the Messiah, the Anointed of God. That Paul has these messianic ideas, promises, and images in view is highlighted by the fact that he states that Jesus and His gospel were "promised before through [God's] prophets in the Holy Scriptures, concerning His Son" (Rom. 1:2–3a). Paul does not make a unique point, as Jesus Himself stated this during His own ministry when the Jews were seeking to kill Him because He was "making Himself equal with God" (John 5:18). Jesus told His persecutors: "For if you believed Moses, you would believe Me; for he wrote about Me" (John 5:46). When Jesus was on the road to Emmaus, Luke tells us that Jesus, "beginning at Moses and all the Prophets…expounded to them in all the Scriptures the things concerning Himself" (Luke 24:27). It is one thing, however, for Paul to claim that Jesus was the Messiah. Some might doubt his assertion. But Paul does not appeal only to the Old Testament Scriptures. He also appeals to Christ's lineage and His resurrection from the dead.

Paul first identifies Jesus as one who was "born of the seed of David according to the flesh" (Rom. 1:3b). In some contexts the term *flesh* has a negative connotation, as Paul uses it to characterize sinful conduct such as the infamous "works of the flesh" (Gal. 5:19–21). In this context, however, the term does not bear negative overtones but instead refers to the incarnation of the Son of God. But note that Paul mentions the incarnation and also identifies Jesus as a descendant of David, no ordinary citizen of Israel. A long time ago, during the reign of David, Yahweh made a promise: "When your days are fulfilled and you rest with your fathers, I will set up your seed after you, who will come from your body, and I will establish his kingdom. He shall build a house for My name, and I will establish the throne of his kingdom forever" (2 Sam. 7:12–13). That Paul identifies Jesus as both the Messiah and the descendant of David tells the reader that Jesus is the embodiment of the fulfillment of God's covenant promises to His people.

But Paul continues and identifies Jesus as one "declared to be the Son of God with power according to the Spirit of holiness, by the resurrection from the dead" (Rom. 1:4). Even though Jesus, the son of David, was unrecognized by Israel as the legitimate heir to His Father's throne and was falsely arrested, convicted, and crucified, God overturned the wicked verdict. God the Father not only openly told the crowds gathered at Christ's baptism, "You are My beloved Son, in whom I am well pleased" (Mark 1:11), but also bellowed from the heavens that Jesus is His only begotten Son by

His resurrection from the dead. The religious leaders declared Jesus guilty of blasphemy, and God the Father reversed the verdict and declared His Son righteous. The resurrection from the dead was Jesus's inauguration as the King of kings. Because Jesus was obedient unto death, even death on the cross, God the Father exalted Him and bestowed on Him the name that is above all other names (Phil. 2:8–9). In the words of the psalmist: "I will declare the decree: The LORD has said to me, 'You are My Son, Today I have begotten You'" (Ps. 2:7). As the apostle Paul elsewhere explains, the psalmist's words, "today I have begotten You," refer to the resurrection of Christ (Acts 13:33).

But Paul's designation of Jesus as the descendant of David and the Son of God is not exhausted in terms of His identity alone. Rather, Paul also has in mind the two great epochs of redemptive history evident by his employment of the flesh-Spirit contrast.[1] Note, for example, the parallel that Paul presents:

who was born of the seed	declared
of David	to be the Son of God
according to the flesh	according to the Spirit of holiness
	by the resurrection from the dead

Jesus entered the world under the dominion of the fallen reign of Adam. During Jesus's temptation, Satan offered all the kingdoms of the world if only He would bow down and worship him (Matt. 4:1–11). Jesus refused; obeyed only His Father, even to the point of death on the cross; and was therefore exalted to His Father's right hand. In the words of Revelation, the great dragon, the serpent of old (Rev. 12:9), has been cast down from heaven—he no longer stands before God to accuse the saints (cf. Job 1:6–12; Matt. 12:25–29; Luke 10:18; Rev. 20:1–2). Rather, all authority in heaven

1. See Geerhardus Vos, "The Eschatological Aspect of the Pauline Conception of the Spirit," in *Redemptive History and Biblical Interpretation: The Shorter Writings of Geerhardus Vos*, ed. Richard B. Gaffin Jr. (Phillipsburg, N.J.: Presbyterian and Reformed, 1980), 91–125, esp. 103–5.

and earth has been given to King Jesus (Matt. 28:18–20). This means that the resurrection is one of the ways God has indicated that the last days are upon us. Christ has come in the flesh and has inaugurated the age of the Spirit, the new creation, the new heavens and earth. And with the new creation, God the Father has also inaugurated the reign of His Son, Jesus.

His Royal Ambassador

The long-awaited Messiah has come, and now the nations must submit to his reign. As the psalmist writes: "Serve the LORD with fear, And rejoice with trembling. Kiss the Son, lest He be angry, And you perish in the way, When His wrath is kindled but a little. Blessed are all who put their trust in Him" (Ps. 2:11–12). Indeed, Paul adds the title *Lord* to Jesus in Romans 1:3, an Old Testament title that belongs exclusively to Yahweh. What else is a person to do but bend the knee and serve this great King? This is why Paul identifies himself as the "bondservant" (literally, "slave") of Jesus Christ (Rom. 1:1). While this term might at first bear negative connotations, especially in our own day in which people view servitude or slavery quite negatively, read in their biblical context the appellation places Paul in a great line of godly servants of God including Moses, Joshua, Elijah, King David, and Nehemiah (Josh. 14:7; 24:29; 2 Kings 10:10; 18:12; Neh. 1:6).[2] Paul explains that he is, in effect, the royal ambassador, chosen by the King to herald the gospel; he has specifically "received grace and apostleship" (Rom. 1:5) from "Jesus Christ our Lord" (Rom. 1:3a). Paul did not take the office of apostle, or royal ambassador, for the Messiah on himself. He did not seek the job. In fact, the very opposite is true—Paul persecuted and sought to destroy the church. Instead, Christ Himself sought Paul, called him from the womb, set him apart as a prophet to the nations, and personally confronted Paul on the road to Damascus (Gal. 1:15–16; Acts 9:1–19).

---

2. Douglas Moo, *The Epistle to the Romans*, New International Commentary on the New Testament (Grand Rapids: Eerdmans, 1996), 41n7.

The Obedience of Faith

God chose Paul to herald the inaugurated reign of the Messiah—to call the nations away from their vain plotting against the Lord and His Anointed. But God set Paul apart both to call the nations unto repentance and to call them to obedience. Paul writes he was given his apostolic office "for obedience to the faith among all nations for His name" (Rom. 1:5). If Psalm 2 tells us anything, obedience does not come naturally to fallen man—the nations plot in vain and set themselves against the Lord and His Anointed (Ps. 2:2). Paul was certainly a microcosm of Psalm 2—one of the religious leaders of Israel setting himself up against the Lord and His Messiah. But God poured out His mercy on Paul and opened his eyes that he might believe in Jesus, the crucified and resurrected Messiah, and that Paul, by faith, would yield the obedience God desired—the obedience Paul was incapable of offering apart from God's grace in Christ. As we will see in the verses and chapters that follow, only by God's sovereign grace can someone turn and kiss the Son, the Messiah, and "put their trust in Him" (Ps. 2:12).

Nevertheless, Paul wrote to the church at Rome to continue his apostolic mission because they belonged to Jesus Christ—God loved and called them to be saints (Rom. 1:6–7a). It was the body of believers at Rome—both Jew and Gentile, slave and free, male and female, young and old—that had the longing of every faithful Israelite resting on them: "Grace to you and peace from God our Father and the Lord Jesus Christ" (Rom. 1:7b). The longing of the Aaronic blessing now rested on them, as the Lord shone the light of His face on His people and gave them peace in the face of His Son, Jesus Christ (Num. 6:24–26). They were no longer among those who set themselves against the Lord and His Anointed but were now among those who took refuge in the Messiah—they were no longer God's enemies but drew near through the shed blood of Christ. Paul wrote to these Roman Christians both to remind them of the tremendous blessings they had received and to give them a greater understanding of the faith they professed so that they might continue to yield the obedience of faith.

Conclusion

Despite the antiquity of Paul's message, one that stretches back two thousand years to the first century and beyond to the prophecies of the coming Messiah, it is still just as relevant today. We no longer live in the shadow lands of the Old Testament in which we behold Christ in types, sacrifices, the priesthood, or in promises yet to be fulfilled. We no longer wait with eager anticipation with the Old Testament saints for the dawning of the last days, the inauguration of the new creation, and the advent of the Messiah, King Jesus. We live in the wake of the advent of Christ. Yet we still face many of the prejudices and outright rebellion that Christ and Paul faced in their own day. Many regard Jesus as if He were a mere man, others as if He were simply a good man who died a martyr's death, and still yet others who look on Him and His claims with derision and outright hatred.

Yet God has called us, like Paul, by His grace and united us to the Messiah by faith. God has joined us to His body, a body called to give corporate witness to the gospel of Christ—a gospel that goes into the nations. This means that, humanly speaking, no matter the cost, we must support the corporate mission of the church. We must promote the gospel at every turn. We should pray, therefore, for faithful preachers. As Martin Luther once wrote, "If only the preachers remain orthodox and the doctrine is preserved, God will grant grace that among the multitude there will always be some who will accept the Word; for where the Word is pure and unadulterated, it cannot be without fruit."[3] In the face of opposition, persecution, rejection, and derision, we must never look on Jesus the way the world looks on Him. In the end, no matter how much they might offer empty praise, the world looks on Jesus as a mere man, a crucified fool. But we must pray that God in Christ would grant us the ability to look beyond what the world sees—that by faith we would behold the crucified and risen Messiah—the son of David

3. Martin Luther, *What Luther Says: An Anthology*, ed. Ewald M. Plass (St. Louis: Concordia, 1959), 3:1125, no. 3506.

and the Son of God. We should revel in God's faithfulness to His promises throughout the ages and be girded with hope knowing that He will be faithful to the end. We should praise God our heavenly Father in the knowledge that His Anointed sits on the throne and rules in the midst of His enemies. Armed with this knowledge, we must remember that nothing will ever separate us from the love of God in Christ—for we have peace with God in Christ, and He reigns over heaven and earth. When your sins rise up against you, remember that Christ has ascended His throne and cast down the accuser, Satan. Seek the forgiveness of your sins, kiss the Son, and put your trust in Him, the royal emissary of God's peace and love.

2

Setting the Agenda

ROMANS 1:8–15

First, I thank my God through Jesus Christ for you all, that your faith is spoken of throughout the whole world. For God is my witness, whom I serve with my spirit in the gospel of His Son, that without ceasing I make mention of you always in my prayers, making request if, by some means, now at last I may find a way in the will of God to come to you. For I long to see you, that I may impart to you some spiritual gift, so that you may be established—that is, that I may be encouraged together with you by the mutual faith both of you and me. Now I do not want you to be unaware, brethren, that I often planned to come to you (but was hindered until now), that I might have some fruit among you also, just as among the other Gentiles. I am a debtor both to Greeks and to barbarians, both to wise and to unwise. So, as much as is in me, I am ready to preach the gospel to you who are in Rome also.

In the business world the most efficient companies have effective meeting facilitators, and one of the keys to a successful meeting is setting a good agenda. In a similar fashion, Paul sets the agenda for his letter to Rome in the passage before us—he wants the recipients of his letter to know of his personal desire to see them, the reason for his desired visit, and the overall thrust of Paul's gospel ministry. At the heart of Paul's agenda in his letter to Rome, as well as his own ministry, is his passion to preach the gospel to the nations. Paul wanted the Romans to know of his desire not so they could be aware of Paul's personal hobby but so they could know the apostle's and their own divinely given agenda: to spread the gospel to the ends of the earth. Apart from this mission, Paul and the church in Rome were liable to drift from their godly purpose in life.

Paul's Desire to Visit

In our own communication-driven age, people can interact, sometimes for years, without ever meeting face-to-face. People send e-mails and texts, post comments on Facebook pages, or talk on the phone, but they might never meet in person. As a pastor-missionary, Paul's desire was to communicate with the church at Rome via his letter and also visit them. Paul received reports of the church's faith in Christ, as he writes, "Your faith is spoken of throughout the whole world" (Rom. 1:8b). Paul undoubtedly encountered the scorn and rejection of many in his ministry, as the Scriptures attest. It must have been greatly encouraging, therefore, to receive this good report: "The church in Rome is thriving!" When Christians adorn their faith in Christ with the fruit of good works, they are lamps shining in the darkness—lights that point back to Christ and His gospel. This is the obedience of faith (cf. Rom. 1:5). But on a darkened battlefield, bright light draws enemy fire; light immediately lets the enemy know where he needs to concentrate his fire. The light of Job's righteousness, for example, drew the persecution of Satan in his desire to extinguish Job's faith and embarrass God. Paul, therefore, made constant mention of the church in his prayers. "Without ceasing," writes Paul, "I make mention of you always in my prayers" (Rom. 1:9c–10a). Paul likely prayed that God would strengthen the church in Rome so they would serve as a faithful witness to Christ (Rom. 1:11b).

The Reason for Paul's Visit

But ultimately, to what end did Paul want to visit the church in Rome? He states that one of the chief objects of his incessant prayers was petitioning the Lord that he might visit Rome so that he could impart "some spiritual gift" (Rom. 1:11). Paul does not mean that he wanted to give the church spiritual gifts such as prophecy, tongues, and discernment, as he lists the gifts of the Spirit elsewhere (e.g.,

1 Cor. 12:4–10). Rather, Paul explains in the immediate context what he means by *spiritual gift*: "That I may be encouraged together with you by the mutual faith both of you and me" (Rom. 1:12). Paul was keenly aware how easily a Christian could be discouraged, whether by persecution, suffering, or tragedy. When Christians feel alone and isolated, these trials can have a deleterious effect on a church. Like beleaguered athletes at halftime, a team without someone to lead, encourage, and spur them on can falter in the face of adversity. Paul's role, however, was not merely that of a cheerleader or motivational speaker. Rather, as the rest of his epistle shows, Paul's desire was to bring the gospel as a source of encouragement—to bring spiritual sustenance, Christ, the manna from heaven, to those who were hungering and thirsting for righteousness. The gospel is not merely for the entry point to the Christian life; that is, the gospel does not become irrelevant once it is preached and converts are won to Christ. While such an idea might be common in the church today, it was utterly foreign to Paul's ministry and is at odds with the message of the Scriptures. But as much as Paul desired to visit the church in Rome, he was unable to do so (Rom. 1:13a–b). Paul's absence, however, was no impediment to conveying to the church the overall thrust of his ministry (his agenda, if you will).

The Thrust of Paul's Ministry

In this respect, Paul explains what his agenda is for his own ministry. He first says, "I am a debtor both to Greeks and to barbarians, both to wise and to unwise" (Rom. 1:14). When Paul writes that he was "a debtor," he refers to Christ's call on his life. Paul explained to the Galatians that he advanced in Judaism beyond many of his peers, persecuted the church, and tried to destroy the Christian faith (Gal. 1:13). But God set Paul apart before he was born so that he might preach Christ among the Gentiles (Gal. 1:15). In a dramatic fashion, Christ confronted Paul on the road to Damascus while he was "still breathing threats and murder against the disciples of the Lord" (Acts 9:1). Christ blinded Paul and told him to enter Damascus, where he would be told what to do (Acts 9:6). What Paul did not know was that around the same time a godly man named Ananias received a vision from the Lord in which he was told that Paul was God's chosen instrument to carry the name of God before the Gentiles, kings, and the children of Israel (Acts 9:10–16). Paul was under obligation to preach the gospel. Paul elsewhere writes: "For necessity is laid upon me; yes, woe is me if I do not preach the gospel!" (1 Cor. 9:16).

As recounted in the book of Acts, Paul's obligation was to preach the gospel both to Israel and the nations. There are a number of indicators in this passage that point us in this direction. Note that Paul congratulates the church in Rome because their "faith is spoken of throughout the whole world" (Rom. 1:8). Paul also mentions that his desire was to come to Rome that he might reap a harvest among them "just as among the other Gentiles" (Rom. 1:13). "Gentile," of course, is a term that encompasses all non-Jews—in effect, anyone not from Israel. Hence, Paul was under obligation "both to Greeks and to barbarians" as well as to "wise and to unwise" (1:14). Paul's terms cut across both racial boundaries and lines of human estimation and worth. In Paul's day, the "wise" were educated philosophers, such as the people he encountered at Mars Hill in Athens (Acts 17). The "unwise" were those of low esteem, means, or worth in the eyes of the cultured and educated classes of the ancient Greek world. Yet the gospel cuts across all such lines of division: Jew, Gentile, slave, free, male, female, young, old, wealthy, poor, high class, low class, cultured, or uncultured. For Paul, the gospel brings unity in place of division and strife, but that unity comes only in Christ.

The gospel of Christ consumed Paul's ministry. How differently his life compares to so many churches these days! Sadly, racial, economic, and cultural lines still divide many churches today. All too often churches spend great amounts of money, or go into significant debt, to build massive facilities, while their foreign and home missions budgets, by comparison, are paltry. What if a church spent ten million dollars on foreign or home missions instead of the same amount on a new building? The same can be said of individuals. While people undoubtedly have bills and all sorts of financial obligations, instead of taking that next vacation, buying that new car, or getting that new big screen TV, why not instead give that same money to support missions? In these two different scenarios involving churches and individuals, their actions are driven by agendas, whether formal or informal. A church may have an agenda to build a bigger sanctuary, or a person might have an agenda to increase his social status by acquiring a new car. However, just because a church builds a new facility or a person purchases a new car does not automatically mean they are driven by sinful agendas.

It is important for churches and people to ask what their agendas are. As D. A. Carson notes regarding Western evangelicalism's penchant for plans and fads for ministry success, "I fear that the cross, without ever being disowned, is constantly in danger of being dismissed from the central place it must enjoy, by relatively peripheral insights that take on far too much weight. Whenever the periphery is in danger of displacing the center, we are not far removed from idolatry."[1] Carson's insight is profoundly applicable to the question of what agenda drives our lives and those of our churches.

Do we align ourselves with the divinely given agenda of the church in the Great Commission? We, like Paul, have received a personal commission from the risen Christ. The church has been given the task to be a light unto the nations—to see that people of every tribe, tongue, and nation hear the proclamation of the gospel. This was Paul's commission and heart's desire, so much so that he was in anguish throughout his ministry for the lost as well as for the church (e.g., Acts 17:16; Rom. 9:3; Gal. 4:19). But bringing about a radical reprioritization in the agenda of a church or individual is not simply a matter of making a motion at a church business meeting or allocating money to a different place in one's personal budget.

Paul was eager to preach the gospel in Rome and to reap a harvest among them and the Gentiles in that city for a reason

1. D. A. Carson, as quoted in Paul Keidel, *Career-Defining Crises in Mission: Navigating the Major Decisions of Cross-Cultural Service* (Pasadena, Calif.: William Carey Library, 2012), 173.

(Rom. 1:13, 15). Recall that Paul wrote in the opening verses of his epistle that he was set apart by God's grace "for obedience to the faith among all nations for [Christ's] name" (Rom. 1:5). In other words, only God's grace in Christ and the gospel enables sinful people to repent, embrace Christ, change their ways, and reorder their lives according to the gospel. Only God's grace in Christ enabled Paul to see his own sinfulness, repent, and make the gospel the chief priority in his life. Only the gospel has the power to change lives and congregations to embrace Christ's agenda for the church—baptizing the nations, preaching, and teaching people to believe in Christ and do all that He commands (Matt. 28:18–19). The reliance on God's grace in Christ and the gospel was exhibited in Paul's own conduct. Paul prayed fervently and unceasingly for the church in Rome, for he knew that only by God's grace in Christ would the church grow, mature, and add to its numbers.

Conclusion

Our desire, both corporately and individually, should be that Christ's agenda orders and prioritizes our lives. Pray that Christ conforms us to His image and that we reflect His holiness and righteousness. Pray that God gives us a passion and zeal for the lost, a concern that manifests in our prayer lives and conduct. And pray that our churches cease to look like us but instead reflect the image of God as it shines forth in the divine image bearers of every tribe, tongue, nation, and walk of life. In the end, our prayer should be that Christ would set the agenda for our lives.

3

The Thesis of Paul's Letter

ROMANS 1:16–17

For I am not ashamed of the gospel of Christ, for it is the power of God to salvation for everyone who believes, for the Jew first and also for the Greek. For in it the righteousness of God is revealed from faith to faith; as it is written, "The just shall live by faith."

One of the more difficult things for seminary students to learn is how to write a solid research paper. When I am grading, one of my standard comments is, "Where is your thesis statement?" In other words, what are you trying to prove? What is the point of your paper? A good research paper states its thesis, its purpose, the whole reason for the paper at the outset. This way the reader knows where things are headed. Over the centuries, theologians have called the two verses before us the thesis statement of Paul's epistle to the Romans. While we do not want to hold Paul to the writing standards of our own day, we can certainly appeal to the idea of a thesis statement and appreciate that most of what Paul writes in the chapters that follow, in one way or another, emanates from these two short verses.

What is Paul's thesis? In a nutshell, Paul's chief point is the power, scope, and nature of the gospel. What is so special about the gospel? It is the power of God unto salvation. What is the scope of the gospel? It has been given to all who believe: first to the Jew, then to the Greek. And what is the nature of the gospel? In the gospel God reveals His righteousness, from faith to faith, which is that the righteous shall live not by works but by faith in the One whom God has sent to redeem fallen people from their sin. But lest we think that Paul's thesis is merely an academic endeavor and that we only read a research paper, I think it is helpful to descend into the original context of the last words of verse 17—namely, "The just shall live by faith." In so doing, we will have a proper frame of reference for understanding the grandeur and significance of Paul's thesis statement for Romans.

The Old Testament Background

We should always remember that for Paul, his Bible was the Old Testament. This fact is evident by virtue of his constant use of the Old Testament in his letters. In this case, Paul ends verse 17 with a quotation from Habakkuk 2:4, "The just shall live by his faith." What has this Old Testament verse to do with the thesis of Paul's letter? What has this statement to do with the gospel? In its original context, the prophet Habakkuk poured out his despair to the Lord. The prophet was gravely concerned for the spiritual state of Israel. He looked on the land and did not see righteousness, holiness, or godliness—only violence, iniquity, and persecution of the righteous (Hab. 1:2–4). Recall the stipulations of the Mosaic covenant: If Israel obeyed, she would enjoy long life in the land, but if she disobeyed she would suffer the curses of the covenant (Deuteronomy 28). Habakkuk was well aware of these stipulations and therefore knew Judah was in grave danger. The northern kingdom of Israel had already been taken away into exile; hence, Habakkuk knew the real dangers of the Mosaic covenant's curses. Habakkuk consequently cried out to the Lord and pleaded that He would intervene (Hab. 1:2). God responded to Habakkuk's prayers but in an unexpected way. The Lord told Habakkuk that He would raise up the Chaldeans (the Babylonians), a pagan Gentile people, to attack Israel and carry them off into captivity.

Habakkuk was stunned, shocked, and perplexed. How could Yahweh, One who cannot bear to look on evil, allow the Babylonians, a wicked pagan nation, to invade, destroy, and carry Judah away into captivity (Hab. 1:13)? We could even say that Habakkuk was angry at God's announcement of judgment. Sure, Judah was wicked, but how could Yahweh tolerate and use a people even more wicked than Judah, a people who would not only sweep away Judah's covenant breakers but also the righteous? Despite the impropriety of Habakkuk's complaint (after all, what right has the creature to question the righteousness of the Creator?), God nevertheless mercifully replied to Habakkuk: "Behold the proud, His soul is not upright in him; But the just shall live by his faith" (Hab. 2:4). Despite the apparent moral complexity of God's actions, His answer is simple yet profound.

God tells Habakkuk that He is fully aware that the Babylonians are proud, puffed up, arrogant, and wicked (cf. Hab. 1:10–11). But by contrast, God also knows that the just (or righteous) will live by faith. In other words, God is not blind to the condition of His people nor has He forgotten His covenant promises. In fact, God's words to Habakkuk echo the description of Abraham. The great patriarch looked on his own life with utter despair. He had no male heir; God had entered into a covenant with him and promised him many offspring (Gen. 12:2), but Abraham was still childless. Abraham and Sarah were as good as dead—they were well beyond childbearing age. Yet even in the absence of the realization of God's promise, Abraham took God at His word: "And he believed in the LORD, and He counted it to him for righteousness" (Gen. 15:6). Abraham believed in the promise of the gospel, as Paul tells us later in Romans (4:3) and in Galatians (3:6–8), and therefore God "counted" or imputed righteousness to Abraham. God did not see the deceitful contriver but rather one who was perfectly righteous and holy (Gen. 12:10–20; 16:1–4; 20:1–17; Deut. 6:25). Abraham did not receive this righteous status by his own works but by faith alone in Christ alone. This faith and trust in Yahweh was strong, as it did not waver in the face of Abraham's childless situation. In the absence of the fulfillment of God's promise, Abraham nevertheless believed in the Lord. This was God's message to Habakkuk, "Continue to trust me even in the face of circumstances that might lead you to believe that I have forgotten you. I have not and will not forget My covenant promises to you, My people." This message lies at the heart of Paul's epistle to the Romans and is the reason he quotes Habakkuk 2:4 in the thesis statement of his letter.

The Power of the Gospel

Given the Old Testament background of Paul's quotation of Habakkuk 2:4, we are in a better position to understand the power of the gospel. Far too many people look on the church and its preaching as empty talk—people gathering to hear someone in a suit deliver platitudes and good advice. Karl Marx (1818–1883) once wrote: "Religion is the sigh of the oppressed creature, the heart of a heartless world, and the soul of soulless conditions. It is the opium of the people."[1] In other words, in the face of suffering, illness, and tragedy, if you tell people about heaven, a place free from all earthly troubles, a place where they will one day go, then they will endure their present circumstances. Tell people of utopia, a place where one day in the sweet by and by they will go to that wonderful place in the sky, and they will forget about the pain they feel from hunger, the cold they feel from lack of adequate clothing, and the absence of justice they have in the face of oppression.

But notice that this is precisely what Paul does not say. Paul does not apply a bandaid to the mortal wounds of humanity. Paul writes that the gospel is "the power of God to salvation for everyone who believes" (Rom. 1:16b). The gospel is the means by which God frees sinners from bondage and raises people from death in sin to life in Christ. The same power that brought worlds into existence, what we see all around us in this sin-fallen but nevertheless beautiful and awe-inspiring creation, is the same power set loose in the gospel of Jesus Christ: "For it is the God who commanded light to shine out of darkness, who has shone in our hearts to give the light of the knowledge of the glory of God in the face of Jesus Christ"

1. Karl Marx, introduction to *A Contribution to the Critique of Hegel's Philosophy of Right*, in *Collected Works*, ed. Joseph O'Malley (1843–44; repr., Cambridge: Cambridge University Press, 1970), 3:3.

(2 Cor. 4:6). The gospel brings the transformative power of God to bear on the lives of sinners. Certainly, Paul's own life was dramatically changed by the gospel. One moment Paul was persecuting the church, seeking to imprison and even kill Christians, and the next moment he was in the grip of Christ's grace, transformed (Acts 9:1–19). He became a shepherd willing to lay down his life for his sheep; Paul was transformed according to the image of his Savior, Jesus Christ. And for this reason, Paul was unashamed of the gospel of Christ (Rom. 1:16a).

The Scope of the Gospel

But as powerful as the gospel of Christ is, a person must still place his faith in Christ. Faith is, of course, a divinely given gift (Eph. 2:8–10). Nevertheless, a person cannot be saved apart from faith in Christ. This is one of the drumbeats that Paul sounds throughout the whole of the epistle of Romans and one that he begins to pound in his thesis statement of the letter, as the gospel is "the power of God to salvation for everyone who believes" (Rom. 1:16b). Paul highlights the importance of salvation by faith alone in Christ alone here in his thesis statement. Abraham and Habakkuk illustrate the importance of salvation by faith alone. God does not save us by our obedience but by believing that Christ's obedience saves us.

God's mercy is wide and great, and He has dispensed it universally through the preaching of the gospel—the message has gone out to every tribe, tongue, and nation. The sun used to set on the borders of the gospel, as only Israel possessed it and the surrounding pagan nations did not. But ever since Pentecost and the reversal of the curse of Babel, the nations are no longer divided according to race and language but are united in Christ through the gospel in whom there is neither Jew nor Greek, slave nor free, male nor female (Gal. 3:28). But in case we might think God has forgotten about Israel in the universal dispensation of the gospel, Paul explains that the gospel is the power of God unto salvation for everyone who believes, "for the Jew first and also for the Greek" (Rom. 1:16c).

God first came to Abraham, the great patriarch of Israel. He then made His covenant with Israel as they stood at the foot of Sinai beneath the ominous dark clouds of His holy presence. Jesus did not descend from the Gentile nations but from Abraham, Isaac, Jacob, and David. Paul writes that from Israel "are the fathers and from whom, according to the flesh, Christ came, who is over all, the eternally blessed God. Amen" (Rom. 9:5). And though Gentiles have been received into the covenant people of God, we must not forget that we were aliens from the commonwealth of Israel and covenants of promise who have been brought near by the blood of Christ (Eph. 2:12–13). These are all themes that Paul unpacks in greater detail in the coming chapters, but the point still stands—the scope of the gospel is universal, but it does go to the Jew first and then to the Greek, the Gentile. Therefore, no one can claim that the gospel is irrelevant. No one can claim he does not need Christ, because all people, both Jew and Gentile, lie under God's just judgment for their sin.

The Nature of the Gospel

The power and the scope of the gospel, then, hopefully will help us understand its nature. Paul explains that God reveals His righteousness in the gospel in terms of His faithfulness to His covenant promises to His people—this point is evident in Paul's quotation of Habakkuk 2:4, which also has allusions to Genesis 15:6 and God's faithfulness to His promises to Abraham. A person would not be righteous if he promised to do something and then reneged on his promise. But what does it mean when we say that God is righteous in fulfilling His covenant promises? What did God promise to do? Did He merely promise to vindicate Israel against the pagan Babylonians? Did He only promise to give Abraham an heir, which would eventually lead to descendants as numerous as the sands on the seashore? In particular, if we dig into the bedrock of God's statement to Habakkuk, that the righteous will live by faith, all the way to His promise to Abraham, I believe we find an answer.

In God's covenant dealings with Abraham, He had the patriarch cut animals in two and line them up. Ordinarily, the two parties of a covenant walked between the severed animal halves indicating what would happen if either person violated the terms of the agreement. But in that Genesis narrative, who alone walked between the severed animal halves? God, represented by the flaming torch, walked between the animal halves while Abraham was fast asleep (Gen. 15:9–21). God took the oath of self-malediction and in effect said, "If I break My word, may this curse fall upon Me, and if you, Abraham, break your word, may this curse fall upon *Me*." But God did not promise merely to bear the curse of the covenant, as amazing as such a promise is. He also promised and gave to Abraham his legal standing: "And he believed in the LORD, and He accounted it to him for righteousness" (Gen. 15:6). God promised and gave to Abraham righteousness. That is, when God looked on Abraham He viewed him as one who was in perfect conformity to the law, not merely innocent. In other words, the gospel reveals the righteousness that God gives to His people, the perfect obedience of Christ. This is a righteousness, Paul says, that comes by faith alone, which he emphasizes by the phrase, "from faith to faith" (Rom. 1:17a; cf. 2 Cor. 2:16).

Here the Heidelberg Catechism is helpful in its question and answer, "How are you righteous before God?" The catechism responds:

> Only by a true faith in Jesus Christ; that is, though my conscience accuse me that I have grievously sinned against all the commandments of God and kept none of them, and am still inclined to all evil, yet God, without any merit of mine, of mere grace, grants and imputes to me the perfect satisfaction, righteousness, and holiness of Christ, as if I had never had nor committed any sin, and myself had accomplished all the obedience which Christ has rendered for me; if only I accept such benefit with a believing heart. (Q. 60)[2]

2. This and subsequent quotations from the catechism come from the version contained in *Ecumenical and Reformed Creeds and Confessions: Classroom Edition* (Dyer, Ind.: Mid-America Reformed Seminary, 1991).

I can think of no more terrifying moment than to stand before a holy God, stained with guilt and sin, knowing that I am worthy of condemnation. But I can think of no greater blessing than to know that because of what Christ has done for me I stand righteous in God's sight and no longer know of the law's condemnation or God's wrath against my sin. I no longer know God as judge but only as my loving father and Christ as my loving brother who laid down His life for me, the prodigal son who refused to come home. This same truth holds true for *anyone* who believes in Christ—we are no longer rebels but sons of the living God.

Conclusion

This is the righteousness that God reveals in the gospel, and this is why Paul was unashamed of the gospel, for he personally knew that it was the power of God unto salvation, first for the Jew, then for the Greek. This is Paul's thesis statement for the whole of his epistle to the Romans. This message was the heartbeat of Paul's preaching, and he wanted to expound on this central truth in terms of our redemption as well as its significance for the Christian life. Faith is both the exclusive means by which we receive the imputed satisfaction, righteousness, and holiness of Christ, and the lens through which we must live our entire lives. We must trust Christ not only for our salvation but also with our very lives. In the face of suffering, persecution, a guilt-stricken conscience, a need for wisdom, great fear, severe illness, and anything that we encounter in life, we must remember that the righteous shall live by faith. This is the thesis of Paul's epistle to Rome, but it should be the thesis for our entire lives.

4

The Revealed Wrath

ROMANS 1:18–32

For the wrath of God is revealed from heaven against all ungodliness and unrighteousness of men, who suppress the truth in unrighteousness, because what may be known of God is manifest in them, for God has shown it to them. For since the creation of the world His invisible attributes are clearly seen, being understood by the things that are made, even His eternal power and Godhead, so that they are without excuse, because, although they knew God, they did not glorify Him as God, nor were thankful, but became futile in their thoughts, and their foolish hearts were darkened. Professing to be wise, they became fools, and changed the glory of the incorruptible God into an image made like corruptible man—and birds and four-footed animals and creeping things. Therefore God also gave them up to uncleanness, in the lusts of their hearts, to dishonor their bodies among themselves, who exchanged the truth of God for the lie, and worshiped and served the creature rather than the Creator, who is blessed forever. Amen. For this reason God gave them up to vile passions. For even their women exchanged the natural use for what is against nature. Likewise also the men, leaving the natural use of the woman, burned in their lust for one another, men with men committing what is shameful, and receiving in themselves the penalty of their error which was due. And even as they did not like to retain God in their knowledge, God gave them over to a debased mind, to do those things which are not fitting; being filled with all unrighteousness, sexual immorality, wickedness, covetousness, maliciousness; full of envy, murder, strife, deceit, evil-mindedness; they are whisperers, backbiters, haters of God, violent, proud, boasters, inventors of evil things, disobedient to parents, undiscerning,

> *untrustworthy, unloving, unforgiving, unmerciful; who, knowing the righteous judgment of God, that those who practice such things are deserving of death, not only do the same but also approve of those who practice them.*

Many are under the impression that eschatology, or the "end times," is entirely a future phenomenon. For example, many God-fearing evangelical Christians believe that God's judgment against the wicked awaits the second coming of Christ. While it is true that we await the second coming of Christ and the final judgment of the wicked and the vindication of the righteous, we must realize that the last days are already upon us. The eschatological age has dawned with the advent of Christ. The kingdom of God was inaugurated in the ministry of Christ—with the arrival of the king you get the kingdom, and with the arrival of the kingdom you have the arrival of the end of the age.

Events such as the resurrection of the dead are not entirely future but have begun with the resurrection of Christ (1 Cor. 15:20). The head has been raised, and now we await the resurrection of the body, or the church. The point is this: Those things that pertain to the last days are not an exclusively future phenomenon. The eschatological age has dawned and brought both the beginnings of the blessings as well as the initial stages of God's judgment on the wicked. Thus, the wicked do not experience the wrath and judgment of God as an exclusively future event. On the contrary, Paul shows us in this portion of Romans that God presently reveals His wrath and judgment. Paul explains that God's wrath falls on the wicked even now and that this is a foretaste of the final judgment at the second coming of Christ. In this portion of Romans Paul expounds on the nature of this judgment, which demands that we give it careful consideration, as it seems to be an immensely practical thing to consider the wrath and judgment of God and the means He has given to escape it.

The Consequences of Unrighteousness

At the outset of this section Paul writes of the wrath of God that is revealed against all ungodliness and unrighteousness, and against those who wickedly suppress the truth (Rom. 1:18). This statement should be read against the context of its antithetical counterpart in verse 17—namely, that God's righteousness is "revealed from faith to faith." Fallen humanity represents the inverse reflection of God's holiness and righteousness, a contrasted light versus darkness. But verse 17 also reminds us that, even though Paul invokes the category of wrath, this does not mean that God acts unjustly. Human expressions of wrath are typically sinful, but this is not the case with God's wrath. In this case God manifests His righteousness both in the mercy He extends to the elect and in the judgment He pours out on the wicked. God is righteous both in His mercy and wrath. But what, specifically, does Paul mean by God's *wrath*?

God's wrath is not the fitful explosion of passion and rage that might be associated with sinful human expression. Rather, it is "the holy revulsion of God's being against that which is the contradiction of his holiness."[1] Why does God reveal His wrath against those who suppress the truth in unrighteousness? Paul answers this question in the following verse: "Because what may be known of God is manifest in them, for God has shown it to them" (Rom. 1:19). Contrary to the agnostic belief that there is insufficient data either to confirm or deny God's existence, there is an abundance of evidence. God manifests the knowledge of His existence not only *in* man (e.g., Rom. 2:14–15) but also *to* man.

Paul explains how God demonstrates His existence: "For since the creation of the world His invisible attributes are clearly seen, being understood by the things that are made, even His eternal power and Godhead, so that they are without excuse" (Rom. 1:20). God clearly manifests His attributes in and throughout creation. Here Paul echoes the psalmist, who writes: "The heavens declare the

---

1. John Murray, *The Epistle to the Romans*, New International Commentary on the New Testament (Grand Rapids: Eerdmans, 1968), 35.

glory of God; And the firmament shows His handiwork. Day unto day utters speech, And night unto night reveals knowledge. There is no speech nor language Where their voice is not heard. Their line has gone out through all the earth, And their words to the end of the world" (Ps. 19:1–4). The sixteenth-century Reformer John Calvin (1509–1564) echoes these sentiments in his own explanation of Paul's words when he writes that God's

> wisdom is seen, because He has arranged all things in perfect order; His goodness, because there is no other cause for His creation of all things, nor can any other reason than His goodness itself induce Him to preserve them. His justice is evident in His governing of the world, because He punishes the guilty and defends the innocent; His mercy because He bears the perversity of men with so much patience; and His truth, because He is unchangeable.[2]

Paul joins the symphonic chorus with all created things that heralds the existence and attributes of its wise, powerful, and just Creator.

Given Over to Sin

But despite the clarity of the revealed knowledge of God through the creation, humanity does not glorify God as it should. Even though humans knew God, they became futile in their thinking, their foolish hearts were darkened, and they refused to worship the one true God, their Creator—they became fools (Rom. 1:20–21). Keep in mind, we sometimes use the term *fool* to denote a lack of intelligence. According to Scripture, however, the fool does not lack information or intelligence but rather wisdom—the wisdom to fear God: "The fool has said in his heart, 'There is no God'" (Ps. 14:1). Humanity, in all its claims to wisdom, does not turn its gaze to the heavens to worship the Creator as it ought but instead looks down on the earth and worships creatures. Humanity, writes

---

2. John Calvin, *Romans and Thessalonians*, Calvin's New Testament Commentaries (1960; repr., Grand Rapids: Eerdmans, 1996), 32.

Paul, "changed the glory of the incorruptible God into an image made like corruptible man—and birds and four-footed animals and creeping things" (Rom. 1:23). In a sense, Paul paints a picture of the creation that has been turned upside down, as he uses virtually the same language of the Genesis creation account that appears in the Greek translation of the Old Testament. In the original Genesis creation narrative in which God created "cattle and creeping thing and beast of the earth, each according to its kind" (Gen. 1:24), the whole point of the text was to demonstrate that the creatures were lowly, that they paled in comparison to humanity, which alone was created in the image of God (Gen. 1:27). Rather than worship the lowly creatures or even bow down to worship man, as lofty and exalted as his place was in creation (e.g., Psalm 8), humanity was supposed to worship God. But instead of worshiping God, humanity has turned to worship creatures and things—idols fabricated by the twisted imagination of fallen people.

This wanton disregard for God's sole place as the rightful recipient of worship does not go unnoticed or unpunished. In the verses that follow, Paul explains the other side of God's righteous and holy character—His wrath unleashed against wickedness. The just, who live by faith (Rom. 1:17), receive God's righteousness through Christ and by faith alone, which is revealed in the gospel. Conversely, the unrighteous, who do not live by faith, receive the revealed wrath of God: "Therefore God also gave them up to uncleanness, in the lusts of their hearts, to dishonor their bodies among themselves, who exchanged the truth of God for the lie, and worshiped and served the creature rather than the Creator, who is blessed forever. Amen" (Rom. 1:24–25). God reveals His wrath against the wicked in divine abandonment—He gives them over to the wicked lusts of their hearts and no longer restrains their sin.

Homosexuality and Idolatry

Paul indicates that there is a cause-and-effect relationship between idolatry, wrath, and judgment when he begins verse 26 with the words, "For this reason," and then follows with the revealed judgment: "God gave them up to vile passions. For even their women exchanged the natural use for what is against nature. Likewise also the men, leaving the natural use of the woman, burned in their lust for one another, men with men committing what is shameful, and receiving in themselves the penalty of their error which was due" (Rom. 1:26–27). Paul's characterization of God's judgment against idolatry has frequently been maligned, misunderstood, and ridiculed. Perhaps in his day, some have said, Paul's fears of homosexual expressions of "love" were common, but in our own supposedly advanced understanding of sexuality, such opinions are false and prejudicial—even downright hateful.

But once again, people infrequently factor in the background and theological point of Paul's statements. Remember, for Paul (and any other first-century theologian), the Old Testament was his Bible. Paul may not have footnoted or cited a specific Old Testament passage, but his language about unnatural male and female relations invokes the recollection of the judgment that fell on Sodom and Gomorrah (Genesis 19). Recall that the men of the city approached Lot's home when they learned that he had two male visitors—their desire was to rape them (Gen. 19:4–5). This incident was only the tip of the iceberg, as it revealed the wicked hearts of the inhabitants of the city, people who were prideful, gluttonous, materialistic, willfully ignorant of the plight of the poor and needy, and idolatrous in addition to being sexually immoral (cf. Ezek. 16:48–50; Lev. 18:22, 26–27; Deut. 7:25–26). One point to note is that Paul develops these themes as he writes his epistle, especially in chapter 3. Giving idolaters over to unnatural relations and its consequent judgment was not something for Gentiles alone, such as the inhabitants of Sodom and Gomorrah, but also for Israel (Isa. 1:10; Jer. 23:14). In other words, at this point Paul does not play favorites but offers a universal indictment against all of humanity.

Another important consideration that demonstrates that Paul is not homophobic is the language that he uses to characterize homosexual relations; he describes it as uncleanness (*akatharsian*). A theology of worship grounds Paul's aversion to homosexuality.

The Greek term Paul employs appears in numerous Septuagint (LXX, the Greek translation of the Old Testament) texts that govern worship and dwelling in the presence of the one, true, holy God (e.g., Lev. 5:3; 7:21; 15:30; Num. 19:13; Judg. 13:7; 2 Chron. 29:5; Ezra 9:11; Prov. 6:16). What ultimately lies at the heart of God's judgment is false worship—man turns to worship the creature and things made by his own hands rather than the Creator, so God abandons him to his idolatry and man turns to worship himself. If unchecked, sinful, idolatrous man will look into the proverbial mirror, fall in love with himself, worship himself, and engage in idolatry through unnatural sexual relations. Sinful humanity, male and female, turns and worships itself and becomes smitten with its own image.

In a world that likes to compartmentalize our lives, Paul knows nothing of private and public conduct—"What a person does in the privacy of his own home, so long as it does no one harm, is his own business." Rather, sexual sin and idolatry go hand in hand. Homosexuality, then, is a precursor of God's end-time judgment on wicked people for their theological narcissism—He allows them to worship themselves. As a consequence, humanity collectively goes into a free fall with all other sorts of attendant wickedness and sin: unrighteousness, sexual immorality, wickedness, covetousness, maliciousness, envy, murder, strife, deceit, evil-mindedness—all of which are a manifestation of humanity's hatred of God (Rom. 1:29–30). This index of vices defines what Paul means when he writes that as a consequence of their idolatry God gave humans over "to a debased mind, to do those things which are not fitting" (Rom. 1:28).

The irony of all this is that, despite its fallen state, humanity still knows that its sinful conduct is worthy of God's judgment, and in many cases, even deserving of death. But rather than repent of their sin, humanity collectively approves of this conduct (Rom. 1:32). Although people look out on creation and see God's wisdom, power, and might, and they can look within to the law written on their hearts because they are created in the image of God (Rom. 2:14–15), humanity willfully suppresses the truth and embraces the lie. As John Murray writes: "To put it bluntly, we are not only bent on damning ourselves but we congratulate others in the doing of those things that we know have their issue in damnation. We hate others as we hate ourselves and render therefore to them the approval of what we know merits damnation."[3]

The Church's Response

As we reflect on this portion of Paul's letter to Rome, my hope is that his words would radically reconfigure the way most Christians evaluate idolatry. Within the church there are a number of different reactions to this type of sin. Officially, most Christians reject homosexuality. But even though some Christians reject it, they do so inconsistently. On the one hand, Christians oppose same-sex marriage, but on the other they tolerate homosexuality in their entertainment, whether in movies or TV. Perhaps we have even been amused or laughed at humor that takes homosexuality as a light matter. Would or should we watch a manifestation of God's wrath and consider it entertainment or find it humorous? If someone were to watch an execution as a form of entertainment and humor, people would think such a person to be mad or deranged. Yet why do some within the church who oppose homosexuality nevertheless spend their time, money, and resources viewing and consuming entertainment that exalts or normalizes this sin? If we find ourselves entertained or laughing at a manifestation of God's wrath, we should turn off the TV or walk out of the movie and meditate on Paul's words.

Another response that Christians have to homosexuality involves revulsion or disgust. Many believe, for example, given Paul's words here in Romans, that homosexuality represents the nadir of human sin. Other Christians treat homosexuals with derision and ridicule because of the effeminate behavior that gay men sometimes exhibit. There are two thoughts that come to mind in the face of these reactions. First, people likely zero in on Paul's

3. Murray, *Epistle to the Romans*, 53.

explanation of homosexuality and frequently miss the catalog of other sins that are equally reprehensible in God's eyes. In His just wrath God not only turns sinful people over to unnatural relations but to murder, covetousness, pride, sexual immorality, and something as seemingly innocuous as being disobedient to one's parents (Rom. 1:29–31). How many Christian men, for example, condemn homosexuality and then give a wink of the eye to one another as they lust after women?

Second, if we recognize with Paul that idolatry is the root cause of homosexuality, perhaps we will look on such people with greater compassion. Hopefully, as we see the sin in others, we will first fall on our knees and seek the forgiveness for our own sins, some of which likely appear in verses 29–31. Christ's advice regarding logs and specks in the eye is something that we should always keep in the forefront of our minds: "First remove the plank from your own eye, and then you will see clearly to remove the speck from your brother's eye" (Matt. 7:5). Read in context, Romans 1:18–32 comes after the glorious announcement of the gospel of Christ and its power unto salvation. How can a recipient of God's grace think himself better than others when he too has received God's free grace in Christ?

Such reflection, I believe, should strike us at the very core of our being as we think on the rampant sin around us. When righteous Lot dwelled in Sodom, he was not driven to revulsion but compassion—his heart broke for the people around him (2 Peter 2:7). Our response to the idolatry all around us, in whatever form it may appear—pride, materialism, covetousness, or sexual immorality—should be like Lot or like Paul when he arrived at Athens: "His spirit was provoked within him when he saw that the city was given over to idols" (Acts 17:16). Rather than revulsion and disgust, our response should be one of compassion, intercession, prayer, and evangelism for the lost. Paul's words to the Corinthians should echo in our hearts:

> Do you not know that the unrighteous will not inherit the kingdom of God? Do not be deceived. Neither fornicators, nor

> idolaters, nor adulterers, nor homosexuals, nor sodomites, nor thieves, nor covetous, nor drunkards, nor revilers, nor extortioners will inherit the kingdom of God. *And such were some of you. But you were washed, but you were sanctified, but you were justified in the name of the Lord Jesus and by the Spirit of our God.* (1 Cor. 6:9–11, emphasis added)

Paul's words should be a constant reminder that the adulterer or the liar is just as detestable to God as the homosexual, but that all of them, regardless of their sin, can find salvation through the mercy of the gospel of Christ.

Conclusion

When we consider the truth of this passage, it should cause us to fear the Lord. So often people, even Christians, believe that God is an absentee landlord or that things will eventually get settled at the final judgment—if and when God returns, and if He actually condemns anyone for sin. Yet this passage shows that God is meting out salvation and damnation, revealing His righteousness in the gospel and His wrath against unrighteousness, right now! We should fear the Lord and take shelter in the embassy of peace—the Lord Jesus Christ. Recall that God reveals His wrath against all unrighteousness and delivers unbelievers over to judgment. At the same time, do not forget what Paul has written—namely: "For I am not ashamed of the gospel of Christ, for it is the power of God to salvation for everyone who believes, for the Jew first and also for the Greek. For in it the righteousness of God is revealed from faith to faith; as it is written, 'The just shall live by faith'" (Rom. 1:16–17). So, if you know homosexuals, lovingly implore them to flee from God's wrath by repenting of their sin and fleeing to Christ. Pray fervently for those who are gripped by this sin, because it is a manifestation of God's wrath here in this life, and if they do not repent they will forever suffer His wrath in the life to come. If you entertain, laugh at, or dally in unrighteousness, repent and flee from God's wrath by seeking shelter beneath the mighty wings of Christ.

At the same time, we should also pray that the Lord would strengthen our marriages. How many people turn to the idolatry of homosexuality because of bad experiences in marriages? If God designed marriage to be a portrait of Christ's marriage to his bride, the church, then how does that inform our marital conduct (Eph. 5:28–32)? When Adam and Eve first sinned, they introduced strife and enmity into their relationship. Adam blamed his wife for his transgression rather than take responsibility for it. Yet, by God's grace, even in a fallen world Christians have the opportunity to shine forth God's intended design and goals for marriage when they turn away from their own idolatry and sacrificially love one another as Christ has loved them. If we walk away from Romans 1:18–32 and think only people guilty of homosexuality need to heed its message, then we have missed Paul's point.

5

No Partiality with God

ROMANS 2:1–16

Therefore you are inexcusable, O man, whoever you are who judge, for in whatever you judge another you condemn yourself; for you who judge practice the same things. But we know that the judgment of God is according to truth against those who practice such things. And do you think this, O man, you who judge those practicing such things, and doing the same, that you will escape the judgment of God? Or do you despise the riches of His goodness, forbearance, and longsuffering, not knowing that the goodness of God leads you to repentance? But in accordance with your hardness and your impenitent heart you are treasuring up for yourself wrath in the day of wrath and revelation of the righteous judgment of God, who "will render to each one according to his deeds": eternal life to those who by patient continuance in doing good seek for glory, honor, and immortality; but to those who are self-seeking and do not obey the truth, but obey unrighteousness—indignation and wrath, tribulation and anguish, on every soul of man who does evil, of the Jew first and also of the Greek; but glory, honor, and peace to everyone who works what is good, to the Jew first and also to the Greek. For there is no partiality with God. For as many as have sinned without law will also perish without law, and as many as have sinned in the law will be judged by the law (for not the hearers of the law are just in the sight of God, but the doers of the law will be justified; for when Gentiles, who do not have the law, by nature do the things in the law, these, although not having the law, are a law to themselves, who show the work of the law written in their hearts, their conscience also bearing witness, and between themselves their thoughts accusing or else excusing them)

> *in the day when God will judge the secrets of men by Jesus Christ, according to my gospel.*

Some think the New Testament is utterly different from the Old Testament. Yet when we make a comparison between the two we find a great degree of similarity, especially in the forms of address and preaching. For example, when the prophet Amos addresses the nation, he begins by condemning the sins of the Gentile nations: "Thus says the LORD: 'For three transgressions of Damascus, and for four, I will not turn away its punishment, Because they have threshed Gilead with implements of iron'" (Amos 1:3). Amos then condemns the Gentile nations of Gaza, Tyre, Edom, Ammon, and Moab (Amos 1:3–13). As you can imagine, the Jews cheered Amos and approved his message. Amos, however, did not stop with these Gentile nations but eventually turned his attention to Israel:

> Thus says the LORD: "For three transgressions of Judah, and for four, I will not turn away its punishment, Because they have despised the law of the LORD, And have not kept His commandments. Their lies lead them astray, Lies which their fathers followed. But I will send a fire upon Judah, And it shall devour the palaces of Jerusalem." Thus says the LORD: "For three transgressions of Israel, and for four, I will not turn away its punishment, Because they sell the righteous for silver, And the poor for a pair of sandals. They pant after the dust of the earth which is on the head of the poor, And pervert the way of the humble. A man and his father go in to the same girl, To defile My holy name. They lie down by every altar on clothes taken in pledge, And drink the wine of the condemned in the house of their god." (Amos 2:4–8)

The prophet did not reserve his words of judgment for the Gentiles alone but also condemned the Jews for their wickedness. This is the very pattern that Paul follows, just like an Old Testament prophet.

Paul spent Romans 1:18–32 condemning the practices and the wickedness of the Gentiles. He also explained that God's judgment and wrath fell on them in the form of giving them over to their wicked lusts that resulted in homosexuality and a host of other sins. Yet, just like Amos, Paul addresses Jewish sinfulness. He challenges the Jewish notion that they were exempt from God's judgment either because they were members of the covenant (their genealogical descent) or because they possessed the law. Paul explains that God shows no favoritism to the Jews for any of these reasons but instead grants His favor and mercy only to those who are in Christ.

The Covenant

As we cross the threshold into the second chapter of Romans, we must remember that the opening verse grows out of Paul's statements in chapter 1: "Who, knowing the righteous judgment of God, that those who practice such things are deserving of death, not only do the same but also approve of those who practice them" (Rom. 1:32). Paul condemned the sinful conduct of the Gentiles and then states: "Therefore you are inexcusable, O man, whoever you are who judge, for in whatever you judge another you condemn yourself; for you who judge practice the same things" (Rom. 2:1). Israelites would likely approve of Paul's words of judgment against presumably Gentile sinfulness, and as members of God's covenant they would have thought themselves immune from such conduct. But Paul reminds his readers that the one who passes judgment on such conduct is also guilty of the same. Recall from the previous chapter (Rom. 1:18–32) that the wickedness of Sodom and Gomorrah also occurred within Israel (cf. Gen. 19:1–29; Judges 19).

Paul does not want the Jews to think they are exempt because they are in covenant with God. Yes, the Jews know the truth of God's law and therefore condemn the Gentiles for these sins. Nevertheless, they practice the very same things. Paul, fully aware of this hypocrisy, levels judgment against his fellow countrymen: "But we know that the judgment of God is according to truth against those who practice such things. And do you think this, O man, you who judge those practicing such things, and doing the same, that you will escape the judgment of God?" (Rom. 2:2–3). Paul indicts the

Jews for their hypocrisy and explains that God judges "according to truth," not according to the lip service the Jews give the law or the fact that they are in covenant with God. Paul's words dismiss a common Jewish idea that just because they were in covenant with God meant that He would overlook their sins. Uninspired Jewish intertestamental literature states: "For even if we sin we are yours, knowing your power" (Wis. 15:2a NRSV).

Many Israelites thought they could take advantage of God's mercy, so Paul confronts their presumption head-on: "Or do you despise the riches of His goodness, forbearance, and longsuffering, not knowing that the goodness of God leads you to repentance?" (Rom. 2:4). Sadly, many professing Christians hold similar erroneous notions. They believe that because they attend church, tithe, and participate in church functions they will not fall under God's wrath. Church membership is as equally unsuitable as covenant membership as a shield against God's wrath. The only thing that ultimately serves as a shield is faith in Christ. God often withholds immediate judgment or discipline to afford a sinner time and opportunity to repent, not so that the sinner can continue to engage in his sinful conduct. Yet the Jews continued headlong in their sin and, in essence, despised God's kindness and forbearance. So often unrepentant sinners think they can tarry and dally in sin given that God is so patient, but Paul informs his readers that they are actually stockpiling judgment: "But in accordance with your hardness and your impenitent heart you are treasuring up for yourself wrath in the day of wrath and revelation of the righteous judgment of God" (Rom. 2:5). God's patience is not infinite, and because of sinners' hard hearts and recalcitrance, in the end they only accrue greater judgment on themselves. Paul tells his readers the righteous judgment of God will be revealed, which means there is no fault in God's wrath against unrepentant sinners. We cannot and should not disconnect God's revealed wrath from His righteousness. God is perfect in all of His ways, even in His dispensation of wrath and judgment.

Jewish Heritage

Paul explains in Romans 2:6–11 how God's judgment works. Whether one is in covenant with Him, as Israel was through the Mosaic covenant, or is an alien to the promises, God judges a person according to his works: "Who 'will render to each one according to his deeds': eternal life to those who by patient continuance in doing good seek for glory, honor, and immortality; but to those who are self-seeking and do not obey the truth, but obey unrighteousness—indignation and wrath" (Rom. 2:6–8). The law is very simple—obedience yields eternal life, and disobedience produces condemnation and hell (cf. Lev. 18:5). At this point Paul does not address the question of whether fallen sinners are capable of rendering obedience to the law so that they might receive eternal life. He merely explains how the law functions. Regardless of a person's status, place in life, or genealogical pedigree, there will be "tribulation and anguish, on every soul of man who does evil, of the Jew first and also of the Greek; but glory, honor, and peace to everyone who works what is good, to the Jew first and also to the Greek" (Rom. 2:9–10). Paul does not give the Jew, one who is in covenant with God through the Mosaic law, an advantage over the Gentile—all lawbreakers, Jew or Gentile, will suffer God's righteous judgment. Just like an Old Testament prophet who leveled his message of condemnation against the unrepentant, Jew and Gentile alike, Paul delivers the same message. The import of his message is simple: "There is no partiality with God" (Rom. 2:11).

Possession of the Law

Given that God's impartial judgment will fall on the Jew and the Gentile, what about Israel's favored status as God's covenant people? What about God's covenant with Israel? What about their possession of the law? Does not the law give Israel preferential treatment? Paul addresses the substance of these questions when he writes: "For as many as have sinned without law will also perish without law, and as many as have sinned in the law will be judged by the law" (Rom. 2:12). Paul's use of prepositions is key to understanding what he means, specifically being *without* (*anomos*) and *in* (*en nomo*) the law. Gentiles are "without the law," as they did not stand at the foot of Sinai and receive the law of God. Therefore, wicked and sinful Gentiles will be judged as those who did not have the law—they will be judged according to the knowledge of God's law that they possess by virtue of their creation—the law of God written on their hearts. The people of Israel, on the other hand, did receive God's law and as such were in the law (cf. Gal. 3:23). Unrepentant Israelites, then, will be judged according to the revealed standard of the law. But regardless of how one receives the law, naturally or specially revealed, Paul reiterates his earlier point: "For not the hearers of the law are just in the sight of God, but the doers of the law will be justified" (Rom. 2:13).

In the verses that follow Paul explains how God holds Gentiles accountable on the day of judgment: "(For when Gentiles, who do not have the law, by nature do the things in the law, these, although not having the law, are a law to themselves, who show the work of the law written in their hearts, their conscience also bearing witness, and between themselves their thoughts accusing or else excusing them) in the day when God will judge the secrets of men by Jesus Christ, according to my gospel" (Rom. 2:14–16). By virtue of humanity's creation in God's image, people inherently know the law. As C. S. Lewis once observed: "Human beings, all over the earth, have this curious idea that they ought to behave in a certain way, and cannot really get rid of it."[1] Lewis goes on to write:

> If no set of moral ideas were truer or better than any other, there would be no sense in preferring civilized morality to savage morality, or Christian morality to Nazi morality. In fact, of course, we all do believe that some moralities are better than others.... The moment you say that one set of moral ideas can be better than another, you are in fact, measuring them both by

1. C. S. Lewis, *The Quotable Lewis: An Encyclopedic Selection of Quotes from the Complete Published Works of C. S. Lewis*, ed. Wayne Martindale and Jerry Root (Wheaton, Ill.: Tyndale, 1989), 438.

> a standard...comparing them both with some Real Morality, admitting that there is such a thing as a real Right, independent of what people think and that some people's ideas get nearer to that real Right than others.[2]

What Lewis calls "Real Morality" is what Paul calls the works of the law of God written on the heart. All people know of God's law because he has written on every human heart.

For example, it does not matter what culture you examine, everyone knows that stealing is wrong. Even among thieves there is a code of conduct—it may be acceptable to steal from others, but thieves do not want anyone to steal from them! John Calvin offers helpful insights in this respect when he argues that the presence of the law on the human heart

> is evidenced by such facts as these, that all the Gentiles alike institute religious rites, make laws to punish adultery, theft, and murder, and commend good faith in commercial transactions and contract. In this way they prove their knowledge that God is to be worshipped, that adultery, theft, and murder, are evils and that honesty is to be esteemed.[3]

Along these lines, apart from reading the Ten Commandments, even thieves know stealing is wrong. Otherwise, why do thieves sneak around, seek opportunities when no one is looking, and lie and deceive others to carry out their thievery? The thief's skulking is evidence that his conscience knows better. But regardless of what a person might get away with, whether he is conscience-stricken or not, at the final judgment God will reckon according to people's works and will reveal the secret, sinful thoughts of all men.

There will be no escape from God's all-seeing knowledge. He will judge all men by Christ, whether they possess the law of God

---

2. Lewis, *Quotable Lewis*, 439–40.

3. John Calvin, *Romans and Thessalonians*, Calvin's New Testament Commentaries, ed. David W. Torrance and T. F. Torrance (1960; repr., Grand Rapids: Baker, 1996), 48.

as revealed in His Word or written on the heart. In the face of the prospects of going before the throne of God for judgment, the first thing we must realize is that God is a just and fair judge. He does not unfairly condemn people. As we saw in Romans 1:18–32, fallen humanity knows of God's existence. Fallen man cannot claim ignorance. Moreover, Paul clearly explained that all people inherently know the law because God has written on their hearts. Newborn infants are not, as some people claim, blank slates. The slate is filled with the natural knowledge of God's law; the creation proclaims God's existence. These two witnesses herald that God exists and deserves worship. Those Gentiles who refuse to turn to God in obedience will fall under God's just judgment according to this naturally revealed standard.

The same just judgment against unbelief and disobedience will fall on Israel, but God will hold them to a higher degree of accountability. They cannot claim ignorance of God's law at any level, because it has not only been written on their hearts but also revealed at Sinai and inscripturated in God's Word. In all His ways, especially with His judgment against unbelief, God shows impartiality, and His judgment is righteous and holy. Whether in the scope of general or special revelation, no one can claim that God is unfair. God's righteous judgment is certainly an idea and work of God on which all Christians should meditate. As Wilhelmus à Brakel (1635–1711), a seventeenth-century Dutch Reformed theologian, explains:

> Believers, may you who know this way—the way by which you go to God—increasingly penetrate the truth of God's justice until you may perceive its purity, glory, and preciousness. Magnify God in His justice, and rejoice in the fact that God is just. Love His righteousness as you love His goodness and mercy, especially in that this righteousness has been satisfied on your behalf. Give thanks to God that the Lord leads you and all His elect along such a holy way unto salvation. Do not

> consider the justice of God to be against you, but as being for you—to give you salvation and justly punish your enemies.[4]

As we contemplate the justice of God, hopefully it will fill us with praise and thanksgiving because God has delivered us from His righteous judgment through His mercy in the gospel of Christ.

While Paul has not yet expounded in great detail the solution to fallen humanity's problem with sin and corruption, do not forget what he has written at the beginning of the epistle: "For I am not ashamed of the gospel of Christ, for it is the power of God to salvation for everyone who believes, for the Jew first and also for the Greek. For in it the righteousness of God is revealed from faith to faith; as it is written, 'The just shall live by faith'" (Rom. 1:16–17). Just as God's judgment against unbelief covers Jew and Gentile, so too the mercy He has given in and through Christ. Paul will explain how Christ delivers us from the curse of the law. But for now, suffice it to say that if God grants eternal life to those who perform the law, then Christ has come not only to pay the debt for His bride, the church, but also to fulfill the law on her behalf. Only in Christ do we find deliverance from the demands of the law and the curse for breaking it.

Conclusion

This passage of Scripture should give us confidence that God is a just judge. Any time we come across those who deny God's existence, we should remember the truths contained herein. No one can claim ignorance about rebellion against God. In light of human sinfulness, we should explain how God's law functions: If you obey, you will live, but if you disobey, God will curse you. Given the demand for perfection regarding the requirements of the law, this would undoubtedly leave people recognizing that they all fall short and are in desperate need of someone to fulfill the law's demands

---

4. Wilhelmus à Brakel, *The Christian's Reasonable Service* (Morgan, Pa.: Soli Deo Gloria Publications, 1992), 1:130.

on their behalf. As such, this is when we must point people to Christ. But before we turn our attention to Christ, we still have to examine further Paul's indictment against his fellow Jews in Romans 2:17–29.

6

No Place for Hypocrisy or Pride

ROMANS 2:17–29

Indeed you are called a Jew, and rest on the law, and make your boast in God, and know His will, and approve the things that are excellent, being instructed out of the law, and are confident that you yourself are a guide to the blind, a light to those who are in darkness, an instructor of the foolish, a teacher of babes, having the form of knowledge and truth in the law. You, therefore, who teach another, do you not teach yourself? You who preach that a man should not steal, do you steal? You who say, "Do not commit adultery," do you commit adultery? You who abhor idols, do you rob temples? You who make your boast in the law, do you dishonor God through breaking the law? For "the name of God is blasphemed among the Gentiles because of you," as it is written. For circumcision is indeed profitable if you keep the law; but if you are a breaker of the law, your circumcision has become uncircumcision. Therefore, if an uncircumcised man keeps the righteous requirements of the law, will not his uncircumcision be counted as circumcision? And will not the physically uncircumcised, if he fulfills the law, judge you who, even with your written code and circumcision, are a transgressor of the law? For he is not a Jew who is one outwardly, nor is circumcision that which is outward in the flesh; but he is a Jew who is one inwardly; and circumcision is that of the heart, in the Spirit, not in the letter; whose praise is not from men but from God.

Throughout history, the Jewish people have been one of the most insignificant races among the nations. Writing of Israel's mean estate, the prophet Ezekiel tells us: "As for your nativity, on the day you were born your navel cord was not cut, nor were you washed in water to cleanse you; you were not rubbed with salt nor wrapped in swaddling cloths. No eye pitied you, to do any of these things for you, to have compassion on you; but you were thrown out into the open field, when you yourself were loathed on the day you were born" (Ezek. 16:4–5; cf. Deut. 7:7; 9:4–6). Ezekiel describes Israel in very lowly terms. Yet, despite their humble origins, the Jewish people had a tendency toward pride. While some might bristle at such a characterization, the fact that the Scriptures characterize Israel as "stiff-necked" informs us of their hard-hearted state. The prophet Nehemiah, for example, writes: "And [You] testified against them, That You might bring them back to Your law. Yet they acted proudly, And did not heed Your commandments, But sinned against Your judgments, 'Which if a man does, he shall live by them.' And they shrugged their shoulders, Stiffened their necks, And would not hear" (Neh. 9:29).

Why were the Jews like this? The answer lies in the fact that they were the recipients of the blessings and riches of God in their election as a nation. But as is the case with the recipients of great mercy, sinful attitudes creep in and people begin to think that God chose them because of their own worthiness rather than because of His unconditional mercy. Once the cancer of pride attacks, it soon grows into a gross, consuming disease and demands ever greater amounts of attention. As a result, the Jews did not place their faith in Christ but in themselves. Paul was well aware of this pattern, as he had not been averse to boasting about his own accomplishments in his life prior to Christ. He was, after all, circumcised on the eighth day, of the chosen people of Israel, of the tribe of Benjamin, a Hebrew of Hebrews, a Pharisee, and blameless in his own eyes before the law (Phil. 3:5–6). Paul knew the prideful heart that beat in the chest of the average Israelite, and he needed to confront it head-on.

If he leveled the charges of sinfulness, idolatry, and disobedience at the feet of fallen humanity in the earlier portions of Romans, then he knew that the average Jew would find reason to dismiss these charges against the Jewish people. After all, they were God's chosen race, the one holy nation chosen out of all the other nations of the earth. Paul's desire to rebuke his fellow Jews for their hypocrisy, therefore, was not out of a sinful zeal to embarrass his countrymen. On the contrary, he wanted his kinsmen in the flesh to recognize that they were infected with sin and consequently in need of the redemption that could heal them of their disease. Or, in the words of Jesus, "Those who are well have no need of a physician, but those who are sick" (Luke 5:31). In this portion of Romans, Paul sets forth his case against the hypocrisy of his fellow Jews to show them their need of Christ, of a Savior.

The Indictment

Paul begins this portion of chapter 2 with an indictment against his fellow Jews: "Indeed you are called a Jew, and rest on the law, and make your boast in God, and know His will, and approve the things that are excellent, being instructed out of the law" (Rom. 2:17–18). Paul reminds his Jewish audience about their intimate knowledge of God's law, which he links to what he wrote earlier in the chapter—namely, God will justify only those who perform and obey the law (Rom. 2:13). In other words, if the law is the standard, and the Jews boast about their conformity to it, then Paul holds the law up against their conduct to see how well they do. Do they receive a passing mark?

Recall the quotation from the Apocrypha I cited in the previous section, "For even if we sin we are yours, knowing your power" (Wis. 15:2 NRSV). In other words, because Jews were insistent on their special place of favor, Paul had to level his hammer against this pride: "[You] are confident that you yourself are a guide to the blind, a light to those who are in darkness, an instructor of the foolish, a teacher of babes, having the form of knowledge and truth in the law" (Rom. 2:19–20). Paul recognizes the flurry of their instructive activity—they are confident in their ability to tell others how they must follow God and obey His commands. Paul notes that the problem with his fellow Jews is not their lack of knowledge—the insufficiency lies not with the law, which is the "form of knowledge and truth," but with their wicked hearts. They teach the law but fail to teach themselves—they fail to practice what they preach. Paul's indictment does not center on the intricacies and technicalities of the law but on its fundamental points: thievery, adultery, and idolatry (Rom. 2:21–23; cf. Ex. 20:3–6, 14–15). Paul's accusation repeats what he wrote at the beginning of the chapter: "Therefore you are inexcusable, O man, whoever you are who judge, for in whatever you judge another you condemn yourself; for you who judge practice the same things" (Rom. 2:1).

Supporting Evidence

Despite their boasting, Paul shows his fellow Jews that they practice the very sins they condemn. But in case his audience is doubtful, Paul, as a good prosecuting attorney, brings supporting evidence. In this case, he brings in an early witness, the testimony of Isaiah the prophet: "For 'the name of God is blasphemed among the Gentiles because of you,' as it is written" (Rom. 2:24). Paul quotes Isaiah 52:5 to show that Israel's pattern of prideful hypocrisy is not a recent development but one with ancient pedigree. Israel boasted about their false fidelity to the Lord for hundreds of years, so much so that the prophet long ago informed them that their conduct led the Gentile nations to blaspheme the name of God. That is, they failed to set a godly example for the surrounding Gentile nations, and so these nations believed that wanton disregard for God's law was the acceptable norm.

Paul then zeroes in on what he perceives is Israel's chief problem—their formalism. In other words, sometimes people believe that, so long as everything on the outside looks acceptable, so long as public perception is acceptable, it matters not what occurs on the inside. In this case, Paul goes after the Israelite pride in the sign of the covenant, their God-given mark that distinguished them from the surrounding nations: circumcision. This sign, Paul writes, was certainly beneficial—if a person kept the law. By taking the sign of circumcision, a person was binding himself to God's covenant and to the entirety of the law. Again, we must remember the framework of this second chapter in Paul's letter: Only the doers of the law will be justified (Rom. 2:13). Hence, if a man receives circumcision, he enters God's covenant and vows to perform the law. But what happens when he fails to live up to his covenant oath? Paul writes that his circumcision becomes "uncircumcision" (Rom. 2:25). Rather than serve as a sign of covenant blessing, circumcision becomes a sign of covenant curse. Recall that the uncircumcised male was cut off from the people of God (cf. Gen. 17:14 LXX). Paul's swift argument reveals the Jewish ignorance about their very point of boasting. They misunderstood the significance of circumcision. It was not merely a sign of their special status—it was a sign of their need to obey the law, a point at which they were failing miserably. Hence, the sign of their boasting was actually a sign of their curse and the judgment that was on them.

Unlikely Righteous Gentiles

But Paul then posits something unthinkable to his fellow Jews. What would happen if an uncircumcised Gentile kept the righteous requirements of the law? How would the law view this uncircumcised stranger to the covenant? Would not the law look past his uncircumcised state and view him as being "circumcised" (Rom. 2:26)? For his Jewish countrymen who believed that the bare sign of circumcision would save them, Paul shows that the law is all about actual conformity to God's decrees, not simply bearing the sign of the covenant. Mere possession of the covenant sign would not save them, especially in light of their covenant infidelity, thievery, adultery, and idolatry. Only the doers of the law will be justified (Rom. 2:13). In this case, even the Gentile doer of the law would rise up, judge, and condemn the Jew, the one who possessed the "written code and circumcision" (Rom. 2:27).

However veiled Paul's charges have been against Israel's formalism, he comes to the heart of his accusation when he writes: "For he is not a Jew who is one outwardly, nor is circumcision that which is outward in the flesh; but he is a Jew who is one inwardly;

and circumcision is that of the heart, in the Spirit, not in the letter; whose praise is not from men but from God" (Rom. 2:28–29). Circumcision was not about external conformity to God's law but was supposed to be indicative of a positively disposed heart, one marked by humility and obedience. This is why Moses used circumcision language to characterize Israel's lack of obedience: "Circumcise the foreskin of your heart, and be stiff-necked no longer" (Deut. 10:16). Paul echoed Mosaic charges against Israel's external conformity to God's law. The mere possession of circumcision alone does not fool the supreme Judge of the cosmos. Rather, God will justify only the doer of the law (Rom. 2:13).

But at this point Paul only hints at how his fellow Israelites might obtain the righteousness that they so desperately claim to possess. Paul indicates that these uncircumcised Gentiles have a circumcised heart "in the Spirit, not in the letter" (Rom. 2:29), which means that circumcision and mere possession of the law do not change the heart. What is curiously absent at this point in chapter 2, and a subject that he will not yet raise until the third chapter, is faith in Christ. But remember how Paul started his epistle: "For I am not ashamed of the gospel of Christ, for it is the power of God to salvation for everyone who believes, for the Jew first and also for the Greek. For in it the righteousness of God is revealed from faith to faith; as it is written, 'The just shall live by faith'" (Rom. 1:16–17). Paul's failure to mention faith in Christ at this point in his letter is not an oversight; it is quite deliberate. He wanted his fellow Jews to realize the depth of their sin so that they would see their utter need for Christ.

The Dangers of Hypocrisy

When we consider the implications of this passage for our own context several things deserve our attention. The overall thrust of the passage should warn us against the sins of hypocrisy and pride. People in any age can fall into formalism. Wilhelmus à Brakel (1635–1711) once observed this type of conduct in his own day:

> We practice this when in the engagement of religious exercise we have ourselves in view so that we may be honored by men. This occurs when a minister stirs up his gifts, appears to be filled with the spirit in prayer, preaches with much fire, but with all this, his objective is to be esteemed as godly and learned and to have the praise and esteem of the people. How abominable! This occurs when a person faithfully comes to church and sits there gravely and attentively in order to gain the reputation of being pious, or sings to let his voice be heard and how well he knows the tune. This also occurs when one sighs loudly during prayer, and makes worshipful and even foolish gestures in order to be seen and heard. This takes place when a person puts on a show of being very attentive during the sermon, while in the meantime, he is secretly looking about to observe whether others see him. It is also the case when one casts but little in the basket of the deacon and is desirous that it sounds as if it were a great gift. In one word, hypocrisy is to create the appearance of serving God while in reality having men in view, and thus one's self.[1]

Many self-professing Christians have been baptized and regularly take the Lord's Supper, in their minds performing the things that God requires for salvation. They do these things because they want the people around them to believe they are something they are not.

The perfect biblical illustration of this type of person is Cain—he brought his offering before God just as his brother Abel did (Gen. 4:1–7). Yet Cain did not fool God by his hypocrisy, nor does our own duplicity deceive God. As Paul said, there are only two ways that a person can satisfy God: either perfectly fulfilling the law or having a circumcised heart, something only God does (cf. Deut. 30:6). A dog and pony show, merely putting on good appearances for God, will not suffice. God sees past all the hypocrisy, and no one will be able to pull the wool over His eyes. As Christ once said, "Many will say to Me in that day, 'Lord, Lord, have we

1. à Brakel, *Christian's Reasonable Service*, 3:315.

not prophesied in Your name, cast out demons in Your name, and done many wonders in Your name?' And then I will declare to them, 'I never knew you; depart from Me, you who practice lawlessness!'" (Matt. 7:22–23).

The Dangers of Pride

Closely related to hypocrisy is the sin of pride. People often want others to think well of them. The sin of pride is a dangerous cancer that can infect the humblest saint. The Scriptures, for example, extol Moses as the humblest of men (Num. 12:3), yet his pride drove him to strike the rock at Meribah (Num. 20:8–12): "And Moses and Aaron gathered the assembly together before the rock; and he said to them, 'Hear now, you rebels! *Must we bring water for you out of this rock?*'" (Num. 20:10, emphasis added). Moses sinfully took credit for bringing water out of the rock. This type of pride was at the root of Paul's Jewish audience. Rather than look to the mercy of God in Christ, Paul's fellow Jews took pride in their circumcision and their possession and knowledge of the law, but they did not have much concern for its actual performance. Because of these prized possessions, they thought they were separate from the Gentile nations and therefore above God's judgment. In the end, what was supposed to be a sign of God's grace became instead a sign of His judgment against them.

Pride is an illness that is alive and well today. It is the opposite of what a Christian is supposed to be, which is why Paul removes all reason for boasting from the Jews in this passage and sets the stage for the only thing in which a person should have pride—Christ. Paul strips away anything that they might have taken shelter in: their heritage, possession of the law, ability to teach, or the sacrament of circumcision. It is even necessary to strip away false humility, as C. S. Lewis writes: "A man is never so proud as when striking an attitude of humility."[2] When stripped of our pride, then we can see our depravity and sinfulness. Again, as á Brakel writes,

2. Lewis, *Quotable Lewis*, 495.

> What abominations this wicked heart has brought forth—not only prior to my conversion, but also yet after my conversion.... How void of desire and spirituality, and how sinful I am in my religion; that is, in hearing and reading the Word of God and in praying and singing! How unfaithful I am in reference to grace received, and how I have grieved the Holy Spirit! Truly, I am not worthy that God would look down upon me and bestow any grace upon me at all.[3]

When there is pride in the heart, it leaves little to no room for grace. This is why Proverbs says: "Better to be of a humble spirit with the lowly, Than to divide the spoil with the proud" (Prov. 16:19). Only in the contemplation of our sinfulness, not our self-worth, can we then rejoice in the grace that we have received in Christ. As the words of Isaac Watts's hymn so powerfully capture:

> Alas! And did my Savior bleed,
> And did my Sovereign die!
> Would he devote that sacred head
> For such a worm as I?
>
> Was it for crimes that I had done
> He groaned upon the tree?
> Amazing pity! Grace unknown!
> And love beyond degree![4]

Only those who are ill need a physician; only when God lays us low do we see our utter need for Christ.

Conclusion

When we look at a passage such as this, we should remember that God placed it here as a message for His people throughout the ages. It should be a warning to us all to guard against the sins of hypocrisy

3. à Brakel, *Christian's Reasonable Service*, 2:585.

4. Unless otherwise noted, all hymn quotations are taken from the *Trinity Hymnal* (Atlanta: Great Commission Publications, 1990).

and pride, as we are all very capable experts in these deadly arts. If we think we are above such sins, then we are already neck deep in them. We must remember to pursue and desire humility above all else—to exhibit this characteristic is not only proper, given our sinfulness, but also most desirous because it is how we are most like our Savior. A gospel-powered humility is evidence that God is conforming us to the image of His Son (Phil. 2:8–11).

7

God's Judgment against Israel

ROMANS 3:1–8

What advantage then has the Jew, or what is the profit of circumcision? Much in every way! Chiefly because to them were committed the oracles of God. For what if some did not believe? Will their unbelief make the faithfulness of God without effect? Certainly not! Indeed, let God be true but every man a liar. As it is written: "That You may be justified in Your words, And may overcome when You are judged." But if our unrighteousness demonstrates the righteousness of God, what shall we say? Is God unjust who inflicts wrath? (I speak as a man.) Certainly not! For then how will God judge the world? For if the truth of God has increased through my lie to His glory, why am I also still judged as a sinner? And why not say, "Let us do evil that good may come"?—as we are slanderously reported and as some affirm that we say. Their condemnation is just.

Within church history the pendulum swings back and forth from one extreme to another on various doctrines. For example, in the early years of the church, theologians defended the doctrine of Christ's deity. About one hundred years later, the pendulum swung in the opposite direction and the church had to protect the doctrine of Christ's humanity. Throughout history the church has guarded itself against the swing of the pendulum to extremes. Another such example comes from the writing of the Westminster Confession of Faith. Orthodox theologians defended the truth against the teachings of Arminianism. Arminians assigned man half the credit of saving himself. Shortly after this period, however, the church once again had to take up a defense against the swing of the pendulum.

This time, however, the threat came from within the Reformed church—hyper-Calvinism.

Hyper-Calvinists emphasized the sovereignty of God to such a degree that they eliminated the important scriptural teaching of human responsibility. Many within the church believed that they did not need to obey the law and therefore did not exhort men to repent of their sins. This error, of course, was the error of antinomianism, or lawlessness. Why? Because the Word clearly enjoins obedience to God's law. Antinomianism began to spread into other areas of church life. Andrew Fuller (1754–1815) tells the story of a church member reeling in a drunken stupor whom he confronted. The church member claimed he was incapable of sobriety and then rebuked Fuller for meddling. The drunken church member said there was no use in trying to fight off his sin.[1] What is perplexing is that antinomian episodes such as this occurred within the covenant community. As we will see from this passage of Scripture, this type of sin is not new. The Jews were well known for their legalism, but antinomianism is often soon to follow. Let us see how Paul deals with the antinomianism within the covenant community and reflect on its relevance for the church.

Paul Answers Objections

Paul begins this portion of his epistle by answering an imaginary interlocutor, or debate partner. Given that in the first chapter he spelled out the sinfulness of humanity, and the idolatry they engaged in, the likely response would have been, "That's all fine and unsurprising. Pagans, of course, are naturally sinful." But Paul then turned his attention to his fellow Jews to demonstrate that they, too, were guilty of gross sin: thievery, adultery, and idolatry. And despite their privileged status as God's chosen people, their possession of the law and circumcision—the sign of God's covenant—was not enough. In the face of these statements, Paul's Jewish audience would have

1. Andrew Fuller, as cited in *Puritan Papers*, ed. D. Martin Lloyd Jones (Phillipsburg, N.J.: P&R Publishing, 2000), 1:273.

responded, "Of what benefit is our privileged status? If we are just as sinful as the pagan, 'what advantage then has the Jew, or what is the profit of circumcision?'" (Rom. 3:1). Paul's response is simple and to the point: Israel's chief advantage lies in the fact that God committed His oracles, His revelation and Word, to them (Rom. 3:2). They had the privilege of knowing the will of God when for thousands of years the Gentile nations sat in darkness.

But Paul asks a rhetorical question, "For what if some did not believe? Will their unbelief make the faithfulness of God without effect?" (Rom. 3:3). In other words, yes, Israel possessed the Old Testament Scriptures, but how was this an advantage? Moreover, if God is the only One who can grant a circumcised heart, yet there are many Jews who do not believe, does this not negate God's faithfulness to His promises? Paul's answer is swift and direct: "Certainly not! Indeed, let God be true but every man a liar. As it is written: 'That You may be justified in Your words, And may overcome when You are judged'" (Rom. 3:4). Just because some of the Jews did not believe does not disprove God's faithfulness to His word, promises, or covenant. To punctuate his point Paul responds with his famous "Certainly not!" or as other translations have it, "May it never be!" (NASB) or "God forbid" (KJV). Paul asserts the faithfulness of God by saying that all men are liars in comparison with His truthfulness and veracity. To substantiate his point, Paul quotes Psalm 51:4.

The original context of the quote comes from David's prayer of repentance when he committed adultery with Bathsheba and killed her husband, Uriah the Hittite. David's point is that, when people sin, God is justified in judging them for their disobedience because ultimately all sin is against God. Therefore, God faithfully fulfills His promises to grant salvation by circumcising the hearts of His people, and He is also faithful and righteous when He punishes unbelief. In other words, in line with Paul's thesis (i.e., Rom. 1:17), the gospel reveals God's righteousness, which He demonstrates in the salvation of His covenant people and the judgment of unbelievers, even those within the covenant community.

Recall that when God gave His covenantal promises of salvation, He also promised to judge unbelief. Through Moses God told Israel, "Therefore keep the words of this covenant, and do them, that you may prosper in all that you do" (Deut. 29:9). But Moses also issued warnings against covenant infidelity:

> So that there may not be among you man or woman or family or tribe, whose heart turns away today from the LORD our God, to go and serve the gods of these nations, and that there may not be among you a root bearing bitterness or wormwood; and so it may not happen, when he hears the words of this curse, that he blesses himself in his heart, saying, "I shall have peace, even though I follow the dictates of my heart"—as though the drunkard could be included with the sober. "The LORD would not spare him; for then the anger of the LORD and His jealousy would burn against that man, and every curse that is written in this book would settle on him, and the LORD would blot out his name from under heaven." (Deut. 29:18–20).

If we have not noticed already, the doctrine of election and God's justice in choosing some and rejecting others stands behind these verses—themes that Paul develops in chapter 9. In fact, he develops these themes in connection with quotations from Deuteronomy 30 in chapter 10. But another thing to observe is Paul's contrast: Israel has been unfaithful to God and His covenant whereas God has been faithful; Israel has been unrighteous and God has been righteous.

Divine Sovereignty and Human Responsibility

But God's sovereign election does not invalidate the vital truth of human responsibility, which is the next question that Paul anticipates and answers in the verses that follow: "But if our unrighteousness demonstrates the righteousness of God, what shall we say? Is God unjust who inflicts wrath? (I speak as a man.) Certainly not! For then how will God judge the world? For if the truth of God has increased through my lie to His glory, why am I also still judged as a sinner? And why not say, 'Let us do evil that good may come'?—as we are slanderously reported and as some affirm that we say. Their condemnation is just" (Rom. 3:5–8).

In these verses, Paul refutes two abuses of the doctrine that he has just explained. The false idea is, How can God judge us for our sin if it helps Him by showing forth His righteousness? Moreover, if it is only by God's electing grace that He circumcises a man's heart, then how can God judge us for our sin?

Paul, of course, responds with his booming, "Certainly not!" Otherwise, how could God judge unbelief and disobedience if He was supposed to reward it? He answers the second question, Why not do evil so that God's glory is more conspicuous? in a similar fashion. That is, Does not my sin provide the perfect dark canvas on which God the grand artist can apply the brushstrokes of His light, mercy, and grace? If so, then should we not sin all the more that God's grace shines all the more brilliantly? As crazy as the question sounds, Paul was not dealing with a hypothetical situation, because he had to deny the charge that this was the nature of the apostolic teaching (Rom. 3:8). Paul's opponents accused him of antinomianism most likely because of what he said about circumcision as well as his teaching on divine sovereignty. These questions and accusations were a perversion of apostolic teaching, which is why it warranted Paul's brusque and direct "Certainly not!"

Beware of Antinomianism

Throughout the first two chapters of Romans Paul challenges the various areas in which the Jews would try to take refuge in order to secure their salvation. He said that a person could not be saved because of his heritage, mere possession of the law, or circumcision. So, yes, the Jews had a tendency toward works-righteousness—trying to add their moral effort to God's grace. Paul's fellow Jews, however, also had a tendency toward antinomianism. They would, for example, preach against certain sins yet commit those very sins themselves (Rom. 2:17–23). They thought God would overlook their sin because they were His covenant people. Yet, as Paul clearly demonstrates, antinomianism is equally unacceptable to God, even if thinly veiled behind a veneer of pretended piety. Moreover, the Jews could not take refuge in the fact that God had not given them circumcised hearts. Yes, there is divine sovereignty; but as Paul has shown us here, there is also human responsibility.

This should be a warning to us: We should not take it for granted that God will overlook our sins just because we are members of the church. The false notion can be described in the following terms: "God is in the business of forgiving sins; I'm a sinner, therefore I'm OK." This is where we must remember that there are both covenantal blessings and curses. Just as a Jew could turn his circumcision into uncircumcision, a person can, for example, turn the blessing of the Lord's Supper into a curse. Any time we become indifferent toward God's law we wade into the dark, murky waters of antinomianism. We might say, "I don't really think that antinomianism is all that rampant in the church today. Is this really a problem we have to worry about?" The answer to this is yes.

Which one of the Ten Commandments is probably broken every single week by Christians, even by good Reformed Christians? The fourth commandment (Ex. 20:9–11; cf. Matt. 28:1; Acts 20:7; Rev. 1:10). Most of the church is familiar with this command, yet many Christians believe that it no longer applies. They believe that Christians have only nine commandments, not ten. This is a form of antinomianism. Yet a grosser form of antinomianism goes on in many churches. Like the Jews in Paul's day, far too many Christians think their church attendance will cover their sins—they construct a façade of conformity to the law, but during the week they live like an unbeliever. On Sunday they promote the law and teach others not to steal, commit adultery, or worship false gods, and then Monday through Saturday they practice what they condemn on Sunday. Along these lines Terry Johnson observes, "Christian people think nothing of cheating on their taxes, stealing from their employer, over-drinking, viewing perversions on television and the cinema, breaking the Sabbath, and breaking their marriage vows. Challenge any of this and one is labeled 'unloving,' 'judgmental,' and 'legalistic,' or, the most damning of twentieth century indictments, 'insensitive.'"[2] This pattern undoubtedly falls short of the mark. The question, though, is how we will respond. Will we take an indifferent attitude toward the law of God, or will we strive to seek God's kingdom and His righteousness? Paul's warnings to his fellow Israelites are equally applicable to the church in our own day.

Christ the Only Refuge

This leads to a second point—namely, we must not take refuge in anything or anyone but Jesus Christ. Note, at this point Paul has not mentioned the term *faith* or *Christ*.

He has stripped away every single thing in which the Jews might try to take shelter. Paul's countrymen erroneously believed that just because they were Jews they would somehow be exempt from God's judgment. These Jews forgot that although being in the covenant community is a tremendous blessing, their presence in this blessed community was not the ground of their redemption. All throughout Scripture the seed of the serpent has *always* surfaced within the covenant community. When God judged the world by the flood, He placed Noah and his family in the ark. The visible covenant community was spared. But even then, the seed of the serpent reared its ugly head when Ham committed gross sexual sin against his father, Noah (Gen. 9:21–27; cf. Leveticus 18). Both Jacob and Esau were born within the covenant community, yet God loved Jacob and hated Esau, a point Paul later develops and explains (Romans 9). Again, mere presence within the church does not shelter one from God's wrath. Proximity to Christ and the gospel guarantees nothing. Only faith alone in Christ alone by God's grace alone constitutes the divine embassy of peace and refuge from our sin and God's judgment.

---

2. Terry Johnson, *When Grace Comes Home* (Fearn, Scotland: Christian Focus, 2002), 122.

Conclusion

So, when we walk away from this passage we should be mindful of the dangers of antinomianism. As I said before, it is the twin heresy to legalism. We must understand that we cannot be saved by obedience to the law, but neither can we scuttle the law. We can be saved only by faith in Christ—we are saved by faith alone, *sola fide*. But we do not have a faith that is alone—a true believer will produce good works and desire to obey the law, a subject that Paul addresses in the chapters to come (Romans 12–16). We should also remember that God is always faithful to His word, whether in His promises to save His people or to judge unbelief and disobedience. Rather than try to establish our own righteousness through observing the law or disregarding the law, seek shelter in Christ and pray that He would equip us to glorify Him in all that we do. A Puritan prayer aptly captures a proper attitude toward Christ and the law:

> Have mercy on me, for I have ungratefully received thy benefits, little improved my privileges, made light of spiritual things, disregarded thy messages, contended with examples of the good, rebukes of conscience, admonitions of friends, leading of providence. I deserve that thy kingdom be taken away from me. Lord, I confess my sin with feeling, lamentation, a broken heart, a contrite spirit, self-abhorrence, self-condemnation, self-despair. Give me relief by Jesus my hope, faith in his name of Savior, forgiveness by his blood, strength by his presence, holiness by his Spirit: and let me love thee with all my heart.[3]

In light of Paul's indictment against Israel, we should give a hearty amen to this prayer.

---

3. Arthur Bennett, *Valley of Vision: A Collection of Puritan Prayers and Devotions* (Edinburgh: Banner of Truth, 1975), 192.

8

The Depravity of Humanity

ROMANS 3:9–20

What then? Are we better than they? Not at all. For we have previously charged both Jews and Greeks that they are all under sin. As it is written: "There is none righteous, no, not one; There is none who understands; There is none who seeks after God. They have all turned aside; They have together become unprofitable; There is none who does good, no, not one." "Their throat is an open tomb; With their tongues they have practiced deceit"; "The poison of asps is under their lips"; "Whose mouth is full of cursing and bitterness." "Their feet are swift to shed blood; Destruction and misery are in their ways; And the way of peace they have not known." "There is no fear of God before their eyes." Now we know that whatever the law says, it says to those who are under the law, that every mouth may be stopped, and all the world may become guilty before God. Therefore by the deeds of the law no flesh will be justified in His sight, for by the law is the knowledge of sin.

Friedrich Nietzsche (1844–1900), famous atheist philosopher, once opined that the concept of sin was something that the church invented to hold man in check—to keep him demoralized and under the thumb of the church:

> The concept of guilt and punishment, the entire "moral world-order," was invented in opposition to science—in opposition to the detaching of man from the priest.... Man shall not look around him, he shall look down into himself; he shall not look prudently and cautiously in to things in order to learn, he shall not look at all: he shall suffer.... And he shall suffer in

> such a way that he has need of the priest at all times.—Away with physicians! One has need of a Savior.—The concept of guilt and punishment, including the doctrine of "grace," of "redemption," of "forgiveness"—lies through and through and without any psychological reality.... Sin, to say it again, that form par excellence of the self-violation of man, was invented to make science, culture, every kind of elevation and nobility of man impossible; the priest rules through the invention of sin.[1]

Within Nietzsche's idea is the kernel of the inherent goodness of man. If there is no sin, then there is no guilt; if there is no guilt, then there is no judgment; if there is no judgment, then there is no need of redemption. Ethically, therefore, humanity can decide what is good and what is bad, or even decide that nothing is truly evil. Nietzsche's views are not uncommon. All we have to do is look around us; everywhere people assert the basic and intrinsic goodness of humanity. People define ethical right and wrong based on how they feel, not on any objective ethical standards.

Yet, surprisingly enough, there has been a string of theologians, even those praised by conservative evangelicals, who affirm the inherent goodness of man. Charles Finney (1792–1875), touted as America's greatest revivalist, for example, writes: "The human will is free, therefore men have power or ability to do all their duty. The moral government of God everywhere assumes and implies the liberty of the human will, and natural ability of men to obey God. Every command, every threatening, every expostulation and denunciation in the Bible implies and assumes this."[2] Paul paints an entirely different picture. In case Paul's recipients had not been paying attention to what he wrote in Romans 1:18–3:8, he makes his point explicitly clear here in 3:9–20. Paul caps his argument by demonstrating the universal sinfulness of all humanity, Jew and Gentile. Paul's indictment, moreover, has no expiration date, no

1. Friedrich Nietzsche, *Twilight of the Idols / The Anti-Christ* (New York: Penguin Books, 1990), 177–78.

2. Charles Finney, *Lectures on Systematic Theology* (London: William Tegg and Co., 1851), 484–85.

shelf life that would confine his words to the first century. Rather, his words possess abiding authority unto the end of the age; hence, they are relevant even to this day.

Universal Sinfulness and Guilt

If the creation narrative is any indication of human nature, once God levels a charge of guilt at a person's feet he immediately seeks a way to avoid, squirm away, or shift the blame. Fully aware of this habit, Paul makes his point abundantly clear: "What then? Are we better than they? Not at all. For we have previously charged both Jews and Greeks that they are all under sin" (Rom. 3:9). In a sin-fallen world, sometimes the obvious is not so obvious. Paul therefore makes his point clear: All people, whether Jew or Gentile, are guilty of sin and therefore liable to God's judgment. To support his point Paul draws on the Old Testament, particularly the book of Psalms, to prove humanity's universal guilt.

Paul loosely quotes Psalm 14:1–3: "There is none righteous, no, not one; There is none who understands; There is none who seeks after God. They have all turned aside; They have together become unprofitable; There is none who does good, no, not one" (Rom. 3:10–12). When a New Testament author quotes an Old Testament passage, he does not merely have the specifically cited words in mind but often the entire chapter, or even larger portions, such as an entire book of the Bible. In this case, it is instructive that Psalm 14:2 states, "The LORD looks down from heaven upon the children of men," which means that Paul accurately uses the text. God through the psalmist testifies to humanity's universal guilt. What rabbi or pious Jew would disagree with God's authoritative Word? And in case someone might try to squirm away from God's all-knowing and all-seeing judgment, the psalmist very clearly states that no one, "not one," is righteous. There is one exception to this rule, but we will consider this below.

Paul adds further authoritative testimony from the Psalms when he writes: "'Their throat is an open tomb; With their tongues they have practiced deceit'; 'The poison of asps is under their lips';

'Whose mouth is full of cursing and bitterness'" (Rom. 3:13–14). Paul does not randomly quote this series of statements from the Old Testament (Ps. 5:9; Jer. 5:16; Ps. 140:3; 10:7) but specifically focuses on the *mouth*. Paul compares the collective mouth of sinful humanity to an open tomb, which if Lazarus's postmortem state is any indicator, it is rank with the malodorous stench of death (John 11:39). Paul's word picture stands in stark contrast to the pleasant aroma of the prayers of the saints (cf. Ex. 25:6; 30:7; Rev. 8:3–4). In this vein, recall that when the prophet Isaiah beheld the preincarnate Christ he cried out, "Woe is me, for I am undone! Because I am a man of unclean lips, And I dwell in the midst of a people of unclean lips; For my eyes have seen the King, the LORD of hosts" (Isa. 6:5; cf. John 12:41).

Why do Isaiah and Paul focus on the mouth and lips? Because they are a window into the soul. Remember Christ's words drawn from Isaiah the prophet: "Well did Isaiah prophesy of you hypocrites, as it is written: 'This people honors Me with their lips, But their heart is far from Me'" (Mark 7:6). A façade of insincere praise, a whitewashed tomb, does not fool God. The seraphim, for example, continually uttered forth the praise of God with their lips: "Holy, holy, holy is the LORD of hosts; The whole earth is full of His glory!" (Isa. 6:3). This is precisely what we are supposed to do with our own lips according to the book of Hebrews: "Therefore by Him let us continually offer the sacrifice of praise to God, that is, the fruit of our lips, giving thanks to His name" (Heb. 13:15). Yet, far from praise, which reflects a heart positively disposed to loving and fearing God, Paul demonstrates that unbelieving man is totally sinful. Praise does not fill his lips; rather, the poison of asps, or serpents, is under his lips.

If sinful humanity has the wretched stench of death rising from its mouth and the caustic poison of serpents under its lips, then it should be no surprise that violence marks fallen man. Once again, Paul draws damning testimony from the Old Testament, Proverbs 1:16 and Isaiah 59:7–8, to prove his point. Like an expert attorney in the courtroom, Paul elicits irrefutable evidence against the accused through his witness, Holy Scripture: "Their feet are swift to shed blood; Destruction and misery are in their ways; And the way of peace they have not known" (Rom. 3:15–17). Paul employs the infallible and authoritative testimony of Scripture to substantiate the charge that fallen humanity has wickedness that not only remains in its heart but gushes out and gives birth to violence and murder. Like an overrun sewer, the vile contents of man's heart flows out into the streets, and wicked thoughts become manifest in sinful action. Quoting Psalm 36:1, Paul summarizes the chief problem of sinful humanity: "There is no fear of God before their eyes" (Rom. 3:18). Rather than fearing the Lord, which is the beginning of knowledge (Prov. 1:7), and hating evil (Prov. 8:13), humanity proudly stands before its Maker and spews forth curses and sings its own praise as people violently strike one another and lather their hands in the blood of their fellow man.

Paul excuses his witness from the stand and offers his closing argument, summarizing Romans 3:9–18 as well as the entirety of 1:18–3:18. He writes: "Now we know that whatever the law says, it says to those who are under the law, that every mouth may be stopped, and all the world may become guilty before God" (Rom. 3:19). Paul has appealed to the law, the Torah, which he cited in Romans 2:22–23: "You who say, 'Do not commit adultery,' do you commit adultery? You who abhor idols, do you rob temples? You who make your boast in the law, do you dishonor God through breaking the law?" But in this case, when Paul writes of the law it likely means the *teaching of Scripture*, to which he has appealed through his quotations from Psalms, Proverbs, and Jeremiah. We should not forget, however, Paul's appeal to the work of the law written on the hearts of all people (Rom. 2:14–15). Given this twofold testimony from the books of nature and Scripture, Paul confidently concludes that everyone is under God's law, and given humanity's sinful condition, all people stand accountable before the divine bar.

Sinful people might think they can somehow curry God's favor through their own good works, and therefore Paul informs his recipients: "By the deeds of the law no flesh will be justified in His sight, for by the law is the knowledge of sin" (Rom. 3:20). Paul offers one last quotation from Psalm 143:2 to prove his point. In its original context, David pleaded with God not to judge him, because he knew he would never be able to meet the law's standard—absolute and perfect obedience. Given David's intimate familiarity with his own sinfulness as well as that of his fellow man, amply evident in Paul's earlier quotations from Psalms 5 and 14, David knew that no sin-fallen person could be justified, or declared righteous, in God's sight on the basis of his own works. Even though Paul has explained how the law functions—namely, the doers of the law will be justified (Rom. 2:13)—he did not say that sinful human beings could successfully withstand God's judgment. Paul has merely stated that *if* a person is obedient, then he will be justified. But given the amassed evidence in Romans 1:18–3:18, it is impossible for sinful man to be justified by his works. For sin-fallen people, the law only identifies and accuses—hence Paul's words, "by the law is the knowledge of sin."

Abiding Relevance

Even though Paul wrote this almost two thousand years ago, people still try to claim that humanity is inherently good. "All we need is the further evolution of humanity," cries the world. "With more evolution we can eliminate all of our problems!" Yes, we stand at the edge of some of the world's greatest scientific, electronic, and medical advances ever known to man. Yet, despite all the progress, we also look back on the twentieth century—in which 180 million people died as a result of war—the bloodiest century in all of human history. People still pursue the fool's errand and believe that man needs only a better education and that learning will eradicate his lust for evil. But look back in history and you will find that some of the world's most educated people have perpetrated some of the world's most heinous evils.

While Karl Barth (1886–1968) carried no banner for traditional orthodox theology, he nevertheless offers excellent insights into the nature of humanity's universal sinfulness based on Paul's analysis here in Romans 3. He begins by asking the question, What would all the prophets, philosophers, church fathers, Reformers, poets, and artists say about the claim that humanity is inherently morally good? Is Paul's doctrine of sin merely one among many? What would an honest study of world history yield? Would we not come to the conclusion that there are some people that are like God and love Him? Barth responds:

> No, but that—*There is none righteous, no, not one*. Does it teach that men possess a deep perception of the nature of things? or that they have experienced the essence of life? No, but that—*There is none that understand.* Does it provide a moving picture of quiet piety or of fiery search after God? Do the great witnesses to the truth furnish a splendid picture, for example, of "Prayer"? No:—*There is none that seeks after God.* Can it describe this or that individual and his actions as natural, healthy, genuine, original, right-minded, ideal, full of character, affectionate, attractive, intelligent, forceful, ingenious, of sterling worth? No:—*They have all turned aside, they are together become unprofitable; There is none that does good, no, not so much as one*. Can it not unearth, perhaps, some secular or spiritual human characteristics more beautiful than these—whether in the inner realm of intelligence or in the outer realm of conduct—conscious or unconscious—active or passive—theoretical or practical? No:—*Their throat is an open sepulcher; With their tongues they have used deceit; The poison of asps is under their lips: Whose mouth is full of cursing and bitterness*. And in final judgment upon the thoughts and words of men—*Their feet are swift to shed blood; Destruction and misery are in their ways; And the way of peace have they not known*. This is the final judgment upon the deeds and works of men.[3]

This should lead us to several conclusions.

---

3. Barth, *Epistle to the Romans*, 85–86.

We Are Slaves to Sin

Unlike Finney, who argued that man had the ability to choose freely between good and evil, this passage of Scripture clearly says otherwise. As Paul wrote, "There is none who seeks after God." Therefore, if no one seeks after God, then this means that sinners cannot and will not seek God—ever. In case some might try to drive a wedge between the teaching of Jesus and Paul on this matter, we should note that they both teach the same thing. Jesus told the crowds, "Most assuredly, I say to you, whoever commits sin is a slave of sin" (John 8:34). Paul similarly writes that before our effectual calling and union with Christ, "we all once conducted ourselves in the lusts of our flesh, fulfilling the desires of the flesh and of the mind, and were by nature children of wrath, just as the others" (Eph. 2:3).

For these reasons the historic Reformed faith has confessed man's inability to seek after God: "Man, by his fall into a state of sin, hath wholly lost all ability of will to any spiritual good accompanying salvation; so as a natural man, being altogether averse from that good, and dead in sin, is not able, by his own strength, to convert himself, or to prepare himself thereunto" (Westminster Confession of Faith [WCF] 9.3). Humanity's enslavement to sin is ultimately the reason why our world will never improve on its own. Humanity will never educate, discover, or invent its way out of its bondage to sin. Our tendency is to look at how awful the world is and shake our heads in disapprobation of its wickedness. Yet we should recognize that this is a portrait not only of the world's wickedness but also of our own.

Look in the Mirror

For some of us, this is an all-too-gruesome reminder of who we were before we were saved. For those of us who have grown up in the church, it should also be a reminder of who we were before Christ. Yes, being born within the covenant community is a tremendous blessing. Being born within the covenant community, however, does not automatically save us. Paul's montage of Old Testament passages concerning the universal sinfulness of humanity is as much a portrait of the unsaved as it is of ourselves before our salvation. We were by nature children of wrath, unrighteous, and we did not seek God. We did not have understanding; we had throats that were open sepulchers, with the poison of asps under our lips; and we did not know the way of peace. We were slaves to sin and were blind to the kingdom of light. The only reason we are not like Paul's description is because God the Father sent Christ the Son to pay the penalty for our wickedness and sent God the Holy Spirit to replace our sin-hardened hearts of stone with Spirit-wrought hearts of flesh. This is why Paul writes: "By the deeds of the law no flesh will be justified in His sight, for by the law is the knowledge of sin" (Rom. 3:20). Or, in the words of the hymn "Rock of Ages" by Augustus Toplady:

> Not the labors of my hands
> Can fulfill thy law's demands;
> Could my zeal no respite know,
> Could my tears forever flow,
> All for sin could not atone;
> Thou must save, and thou alone.
>
> Nothing in my hand I bring,
> Simply to thy cross I cling;
> Naked, come to thee for dress;
> Helpless, look to thee for grace;
> Foul, I to the Fountain fly;
> Wash me, Savior, or I die.

When we look into the mirror of the law of God, the last thing we would want to do is walk away and forget what we have seen or try to perfume the foul stench of death in the hopes that God will not notice. Rather, Christ is our only refuge.

The Authority and Power of the Word

This passage should also serve as a paradigm to ministers of the Word as we examine how Paul prosecutes his case. Paul could have simply stood on the platform of his own apostolic authority to support his claims. Paul, after all, was personally ordained by Christ Himself to be "a bondservant of Jesus Christ, called to be an apostle" (Rom. 1:1). But Paul ultimately relied on the authority and power of God's Word—his numerous quotations of the Old Testament show us that he relied on God to convict people of their sin. He did not try to convince people simply by rhetoric, persuasive arguments, or even by his own apostolic authority. As ministers of the Word, our inclination might be to try to persuade people of the truth by whatever means we can rather than rest in the power of God's Word. But if God's Word has the power to create worlds out of nothing, then why would we seek other means when we have His infallible, inerrant, and all-powerful Word at our disposal to save fallen sinners? If we truly believe that the gospel is the power of God unto salvation, then we will seek no other instrument by which to convict people of their sin.

Conclusion

This passage of Scripture should be permanently engraved on our hearts. It should be a reminder to us that man is and always will be wicked apart from the saving grace of God. It should also be a reminder that it is a portrait of ourselves prior to our conversion. The fact that we have been delivered from spiritual death should give us great reason to praise our triune Lord: "Behold what manner of love the Father has bestowed on us, that we should be called children of God" (1 John 3:1).

9

Saved from God by God

ROMANS 3:21–31

But now the righteousness of God apart from the law is revealed, being witnessed by the Law and the Prophets, even the righteousness of God, through faith in Jesus Christ, to all and on all who believe. For there is no difference; for all have sinned and fall short of the glory of God, being justified freely by His grace through the redemption that is in Christ Jesus, whom God set forth as a propitiation by His blood, through faith, to demonstrate His righteousness, because in His forbearance God had passed over the sins that were previously committed, to demonstrate at the present time His righteousness, that He might be just and the justifier of the one who has faith in Jesus. Where is boasting then? It is excluded. By what law? Of works? No, but by the law of faith. Therefore we conclude that a man is justified by faith apart from the deeds of the law. Or is He the God of the Jews only? Is He not also the God of the Gentiles? Yes, of the Gentiles also, since there is one God who will justify the circumcised by faith and the uncircumcised through faith. Do we then make void the law through faith? Certainly not! On the contrary, we establish the law.

One of the false doctrines that periodically surfaces within the broader church is that humanity is essentially good. Within academic circles, theologians in the broader church claim that humanity's problem is not original sin but original selfishness. They deny the biblical doctrine that all human beings are sinful because of Adam's first transgression and instead argue that God created human beings with a proclivity toward self-preservation—a biological necessity to ensure the existence of the human race, but an inclination that also results in selfishness. People must look to Christ's example of selflessness and follow His example in order to attain their salvation. Such claims might sit well with many in the scientific community who embrace evolutionary theories of humanity's origins, but they ultimately clash with the Bible's teaching. The claim rests on the assumption that human beings are inherently good and act in a selfish manner only because they were made this way.[1] In such a conception, we must reconfigure the doctrine of atonement. No longer does Christ come as a propitiation for sinners but only as a moral exemplar—He shows the way but does not actually save. Is Christ merely an example of moral living, or does He actually come to save sinners who lie under the righteous condemnation of God and are thus subject to His wrath? In this portion of Romans, Paul sets forth the very heart of his epistle and, indeed, the very heart of the gospel.

Righteousness Apart from the Law

As we explore this section of Paul's epistle, it is important that we recall the chief points he raised in the preceding section. First, Paul indicts all humanity—they are all guilty of sin: "There is none righteous, no, not one" (Rom. 3:10). Correlatively, given the universal sinfulness of mankind, no one can be justified by personal obedience: "By the deeds of the law no flesh will be justified in His sight, for by the law is the knowledge of sin" (Rom. 3:20). Not even Israel's special identity as God's chosen people, circumcision, or possession of the law, curries divine favor. For sin-fallen creatures, therefore, "in justification there is no contribution, preparatory, accessory, or subsidiary, that is given by the works of the law."[2] As sin-fallen creatures look into the mirror of the law, it offers no hope, no respite, and no shelter.

---

1. See Daryl P. Domning and Monika K. Hellwig, *Original Selfishness: Original Sin and Evil in the Light of Evolution* (Aldershot, UK: Ashgate, 2006).

2. Murray, *Epistle to the Romans*, 109.

But then Paul pens what are some of the most glorious words in Scripture: "But now the righteousness of God apart from the law is revealed, being witnessed by the Law and the Prophets, even the righteousness of God, through faith in Jesus Christ, to all and on all who believe" (Rom. 3:21–22a). Paul's words are as the sun bursting over the horizon and piercing the darkness when he states that God's righteousness comes apart from the law. Clearly, Paul states that the law and the prophets bear witness to it. By what means can sin-fallen people access this righteousness? We can access and lay hold of this righteousness only by faith alone in Christ alone. Moreover, laying hold of God's righteousness in Christ by faith is effective not just for a small subset of humanity. Rather, for each and every person of the human race, faith alone in Christ alone is the only means by which we can lay hold of this righteousness. Why? Because as Paul writes, "For there is no difference; for all have sinned and fall short of the glory of God" (Rom. 3:22b–23). All of us are more interested in glorifying ourselves and turning our own will into an idol rather than glorifying God. Instead of loving God, we sinfully love ourselves (Deut. 11:13; 1 John 5:2).

Remember what Paul has written: "The doers of the law will be justified" (Rom. 2:13)—but sin-fallen people are incapable of perfectly fulfilling the law. So this is why God has poured out His mercy and we are "justified freely by His grace through the redemption that is in Christ Jesus" (Rom. 3:24). Note the antithetical relationship between faith and works, between moral effort and God's gift of grace. Rather than look introspectively to our own moral efforts, Paul instead points us extrospectively to the redemption that comes through Christ. Paul's use of the term *redemption* (*apolytrowseows*) is apt, given that the New Testament uses it in connection with liberating slaves (cf. Luke 24:21; Eph. 1:7). This language likely would have brought Israel's liberation from Egypt to the minds of most first-century Jews—an emancipation, mind you, wrought entirely by God. All people were under the condemnation of the law given their sinfulness; hence, the law was like Pharaoh to them (cf. Rom. 7:6; Gal. 3:23; 4:9).

But God freed us by one greater than Moses, Jesus Christ, "whom God set forth as a propitiation by His blood, through faith" (Rom. 3:25). Paul's use of the term *propitiation* (*hilasteœrion*) is quite important, a term often otherwise translated as "mercy seat" (NET), "sacrifice of atonement" (NIV, NRSV), "expiation" (RSV), and "sacrifice" (NLT). These other terms approach the nature of Christ's redemption. The Greek translation of the Old Testament uses the term *hilasteœrion* for the cover of the ark of the covenant, which was sprinkled with blood and therefore called the "mercy seat" (Ex. 25:17–19 LXX). This connection draws us into the sacrificial protocols of the Day of Atonement (Lev. 16:14–15). On that day of days, the high priest entered the holy of holies and offered a blood sacrifice to cover Israel's sins and avert God's wrath (Lev. 16:34). But as the book of Hebrews reminds us, the blood of bulls and goats was ultimately of no avail, as it could not cleanse a person of sin (Heb. 10:4). God never intended these sacrificial animals to cleanse people from sin. Rather, He implemented the sacrificial system to point forward to the once-for-all sacrifice of His Son, Jesus Christ, which would not only remove the people's sins but also placate God's wrath. This is why the NKJV's choice to translate *hilasteœrion* by the term *propitiation* is an apt one. Christ's sacrificial work is not merely an *expiation*, something that takes away sin. His shed blood is a *propitiation*, something that takes away sin and appeases God's wrath against sin.

Christ's role as propitiation is significant. When we acknowledge Christ's role as a propitiation, it means that once Christ forgives us of our sin, it can rise against us no more. Christ's sacrifice nullifies the law's condemnation against us. This means that Christ's sacrifice conveys peace for all who seek shelter in Him. If Christ were merely a moral exemplar, then we would have no peace with God. Salvation would be a long, perilous, and arduous journey that no one would complete. Strip humanity of sin and you strip humanity's need for Christ. Acknowledge the depth and debt of our sin and you tacitly admit your utter and irreplaceable need for Christ.

God—Just and Justifier

Paul then explains why God would send His only begotten Son to bring us eternal life: "To demonstrate His righteousness, because in His forbearance God had passed over the sins that were previously committed, to demonstrate at the present time His righteousness, that He might be just and the justifier of the one who has faith in Jesus" (Rom. 3:25b–26). In Christ's sacrificial work, God reveals His righteousness. Recall, this is one of the chief themes of Paul's epistle to Rome. Paul set forth his thesis at the beginning of his letter when he wrote that in the gospel, "the righteousness of God is revealed from faith to faith" (Rom. 1:17). The gospel reveals both the mercy and justice of God, His wrath and His grace. When Christ shed His blood on the cross, God demonstrated to the world that He was just, that He was righteous—He did not merely write off sin. God punished the sins of His people when Jesus willingly suffered on their behalf. But at the same time, God mercifully granted access to Christ's representative and intercessory work through the gift of faith alone, and for this reason He is also the justifier. God is both "just and the justifier of the one who has faith in Jesus" (Rom. 3:26). In fact, God was so desirous to demonstrate His love for His people that Paul tells us, "In His forbearance God had passed over the sins that were previously committed" (Rom. 3:25b). In other words, He did not immediately judge the world for its sin but rather patiently waited for His plan to unfold so that Christ, the God-man, would intercede on behalf of God's people.

Now if all of these things are true, then how can sinful man conceivably boast in anything that he might do apart from God's grace in Christ? As Paul writes, "Where is boasting then? It is excluded. By what law? Of works? No, but by the law of faith" (Rom. 3:27). How can we boast in our ineffective efforts to secure our justification by our works if the only way we can be saved is by faith alone? Paul sets forth the two mutually exclusive paths: We are justified either by the law (or principle) of works or by the law (or principle) of faith. And given our sin-fallen condition, the principle of justification by works is out of the question; hence, Paul writes, "Therefore we conclude that a man is justified by faith apart from the deeds of the law" (Rom. 3:28). These are some of the most glorious words in all of Scripture—a fount of water to the thirsty, words that bring life to the dead! If we are justified by faith alone in Christ alone by God's grace alone, then we have no ground whatsoever for boasting in ourselves. And Paul's point applies universally to all, to Jew and Gentile, circumcised and uncircumcised, as God will only justify both by faith alone in Christ alone (Rom. 3:29–30). And Paul's argument thus far in no way overthrows the law (that is, the collective teaching of the Old Testament) but rather upholds it (Rom. 3:31). Paul's repeated references to and quotations of the Old Testament manifestly demonstrate that the gospel is nothing new but rather was God's plan from the outset.

This passage of Scripture clearly demonstrates the fact that God is not a doting father trying to win the acceptance of His wayward children. Or, as H. Richard Niebuhr (1894–1962) once characterized the gospel as it was preached in America, as "a God without wrath who brings humans without sin into a kingdom without judgment through a Christ without a cross."[3] Nothing could be further from the truth. What might be commonplace in American churches does not at all reflect the teaching of Scripture. According to Paul, God is our judge, and a guilty verdict and death sentence hang over us. Rather than punish us as we rightly deserve, God lovingly and mercifully sends His Son, Jesus Christ, who willingly takes our place and bears the punishment that is rightly ours. And, if this were not enough, God also gives us His righteousness in Christ as if it were our own. This is a subject on which Paul will elaborate in the chapters to come.

But suffice it to say that the righteousness we receive is not our own; it is an alien righteousness because it comes from outside of us. As Martin Luther explains, "Is not this a beautiful, glorious exchange, by which Christ, who is totally innocent and holy, not

3. H. Richard Niebuhr, *The Kingdom of God in America* (Indianapolis: Wesleyan Publishing House, 1988), 193.

only takes upon himself another's sin...but also clothes and adorns me...with his own innocence and purity? Through this blessed exchange...and through nothing else, are we freed from sin and death and given his righteousness and life as our own."[4] What is wonderful about all of this is that God Himself saves us from His terrible wrath and destruction! God saves us from God. This has been the message from the very beginning of redemptive history, when God alone walked between the severed animal halves while Abraham slumbered (Gen. 15:7–17). God's message to Abraham was that He would bear his sins and communicate His righteousness to him, and this is the message that Paul heralds. The only way, therefore, that we can be saved is not by our own works but by placing our faith and trust in the work of Christ. This passage and others like it lead the sixteenth-century Reformers to conclude that salvation is by Christ alone by grace alone through faith alone—*solus Christus*, *sola gratia*, and *sola fide.*

Conclusion

So, then, do we realize that we have been saved from God by God? Do we realize that Christ bore the penalty for our sin and that God did not merely write off our rebellion? Do we recognize that God is not the doting father trying to win our affections but that apart from Christ's intercessory work He is our Judge? Do we recognize that Christ is far more than a moral example? On the great day of the Lord, God will judge the world (e.g., Zeph. 1:14–18). We either bear this judgment ourselves or we can take shelter in Christ—for He has borne it for His people. We will not be able to say, "You can't hold me responsible for my sin—you made me this way!" Too many people try to cut these words from the same cloth as Adam's failed self-defense in the garden of Eden. By God's grace Adam eventually placed his faith in the promised deliverer, the seed of the woman who would crush the head of the serpent. Praise be to

4. Martin Luther, *Luther's Works*, vol. 51, ed. John W. Doberstein (St. Louis: Concordia Publishers, 1959), 315.

God the Father for giving us His Son and His Holy Spirit, that we may see Christ's work and take refuge in it by faith alone. Therefore, seek shelter in Christ and not in your own so-called good works. Rest in Him.

10

Sola Fide

ROMANS 4:1–8

What then shall we say that Abraham our father has found according to the flesh? For if Abraham was justified by works, he has something to boast about, but not before God. For what does the Scripture say? "Abraham believed God, and it was accounted to him for righteousness." Now to him who works, the wages are not counted as grace but as debt. But to him who does not work but believes on Him who justifies the ungodly, his faith is accounted for righteousness, just as David also describes the blessedness of the man to whom God imputes righteousness apart from works: "Blessed are those whose lawless deeds are forgiven, And whose sins are covered; Blessed is the man to whom the Lord *shall not impute sin."*

In the history of the church there have been times when the faithful defended the truth from the attacks of the enemy. One such time, of course, was the sixteenth-century Reformation in which the doctrine of justification by faith alone was under attack. According to Martin Luther, "the article of justification is the master and prince, the lord, the ruler, and the judge over all kinds of doctrines; it preserves and governs all Church doctrine and raises up our conscience before God. Without this article the world is utter death and darkness."[1]

1. Luther, *What Luther Says*, 2:703.

Likewise, John Calvin said that the doctrine of justification was "the principal hinge by which religion is supported."[2] Elsewhere Calvin wrote, "Whenever knowledge of it is taken away the glory of Christ is extinguished, religion abolished, the Church destroyed, and the hope of salvation utterly overthrown."[3] Surely, Luther and Calvin exaggerate, right? Could we not say that this was all a tempest in a teapot? Have we not moved beyond such rhetoric and theological debates? The simple answer to these questions is no. Luther and Calvin did not exaggerate. The debates over justification between the Reformers and the Roman Catholic Church were not a tempest in a teapot, and we cannot characterize their statements as overheated rhetoric. But in order to substantiate this claim, we must first understand the nature of the doctrine of justification by faith alone according to what Paul has written in these opening eight verses of the fourth chapter. Second, we must then examine the nature of the ongoing debate between a Reformed and Roman Catholic understanding of justification. Lastly, we should contemplate what this means for us personally.

The Nature of Justification

Before we proceed to Paul's opening statement, we should first remember what he has argued thus far. Paul has just spent the third chapter arguing two key points. First, because of the universal sinfulness of humanity (Rom. 1:18–3:19), no one can be declared righteous in God's sight based on his own obedience to the law: "By the deeds of the law no flesh will be justified in His sight, for by the law is the knowledge of sin" (Rom. 3:20). We might walk away from such a conclusion sapped of all hope, but Paul does not end here, praise God. He continues with a second point: "For all have sinned and fall short of the glory of God, being justified

2. John Calvin, *Institutes of the Christian Religion*, trans. John Allen (Grand Rapids: Eerdmans, 1949), 3.11.1.

3. John Calvin, "Reply by John Calvin to Cardinal Sadolet's Letter," in *John Calvin: Tracts and Letters*, vol. 1, ed. and trans. Henry Beveridge (1844; repr., Edinburgh: Banner of Truth, 2009), 41.

freely by His grace through the redemption that is in Christ Jesus" (Rom. 3:23–24). What sinful people are unable to do, God has done in and through Christ. Christ offers the perfect obedience that God requires, and we receive this righteousness by faith alone in Christ alone.

But if this blessing is available to both Jew and Gentile, then what advantage does Israel have over the Gentile nations? Paul poses this question and draws his readers' attention to Abraham, the great patriarch of Israel: "What then shall we say that Abraham our father has found according to the flesh?" (Rom. 4:1). Paul expounds the blessings that Abraham received by explaining the nature of justification and connecting it to the lives of Abraham and King David, another Israelite greatly esteemed by all.

Paul explains the nature of justification by delving into the life of Abraham, arguably Israel's greatest patriarch. He first sets forth a hypothetical argument in which he contemplates, What *if* Abraham had been justified by works? *If* God justified Abraham by works, then the patriarch would have grounds for boasting: "For if Abraham was justified by works, he has something to boast about" (Rom. 4:2). He would, after all, stand before the divine bar and pass the test under his own strength. But almost as quickly as the words fall from the quill to the parchment, the apostle denies the possibility by saying that Abraham has no grounds for boasting. He then proves his point by going back to the Old Testament, quoting Genesis 15:6: "Abraham believed God, and it was accounted to him for righteousness" (Rom. 4:3).

This verse mentions *nothing* about Abraham's justification by works. In fact, the Greek word here that is translated as "counted" can also be translated as "imputed" or "reckoned" (RSV) or "credited" (NIV). Moreover, the Greek verb is in the passive voice, which means that the imputation is not an act performed by Abraham (such as his own obedience); rather, he is the recipient of the action. Paul's point is therefore this: Righteousness comes through faith, not by works. He proves this with the Israelite of Israelites, the great patriarch Abraham. This bolsters his two main points from chapter 3—namely, God will not justify anyone in His sight by his works (Rom. 3:20). All have sinned and fallen short of God's glory and are justified freely by His grace through the redemption that has come through Christ (Rom. 3:23–24).

To drive his point home, Paul offers an illustration: "Now to him who works, the wages are not counted as grace but as debt. But to him who does not work but believes on Him who justifies the ungodly, his faith is accounted for righteousness" (Rom. 4:4–5). Paul sets forth a simple mathematical formula that builds on what he has already stated in Romans 2:13b: "The doers of the law will be justified." In other words, law + works = justification. When a person works, Paul tells us, God counts his wages as his just reward, not as a gift. This is one path to justification. But Paul sets forth a second path to justification—by faith alone in Christ alone (Rom. 4:5). If you believe in what Christ has done in His life, death, resurrection, and ascension, then you will be justified—declared righteous. Paul places this second path of justification in stark contrast and antithesis to the first. Notice how he characterizes this second path: "To him who does not work but believes on Him," God justifies this "ungodly" person. Paul places the strongest antithesis between faith and works, between obedience and trusting in Christ. A person cannot be the recipient of grace if he works for his salvation, because his salvation is owed to him. On the contrary, as Paul affirmed in Romans 3:23–24, God freely justifies the ungodly. Also notice the implication here: Paul indirectly calls Abraham ungodly. This continues to challenge the idea that Abraham earned his salvation in any way and echoes the truth of Romans 3:23, "For all have sinned and fall short of the glory of God," which includes the great patriarch of Israel, Abraham.

Paul's characterization of Abraham was quite different from the estimation of his Jewish first-century peers. In one statement, we find the following: "Was not Abraham found faithful when tested, and it was reckoned to him as righteousness" (1 Macc. 2:52 NRSV). In another uninspired Jewish writing we find the following description:

> Abraham was the great father of a multitude of nations, and no one has been found like him in glory. He kept the law of the Most High, and entered into a covenant with him; he certified the covenant in his flesh, and when he was tested he proved faithful. Therefore the Lord assured him with an oath that the nations would be blessed through his offspring; that he would make him as numerous as the dust of the earth, and exalt his offspring like the stars, and give them an inheritance from sea to sea and from the Euphrates to the ends of the earth. (Sir. 44:19–21 NRSV)

These two descriptions mirror what we find in another statement from intertestamental Jewish literature: "For Abraham was perfect in all of his actions with the LORD and was pleasing through righteousness all of the days of his life (Jub. 23:10a; cf. 16:28). For first-century Jews, Abraham was a righteous and godly man who secured his righteous status by his obedience. For Paul, Abraham was "ungodly," and he secured his righteous status by faith alone in God's promise.

If this is insufficient evidence, Paul invokes a second Old Testament example. He calls King David, Israel's greatest earthly king, to the witness stand: "Just as David also describes the blessedness of the man to whom God imputes righteousness apart from works: 'Blessed are those whose lawless deeds are forgiven, And whose sins are covered; Blessed is the man to whom the LORD shall not impute sin'" (Rom. 4:6–8). Paul invokes King David's testimony from Psalm 32:1–2, where Israel's former king characterizes justification in terms of the forgiveness of sins—not merely in wiping the slate clean but in covering the sins with positive righteousness, or obedience. The law knows nothing of neutrality—one may not be indifferent toward it. Rather, the law knows only of positive fulfillment or negative transgression. And if we have transgressed the law, then we are guilty of violating it, and only positive righteousness, or obedience, can cover our sins. Hence, God blesses us when He does not count, or impute, sin to us. This non-accounting of sin is not on the basis of our own good works but only on the basis of Christ's perfect obedience to the law.

The Ongoing Debate

In light of what Paul has written, do we understand that the Reformation debate was not a tempest in a teapot? There is a stark difference between what the Protestant Reformers taught and what the Roman Catholic Church taught and still teaches. For example, note what the Westminster Larger Catechism (WLC) states on this point when it asks the question, What is justification? It answers: "Justification is an act of God's free grace unto sinners, in which he pardoneth all their sins, accepteth and accounteth their persons righteous in his sight; not for any thing wrought in them, or done by them, but only for the perfect obedience and full satisfaction of Christ, by God imputed to them, and received by faith alone" (Q. 70). This question and answer reflects the very points that Paul sets forth in Romans 3:20–4:8. In justification God pardons our sins and accepts and accounts us righteous in His sight, not because of our own good works or obedience but only for the perfect obedience and suffering of Jesus—His perfect fulfillment of the law and His suffering the penalty of the law on our behalf.

The Larger Catechism continues and explains how God justifies us: "How doth faith justify a sinner in the sight of God?" The catechism responds: "Faith justifies a sinner in the sight of God, not because of those other graces which do always accompany it, or of good works that are the fruits of it, not as if the grace of faith, or any act thereof, were imputed to him for his justification; but only as it is an instrument by which he receiveth and applieth Christ and his righteousness" (Q. 73). This echoes, of course, the teaching of the Reformation that we are justified by faith alone, or *sola fide*. Our works do not justify us, as Paul clearly writes here. If our works justified us, this would completely contradict Paul's point.

But not every church that claims fidelity to the Scriptures teaches the same doctrine. In its official response to the Protestant Reformation, the Roman Catholic Church at the Council of

Trent (1547) issued the following declarations concerning the doctrine of justification: "Justification itself, which is not remission of sins merely, but also the sanctification and renewal of the inward man, through the voluntary reception of the grace, and of the gifts, whereby man of unjust becomes just, and of an enemy a friend, that so he may be an heir according to hope of life everlasting."[4] Rome specifically insists that justification consists in both the forgiveness of sins *and* the sanctification and renewal of the inward man. In contradiction to Paul's clear statements here, they claim that in order to be justified a person must contribute to the process with his own good works. Trent states this point quite clearly when it claims, "They, through the observance of the commandments of God and of the Church, faith co-operating with good works, increase in that justice which they have received through the grace of Christ, and are still further justified."[5]

The Council of Trent also rejects another key teaching that Paul describes here in the fourth chapter—namely, the imputed obedience of Christ. Paul opens this subject here but will elaborate later, especially in chapter 5. Nevertheless, Trent states, "If any one saith, that men are justified, either by the sole imputation of the justice of Christ, or by the sole remission of sins, to the exclusion of the grace and the charity which is poured forth in their hearts by the Holy Ghost, and is inherent in them; or even that the grace, whereby we are justified, is only the favor of God: let him be anathema."[6] Rome is clear—the obedience and suffering of Christ is insufficient for our salvation, and anyone who claims that we are saved by Christ's work alone (*solus Christus*) lies under the condemnation of the Roman Catholic Church. I know that Roman Catholics would

---

4. Council of Trent, Sixth Session, chap. 7 in Philip Schaff, ed., *Creeds of Christendom*, vol. 2, *The Greek and Latin Creeds* (1931; repr., Grand Rapids: Baker, 1990), 94.

5. Council of Trent, Sixth Session, chap. 10 in Schaff, *Greek and Latin Creeds*, 2:99.

6. Council of Trent, "On Justification," in Schaff, *Greek and Latin Creeds*, 2:112–13.

reject the conclusion, but it is difficult to see how the apostle does not stand condemned before the Council of Trent. I suspect Paul would not be terribly concerned about Rome's condemnation; he knows that he stands guilt-free before the divine bar because of the all-sufficient obedience and suffering of Christ imputed to him by faith alone. Roman Catholic teaching accords neither with Paul's teaching nor the rest of Scripture. Abraham did not add good works to his justification, nor did he merit God's favor. Rather, as Paul says, "But to him who does not work but believes on Him who justifies the ungodly, his faith is accounted for righteousness" (Rom. 4:5). Rome denies what Paul so clearly affirms—God declares the *ungodly* righteous.

Now, we have moved past this contentious period, and the flames of this sixteenth-century debate are certainly nothing but smoldering embers, right? Unfortunately, the answer to this question is no. A number of years ago a group of evangelicals and Roman Catholics produced a document titled "Evangelicals and Catholics Together" (ECT), which declared the following: "We affirm together that we are justified by grace through faith because of Christ." Absent from this statement is the one word *alone*. Yes, we are justified by God's grace *alone* through faith *alone* because of Christ *alone*. To put it mildly, you can drive a truck through this ECT statement. It only affirms that Protestants and Roman Catholics believe that salvation is by grace, which very few in the history of the church have denied. This document also contended that evangelicals and Roman Catholics should leave one another alone: "We condemn the practice of recruiting people from another community for purposes of denominational or institutional aggrandizement." Rather than try to evangelize one another, evangelicals and Roman Catholics should instead focus their energies on converting the lost: "In view of the large number of non-Christians in the world and the enormous challenge of our common evangelistic task, it is neither theologically legitimate nor a prudent use of resources for one Christian community to proselytize among active adherents of another Christian community."[7] True, some of the high-profile evangelicals who signed this document withdrew their names from it, but the fact that they signed it in the first place shows us that they were not acutely aware of the major differences between Roman Catholicism and Protestantism. Even to this day prominent Roman Catholics claim there are no great differences between Rome and Protestantism.[8]

Personal Implications

We must not surrender the doctrine of justification under any circumstances. Luther and Calvin were correct: Justification is the article on which the church either stands or falls and the main hinge on which all true religion turns. When we read this passage and consider its implications for the church as a whole and what it teaches us personally, we can easily get swept up in polemics and forget to relish the sweet thoughts of what it means to be justified in God's sight. Never forget that our justification, our ability to stand in the presence of a holy God, is not at all predicated on our good works. Rather, we receive the forgiveness of sins and the imputation of Christ's righteousness through faith: "Blessed are those whose lawless deeds are forgiven, And whose sins are covered; Blessed is the man to whom the LORD shall not impute sin" (Rom. 4:7–8). For the fornicator, idolater, adulterer, homosexual, thief, coveter, and drunkard, there is no more guilt and burden of sin when they look to Christ by faith alone and trust in His perfect obedience and suffering (1 Cor. 6:9–11). What glorious grace there is in the forgiveness, justification, and imputed righteousness that comes by faith alone. The famous Reformed hymn writer Augustus Toplady (1740–1778) poetically captures this point in his hymn, "Fountain of Never-Ceasing Grace." Toplady writes:

---

7. All quotations taken from "Evangelicals and Catholics Together: The Christian Mission in the Third Millennium," *First Things* 43 (May 1994): 15–22.

8. John Richard Neuhaus, "Interview with John Richard Neuhaus," *Modern Reformation* 11, no. 2 (2002): 36.

Fountain of never ceasing grace,
Your saints exhaustless theme,
Great object of immortal praise,
Essentially supreme;
We bless you for the glorious fruits
Your incarnation gives
The righteousness which grace imputes,
And faith alone receives.

Conclusion

This passage should remind us to appreciate our theological history and heritage—to appreciate those great saints who have defended the faith from the enemy. It should remind us not to forget the lessons and battles of the past. If we fail to remember, we will be doomed to repeat the same errors. Lastly, we should not forget that these battles were not simply about rhetoric or academic musings but were vital battles for the very essence of the gospel itself. This has implications not only for the corporate body but also for us as individuals. Indeed, where would we be without justification by faith alone? We, of course, would be lost in utter darkness. Instead, we receive the riches of God's mercy in Christ, His imputed righteousness, by faith alone!

11

The Seal of Righteousness

ROMANS 4:9–12

Does this blessedness then come upon the circumcised only, or upon the uncircumcised also? For we say that faith was accounted to Abraham for righteousness. How then was it accounted? While he was circumcised, or uncircumcised? Not while circumcised, but while uncircumcised. And he received the sign of circumcision, a seal of the righteousness of the faith which he had while still uncircumcised, that he might be the father of all those who believe, though they are uncircumcised, that righteousness might be imputed to them also, and the father of circumcision to those who not only are of the circumcision, but who also walk in the steps of the faith which our father Abraham had while still uncircumcised.

"The pen is mightier than the sword" is a proverb that captures the idea that words can be more powerful than someone wielding violence against others. One person wielding a weapon might affect the lives of those immediately around him, but that same person can use words to rally his peers, even a nation, to war. Or words can be powerful enough to calm a nation's fears and thereby avert war. Words have the power to persuade, to change minds, and even to change our circumstances. For example, think about an ordinary citizen taking the oath of office and becoming president of the United States. He becomes one of the world's most powerful leaders merely by uttering a few words. Words are not merely things to be mumbled; they are a powerful force, and they are even more powerful in the mouth of our Savior, Jesus Christ. The Scriptures liken the spoken word in Christ's mouth to a sharp, two-edged sword, one that has the power to divide what is seemingly indivisible (Ps. 2:9; Heb. 4:12; Rev. 2:16; 19:15). In this passage Paul explores the life-giving power of the verdict of our justification by faith alone—what it means when God says, "You are righteous!" He explains the connection between the spoken word, God's verbal verdict, and the visible word—that is, the sacrament of circumcision. Paul explains the significance of circumcision as a sign and seal of the righteousness that Abraham had by faith.

In the apostle Paul's day there were grave errors that continually danced around the truth in an effort to shroud it under a veil of false piety. One of the serious errors that Paul confronted early in his ministry was the relationship between justification and the Old Testament rite of circumcision. Paul planted the Galatian churches and gave them the gospel—he heralded the message of justification by grace alone through faith alone in Christ alone. But soon after Paul departed, false teachers descended on the Galatian churches and started teaching that a person was justified by believing in Christ *and* by receiving circumcision. In other words, a person was no longer justified *sola fide*, by only believing in the work of Christ. Rather, believers had to add something else to the equation. The Jewish Christians taught that Gentile Christians had to be circumcised because they believed it was unthinkable that God would set aside the sign of His covenant, a sign that was in place for almost two thousand years.

The false teachers failed to grasp two key elements regarding the place and function of circumcision. First, they failed to understand that as a sign and seal of the Abrahamic covenant, circumcision pointed to Abraham's future seed, Jesus Christ (Gal. 3:16). Now that Christ had come, circumcision was no longer required because the sign was fulfilled. The fact that the apostles baptized people into the name of Christ implicitly demonstrates the designed obsolescence of circumcision. Second, the false teachers failed to realize that circumcision was not the *source* of Abraham's right standing before God, but, as Paul explains here, it is a *seal* of his standing.

Paul does not employ many words to explain the relationship between circumcision and justification as he does in his epistle to the Galatians, but he nevertheless addresses the subject. Paul does so undoubtedly because the sting, pain, and memories of the Galatian apostasy were still fresh on his mind. But lest we be lulled into a sense of complacency, we should recognize that Paul's words are still profoundly relevant for the church today. True, we no longer circumcise new converts; we baptize them. But in the chest of every Christian beats a heart that is always tempted to look away from Christ in an effort to displace His all-sufficient work. In this case, many Christians, like their first-century counterparts, believe they are saved by their faith in Christ *and* their baptism. Hence, Paul's words about the nature of circumcision are still relevant on two counts. First, he shows us that justification is by faith alone (*sola fide*)—a truth that has no expiration date. Second, the signs of the covenant (circumcision or baptism) serve as *seals*. A seal on a letter is not the actual letter but rather authenticates and gives greater authority to it. These are important truths that Paul explains in the verses before us.

The Nature of Circumcision

Crucial to grasping Paul's point about circumcision is remembering and rehearsing the overall context in which we find this passage. Paul has repeatedly stressed that salvation is not by works but by faith alone in Christ alone. He hammered this point with two Old Testament illustrations, Abraham and David: "For what does the Scripture say? 'Abraham believed God, and it was accounted to him for righteousness'" (Rom. 4:3; cf. Gen. 15:6). Abraham believed God; he did not trot out his good works or obedience. When Abraham believed in God and trusted in the promise of an heir, God counted his faith as righteousness. By faith Abraham laid hold of the promised obedience and suffering of Christ. Paul also stressed that works do not secure justification. Instead, sinners receive their justification through the forgiveness of sins when God covers them with the righteousness, or obedience, of Christ. Paul, quoting King

David, writes: "Blessed are those whose lawless deeds are forgiven, And whose sins are covered; Blessed is the man to whom the LORD shall not impute his sin" (Rom. 4:7–8; cf. Ps. 32:1–2).

In Paul's day, Jewish people, and even Jewish converts to Christianity, probably raised the question, But what about circumcision? What about the sign of God's covenant? Paul anticipates this question by first leveling the playing field—he states that justification, whether for the Jew or the Gentile, is by faith alone: "Does this blessedness then come upon the circumcised only, or upon the uncircumcised also? For we say that faith was accounted to Abraham for righteousness" (Rom. 4:9). Even though justification was initially restricted to Israel, God's intention all along was to bless the nations. Recall His promise to Abraham: "I will make you a great nation" (Gen. 12:2). Concerning this promise Paul elsewhere states, "And the Scripture, foreseeing that God would justify the Gentiles by faith, preached the gospel to Abraham beforehand, saying, 'In you all the nations shall be blessed.' So then those who are of faith are blessed with believing Abraham" (Gal. 3:8–9; cf. Gen. 12:3).

Vital to Paul's point is that both Jews and Gentiles are justified by faith *alone*, and to prove this he draws attention to the timing of Abraham's justification versus when he received circumcision: "How then was it accounted? While he was circumcised, or uncircumcised? Not while circumcised, but while uncircumcised" (Rom. 4:10). In terms of the Old Testament text, God justified Abraham in Genesis 15 and Abraham was later circumcised in Genesis 17, twenty-nine years later, according to Jewish rabbis.[1] Paul's point is this: Abraham was justified *before* and *apart* from his circumcision. The Old Testament rite played no part whatsoever in Abraham's justification. The question that naturally arises on the heels of this statement is, "Why, then, was Abraham circumcised? What was its purpose if it was not to justify Abraham?"

1. Moo, *Epistle to the Romans*, 268.

Paul answers this question in the following verse: "And he received the sign of circumcision, a seal of the righteousness of the faith which he had while still uncircumcised" (Rom. 4:11a). The apostle clearly states that circumcision was a *seal* of the righteousness that Abraham had by faith alone. Think of how a seal functions. When kings, for example, send a letter, they place their royal seal on it. Such a seal authenticates the message in the letter and invests it with authority. The recipient who opens the letter immediately knows that it comes from the king because it bears his royal seal. Paul applies this term to circumcision—the rite in and of itself was neither the means nor instrument by which Abraham was justified. It was not the ground on which his righteous status rested. Rather, it was the seal placed on the righteousness he already had received by faith alone—it authenticated the covenant promise that God gave to Abraham. This is an important point that should not be missed: Circumcision, Paul writes, was "a seal of the righteousness of the faith which he [Abraham] had." Where does the emphasis lie: on Abraham's faith or God's promise? The overall context dictates that the emphasis falls first on God's covenant promise. This was, after all, the source of Abraham's righteousness. Hence, circumcision was God's official royal seal on His covenant promise.

But Paul's main point in identifying circumcision as a seal of the righteousness that Abraham had by faith was to show that his justification was not causally linked to the rite. This is why Paul writes, "That he might be the father of all those who believe, though they are uncircumcised, that righteousness might be imputed to them also, and the father of circumcision to those who not only are of the circumcision, but who also walk in the steps of the faith which our father Abraham had while still uncircumcised" (Rom. 4:11b–12). Paul explains that Abraham's justification is *the* paradigm for all believers, Jew or Gentile, Old Testament or New Testament. There are not two plans for redemption. There are not two different ways that people are saved—there is one plan, one salvation, one Savior, and one doctrine of justification by faith alone. This is why Paul calls Abraham the "father of all those who believe," whether Jew (circumcised) or Gentile (uncircumcised). Paul echoes truths that he first wrote to the Galatian churches when he made the stunning claim that even Gentiles were sons of Abraham: "There is neither Jew nor Greek, there is neither slave nor free, there is neither male nor female; for you are all one in Christ Jesus. And if you are Christ's, then you are Abraham's seed, and heirs according to the promise" (Gal. 3:28–29).

Given what Paul has said about the sign of circumcision and its relationship to the doctrine of justification, we know that baptism functions in a similar manner. Baptism is the sign of the new covenant, evident by Christ's inauguration of the new covenant in the upper room with His disciples (cf. Jer. 31:31; Matt. 26:26–29; Heb. 9:15) and formalized by His command to baptize the nations (Matt. 28:18–19). The seed of the woman who would crush the head of the serpent has arrived and conquered; the seed of Abraham through whom God would bless the nations has accomplished His work. He has been cut off from the land of the living by becoming a propitiation for sin (cf. Gen. 17:14; Isa. 53:8). Christ was circumcised in His crucifixion (Col. 2:11). Now, in the wake of His earthly ministry, He has instituted a new sign of the covenant, baptism. Baptism points to the fact that Christ has poured out the Holy Spirit on creation—especially the church, both young and old, male and female (cf. Joel 2:28–29; Mark 1:8; Acts 2:16–18, 33).

But just because the sign has changed does not mean that it somehow functions differently. Like circumcision, baptism is a sign and seal of the righteousness that we receive by faith alone in Christ alone. Baptism is the divine royal seal of authentication and authority. God places His seal on the message of the gospel as a source of hope, as a proclamation of the gospel of Christ and our justification by faith alone, but it is a message that God preaches to our other senses. What the Word is to our ears, baptism is to our senses of touch and sight. As we hear the message of the gospel and see the water cascading down the face of a new convert or on an infant born within the church, we can receive the double preaching of the

Word—the dual proclamation of the gospel message of justification in Word and sacrament.

The Danger of the Sacrament

As much of a blessing as the sacraments herald, they can also be harbingers of judgment. Recall that Paul said that if the Jews did not keep the law that their circumcision would become uncircumcision (Rom. 2:25). According to God's instruction, any male Jew who was not circumcised on the eighth day was cut off from the covenant community (Gen. 17:14). In this case, faith in the promise motivates obedience. If the sacrament is not joined with faith, then the sign of the covenant is no longer a herald of blessing, but a vehicle of curse and judgment. Abraham received the sign of the covenant, as did Jacob and Esau. Yet Jacob esteemed the covenant and placed his faith in Christ, whereas Esau scorned the covenant and sold his interest in redemption for a bowl of lentil soup (Heb. 12:16). This should be a great warning to us all, but especially as it concerns our covenant children. We must not fall into the trap of thinking like the Jewish Christians to whom Paul wrote. We must not place our faith in a sacrament; rather, we must place our faith in Christ, the One who stands behind the sacrament—the One to whom the sacrament points. Just because you have been baptized and brought up in the church does not mean that you are automatically saved. Like Abraham, you must place your faith in Christ and in His perfect righteousness. You too must remember that you cannot earn your salvation.

Conclusion

Paul showed the recipients of his epistle that they needed to understand the relationship between justification and circumcision. He did this not merely so that they could recognize that no work, even obedience to a command of God, could improve their standing before the divine bar. Only Christ's perfect righteousness and suffering secures the verdict of "Righteous!" in God's sight. But as a sign and seal, circumcision authenticated God's covenant promises, a message that rings true today in the sign of the new covenant, baptism. Never forget that we are saved by grace through faith in Christ and that the sacrament of baptism, like circumcision, is a sign and seal of the righteousness of faith, not a means of justification. Ultimately, Christ's work stands behind the great sign and seal of the covenant.

12

The Life-Giving Verdict

ROMANS 4:13–25

For the promise that he would be the heir of the world was not to Abraham or to his seed through the law, but through the righteousness of faith. For if those who are of the law are heirs, faith is made void and the promise made of no effect, because the law brings about wrath; for where there is no law there is no transgression. Therefore it is of faith that it might be according to grace, so that the promise might be sure to all the seed, not only to those who are of the law, but also to those who are of the faith of Abraham, who is the father of us all (as it is written, "I have made you a father of many nations") in the presence of Him whom he believed—God, who gives life to the dead and calls those things which do not exist as though they did; who, contrary to hope, in hope believed, so that he became the father of many nations, according to what was spoken, "So shall your descendants be." And not being weak in faith, he did not consider his own body, already dead (since he was about a hundred years old), and the deadness of Sarah's womb. He did not waver at the promise of God through unbelief, but was strengthened in faith, giving glory to God, and being fully convinced that what He had promised He was also able to perform. And therefore "it was accounted to him for righteousness." Now it was not written for his sake alone that it was imputed to him, but also for us. It shall be imputed to us who believe in Him who raised up Jesus our Lord from the dead, who was delivered up because of our offenses, and was raised because of our justification.

The irrepressible heart of fallen man needs repeated and constant reminders about his sin-stricken condition. In the previous chapters,

Paul addressed the sinfulness of humanity, the impossibility of justification by obedience to the law, and the antithesis between law and gospel in justification. He continues to address these points in this section of chapter 4, but he does so by emphasizing the all-powerful nature of God's life-giving verdict in our justification. To highlight the ineffectiveness of works-righteousness, Paul returns to the life of Abraham to show how the great patriarch's justification was another manifestation of God's creative word. Just as God called worlds into existence by the power of His word, so God gave life to Abraham when He declared him righteous. Paul explains the power of justification by faith alone in Christ alone but also reminds the recipients of his letter that what happened to Abraham is still relevant for people in first-century Rome. Moreover, as we will also see, Paul's words about Abraham are vital for people in every age.

Law and Gospel

Recall what the apostle covered in the previous sections of his letter. Paul labored to demonstrate that salvation is not by works but by faith alone. Paul brought forward two key witnesses, Abraham and David (Rom. 4:3, 7–8; cf. Gen. 15:6; Ps. 32:1–2). God imputed righteousness to Abraham by faith alone, and David found salvation not in the accumulation of his good works but in the forgiveness of his sins. His sins were covered by a perfect righteousness. Moreover, Paul explained that circumcision was not a means by which people were justified but that it was a sign and seal of the righteousness that Abraham had by faith (Rom. 4:11).

Paul continues to emphasize *sola fide* by what he writes in Romans 4:13: "For the promise that he would be the heir of the world was not to Abraham or to his seed through the law, but through the righteousness of faith." We can paraphrase Paul's statement, therefore, in the following manner: "It was not through obedience that Abraham and his offspring received the promise...but through the righteousness that comes by faith." More simply, you *do* the law and you *believe* the gospel. Paul highlights the antithesis between law and gospel in the verses that follow: "For if those who are of the law are heirs, faith is made void and the promise made of no effect, because the law brings about wrath; for where there is no law there is no transgression" (Rom. 4:14–15). If a person can earn his salvation through obedience to the law, then there is no wrath, and faith in the promise of the gospel is superfluous.

But Paul states that "law brings about wrath," which within the broader context of his epistle, especially the opening portion—"the wrath of God is revealed from heaven against all ungodliness and unrighteousness of men" (Rom. 1:18)—means that salvation through obedience to the law is impossible. Hence, Paul writes: "Therefore it is of faith that it might be according to grace, so that the promise might be sure to all the seed, not only to those who are of the law, but also to those who are of the faith of Abraham, who is the father of us all" (Rom. 4:16). Notice that disobedience and wrath go hand in hand, just as faith and grace are joined together. Salvation rests on grace and therefore must come through faith—that is, we look outside of ourselves to the work of another, to the work of Jesus. This is why Paul writes that the promised salvation comes to all who believe, whether Jew or Gentile. Abraham is the father of all who believe in Christ, which is why Paul quotes Genesis 17:5: "(As it is written, 'I have made you a father of many nations') in the presence of Him whom he believed—God, who gives life to the dead and calls those things which do not exist as though they did" (Rom. 4:17). God never had two plans—plan A for Israel and plan B for the Gentiles in the event that Israel rejected Christ. From the very outset, God planned that the promised seed, Christ, would come through Abraham and bring salvation to all, Jew and Gentile alike.

But buried in Paul's assertion of Abraham's global fatherhood is his characterization of these blessings in terms that evoke the opening creation narrative from Genesis 1. In the beginning there was nothing but the triune God, and only when God said, "Let there be light," did something else other than God begin to exist. Such is the nature of our justification—we do not somehow approach God with our dusty and dingy (but nevertheless sincere) pile of good works, hoping that God will look past our faults. Rather, we were dead in our sins and trespasses, and through His all-powerful Word and the proclamation of the gospel He raises people from death to life and passes a life-giving verdict over them. Imagine a convicted criminal standing before the judge—a brigand who stands bound in chains: the life-giving verdict goes forth, the chains fall off, and the once-bound prisoner goes free! Such is the nature of our justification and its attendant blessings.

The Power of the Verdict

Paul further illustrates this point by drilling down into the life of Abraham when he writes: "Who, contrary to hope, in hope believed, so that he became the father of many nations, according to what was spoken, 'So shall your descendants be.' And not being weak in faith, he did not consider his own body, already dead (since he was about a hundred years old), and the deadness of Sarah's womb" (Rom. 4:18–19). Humanly speaking, the prospects of becoming the father of many nations were an elusive dream, but with God all things are possible. Even though Abraham and Sarah were nearly dead, Abraham looked to the promise: "He did not waver at the promise of God through unbelief, but was strengthened in faith, giving glory to God, and being fully convinced that what He had promised He was also able to perform" (Rom. 4:20–21). Abraham trusted that God could bring life out of death and deliver on His covenant promises. "Therefore 'it was accounted to him for righteousness'" (Rom. 4:22). God looked on Abraham's trust and credited it to him as righteousness—Abraham did not trust in his own good works but trusted in the promises of God. Again, the overriding theme that Paul continues to press is that ungodliness and disobedience merit wrath, not life, whereas God's grace by faith alone brings life.

Abraham's justification, however, was not merely ancient history—something no longer relevant in Paul's day or in our own, for that matter. On the contrary, "Now it was not written for his sake alone that it was imputed to him, but also for us. It shall be imputed to us who believe in Him who raised up Jesus our Lord from the dead, who was delivered up because of our offenses, and was raised because of our justification" (Rom. 4:23–25). Paul reiterates that Abraham is a model for both the Old and New Testament believer. Anyone who believes will receive the imputed righteousness of Jesus Christ. Our salvation is secured not only by the life and death of Christ but also by His resurrection. What is the connection between Christ's resurrection and our justification? His resurrection means that God the Father accepted His sacrifice and that Christ conquered death. If Christ were still in the grave, then His sacrifice would have been null and void. The wages of sin is death; hence, Christ's continued state in death would have signaled that His sacrifice was ineffective and that at some point in His life He transgressed the law of God. But blessedly, the opposite is true: Christ fulfilled every jot and tittle of the law, He suffered the penalty of the law, and therefore the Father and Spirit raised Him from the dead. Christ's resurrection was the Father's reversal of the false verdict that had been passed over His Son. And therefore, Christ's resurrection is intimately tied to our justification. Without the public declaration of His righteousness in His resurrection confirming His perfect obedience to the law, we would have no legal ground for our own justification (cf. Rom. 1:4; 1 Tim. 3:16).

The Gospel's Abiding Relevance

If we meditate on what Paul has written in this portion of chapter 4, one thing that should stand in the forefront of our minds is the power of the gospel, a theme Paul announced in the opening chapter: the power of God for salvation to everyone who believes (Rom. 1:16). The nature of the gospel and its power explains why Paul was so adamant about setting law and gospel in stark antithesis in his explanation of how God justifies us. If we are able to merit our justified status, then what need is there for the grace of God? The power of the gospel unto salvation is simply beyond the reach of fallen sinners. We can no more extract ourselves from our fallen state than a dead man can get up and walk away from his coffin. The fact that Paul likens Abraham's justification to the very act of creation itself should signal to us the power of God's life-giving verdict and our utterly desperate state apart from it. We lie bound in the shrouds of death like Lazarus in his tomb, and only the Word of God that brings the life-giving verdict enables us to rise and walk out of the tomb.

Most people in the church embrace and profess these truths but then practically deny them by the way they live. People do not realize that the gospel of Jesus Christ comes chiefly through the preaching of God's Word. All too often people find reasons and excuses for absenting themselves from corporate worship: They want to rest, sleep in, visit with friends or family, catch up on yard work, play a round of golf, or get a head start on the new work week. Ministers and church leaders exhibit a similar practical denial of the power of the gospel. All too often preachers step into the pulpit unprepared or deliver smooth platitudes or moral advice rather than unashamedly proclaiming the power of God unto salvation. One of the funniest and yet saddest instances of such an ethos occurred during the life and times of Johann Sebastian Bach (1685–1750). In Bach's day a preacher's effectiveness was not measured by his fidelity to the biblical text but by how useful and practical his sermons were. Church historian Jaroslav Pelikan notes that there were sermons in which preachers gave gardening tips. Preachers became paralegals, parafarmers, and paramedics in their efforts to be relevant.[1]

Historically, the Reformed tradition has placed a high premium on the preached Word. On this issue the Westminster Larger Catechism asks the question, How is the Word made effectual to salvation? The catechism responds:

> The Spirit of God maketh the reading, *but especially the preaching of the Word*, an effectual means of enlightening, convincing, and humbling sinners; of driving them out of themselves, and drawing them unto Christ; of conforming them to his image, and subduing them to his will; of strengthening them against temptations and corruptions; of building them up in grace,

1. Jaroslav Pelikan, *Bach among the Theologians* (Philadelphia: Fortress Press, 1986), 35.

> and establishing their hearts in holiness and comfort through faith unto salvation. (Q. 155, emphasis added)

The Westminster divines recognized the power of the preached Word and, correlatively, the power of the gospel unto salvation. If people in the pew and ministers in the pulpit absorbed what Paul has written here, we would all give greater attention to the preached Word of God.

Conclusion

Why deliver moral platitudes when you can have the privilege of heralding the life-giving verdict of justification by faith alone? Why avoid corporate worship when the Word of God is preached and is a fountain of life for all who appropriate it by faith alone? The extent to which we esteem the Word of God and its life-giving verdict in our justification will be manifest by the degree to which we attend to the preaching of the Word. Never forget that the declaration of our justification is from the God who gives life to the dead and calls into existence things that did not exist.

13

Glorifying God through Suffering

ROMANS 5:1–5

Therefore, having been justified by faith, we have peace with God through our Lord Jesus Christ, through whom also we have access by faith into this grace in which we stand, and rejoice in hope of the glory of God. And not only that, but we also glory in tribulations, knowing that tribulation produces perseverance; and perseverance, character; and character, hope. Now hope does not disappoint, because the love of God has been poured out in our hearts by the Holy Spirit who was given to us.

Suffering is one of the most misunderstood phenomena in the Christian church. When we suffer, we look for ways to avoid it. Perhaps our prayers even betray this desire when we do not know how to pray: Do we pray for a person's suffering to end or for strength in the midst of continued suffering? We wage this battle in our hearts and minds because we find a teaching in Scripture that runs contrary to the very fiber of our being. What is that teaching? To rejoice in suffering. How is it possible to rejoice in suffering? Moreover, how is it possible to view suffering as a fruit of our justification? If we are saved and pardoned from sin, then should we not be delivered from all forms of suffering? Yes, sometimes our suffering is the result of our own sin and foolishness—the consequences of our rebellion. But what about those times when we can detect no blatant rebellion? Is God simply making us suffer because we deserve it? No, rather, suffering is an opportunity to glorify God.

Paul explains the reason why God calls us to suffer, and he tells us that we do not suffer alone.

Peace as the Fruit of Justification

Remember the overall context that has led us to this point. Paul argued that God presently pours out His wrath against all unrighteousness (Rom. 1:18) and that His judgment is just because all have sinned and fall short of His glory (Rom. 3:23). No one can extricate himself from this just judgment—no amount of moral effort can somehow secure the "Righteous!" verdict from the Judge of the cosmos. Instead, God, who is both just and the justifier, has given us Christ so that we can be declared righteous by faith: "Abraham believed God, and it was accounted to him for righteousness" (Rom. 4:3; cf. Gen. 15:6). Abraham trusted in God's covenant promise to give him an heir, and God therefore declared him righteous on the basis of Christ's work. A person not only receives the forgiveness of sins and the imputed righteousness of Christ but also has peace with God: "Therefore, having been justified by faith, we have peace with God through our Lord Jesus Christ" (Rom. 5:1). The wrath that once rested on us is taken away because of Christ's intercession on our behalf. God's wrath no longer rests on the person who is in Christ. Lest we forget, peace with God comes through "our Lord Jesus Christ." There is no other avenue of approach to our righteous and holy God—this peace comes only by faith alone in Christ alone.

Paul continually stresses that Christ is the one "through whom also we have access by faith into this grace in which we stand, and rejoice in hope of the glory of God" (Rom. 5:2). We stand in God's presence not by our works but by His grace. Paul continues to emphasize the utter incompatibility between grace and works in our justification. We stand before God through the alien righteousness of Christ, an obedience that is not our own and one that we receive through faith alone. Recognizing this fact should most certainly cause us to burst forth in praise and thanksgiving, reveling in the mercy of God. As Paul elsewhere writes: "He who glories, let him glory in the LORD" (1 Cor. 1:31). This means that the doctrine of justification should lead us to doxology and worship. The connection between salvation and worship lies at the heart of the Westminster Larger Catechism's answer to its first question, regarding the chief end of man: "Man's chief and highest end is to glorify God, and fully to enjoy him forever."

Glorifying God through Suffering

Now at this point, we might leap to a number of hasty conclusions as to how we might glorify God. Acts of private and corporate worship are certainly in order and are legitimate means to glorify God. But Paul takes an unexpected turn onto a path marked by suffering: "And not only that, but we also glory in tribulations, knowing that tribulation produces perseverance; and perseverance, character; and character, hope. Now hope does not disappoint, because the love of God has been poured out in our hearts by the Holy Spirit who was given to us" (Rom. 5:3–5). Paul undoubtedly looked forward to the future glory that will be revealed in the people of God (e.g., Rom. 8:18). That future glory will far surpass the nature of our present suffering, but Paul was not a utopian who looked exclusively to the future as the only time when God reveals His glory. Just as God's end-time wrath is a present reality (e.g., Rom. 1:18–32), so too is His end-time glory. God reveals His glory in and through His people in the midst of their weakness and suffering. As counterintuitive as it might seem, when we are weak, God is strong. As Paul writes: "Therefore I take pleasure in infirmities, in reproaches, in needs, in persecutions, in distresses, for Christ's sake. For when I am weak, then I am strong" (2 Cor. 12:10). Paul did not pity himself, nor did he pity others; instead, he rejoiced in his sufferings because they brought glory to God.

But our sufferings are not merely an opportunity for us to glorify God, as important as this is. Rather, suffering "produces perseverance; and perseverance, character; and character, hope" (Rom. 5:3b–4). In other words, when we suffer we inevitably cry out to the Lord for help, and in the midst of our weakness He pours out

His grace and equips, strengthens, and sustains us. In this process we grow spiritually—our trials and tribulations become the crucible where the smelter's fire burns away our impurities and leaves behind only the very best heat-tempered metal. In this crucible of providentially governed suffering God gives us the opportunity to glorify Him, He further conforms us to the image of Christ, and He also better equips us to demonstrate Christ's love to others.

Paul elsewhere explains the connection between suffering and the ability to assist others in the midst of their own suffering: "For as the sufferings of Christ abound in us, so our consolation also abounds through Christ. Now if we are afflicted, it is for your consolation and salvation, which is effective for enduring the same sufferings which we also suffer. Or if we are comforted, it is for your consolation and salvation. And our hope for you is steadfast, because we know that as you are partakers of the sufferings, so also you will partake of the consolation" (2 Cor. 1:5–7). Paul saw suffering as a window through which God would send His consolation and the means by which He fosters hope in us. Moreover, Paul saw his own suffering as an instrument in God's hands to bring about the salvation of others. But, once again, we should note that these are the sufferings of Christ (2 Cor. 5:5). As we suffer, we follow in the footsteps of our Savior and are conformed into His image. As He suffered, we suffer—as goes the Head, so goes His body. This suffering, however, is not aimless, because it ultimately builds hope within us: "Now hope does not disappoint, because the love of God has been poured out in our hearts by the Holy Spirit who was given to us" (Rom. 5:5). Paul emphasizes the fact that we have peace with God through the intercession of Christ. And for this reason, we can glory in God as we eagerly await and look forward to the coming revealed glory. Our faith, though, is not one that is exclusively locked away in the future; it is also bound up in the present. Naysayers will undoubtedly contend that our present sufferings prove that our faith is empty: If God were truly interested in saving us, then why does He let us suffer? We suffer because we are saved—it is the means by which God providentially conforms us to the image of His Son.

Why We Are Called to Suffer

God calls us to suffer so that He can conform us to the image of Christ. If Christ glorified His Father through His suffering, then we are most like Christ when we glorify God in our suffering. Along these lines, John Calvin writes:

> On occasion the Lord so besets and crushes His people for a time as scarcely to allow them to breathe or recollect their source of consolation; but in a moment He restores to life those whom he had almost submerged in the darkness of death. Thus Paul's affirmation is always fulfilled in them: "We are hard pressed on every side, yet not crushed; we are perplexed, but not in despair; persecuted, but not forsaken; struck down, but not destroyed—always carrying about in the body the dying of the Lord Jesus, that the life of Jesus also may be manifested in our body. For we who live are always delivered to death for Jesus' sake, that the life of Jesus also may be manifested in our mortal flesh." (2 Cor. 4:8–9)[1]

This is why Jesus told His disciples in the Sermon on the Mount: "Blessed are you when they revile and persecute you, and say all kinds of evil against you falsely for My sake. Rejoice and be exceedingly glad, for great is your reward in heaven, for so they persecuted the prophets who were before you" (Matt. 5:11–12). When we suffer for the sake of Christ, we step in the footprints of the giants of the faith and tread where they walked and were conformed into the image of Christ. Therefore, contrary to popular opinion that suffering is shameful, Paul argues that suffering is the arena of God's glory. For when we are weak, God's glory shines forth more brilliantly. To quote Paul again: "For when I am weak, then I am strong" (2 Cor. 12:10). So, then, this is why God calls us to

1. Calvin, *Romans and Thessalonians*, 106.

suffer, though we must also realize an important factor—we do not suffer alone!

We Do Not Suffer Alone

So often in the midst of suffering we think that we are alone—no one knows what we have gone through, are going through, or are about to go through. We think our situation is unique. Or we look for others that have suffered in a similar manner to find some bond of fellowship, camaraderie, or source of support. One theologian by the name of Octavius Winslow (1808–1878) wrote a little gem of a volume titled *The Sympathy of Christ* in which the chapter "The Sensitiveness of Christ to Suffering" offers a number of observations worth quoting at length. Winslow explains the natural propensity and desire for companionship in the midst of our suffering:

> In suffering, we naturally seek companionship; we instinctively yearn for sympathy. And if we but meet the individual whose history bears some resemblance to our own,—who has suffered as we suffer, has sorrowed as we sorrow, and how in both has betrayed like human feelings, infirmities, and weakness with ourselves—we are at once conscious of a support the most sustaining, and of a sympathy the most grateful and soothing. It is just in this particular that Christ meets our case, and meets it as no other being can.[2]

In what way does Christ sympathize with our suffering? Think about it. What about the believer who suffers from cancer so that Christ may be glorified through his weakness? What does Christ have to say about such pain?

Winslow draws a parallel between the sufferings of Christ and the believer to demonstrate that Christ most assuredly knows of our pain:

---

2. Octavius Winslow, *The Sympathy of Christ with Man: Its Teaching and Its Consolation* (London: James Nisbet & Co., 1862), 168.

> Oh, was there no bodily agony in the laceration of the scourge, in the heavy blows of the clenched fist, in the plucking off the hair, in the thorn-crown, in the spikes impelled through the hands and the feet, in the thrust of the spear entering the side and piercing the heat of Jesus? Was there no torture in the long, lingering agony of the cross, the blood oozing from the wounds by drops, and life ebbing slowly by inches?... You, too, may thus be shrinking from bodily suffering. Does the weak flesh recoil from those agonies which no tongue can describe, which no skill can baffle, which no anodyne can soothe, and which no affection can prevent? Jesus can sympathize.[3]

Recall what the author of Hebrews says: "For we do not have a High Priest who cannot sympathize with our weaknesses, but was in all points tempted as we are, yet without sin" (Heb. 4:15). What an amazing reality, that Christ has suffered with us and knows our pains and heartaches. Again, Winslow observes:

> Oh, how my love is awakened! I love Him, because that He, though God, is near to me, near in the valley of tears and suffering, not chiding but sharing, not crushing but sustaining, not repelling but sanctifying my infirmities, feebleness, and sorrow. I love Him for the sympathy that soothes, and for the power that succors me. I love Him who, while He sighs with me, weeps with me, sorrows with me, encircles me with His omnipotent arms, upholds me with His Divine grace, and perfects His strength in my weakness.[4]

This is amazing! This should fill us with awe. The God of the cosmos condescended to weak and sinful creatures and saved us by assuming our flesh and sending forth His abundant love into our hearts! Again, this is precisely what Paul tells us in Romans 5:5: "The love of God has been poured out in our hearts by the Holy Spirit who was given to us." This truth should cause our souls to swell with praise and adoration for our wonderful Savior. He is

3. Winslow, *Sympathy of Christ*, 178–79.
4. Winslow, *Sympathy of Christ*, 185–86.

present in the midst of our suffering, pouring out His love through the Holy Spirit.

These facts should remind us of another important truth—if Christ indwells all believers, and all believers are a part of Christ's body, then no believer who suffers should ever suffer alone. Yes, Christ is with us in the midst of our suffering, but we should look to be an "incarnation," if you will, of Christ to our fellow suffering brothers and sisters. If we had the opportunity to minister to Christ in His suffering, would we not have jumped at the chance? Yet, because all believers are united to Christ by faith through the indwelling presence of the Holy Spirit, we have that opportunity now. Winslow explains this communion in suffering that all believers share by virtue of their union with Christ, and hence with one another:

> You will learn, too, to sympathize with the suffering members of Christ's body. Soothed by such a sympathy as His, our own will flow forth in its tenderness toward all who through weakness and infirmity of the flesh are shrinking from or are drinking the cup of suffering.... Recognize a suffering Christ in His suffering members, a persecuted Christ in His persecuted members, a despised Christ in His downtrodden members, a poor Christ in His poor members, an imprisoned Christ in His imprisoned members; a sick, a naked, a hungry Christ in those whom worldly adversity, penury, and want have smitten and laid low.[5]

Remember, as Christ has told us, "Assuredly, I say to you, inasmuch as you did it to one of the least of these My brethren, you did it to Me" (Matt. 25:40).

Conclusion

So, then, suffering is not a badge of shame. We are called to suffer because we must, as the children of God, be conformed into the

5. Winslow, *Sympathy of Christ*, 188–89.

image of Christ. And we are not alone in our suffering, for Christ has gone before us and sympathizes with us in our pain. He also pours out His abundant love on us, especially in these situations. So, far from being cursed, suffering is a special calling that God sends to His saints where He says, "My child, I have especially chosen you to shine forth My glory and be most like Christ. But rest assured, you have peace with Me because I have justified you by the work of My Son, which has come by My gift of faith." God grant that we would see suffering as a divine calling and that we would rejoice in it, as Paul writes, knowing that we bring glory to Him and that He conforms us to Christ's image.

14

A Different Love Story

ROMANS 5:6–11

For when we were still without strength, in due time Christ died for the ungodly. For scarcely for a righteous man will one die; yet perhaps for a good man someone would even dare to die. But God demonstrates His own love toward us, in that while we were still sinners, Christ died for us. Much more then, having now been justified by His blood, we shall be saved from wrath through Him. For if when we were enemies we were reconciled to God through the death of His Son, much more, having been reconciled, we shall be saved by His life. And not only that, but we also rejoice in God through our Lord Jesus Christ, through whom we have now received the reconciliation.

One of the world's favorite types of stories is a good love story. Perhaps people like the idea of love mesmerizing their hearts; indeed, it is a powerful emotion. There is nothing like winning and capturing the love of another—this idea has gripped the hearts and minds of millions of people. Proof of this appears in the fact that all sorts of media—blogs, movies, books, and TV shows—never grow tired of telling great love stories. Why is there such a fascination with love stories? Perhaps it is because women often look for words or actions that will sweep them off their feet, and men like the idea of playing the hero or the thrill of the chase. I think another reason lies in the fact that, as human beings, we are wired to seek love and companionship. God, after all, created man male and female, which means that most people will seek to live in a lifelong relationship with another person (cf. 1 Corinthians 7). The age-old story usually unfolds in the same manner: boy meets girl, boy wins girl's heart, boy marries girl. The Bible has a number of romance stories: Consider how Jacob was willing to work seven years to marry Rachel, how Boaz married Ruth, or how Solomon describes marital love in Song of Songs—we find romance in the pages of Scripture.

One of the most common elements in the romance stories of Scripture is the fact that there is a strong attraction between the parties involved based on appearance and character. For example, the Genesis narrator notes that Rachel was beautiful in form and appearance (Gen. 29:17b). Boaz admired Ruth's virtue: "For you have shown more kindness at the end than at the beginning, in that you did not go after young men, whether poor or rich" (Ruth 3:10). Solomon's wife enchanted him: "Behold, you are fair, my love!" (Song 4:1a). These three examples all share the idea of beauty and attraction, whether of appearance or character. Yet Paul recounts another love story from Scripture here in this portion of Romans 5. The common element of beauty is missing, which makes the love story very different. It is more like the prophet Hosea and his adulterous wife, Gomer. On the heels of explaining the connections between justification, peace, and assurance in the midst of suffering, Paul rhapsodizes about the greatest love story of all—Christ's love for His bride.

The Greatest Love Story

Recall from the previous section (Rom. 5:1–5) how Paul showed his readers that believers could revel both in the future revelation of God's glory and in their present trials. Paul tells us that in the midst of our present suffering, "the love of God has been poured out in our hearts by the Holy Spirit who was given to us" (Rom. 5:5). As Anders Nygren observes,

> In Christ, God's love has filled the cup to overflowing and been poured out on us. It has poured forth from the heart of God and sought its way to our hearts, true to the very nature of love. God's love now has a representative in our hearts, "the Holy Spirit which has been given to us." The function

> of the Holy Spirit, according to Paul, is to be a "guarantee" in our hearts that we belong to Christ and are "in Him" (2 Cor. 1:21f). When God's love is present with us as an unfailing reality, that is the work of the Holy Spirit.[1]

Paul now shows exactly how God has poured out His love in Christ in Romans 5:6–11. He writes: "For when we were still without strength, in due time Christ died for the ungodly" (Rom. 5:6). When Paul writes of weakness, he does not have our physical but rather our moral inability in mind—our sin-fallen condition that he expounded in Romans 1:18–3:19. We can be sure of this conclusion because Paul states that Christ died for the *ungodly*. This is the second time Paul has invoked this term—the first was when he called Abraham ungodly (Rom. 4:5). This is something that many in the church have a difficulty understanding. Regardless of our misunderstanding, we must recognize that, apart from Christ, we are all ungodly.

Paul elaborates on this thought to highlight the grandeur and depth to which Christ condescended to bring about our redemption: "For scarcely for a righteous man will one die; yet perhaps for a good man someone would even dare to die. But God demonstrates His own love toward us, in that while we were still sinners, Christ died for us" (Rom. 5:7–8). Paul reminds us of a truth that many of us instinctively know but few of us seldom think about. Most people would be willing to risk their lives for another person, say for children trapped in a burning house. Paul recognizes this when he writes, "For scarcely for a righteous man will one die." In other words, if you know innocent children are in a burning house, you will likely do everything you can to rescue them, even at the risk of your own life. But how would this scenario change if you knew that there was a death-row inmate in the burning house? I suspect that you would be slower to react. But what if we further complicate this scenario by asking the question, Would you substitute one of your

1. Anders Nygren, *Commentary on Romans*, trans. Carl C. Rasmussen (Philadelphia: Muhlenberg Press, 1949), 199–200.

very own children to take the place of the death-row inmate in the burning house? I think no one in his right mind would make such a substitution. But this is the nature of God's love for us. As John tells us in his gospel, "For God so loved the world that He gave His only begotten Son" (John 3:16). Or in Paul's words, "While we were still sinners, Christ died for us."

The wholly innocent and righteous Christ died in the place of sinners. Paul expands on Christ's substitutionary death and ties it to the doctrine of justification: "Much more then, having now been justified by His blood, we shall be saved from wrath through Him. For if when we were enemies we were reconciled to God through the death of His Son, much more, having been reconciled, we shall be saved by His life" (Rom. 5:9–10). Paul shows us the degree to which we receive the love of God through the Holy Spirit in the person and work of Christ. If God manifested His love toward us through His Son while we were guilty sinners and in a state of alienation, then how much more will He lavish His love on us as His children? Christ has removed the alienation that separated us from God. And, as indicated before (Rom. 5:1–5), the knowledge of what Christ has done for us should lead us to worship: "And not only that, but we also rejoice in God through our Lord Jesus Christ, through whom we have now received the reconciliation" (Rom. 5:11). Even in the midst of trial and tribulation we should rejoice in God because He has given us so much.

We Are the Ugly Bride

In Paul's explanation of the greatest love story, do you notice the missing element of beauty? Unlike Rachel's beauty or Ruth's virtue, Paul does not ascribe any form of beauty to Christ's bride. In fact, Christ's bride is unattractive—I daresay she's ugly. As fallen sinners, we exhibit nothing appealing or attractive. Like Hosea's adulterous wife, we are whores. This is Paul's point when he writes, "While we were still sinners, Christ died for us" (Rom. 5:8). Think how differently Jacob's estimation of Rachel might have been were she grotesque in form and appearance. And how would Boaz have reacted if Ruth showed him contempt? How might we feel about Solomon's poetic song about his bride if he considered her ugly?

These three counterexamples make the same point that Paul offers here—there was nothing appealing about us, but Christ nevertheless interceded on our behalf and saved us! Recall everything that Paul has written about the sinful condition of all humanity (Rom. 1:18–3:19). Yet Christ died for His monstrous bride—He loved us and gave Himself for us that He might sanctify and cleanse us through the washing of water by His word so that He might present us before His Father as a glorious bride without spot, wrinkle, or blemish (Eph. 5:25–27)! Christ loved us when we were His enemies and were unlovable. Christ's love has made us lovable. He clothed us in beauty, splendor, and righteousness so that the Father no longer sees us as grotesque or hideous in His sight. In the words of Isaiah the prophet: "I will greatly rejoice in the LORD, My soul shall be joyful in my God; For He has clothed me with the garments of salvation, He has covered me with the robe of righteousness, As a bridegroom decks himself with ornaments, And as a bride adorns herself with her jewels" (Isa. 61:10).

Living This Truth

Generally speaking, I believe we are familiar with the truth that we are Christ's ugly bride. Sometimes, however, ideas remain in our minds and do not trickle into our hearts. At the Synod of Dort (1618–1619), one of the prominent members, Franciscus Gomarus (1563–1641), became engaged in a heated debate. He became so angry that he challenged another minister to a pistol duel! Others intervened and cooler heads prevailed. In this moment the gospel undoubtedly rested in Gomarus's mind but failed to reach his heart. Rather than be filled with rage and anger, Gomarus should have been marked by patience and humility. Indeed, the amount of love, grace, and patience that we show others is proportionally reflective of the depths to which we grasp the love, grace, and patience God has poured out on us in Christ (Eph. 4:1–3). Christ told His disciples that if they loved the lovable, they were only doing what tax collectors did, the most despised members of first-century Israelite culture (Matt. 5:43–48). It is quite easy to love those with whom we agree and like. It is quite another thing to demonstrate love toward our enemies—maybe even persecutors. But if Christ has loved us, then we must love others, even the unlovable.

When we encounter the unbeliever who brings trial or tribulation into our lives, we must remember that we look in the mirror. We see the ugly bride in the mirror, yet Christ died for this ugly bride. We must show Christ's love to our enemies. When we have difficulty loving the unlovable, we must once again remember that we are looking in the mirror at ourselves. Yes, as believers we are clothed and adorned as a glorious bride as Paul has explained so far in Romans 3:20–5:11. But we are, as Martin Luther said, *simil iustus et peccator*, at the same time righteous and a sinner. Therefore, we are still hampered by sin and will still see shadows of that ugly bride in the mirror. We must remember that Christ died and gave us His glorious righteousness. While we may disagree with our brothers or sisters, we must love them because Christ was willing to die for them. If He was willing to die for them, then we too must be willing to manifest the love of Christ's gospel to them. We can show this Christlike love to others only by resting in the promises and power of the Spirit-applied gospel of Christ.

Conclusion

Christ's love for His bride is the greatest love story ever told. We are not the beautiful, captivating bride that we often fancy ourselves to be. We are instead grotesque and hideous in appearance and character. Yet, despite our hideousness, Christ still loved us and made us beautiful by giving us His righteousness. And even now the Holy Spirit sanctifies us, and on the last day we will be adorned not as the ugly bride but in total splendor and glory! Or in the words of a recent hymn:

> What God is this from Heaven's realm,
> Who loves me faithfully?
> He is aware of all my sin,

My words and deeds, my thoughts within,
And yet He still loves me.

I've nothing pure to offer Him
Who loves beyond degree.
I only have a selfish heart,
And from God's way I oft depart,
And yet He still loves me.

Although I try to change my ways,
Impure I'll always be;
I've never done the good I should,
The wrong is all I've understood,
And yet He still loves me.

But God has made me right with Him,
His Son has set me free!
For while I was a sinner still,
Christ died for me, as was God's will—
Such is His love for me![2]

---

2. Jonathan Landry Cruse, "He Still Loves Me," accessed July 27, 2017, at http://hymnsofdevotion.com/pdf/He_Still_Loves_Me.pdf.

15

The First and Last Adam

ROMANS 5:12–14

Therefore, just as through one man sin entered the world, and death through sin, and thus death spread to all men, because all sinned—(For until the law sin was in the world, but sin is not imputed when there is no law. Nevertheless death reigned from Adam to Moses, even over those who had not sinned according to the likeness of the transgression of Adam, who is a type of Him who was to come.)

We live in a radically individualistic culture. We regularly hear the creed of individualism preached from media pulpits and the mantra that this country was founded on the principle of "rugged individualism." This idea not only permeates our political culture but also runs rampant in our social culture. Now people have websites, Facebook, Twitter, Instagram, Snapchat, and the like that are devoted to promoting themselves, their own ideas, and their own following. The cult of personality reigns supreme. Not to be outdone by the tech-savvy generation, others express their individualism in another way. People young and old have grown up, moved away from home, and established their own unique identity and existence apart from their families.

In non-Western cultures, however, this is not the case. It is quite common to find multiple generations living under one roof. We are one of the few cultures, for example, that has retirement homes. Other cultures do not have retirement homes because they see it as the responsibility of the family to take care of elderly family members. The highly individualistic nature of American culture is even reflected in a common evangelistic question that we ask: "If you were to die tonight and stand before the throne of God, why should he let you into his Kingdom?" The question suggests that we will stand before God's throne as individuals. This sometimes inadvertently conveys the idea that we are accountable for our personal sin. Now, while this is all true, it is not the only relationship in which we will stand before the throne of God. We will stand before God's throne not only as individuals but also as represented by one of two men, either the first or last Adam. We must recognize that we are both individuals *and* part of a corporate body. This is the important truth contained in the passage of Scripture before us.

Paul spent much of Romans 3:20–5:11 dealing with matters that might lead some to believe that the apostle has only the individual in mind since individuals place their God-given but nevertheless *personal* faith in Christ to receive their justified status. But Paul makes explicit what has been implicit throughout Romans 3:20–5:11. He points to the individual's corporate identity, which can only be connected either to the first or last Adam. Understanding the individual-corporate identity that all human beings possess is vital to comprehending Paul's doctrines of sin and justification and his greater understanding of salvation.

All Have Sinned in Adam

Some may wonder about the connection between the universal sinfulness of man and the doctrine of justification, Paul's chief subject since Romans 3:20. For example, how is it possible that mankind is universally sinful, as Paul tells us in Romans 3? Moreover, why has no one escaped the reach of sin? This is the very doctrine that Paul takes up in this portion of Romans 5. He shows how Christ's righteousness is imputed to believers and how Adam's sin has been imputed to all people. This is what Paul means when he writes: "Therefore, just as through one man sin entered the world, and death through sin, and thus death spread to all men, because all sinned" (Rom. 5:12). How is it possible that all sinned because one man (namely, Adam) sinned? More pointedly, some might ask, "How can I be held personally responsible for Adam's sin when I wasn't even present in the garden, let alone even born?"

We must recognize that Adam was our representative who acted on our behalf. Historically, Reformed theologians have explained this relationship in terms of federalism, or the doctrine of the covenants. Adam did not act alone but was the universal covenantal representative for all humanity. Just as when a politician represents the people who elected him and acts on the behalf of his constituents, God chose and created Adam to act on our behalf. The chief part of this covenantal relationship is the doctrine of imputation. Recall Paul's statement that we received the righteousness of Christ, His perfect obedience, through imputation. God accredits or accounts Christ's righteousness to believers by faith alone: "It [righteousness] shall be imputed to us who believe in Him who raised up Jesus our Lord from the dead, who was delivered up because of our offenses, and was raised because of our justification" (Rom. 4:24b–25). We were absent at the cross when Christ paid the penalty for sin and when He perfectly obeyed the law, yet God imputes His righteousness to all who believe. Likewise, we were absent in the garden when Adam sinned, yet God imputes Adam's sin and guilt to all mankind. This is the nature of the federal and covenantal relationship that we share with Adam and Christ. If we deny our sinful connection to Adam, then by irresistible logic we must deny our connection to Christ.

Paul further elaborates his point in the following two verses: "For until the law sin was in the world, but sin is not imputed when there is no law. Nevertheless death reigned from Adam to Moses, even over those who had not sinned according to the likeness of the transgression of Adam, who is a type of Him who was to come" (Rom. 5:13–14). Paul proves his point regarding the imputation of Adam's sin by surveying the landscape of redemptive history and dividing it into three sections:

Adam   Adam ➔ Moses   Moses ➔ Present day

It is easy to understand why Adam died and why people after the revelation of the Mosaic law died: They all transgressed expressly revealed commandments of God. God explicitly told Adam not to eat of the tree of knowledge lest God punish him with death. And Israel, like Adam in his state in the garden, received expressly revealed commands from God, who threatened them with death for violating them (e.g., Ex. 21:15–17). But what about the people who lived *and died* between Adam and Moses? On what basis did they die when God had not revealed His commands or laws to them as He did to Adam and Israel?

The answer comes from the doctrine of imputation. "Death reigned," writes Paul, "from Adam to Moses, even over those who had not sinned according to the likeness of the transgression of Adam" (Rom. 5:14). The inhabitants of the Adam-Moses gap died even though they did not transgress expressly revealed commands of God like Adam did. But if they suffered the consequences of violating the law—namely, death—then God must somehow credit Adam's first sin to all people. God, therefore, punishes all people as if they disobeyed His revealed law even though they did not personally do so. In short, God imputes Adam's guilt to all humanity. Adam is the universal federal and covenantal head for the entire human race.

The Two Adams Compared

As we look at Adam we would undoubtedly become bereft of all hope were it not for the closing line of Romans 5:14 in which Paul writes that Adam "is a type of Him who was to come." Paul will develop the contradistinctive work of Christ in the verses that follow (Rom. 5:15–21), which we will cover in the next chapter. For the time being, we must understand that Adam is the federal head, the chosen representative, for all humanity, and Christ is the federal head for His people, for all who believe in Him. Those who are in Adam receive his imputed sin and guilt, and those who are in Christ receive His imputed righteousness because He is the "last Adam," as Paul calls Him in 1 Corinthians 15:45. Quite simply, "for as in Adam all die, even so in Christ all shall be made alive" (1 Cor. 15:22). The relationship between the contradistinctive work of the two Adams appears when Paul identifies the first Adam as a *type* of the one to come, the last Adam, Jesus. Adam foreshadows Christ.

We must understand the connection between the first and last Adam as well as the concept of federal headship. If we do not grasp these two concepts, we will be unable to make much sense of the verses that follow in the rest of this chapter. We must realize that God first gave Adam the opportunity to secure a permanent place before Him. Recall God's presence in the garden (Gen. 3:8). God gave Adam and Eve the tree of life and told them to obey. Their obedience would have permanently secured their residence in His benevolent presence for themselves and for their children (Gen. 2:9; 3:22; cf. Rev. 2:7). Adam had to refrain from eating from the tree of knowledge and had to be fruitful, multiply, and take dominion over the earth (Gen. 1:28; 2:16–17). Had Adam obeyed these commands, he would have brought about the consummation of the kingdom of God. As God's vice regent, Adam would have filled the earth with his children, all of whom bore the unsullied image of God, and he would have extended the garden-order of God's first dwelling place throughout the entire world.

Instead, Adam ate from the tree, and through his act of disobedience he ushered in the reign of sin and death, not the kingdom of God. Through Adam's disobedience, "death has ascended the throne in this world; and now, with sovereign authority, it uses its power with terrifying effects."[1] Adam, though created in the very image of God, a reflection of God's holiness, righteousness, purity, and creativity, pursued his own will rather than the will of his Creator. Satan tempted Adam and Eve with the idea that if they ate the forbidden fruit they would "be like God" (Gen. 3:5). Paul recounts the

1. Nygren, *Commentary on Romans*, 216.

accomplished work of the first Adam—"Therefore, just as through one man sin entered the world, and death through sin, and thus death spread to all men, because all sinned" (Rom. 5:12). Because of Adam's act of disobedience, he ushered in the brutal reign of sin:

> Ever since Adam the fate of the race has been to lie in thralldom to the powers of destruction. When man lives in sin, he deludes himself with the belief that he is himself in control; that he is free and can choose sin in one moment and good in another. But in reality the sin which he commits is evidence that sin is the master and man the slave. So also as to death. Man would save his own life; he is always looking out for himself. But all that he does still serves death. Death is the sovereign who rules over man's whole existence. Such is the common lot of man since Adam.[2]

This is a total contrast to the actions of the last Adam, Jesus Christ.

Remember the fact that Paul identifies Adam as "a type of Him who was to come" (Rom. 5:14), which means that Adam points forward to Christ; he prefigures Christ. This means that God intentionally designed and divinely ordained similarities between Adam and Christ. Just as Adam is the federal head, or representative, of humanity, so too Christ is the federal head of the church, His body. God made Adam in His image, a reflection of His being and attributes. Christ, in similar fashion, is not merely the reflection of God but the uncreated eternal image of God. Remember what Jesus told His disciples: "He who has seen Me has seen the Father" (John 14:9). Paul elsewhere tells us that Christ "is the image of the invisible God" (Col. 1:15). And just as Adam was given a task by the Father, so was Christ, though His work was much more difficult.

God told Adam to obey His command that he might merit eternal life. Likewise, the Father commanded the Son to redeem His bride through His obedience to the Father's will. Yet the similarities between Christ and Adam melt away and reveal prominent

---

2. Nygren, *Commentary on Romans*, 213.

dissimilarities. Adam's task was simple: have children, extend the garden-order throughout the creation, and refrain from eating of the tree of knowledge. Christ, however, was perfectly obedient to the entirety of God's law, which according to rabbinic tradition includes 613 commands! Adam's probation took place in Paradise, whereas the pinnacle of Christ's tests of obedience took place in the wilderness, the haunt of wild animals, an arid wasteland. Adam was satiated and lacked nothing because God provided for every one of his needs; he had every tree of the garden—indeed, every animal and plant at his disposal. Christ was hungry and thirsty—He had not eaten for forty days (Luke 4:1–13). Satan tempted Christ with the very same temptation as Adam—to abandon the command of God and establish His place of authority on His own terms. Yet despite His hunger, despite His suffering, and despite the ease with which He could have complied with Satan's temptation, He said no.

Paul wonderfully and succinctly captures the parallels between the first and last Adam in his epistle to the Philippians: "Christ Jesus, who, being in the form of God, did not consider it robbery to be equal with God, but made Himself of no reputation, taking the form of a bondservant, and coming in the likeness of men. And being found in appearance as a man, He humbled Himself and became obedient to the point of death, even the death of the cross" (Phil. 2:5–8). Notice that Paul says that Christ "did not consider it robbery to be equal with God" (v. 6). Robbery involves taking hold of what does not belong to you. Adam did consider it robbery to be equal with God when he heeded Satan's counsel and lawlessly took the forbidden fruit to become like God. Adam did not even have to be obedient to the point of death, yet Christ was obedient to this extent. Adam's federal headship required no condescension to humility, whereas Christ stooped from His heavenly throne to be the federal head for His people. The One of whom it was said, "Holy, holy, holy is the LORD of hosts; the whole earth is full of his glory," and the One whose train of His robe filled the temple and drove the prophet Isaiah to fear for his life condescended to be born under the law and be placed in an animal feeding trough (Isa. 6:3;

cf. John 12:41 NIV). He condescended to the depths of suffering and was obedient unto death. The King of Glory cried out from His derelict estate, "My God, My God, why have You forsaken Me?" (Matt. 27:46) as He ignominiously hung on the cross.

The Importance of Federal Headship

The implication of the dissimilarities between the first and last Adams is ultimately the difference between heaven and hell. So many people believe they will stand before God's throne as individuals on the day of judgment. To a certain extent, this is true—we will, as Christ tells us, have to account for every idle word that we say (Matt. 12:36). Yet this is not the only relationship in which we will stand. As this passage of Scripture clearly teaches, we stand in solidarity and under the representation of either one of two men—either the first or the last Adam. Even if a person were to live a perfect life, were it possible, he would still bear the guilt of Adam's sin—the fact that he dies is evidence of this. We are mortal not because we are finite but because of Adam's sin—he broke the covenant of works (Lev. 18:5; Hos. 6:7; Rom. 10:5; Gal. 3:12). If Adam is our representative, then we will bear the full penalty of the broken covenant of works. God told Adam that if he ate of the tree of knowledge he would die. Those allied with Adam will not only die but also suffer the second death (Rev. 20:14).

Conversely, those allied with the last Adam will not suffer the consequences of the broken covenant of works, because as Paul elsewhere writes: "Christ has redeemed us from the curse of the law, having become a curse for us (for it is written, 'Cursed is everyone who hangs on a tree')" (Gal. 3:13). Moreover, those in Christ will one day eat from the tree of life—He has broken the reign of sin and death that Adam ushered in. For those who are in Christ, the cherubim with their flaming swords no longer guard the path to the tree of life; we no longer dwell east of Eden (Gen. 3:24). As Christ tells us in the book of Revelation: "To him who overcomes I will give to eat from the tree of life, which is in the midst of the Paradise of God" (Rev. 2:7; cf. 22:2, 14).

Conclusion

The whole point of Romans 5:12–14 is that we must abandon any hope that we might somehow fulfill the requirements of the law. We do not stand guilty before the divine bar because we sin. Rather, we stand guilty because of Adam's sin and our own personal sins. We will not stand as individuals before the throne of God on the last day but as individuals corporately tied to one of two Adams—there is no other option. Seeing that Adam even abandoned his own sinking ship and sought the headship of Christ, should this not tell us something (cf. Luke 3:38)? We must therefore abandon our corporate identity in Adam and place our faith in the work of the last Adam, Christ. Only His work, His perfect fulfillment of the law, and His suffering the curse for the law's violation gives us peace with God.

Some might argue that they should not be held accountable for Adam's sin, because they were absent from the garden. Yet this then means that they cannot receive the righteousness of Christ, because they were absent at the cross. If we are in Adam, we will receive the imputed guilt of his sin; if we are in Christ we will receive His imputed righteousness. Place your trust in the last Adam, who was faithful to the law of God, even to the point of death on a cross. Praise our federal head, our Captain (Heb. 2:10), for the wonderful work that He has accomplished on our behalf. Only Christ grants us the access and right to eat from the tree of life so that we may eternally dwell in the presence of our triune covenant Lord.

16

Our Great Champion

ROMANS 5:15–21

(But the free gift is not like the offense. For if by the one man's offense many died, much more the grace of God and the gift by the grace of the one Man, Jesus Christ, abounded to many. And the gift is not like that which came through the one who sinned. For the judgment which came from one offense resulted in condemnation, but the free gift which came from many offenses resulted in justification. For if by the one man's offense death reigned through the one, much more those who receive abundance of grace and of the gift of righteousness will reign in life through the One, Jesus Christ.) Therefore, as through one man's offense judgment came to all men, resulting in condemnation, even so through one Man's righteous act the free gift came to all men, resulting in justification of life. For as by one man's disobedience many were made sinners, so also by one Man's obedience many will be made righteous. Moreover the law entered that the offense might abound. But where sin abounded, grace abounded much more, so that as sin reigned in death, even so grace might reign through righteousness to eternal life through Jesus Christ our Lord.

When we hear of death, it often is distant and removed from us. We hear of people dying all the time, whether due to war, car accidents, or illness. Death is a regular part of life. The only time that death begins to seem unnatural is when it strikes close to home. I will never forget the time I saw a man dying right before my eyes from gunshot wounds. It made a lasting impression on me—it made me realize how finite and fragile life is. Yet I think we fail not only to see the power of death but also to ask why people even die in the first place. In short, death is the most unnatural of human conditions. We have examined Romans 5:12–14 and now understand that death is by no means natural; it was not part of God's initial creation of humanity. Death is an alien, evil presence in God's good world. The first Adam opened the door to sin and death by his own transgression of God's command. But blessedly, we also know of the work of the last Adam. In the verses before us Paul expands on the foundation he laid in Romans 5:12–14. He shows the precise relationship between Adam's one sin and Christ's one act of obedience and the respective outcomes, eternal death and eternal life.

Two Acts and Different Consequences

Remember the discussion in the previous verses—namely, Christ is the last Adam. Paul contrasts the difference between Adam's work and Christ's work. Keep in mind that Paul contrasts the idea of "the one" and "the many"—singularity and plurality. Paul writes: "But the free gift is not like the offense. For if by the one man's offense many died, much more the grace of God and the gift by the grace of the one Man, Jesus Christ, abounded to many" (Rom. 5:15). The action of the one man, Adam, affected humanity, the many. Likewise, one man, Christ, affected those who are in Him. Paul emphasizes the idea of federal headship throughout these verses.

Notice how many words in Romans 5:15 highlight the gracious nature of our redemption in Christ, which is especially evident against the backdrop of Adam's sin: "free gift," "grace of God," and "the gift by the grace of the one Man, Jesus Christ." Paul highlights the legal dimensions of the respective actions of the two Adams: "And the gift is not like that which came through the one who sinned. For the judgment which came from one offense resulted in condemnation, but the free gift which came from many offenses resulted in justification" (Rom. 5:16). Adam's transgression brings condemnation, but Christ's obedience brings justification. When we stand in a court of law, the judge levels his verdict: You are either guilty or innocent. When we stand before the divine bar, however, we are guilty or *righteous*, not merely innocent. In other words, we have either transgressed or fulfilled the law—there is no neutral middle ground. In this case, we understand the nature of God's activity in connection with Adam and Christ. Adam's sin brings condemnation—the pronouncement of a judicial sentence. Conversely, Christ's work brings justification—the pronouncement of a judicial sentence. This teaches us that our justification is therefore based not on our work but rather on the work of another—Christ.

Moreover, there is, of course, a world of difference between condemnation and justification. One sin was sufficient to bring about condemnation, but the justification that we receive by faith alone in Christ brings about the forgiveness of multiple sins: Adam's first sin, and all of our own personal sins. This demonstrates the incredible power of sin—it can bring about the condemnation of an entire race. But it also shows us the incredible power of grace because it can remove the guilt of sin: "For if by the one man's offense death reigned through the one, much more those who receive abundance of grace and of the gift of righteousness will reign in life through the One, Jesus Christ)" (Rom. 5:17). Sin brings about death, though it was only one man who brought sin into the world. But grace and the gift of righteousness have overcome death—they are infinitely more powerful than sin and death.

Paul continues to reiterate his point—namely, the relative effects of the work of each Adam: "Therefore, as through one man's offense judgment came to all men, resulting in condemnation, even so through one Man's righteous act the free gift came to all men, resulting in justification of life" (Rom. 5:18). Paul comes full circle to the point he originally made in Romans 5:12—that death entered the world through the sin of one man, Adam. But Paul then contrasts Adam's one sin with "one Man's [Christ's] righteous act." This particular phrase has vexed people over the ages because they naturally want to know, What was Christ's singular act of righteousness? Was it His crucifixion, for example? Given Paul's emphasis here on Christ's obedience and the fact that the apostle elsewhere tells us that Jesus was born "under the law" (Gal. 4:4), we should not reduce

Christ's work to one singular act. Paul does not have a single event in mind when he writes of Jesus's one righteous act. Rather, his point is rhetorical. Paul compares the one act of Adam to the one "righteous act" of Jesus. In this case, the likely solution is that Paul has in mind the entirety of Christ's ministry (life, death, resurrection) as His one "righteous act."

A second issue also raises its head. At first glance Paul appears to deal in universal categories. All people are guilty of sin because of Adam's one act of disobedience. Does this therefore mean that all people are automatically righteous because of Christ's obedience? Are all people saved? To be clear, Paul does not posit the universal salvation of all people. A number of passages throughout his corpus corroborate this conclusion, though from the immediate context Paul's emphasis on the necessity of faith in Christ should govern our understanding of the "justification and life" for all men. Justification and life comes only to those who are *in Christ*. Note, for example, what Paul later writes: "There is therefore now no condemnation to those who are in Christ Jesus" (Rom. 8:1).

Paul sharpens his point in Romans 5:19: "For as by one man's disobedience many were made sinners, so also by one Man's obedience many will be made righteous." The New King James offers a sound translation of Paul's statement, though attention to the Greek text brings an important detail into sharper focus. Paul does not state that Adam's disobedience *made* sinners but rather *constituted* sinners. *Constitute*, *assign*, or *appoint* better reflects the meaning of the Greek term *katestatheœsan*. In other words, because of Adam's sin all of humanity was placed in the category of *sinner*—God did not somehow make them sinful. Likewise, because of Christ's one act of obedience, many were placed in the category of *righteous*.[1] These are legal categories—Paul has not yet invoked the doctrine of sanctification whereby we become holier. Again, the broader context of this passage confirms and warrants this refined translation because Paul addresses neither our personal sins nor our spiritual

1. Murray, *Epistle to the Romans*, 204–5.

transformation whereby we become more like Christ. Rather, he pounds the drum regarding the consequences that arise from the respective disobedience and obedience of the two Adams—death and life, condemnation and justification.

Paul concludes this section with a statement that might surprise readers at first: "Moreover the law entered that the offense might abound. But where sin abounded, grace abounded much more, so that as sin reigned in death, even so grace might reign through righteousness to eternal life through Jesus Christ our Lord" (Rom. 5:20–21). As much as some might identify the law with righteousness and therefore salvation, Paul tells us that God introduced the law not so that we might use it as a ladder by which we can ascend to the heavens but rather to increase trespasses! How can Paul say such a thing? If we look at the bigger context, especially Romans 5:12–14, recall that Paul divided all of history into three periods: Adam, Adam to Moses, and Moses to the present day. Paul associated Moses with the introduction of the law, and his point is that God did not reveal the law so that sinners could somehow save themselves by their own obedience. Rather, God introduced the law so that sinners would see how far they fell short, and in their desperation cry out to the Lord to save them, that they would turn to Christ and His perfect law keeping. In this way, then, where sin increased, God's grace abounded all the more. Hence, Paul merely reiterates points he made earlier in his epistle—namely, justification does not come through works of the law but by the works, the obedience, and the suffering of Jesus Christ, the faithful last Adam.

Jesus Our Great Champion

So, then, why do people die? We have received that answer from this passage—people die because of Adam's sin. This is a truth worth careful meditation and pondering. Think of the great power of sin. Think of all the violence, deceit, sexual immorality, war, robbery, hatred, malice, and idolatry that we see in the world, not only in our own day but also throughout all recorded history. All this sin and untold wickedness is the result of one seemingly insignificant action—taking a bite of a forbidden piece of fruit. J. R. R. Tolkien captures this idea in his fantasy adventures of *The Hobbit* and *The Lord of the Rings*. Especially with the latter story, a seemingly small, tiny, and insignificant ring is the source of great evil, corruption, and power. Another dimension of Adam's sin and its detrimental effects on humanity is its universal extent. The fact that there are stillborn infants, that children die, that young men and women perish in car accidents, that men and women suffer from cancer and die painful deaths, and every other conceivable form of death occurs in this world is all because of Adam's one sin. No one escapes the clutches of death.

Despite these terrible realities, people, including many Christians, often retreat into anti-reality, euphemism, and sentimentalism when it comes to death. People think that science will eventually find a way to overcome death. Famous people, for example, have been cryogenically frozen after death so that they can be brought back to life. When people die, we say they "kicked the bucket," "bought the farm," "passed away," or "have gone to a better place." Or people try to look past the coffin that rests before them and they eulogize the dead by saying that the person will live forever in our collective memories. All these efforts amount to a fool's errand—like trying to put lipstick on a pig to make it more attractive. At the end of the day, no matter how much lipstick you use, you still have a pig. We must come to grips with reality and recognize that we face the powerful specter of death and suffering because of Adam's one sin, and there is no escape save the one act of righteousness of the last Adam, Jesus.

As powerful and destructive as Adam's one sin is, Christ's obedience and righteousness are more powerful. Christ's faithful obedience has the power to overcome all the sin that we see in the world as well as the den of iniquity that lies within our hearts. Each one of our sins has the power, like Adam's one sin, to bring about death and destruction, yet Christ's grace has the power to overcome all our sins put together! Our foes, sin and death, are great and mighty, strong and powerful, but our great Champion has conquered our powerful foes. Why do I call Christ our great Champion? Because this is what the author of Hebrews calls Christ:

> But we see Jesus, who was made a little lower than the angels, for the suffering of death crowned with glory and honor, that He, by the grace of God, might taste death for everyone. For it was fitting for Him, for whom are all things and by whom are all things, in bringing many sons to glory, to make the captain of their salvation perfect through sufferings. (Heb. 2:9–10)

The author of the Hebrews calls Christ our Captain, or in the Greek, *archeœgon*, the same word used in pagan literature for heroes such as Hercules.[2]

Hence, Christ, our great Champion and Savior, stood before our fierce foe and conquered him. David, Israel's champion, conquered the fearsome Goliath. This Old Testament story is a typological event that ultimately points forward to Christ. The Israelites could not conquer Goliath—it took God's anointed man, David, to do so. Likewise, we could not conquer our great foe, sin and death—this is Paul's point in showing one of the great purposes of the law. The law reveals sin—it is not a means of salvation; it brings only more condemnation. We could not defeat our foe, but Christ has fought on our behalf and has secured our greater victory over sin and death.

How This Should Affect Us

How should this affect us? The answer is twofold. First, we should recognize that we cannot defeat sin and death ourselves. Our foes are powerful: Remember that all the evil and death around us is a result of one sin. We cannot conquer these foes by our own power or righteousness. We must recognize that only Christ, our great Champion, has won the victory. As John Calvin writes, "Paul says that it was by *the one*, because the Father has made Him the fountain out of whose fullness all may draw. He thus teaches us that not even a drop

2. William L. Lane, *Hebrews 1–8*, Word Biblical Commentary (Waco, Tex.: Word, 1991), 56–57.

of life can be found beyond Christ, nor is there any other remedy for our poverty and want than that which He conveys to us from His own abundance."[3] Will we stand alone against sin and death, or will we stand behind our great Champion, Jesus Christ?

Second, even though sin and death constantly surround us and cause us pain, whether self-inflicted or as we receive it from others, we should know that we have a great source of hope. When we stand at a funeral of a dear loved one, we should recognize that we are there because of the one sin of Adam—his one act of rebellion has had powerful and far-reaching effects that cause us fear, pain, and suffering. Yet we may also stand at that same funeral with hope, knowing that for those who are in Christ, Adam's sin, as powerful as it is, does not have the victory. Rather, our Champion, Jesus Christ, has conquered sin and death.

Conclusion

This passage of Scripture, therefore, should cause us to think about the power of sin. It should be a reminder to us, warning us not to give in to the temptation and encouraging us to cry out to the Holy Spirit for a greater degree of sanctification. Sin is no light matter. Yet this passage should also be a source of hope knowing that Jesus Christ, our Champion, has conquered sin and death. God has delivered sin and death into the hands of Christ, who holds the keys of death and hell (Rev. 1:18). He has struck the head of the serpent and defeated our foe. Praise and worship Christ, our Champion, for His victory and the abundant grace that He has poured out on us. This redemption is the grand effect of His one act of righteousness; His perfect obedience has secured eternal life for those who look to Him by faith alone.

---

3. Calvin, *Romans and Thessalonians*, 115.

17

Union with Christ

ROMANS 6:1–4

What shall we say then? Shall we continue in sin that grace may abound? Certainly not! How shall we who died to sin live any longer in it? Or do you not know that as many of us as were baptized into Christ Jesus were baptized into His death? Therefore we were buried with Him through baptism into death, that just as Christ was raised from the dead by the glory of the Father, even so we also should walk in newness of life.

I once had a conversation with an individual who asked me about God's willingness to forgive sin. He wanted to know if God cut people slack when it came to certain vices, so this question gave me a natural segue to present the gospel. When I explained that works play no part in our salvation and that it is entirely a free gift of God because Christ paid the penalty for our wrongdoing, the man seemed to be relieved—though in the wrong way. This man thought that because Christ paid the price for our sins that this gave him license for his vice. I explained that this was not at all the correct way to view salvation. To say the least, this man was an antinomian at heart. In other words, he wanted to use God's grace as a cover for his continued and deliberate sin. We are sinners and God is in the business of forgiving sins—who can think of a better arrangement? The idea that a believer can live a life of lawlessness is antithetical to the gospel and the biblical doctrine of justification. Given what Paul has said thus far, it should come as no surprise that he would encounter the question that leads off the sixth chapter—namely,

"Shall we continue in sin that grace may abound?" That is, if everything that Paul has written from Romans 3:20–5:21 is true, then do we not have a license to sin? Will not such teaching lead to licentiousness and a wanton disregard for God's law and personal holiness? This is the very question that Paul answers in the verses before us. He responds to the charge that his view of salvation and God's grace leads to antinomianism. To counter this erroneous belief, Paul sets the doctrine of justification within the broader context of our union with Christ. We therefore want to understand how justification connects to our union with Christ as well as draw out the implications for how we should live on a day-to-day basis.

Shall We Go on Sinning?

When we come to the shores of chapter 6, we must not forget what Paul has said in previous sections. Paul explained the significance of federal headship—either Adam or Christ represents us. We all receive the imputed guilt of Adam's sin, and only the imputed righteousness of Christ received by faith alone can counteract its deadly effects. Moreover, recall that the law is not a means of salvation but is merely a means of uncovering our sinfulness. When we recognize our sinfulness as we look at ourselves in the mirror of the law, God's grace abounds to us when we repent: "Moreover the law entered that the offense might abound. But where sin abounded, grace abounded much more" (Rom. 5:20).

On the heels of God's abounding grace for sinners, Paul answers his antinomian critics. He writes: "What shall we say then? Shall we continue in sin that grace may abound? Certainly not! How shall we who died to sin live any longer in it?" (Rom. 6:1–2). Paul's critics contend that if God's grace abounds where there is sin, then we should sin all the more so that we can receive God's grace in greater abundance. The more we sin, the more of God's grace we receive, right? Paul's response to this question is his brusque "Certainly not!" Paul does not offer lengthy argumentation but simply rejects the notion because believers are dead to sin. In the same way that a dead body no longer functions, so a Christian can no longer live in reckless, unchecked rebellion because he is dead to sin.

In what way have Christians died to sin? Paul writes, "Or do you not know that as many of us as were baptized into Christ Jesus were baptized into His death?" (Rom. 6:3). Paul draws attention to the closely related doctrines of baptism and union with Christ. When an adult convert hears the preaching of the Word and is baptized, God proclaims and seals His promise with water. What the Word is to the ears, the water is to the other senses. The ordinance of baptism proclaims, signifies, and seals God's gospel promises but also gives the adult recipient the opportunity to testify to the world that he belongs to Christ. Our baptisms testify to the reality that we have been saved from God's wrath and have been united to Christ through the baptism of the Holy Spirit, by which the Spirit indwells us and effectually calls us into the state of grace out of the state of spiritual death. But to be baptized into Christ means to be joined to Him in everything that He is. Paul uses this phrase in other portions of his writings. The Israelites, for example, were "baptized into Moses" (1 Cor. 10:2), which means they were associated with everything for which Moses stood, chiefly the deliverance that came through him. Elsewhere Paul states quite succinctly, "For as many of you as were baptized into Christ have put on Christ" (Gal. 3:27). The idea, then, is that the believer is identified with Christ and everything that is associated with Him. In this case, Paul specifically identifies that the believer has been baptized into the death of Christ.

Why does Paul bring up the death of Christ, and what is the connection to the believer? He answers this question in the following verse: "Therefore we were buried with Him through baptism into death, that just as Christ was raised from the dead by the glory of the Father, even so we also should walk in newness of life" (Rom. 6:4). Paul now explains the rest of the connection regarding our union with Christ. When we are baptized into Christ, we are joined and unified with Him in His life, death, and resurrection. Just as the Israelites were united to Moses in his mission and goals, so too

God unites us to Christ but in a far richer manner. We "put on the uniform of Christ" when God clothes us in His imputed righteousness.[1] We can no longer live in habitual rebellion and sin since we are dead to it. A man can no longer be a child—it is impossible for him to do this. A married man can no longer be a bachelor. A free man can no longer be a prisoner.[2] In a similar fashion, God's grace changes the person who was dead in his sin and trespasses, a God-hater, blind to the truth, and unable to exercise faith. Once he is made alive in Christ, is given the desire to love God, sees the truth, and exercises faith, it is impossible for him to return to his previous state. He is dead to sin.

Why is it impossible? Because anyone who is in Christ is part of the "new creation" (2 Cor. 5:17; cf. Isa. 65:17; 66:22). When God effectually calls people through the sovereign work of the Holy Spirit, they not only are mystically united to His Son through the indwelling of the Spirit but also enter into the new creation—they take their first step into the new heavens and earth. Given our new existence, being raised according to our inner man (2 Cor. 4:16) and entering the new creation by virtue of our union with Christ, a Christian would never use the grace of God as a cover-up for lawlessness—he would never choose the path of antinomianism. This is totally antithetical to the very constitution of the believer who is part of the new creation in Christ. This antinomian conduct is not the obedience of faith.

What Paul Is Not Saying

It is important that we explore the implications of what Paul has written and understand them as best as we can. First, we must understand what Paul is *not* saying. He is not saying that the believer will never sin. Yes, it is true that a man can no longer be a child, but he can be childish. A childish man, however, should eventually

---

1. James Montgomery Boice, *Romans*, vol. 2, *The Reign of Grace* (Grand Rapids: Baker, 1992), 661.

2. Boice, *Reign of Grace*, 2:656.

recognize that he is not a child and stop his immature behavior. Likewise, a person who enters into serious rebellion must recognize the gravity of his sin and turn from it. One of the most famous examples of this is King David: He fell into grave sin—murder and adultery—yet he ultimately repented and turned from his rebellion. The Westminster Confession (WCF) addresses this very issue when it states that Christians,

> through the temptations of Satan and of the world, the prevalency of corruption remaining in them, and the neglect of the means of their preservation, fall into grievous sins; and, for a time, continue therein: whereby they incur God's displeasure, and grieve his Holy Spirit, come to be deprived of some measure of their graces and comforts; have their hearts hardened, and their consciences wounded; hurt and scandalize others, and bring temporal judgments upon themselves. (WCF 17.3)

Therefore, Paul does *not* say that Christians will never sin. Rather, he refutes the accusation that he promotes antinomianism. He refutes the idea that Christians will, with wanton and deliberate disregard for God's law, continue steadfastly in sin because of the free grace of the gospel. Such a conclusion is unthinkable to Paul.

What Is Paul Saying?

A Christian never would or could be an antinomian. For the person who claims to be a Christian but lives like a pagan, with no signs of remorse or repentance on the horizon, by the best use of our judgment and charity, we must conclude that such a person is not a believer. If a believer begins to exhibit antinomian behavior, God will stop him from continuing. In this vein James Boice observes,

> God will not stop you from sinning, but he will stop you from continuing in it. And he will do it in one of two ways. Either he will make your life so miserable that you will curse the day you got into sin and beg God to get you out of it, or God will put an end to your life. Paul told the Corinthians that because they had dishonored the Lord's Supper, God had

> actually taken some of them home to heaven (1 Cor. 11:30). If God did it to them for that offense, he will do it to you for persistence in more sinful things.[3]

God has such a great concern for His holiness and the integrity of His name that He will lovingly discipline His children to preserve the holiness of Christ's church. This reality has important implications regarding the way that we see our sanctification, our conduct, and our selves.

Do we recognize that we are united to Christ by faith? I once heard a powerful line in a movie in which one character said to another, "You are more than you have become." This statement gives us a window of insight into the truth of our union with Christ and its implications for our quest for holiness and greater conformity to Him. Do we recognize that we are dead to sin? Or do we wallow in it and live like the childish man? How we view ourselves will undoubtedly have a great impact on our sanctification and the way that we live our lives.

We must understand that Christ died in our place and paid the penalty for our sins, and that we are united and joined to Him in His representative death. Moreover, we are new creatures in Christ and have put off the sinful nature. If these things are true, then there should be a marked difference about the way we live. Charles Spurgeon (1834–1892) once recounted with great horror about those who do not recognize these truths:

> It shocks me to my very soul when I hear some people talk about the doctrines of grace that are as dear to my heart as life itself. These people uphold the principles of grace while they ignore the practices of godliness, for their lives are inconsistent with their professions. I have known professing believers who never talk so well about theology as they do when they are half drunk and never seem to be so sound in the faith as when they can hardly stand on their legs. They will tell you that good works are nothing and all, and they glory in free grace. Ah,

---

3. Boice, *Reign of Grace*, 2:663–64.

> dear friend, God save you from being Mr. Talkative, who could lecture upon free grace but never felt the power of it. If the grace of God does not save a man from drunkenness, from lascivious conversation, from lies and lewdness, from slandering and scowling at your fellow Christians, then I think the grace of God must be a very different thing from what I read of in this precious Word of God. Either my judgment is at fault or your pretensions are spurious.[4]

Again, it is impossible for a believer to live in the same way as a man who is dead in his sins and trespasses. The grace of God should make the greatest impact on a person's life, even in the most mundane and ordinary matters. Do the members of your household benefit from the fruit of the Spirit in your life—love, joy, peace, patience, kindness, gentleness, faithfulness, and self-control (Gal. 5:22–23)? Are you kinder and gentler to your boss and coworkers? Are you as an employee more respectful and diligent, more scrupulous and honest?[5] All these moral changes are not accomplished by the believer's sheer willpower. Rather, they are the fruit of the work of God—they result because God has created a new creature in Christ.

Conclusion

Our union with Christ, therefore, precludes the possibility of antinomianism. No one receives justification—the imputed alien righteousness of Christ and the forgiveness of sins—apart from being united to Christ. If you are united to Christ, then you are part of the new creation, and you have the indwelling presence of the Spirit to sanctify you. You have been raised from death to walk in the newness of life, not to return to your old, sinful ways. We must therefore strive to look to our union with Christ and desire to be who we are in Him.

---

4. Charles Spurgeon, *A Passion for Holiness in a Believer's Life*, ed. Robert Hall (Lynnwood, Wash.: Emerald Books, 1994), 169–70.

5. Spurgeon, *Passion for Holiness*, 170.

18

Justified from Sin

ROMANS 6:5–11

For if we have been united together in the likeness of His death, certainly we also shall be in the likeness of His resurrection, knowing this, that our old man was crucified with Him, that the body of sin might be done away with, that we should no longer be slaves of sin. For he who has died has been freed from sin. Now if we died with Christ, we believe that we shall also live with Him, knowing that Christ, having been raised from the dead, dies no more. Death no longer has dominion over Him. For the death that He died, He died to sin once for all; but the life that He lives, He lives to God. Likewise you also, reckon yourselves to be dead indeed to sin, but alive to God in Christ Jesus our Lord.

I suspect that all of us at some point have wondered what heaven is like. The fantastic imagery and descriptions of heaven in Scripture stretch the imagination but ultimately leave us wanting to know more. We sing hymns that express our longing to be with our heavenly Father. Unregenerate man searches for heaven in all the wrongs places: love, food, possessions—whatever he can gather as a poor substitute for God. Christians, however, should have their hope firmly set on things above and, with the apostle Paul, long for the consummation of the age, the return of Christ, and the prospects of dwelling in heaven eternally with our God, our Creator and Redeemer. Yet while we await heaven and long for a taste of its richness, we may fail to recognize that we already experience and know heaven at this very moment. In what way do we experience a first taste of the age to come? We should keep this question before our minds as we examine this passage of Scripture and consider the life-giving nature of our justification. When God justifies and declares us righteous in His sight on the basis of Christ's imputed obedience and satisfaction, certain consequences come as a result—namely, our freedom from sin, which allows us to live a life of holiness through the sanctifying power of the Holy Spirit. In a word, our justification is a life-giving verdict.

What Breaks the Legal Power of Sin?

Recall what we examined in the previous section (Rom. 6:1–4): Because of our union with Christ we have been joined with Him in everything that He accomplished. Just as Christ died, so we too have died to sin, and therefore it is inconceivable that the true believer would continue in unchecked rebellion. Paul now continues this thought from Romans 6:4 into the next verse: "For if we have been united together in the likeness of His death, certainly we also shall be in the likeness of His resurrection" (Rom. 6:5). Paul writes that we "have been united," or literally, "planted together" (*symphytoi*) with Christ. We therefore die to sin, as Christ died on the cross, because we have been united to Him in everything that He has done, which also means we have been raised to walk in the newness of life (Rom. 6:4). Notice that Paul uses the future tense when he says, "we also shall be in the likeness of His resurrection" (Rom. 6:5b). Paul's use of the future tense does not denote something yet to occur but rather conveys the certainty of our resurrection-producing union. In other words, the new convert *will certainly* produce the fruit of a regenerate heart. It is important, though, to notice that the newness of life in which the believer walks is a result of the resurrection of Christ, not his own self-generated moral renewal.

Paul restates this truth in a slightly different manner in the following verse: "Knowing this, that our old man was crucified with Him, that the body of sin might be done away with, that we should no longer be slaves of sin" (Rom. 6:6). When people read of their "old man," they question what Paul means by this term. The easiest way to answer this is to appeal to what Paul wrote in Romans

5:12–21. Recall that Paul talked about the respective works of disobedience and obedience of the first and last Adams. The first Adam disobeyed and brought sin, death, and condemnation into the world and on his children. The last Adam obeyed and brought life, justification, and entry to the new creation for those who are united to Him. So when Paul writes that our "old man was crucified with Him," it means that our former existence in Adam was terminated in the crucifixion of Christ. Consequently, because we are no longer united to Adam and the deleterious effects of his first sin, we are no longer slaves to sin because we are now united to Christ and the life-giving effects of His obedience, or imputed righteousness. This is why, again, Paul calls believers "new creation" in Christ (2 Cor. 5:17). They are not merely *a* new creation but rather are part of *the* new creation, the new heavens and earth. Important to note is Paul's use of a purpose clause at the end of the verse, which signals the resultant effects of the believer's crucifixion with Christ: "That we should no longer be slaves of sin" (Rom. 6:6b).

Although Paul discusses matters pertaining to the doctrine of sanctification here in chapter 6, this does not mean he has forgotten justification. In this respect the following verse is key to understanding how and in what way the doctrine of justification relates to the doctrine of sanctification: "For he who has died has been freed from sin" (Rom. 6:7). What does Paul mean when he states that we have been *freed*, literally "justified" (*dedikaioœtai*), from sin? We first must realize the source of sin's power. I think many people believe that sin has a power all its own, and in one sense, this is true—it is a corrupting power and detrimental influence on the lives of anyone it touches. Like a cancerous infection that spreads throughout a body, sin has the power to destroy anyone by its influence. But the specific issue at hand is whence arises sin's *legal* power. Paul elsewhere explains this relationship in his first epistle to Corinth in which he similarly unfolds the significance and impact of the respective works of the first and last Adams: "As was the man of dust, so also are those who are made of dust; and as is the heavenly Man, so also are those who are heavenly. And as we have borne the image of the man of dust, we shall also bear the image of the heavenly Man" (1 Cor. 15:48–49). For those who bear the image of the man of dust, there is only sin, death, and misery. And, according to Paul, "the sting of death is sin, and the strength of sin is the law" (1 Cor. 15:56). Sin would be powerless were it not for the entrance of the law into the world. Recall what Paul wrote about the law in the previous chapter: "The law entered that the offense might abound" (Rom. 5:20a). God's forensic, or legal, declaration that we are free from the law's condemnation by faith alone in Christ alone, by which we receive the imputed righteousness of Jesus, breaks the legal claim and power of sin. We are, as Paul writes, "freed," or justified, "from sin."

Paul speaks in a similar manner when he states, "Therefore let it be known to you, brethren, that through this Man is preached to you the forgiveness of sins; and by Him everyone who believes is justified from all things from which you could not be justified by the law of Moses" (Acts 13:38–39).[1] Our justification frees us from the claims and condemnation of the law, which means that we are no longer bound to serve sin but are free to serve Christ. Paul's point has been succinctly captured by a number of exegetes and theologians over the years. John Calvin has famously noted: "For unless we first of all apprehend in what situation we stand with respect to God, and what his judgment is concerning us, we have no foundation either for a certainty of salvation, or for the exercise of piety toward God."[2] The foundation Calvin has in mind is our justification, which he calls the "principal hinge by which religion is supported" and the "beginning, foundation, cause, proof, and substance of works righteousness."[3] Likewise, Charles Hodge (1797–1878) explains,

1. Robert Haldane, *Exposition of the Epistle to the Romans* (1874; repr., Edinburgh: Banner of Truth, 1996), 248.

2. Calvin, *Institutes*, 3.11.1.

3. Calvin, *Institutes*, 3.11.1, 3.17.9.

> For he who has died (with Christ) is justified, and therefore free from sin, free from its dominion. This is the great evangelical truth which underlies the apostle's whole doctrine of sanctification. The natural reason assumes that acceptance with a holy and just God must be founded upon character, that men must be holy in order to be justified. The gospel reverses this, and teaches that God accepts the ungodly; that we must be justified in order to become holy. This is what Paul here assumes as known to his readers. As justification is the necessary means, and antecedent to holiness, he that is justified becomes holy; he cannot live in sin. And he who is dead, *i.e.*, with Christ, (for it is only his death that secures justification,) is justified from sin. *To be justified from sin* means to be delivered from sin by justification. And that deliverance is twofold; judicial deliverance from its penalty, and subjective deliverance from its power. Both are secured by justification; the former directly, the other consequentially, as a necessary consequence (cf. Gal. 2:19–20; 6:14; Col. 2:13; 3:3; 1 Pet. 4:1).[4]

Calvin and Hodge, and Paul for that matter, believed that the verdict of justification gives life. When an accused criminal stands before the judge shackled in chains and the judge pronounces the verdict of "Not guilty!" the bailiff comes over, removes the shackles, and the prisoner goes free. Similarly, when God declares us righteous, the shackles and bonds of sin and death come off and we are freed in Christ to live lives of holiness and righteousness. We are free to become what we have been declared in Christ. We are free to be holy.

Paul connects not only Christ's death to the believer's newfound freedom but also His resurrection: "Now if we died with Christ, we believe that we shall also live with Him, knowing that Christ, having been raised from the dead, dies no more. Death no longer has dominion over Him" (Rom. 6:8–9). Recall that not only does Christ's death free the believer from the bonds of sin (e.g., Rom.

---

4. Charles Hodge, *Romans* (1835; repr., Edinburgh: Banner of Truth, 1989), 198–99.

3:25a) but so does His resurrection because Christ was "delivered up because of our offenses, and was raised because of our justification" (Rom. 4:25). Christ's complete work—His life, death, and resurrection—is the judicial foundation of our salvation, or justification. It frees us from the power of sin so that we might walk in the newness of life, not so we can continue in sin—far from it: "For the death that He died, He died to sin once for all; but the life that He lives, He lives to God. Likewise, you also, reckon yourselves to be dead indeed to sin, but alive to God in Christ Jesus our Lord" (Rom. 6:10–11). Death is unrepeatable, which means that if Christ died once, then we die once to sin, never to return to that state. Hence, we are dead to sin and alive to God, that we might use this newly given life for righteous service to God. I think one of Paul's chief points is that justification and sanctification are in no way inimical but work together like the proverbial hand in the glove.

Heaven Now!

In what way do we experience and know heaven at this very moment? We should realize that Romans 5:6–11 conceptually hinges on verses 4–5 and is the outworking of what Paul set forth in Romans 5:12–21. Remember, "as sin reigned in death, even so grace might reign through righteousness to eternal life through Jesus Christ our Lord" (Rom. 5:21). And this eternal life is not something for which we wait—it is not entirely future, it is now! God raises believers to the newness of life and frees them from the bondage of sin and death. Through these events we obtain the first taste of heaven, the new creation. The Old Testament teaches us that the resurrection is an end-time event (Dan. 12:1–2). The beginning of the great eschatological harvest starts with the resurrection of the head of the body, Jesus. He is, as Paul writes, the "firstfruits of those who have fallen asleep" (1 Cor. 15:20). Christ's resurrection from the dead signals that the end of the age is upon us. He "gave Himself for our sins, that He might deliver us from this present evil age" (Gal. 1:4). In other words, through His resurrection Christ conquered sin and death, the lords of this present evil age. Christ, then, frees us from both sin and death through our justification so that we can live the life of sanctification, but this new existence occurs as we enter by faith into the new heavens and earth. Indeed, through faith and the indwelling power and presence of the Holy Spirit we enjoy the "powers of the age to come" (Heb. 6:5). All these things signal the fact that the eschatological age has dawned on us and we taste, experience, and know the Spirit's power.

We know His power because we are new creatures in Christ who walk in the newness of life. How do we walk in the newness of life? By the power of Christ's resurrection. This is what Paul meant when he said he sought to live by the power of Christ's resurrection, that he would know the fellowship of His sufferings and be conformed to His death (Phil. 3:8–11). Paul wanted to know the power of Christ's resurrection—that is, to live in the newness of life. The very fact that Christ saves us from this present evil age by raising us from death to life means we can discern good from evil, which informs us that we experience the dawning of the eschatological age. By the power of the resurrection of Christ, which secures our life-giving verdict in our justification by faith alone, we begin to live by the power of the age to come—we experience and know heaven right now. Mind you, this is not to say that we experience the consummation of the age—Jesus has not yet returned. There are still greater salvific realities to come, such as our glorification. But we do not want to diminish the significance of the inaugurated aspects of the eschatological age that have come to those of us who walk in the newness of life.

We must therefore realize the utter incompatibility of sin and the new creation. Sin entered the creation through the disobedience of one man, but by the obedience of Jesus, we receive eternal life—the freedom from sin, the ability to walk in the newness of life, and the hope of the completion of our salvation. If we continue persistently to live in sin after our profession of faith in Christ, then we quite obviously have missed something significant. Not only have we failed to recognize the age-shattering nature of Christ's work, that He has inaugurated the new heavens and earth, but we have also failed to grasp the moral-ethical consequences of what it means to be united to Christ, justified and sanctified. We must die more and more to sin and live more and more unto Christ by seeking the power of His life-giving resurrection and laying hold of the life-giving verdict of our justification. We must seek Christ in the means of grace—Word, sacraments, and prayer—so that we might continue to breathe the air of the new creation and recognize that we are dead to our old existence in Adam.

Conclusion

We live at the dawn of the age to come, the inception of the new heavens and earth. Heaven is upon us, and now we await the consummation of the age and Christ's return. How, then, will we live? We cannot live as though we still belong to this present evil age. We who have experienced the power of the age to come through the ministry of the Holy Spirit must walk in the newness of life. As Paul wrote to the Philippians: "For our citizenship is in heaven, from which we also eagerly wait for the Savior, the Lord Jesus Christ, who will transform our lowly body that it may be conformed to His glorious body, according to the working by which He is able even to subdue all things to Himself" (Phil. 3:20–21). Remember, then, that we do not find heaven in worldly pleasures. Although we long for heaven, we presently know of its power and glory because of our union with Christ—the fact that we walk in the newness of life because of His resurrection from the dead. Therefore, live with a heavenly mind-set, not as inhabitants of this evil age, antinomians at heart, but rather as citizens of heaven, those who desire to please God with every thought, word, and deed. Live in the knowledge that you have been justified from sin—you enjoy the power and benefits of the life-giving verdict of your justification by faith alone in Christ alone.

19

Freed from Bondage

ROMANS 6:12–23

Therefore do not let sin reign in your mortal body, that you should obey it in its lusts. And do not present your members as instruments of unrighteousness to sin, but present yourselves to God as being alive from the dead, and your members as instruments of righteousness to God. For sin shall not have dominion over you, for you are not under law but under grace. What then? Shall we sin because we are not under law but under grace? Certainly not! Do you not know that to whom you present yourselves slaves to obey, you are that one's slaves whom you obey, whether of sin leading to death, or of obedience leading to righteousness? But God be thanked that though you were slaves of sin, yet you obeyed from the heart that form of doctrine to which you were delivered. And having been set free from sin, you became slaves of righteousness. I speak in human terms because of the weakness of your flesh. For just as you presented your members as slaves of uncleanness, and of lawlessness leading to more lawlessness, so now present your members as slaves of righteousness for holiness. For when you were slaves of sin, you were free in regard to righteousness. What fruit did you have then in the things of which you are now ashamed? For the end of those things is death. But now having been set free from sin, and having become slaves of God, you have your fruit to holiness, and the end, everlasting life. For the wages of sin is death, but the gift of God is eternal life in Christ Jesus our Lord.

I once watched a documentary about American prisoners of war during the Vietnam War. The documentary recounted how downed pilots were taken to the main prison in Hanoi, what the Americans called the "Hanoi Hilton." This moniker was by no means indicative of the posh accommodations but was a euphemism for the brutality that these airmen regularly faced. When the captors tried to extract information from the pilots, they regularly beat most prisoners within inches of their lives. One pilot recounts that when he was initially captured the local villagers surrounded him and had blood lust on their minds—they came face to face with the man who had just bombed their country. One man took a sharpened bamboo stick and jammed it into each foot and twisted it as far as it would go. This pilot eventually suffered many broken bones and wished for death. He thought his torture would never end. This particular pilot was held prisoner for more than six years, during which time he suffered a spinal fracture, hundreds of mosquito bites, broken feet, a broken tooth, a rare kidney disorder, and dysentery.[1]

As you can imagine, once he was freed he was overjoyed. When the plane carrying the POWs finally took off, the former captives cheered, clapped, and even wept. Again, the same pilot writes:

> We were whisked off to the large base hospital where we were greeted by an enthusiastic and caring staff. We were assigned rooms and given time to shower (with real hot water!) and change into hospital garb. We then went down to the hospital cafeteria where we could order anything we wanted. I had steak and eggs with bacon and ham, with a side order of potatoes, and a waffle. I then tried to eat pie with ice cream, but had trouble eating it due to the chocolate sundae I had previously devoured. Needless to say, we all had stomach aches from too much rich food, but were ready to do it again that evening.[2]

We can only imagine the utter torment these men faced—as most of them were kept in solitary confinement for the majority of their captivities—and the absolute joy of finally obtaining their freedom. We would rightly consider them fools if the POWs freely

---

1. Col. Gordon "Swede" Larson, *Biography*, accessed August 26, 2013, at http://www.soft-vision.com/hanoi/larson/bio_4.htm.

2. Larson, *Biography*.

decided to return to the Hanoi Hilton. Who in their right mind would return to live under such brutal conditions? We must keep this question in the back of our minds as we examine the passage of Scripture before us. For indeed, we too have been released from a life of bondage and oppression, yet some are tempted to return to that life of death. To place this equation in biblical garb, many Christians who have been freed from bondage in Egypt want to return for "the cucumbers, the melons, the leeks, the onions, and the garlic" (Num. 11:5). Or to put this in Pauline terms, sinners were justified and freed from the bondage of Satan, sin, and death (Rom. 6:7), but some wanted to use their Christ-wrought freedom to return to their former state of oppression. What does Paul have to say to such people?

Ethical Implications of Our Union with Christ

Paul expounded the doctrines of the universal sinfulness of humanity (Rom. 1:18–3:19), justification (Rom. 3:20–5:21), union with Christ and sanctification (Rom. 6:1–4), the foundational nature of justification, and the legal aspect of our union with Christ (Rom. 6:5–10), and now he turns his attention to the ethical implications of all these things. Or, stated more simply, given who we are in Christ, how then should we live? Paul writes: "Therefore do not let sin reign in your mortal body, that you should obey it in its lusts. And do not present your members as instruments of unrighteousness to sin, but present yourselves to God as being alive from the dead, and your members as instruments of righteousness to God. For sin shall not have dominion over you, for you are not under law but under grace" (Rom. 6:12–14). Given our union with Christ, which gives us justification and sanctification, Paul says we must live holy lives. We have been freed from the bondage of sin and death and must therefore use our bodies as instruments of righteousness. Sin is no longer our master—Christ is our Lord and Savior. As Paul succinctly explains, we are "not under law but under grace." But his statement does not mean that believers are completely freed from the obligations of the law and that it can make no demands whatsoever of the believer.

Rather, when he says that we are no longer under law but under grace, this is another way of saying that we are no longer united to Adam and thereby subject to the curse of the law. We are united to Christ and enjoy the fruits and benefits of God's grace in our redemption. Reformed theologians have noted that believers no longer stand in relation to the law as a covenant of works, that which requires personal, perfect, and perpetual obedience (WCF 7.2; 19.1–7). Instead, once Christ redeems, justifies, and sanctifies a person, He delivers him from the law as a covenant; instead, it becomes a rule for life, that which informs the believer of what the Lord desires of His people. The law is no longer an enemy but a friend. But Paul once again bats down the possible objection that the grace of God would somehow be misused as a cover-up for sin and wanton rebellion: "What then? Shall we sin because we are not under law but under grace? Certainly not!" (Rom. 6:15). The Christian is dead to sin, has been raised to the newness to life by the same power that raised Christ from the dead, is part of the new creation, and now lives at the dawn of the eschatological age.

Paul fleshes out this point by explaining what happens when a person submits himself once again to the dominion of sin: "Do you not know that to whom you present yourselves slaves to obey, you are that one's slaves whom you obey, whether of sin leading to death, or of obedience leading to righteousness?" (Rom. 6:16). There are only two options: death or life, disobedience and slavery or obedience and righteousness. A believer is a servant either of sin or of Christ, an antinomian dead in his trespasses or a part of the new creation raised to walk in the newness of life. As our Lord told His disciples: "No servant can serve two masters; for either he will hate the one and love the other, or else he will be loyal to the one and despise the other" (Luke 16:13a). This means that a Christian should never lead a life of unchecked rebellion just because he has been freed from the curse of the law. On the contrary, he is no longer a slave to sin but is instead a slave to righteousness: "But God be thanked that though you were slaves of sin, yet you obeyed from the heart that form of doctrine to which you were delivered. And having been set free from sin, you became slaves of righteousness" (Rom. 6:17–18). The fact that verse 18 is in the passive voice—literally, "you have been enslaved to righteousness"—conveys the idea that *God* frees the sinner from the bondage of sin and makes him a slave of righteousness. Christians are passive in the salvation process—God delivers them from bondage, they do not free themselves. In the event that his readers are still confused or mistaken, Paul restates his point as clearly as he can: "I speak in human terms because of the weakness of your flesh. For just as you presented your members as slaves of uncleanness, and of lawlessness leading to more lawlessness, so now present your members as slaves of righteousness for holiness" (Rom. 6:19). As redeemed sinners now united to Christ, those who breathe the air of the new creation, their whole purpose in life is to pursue holiness, not sin.

Paul pushes the logic of our new existence in Christ in comparison to our former existence in Adam: "For when you were slaves of sin, you were free in regard to righteousness. What fruit did you have then in the things of which you are now ashamed? For the end of those things is death" (Rom. 6:20–21). Prior to their union with Christ, the Roman Christians conducted themselves in shameful ways, perhaps sins like those Paul mentions elsewhere: sexual immorality, idolatry, adultery, homosexuality, greed, drunkenness, reviling, and swindling (1 Cor. 6:9–10). These are certainly sins that Paul mentions earlier in his letter to Rome (Rom. 1:18–3:19). He reminds them that such conduct, and such a connection to Adam and his fallen kingdom, spells certain death and judgment. Paul elsewhere makes this same point in his epistle to the Galatian churches: "Now the works of the flesh are evident, which are: adultery, fornication, uncleanness, lewdness, idolatry, sorcery, hatred, contentions, jealousies, outbursts of wrath, selfish ambitions, dissensions, heresies, envy, murders, drunkenness, revelries, and the like; of which I tell you beforehand, just as I also told you in time past, that those who practice such things will not inherit the kingdom of God" (Gal. 5:19–21). Prior to their conversion, the Roman

Christians engaged in such conduct because they were free from righteousness; they were not united to Christ.

But now that they have been freed from sin, to what end have they been freed? Paul writes: "But now having been set free from sin, and having become slaves of God, you have your fruit to holiness, and the end, everlasting life. For the wages of sin is death, but the gift of God is eternal life in Christ Jesus our Lord" (Rom. 6:22–23). Having been set free to serve God, believers should manifest the fruit of the Spirit: love, joy, peace, patience, kindness, goodness, gentleness, faithfulness, and self-control (Gal. 5:22–24). Such conduct is the fruit of drawing nigh to God through His appointed means, and as such, leads to the end-goal of eternal life.

Shall We Return to Egypt?

Do you see the overall point that Paul makes in this passage? Do you see why Paul says that grace is never a license to sin? The believer has been freed from the dominion of sin and death. Again, think of the POW who was freed after six brutal years in captivity. Would he have willingly returned to his prison? If he did, we would rightly call him insane! Why would a person return to a life of torture and hardship and give up a life of freedom? This is Paul's primary point. Why would you use your Christ-wrought freedom from Satan, sin, and death to return under its dominion?

Paul's didactic precision unfolds in Israel's Old Testament redemption from Egypt, which was ultimately, among other things, a typological portrait of our redemption from Satan, sin, and death. Pharaoh was Israel's cruel taskmaster who held the people of God in bondage. Moses, a type of Christ, led the people out of slavery. When the people who were liberated from Egypt thought about returning, both Moses and Joshua tore their clothes in mourning. They knew that God had delivered them from bondage and was bringing them into the Promised Land. Likewise, we must realize what these typological figures and events mean for us. As Paul elsewhere writes, "Now all these things happened to them as examples [*typos*, literally "types"], and they were written for our admonition, upon whom the ends of the ages have come" (1 Cor. 10:11). Our Mediator, Jesus Christ, has led us in the great exodus from sin and death. If we, for any reason, find ourselves wanting to return to our former captivity, then let us rend our hearts and mourn. We have been freed from the bondage of sin and death and must now walk in the newness of life. A true believer, therefore, would never endlessly abuse God's grace in Christ as a cover-up for his lawless living. On the contrary, a true believer should yearn to manifest the fruit of righteousness in his life, all to the glory of Christ. A true believer should never want to return to Egypt. Perish the thought!

Conclusion

This passage of Scripture should cause us to ask ourselves, Do we ever desire to return to Egypt? We should remember the fact that we are slaves of God and that Jesus Christ has freed us from the bondage of sin and death and their oppressive rule. Should we find ourselves tempted to return to Egypt, under the dominion of sin, we should pray for watchfulness and fidelity as the saints who have gone before us. In the words of one prayer, "O how desirable, how profitable to the Christian life is a spirit of holy watchfulness and godly jealousy over myself when my soul is afraid of nothing except grieving and offending thee, the blessed God, my Father and friend, whom I then love and long to please, rather than be happy in myself."[3]

I am sure there is not a day that goes by in which the former POWs do not live in thankfulness that they were liberated from captivity. So too, we must live in this manner and desire to please God with the fruit of righteousness. As Charles Wesley writes in his famous hymn "And Can It Be,"

> Long my imprisoned spirit lay
> Fast bound in sin and nature's night;
> Thine eye diffused a quick'ning ray;
> I woke, the dungeon flamed with light;

3. Bennett, *Valley of Vision*, 130.

My chains fell off, my heart was free,
I rose, went forth, and followed Thee.

No condemnation now I dread;
Jesus, and all in Him, is mine!
Alive in Him, my living Head,
And clothed in righteousness divine,
Bold I approach th'eternal throne,
And claim the crown, through Christ, my own.

Amazing love! how can it be,
That Thou my God, shouldst die for me?

Give thanks that God has delivered us by the life, death, and resurrection of His Son, and pray that He would enable us, by His grace, to live as slaves of righteousness in the full knowledge that we have died to our old man in Adam and have been united to our living head, Jesus Christ.

20

Freed from the Law

ROMANS 7:1–25

Or do you not know, brethren (for I speak to those who know the law), that the law has dominion over a man as long as he lives? For the woman who has a husband is bound by the law to her husband as long as he lives. But if the husband dies, she is released from the law of her husband. So then if, while her husband lives, she marries another man, she will be called an adulteress; but if her husband dies, she is free from that law, so that she is no adulteress, though she has married another man. Therefore, my brethren, you also have become dead to the law through the body of Christ, that you may be married to another—to Him who was raised from the dead, that we should bear fruit to God. For when we were in the flesh, the sinful passions which were aroused by the law were at work in our members to bear fruit to death. But now we have been delivered from the law, having died to what we were held by, so that we should serve in the newness of the Spirit and not in the oldness of the letter. What shall we say then? Is the law sin? Certainly not! On the contrary, I would not have known sin except through the law. For I would not have known covetousness unless the law had said, "You shall not covet." But sin, taking opportunity by the commandment, produced in me all manner of evil desire. For apart from the law sin was dead. I was alive once without the law, but when the commandment came, sin revived and I died. And the commandment, which was to bring life, I found to bring death. For sin, taking occasion by the commandment, deceived me, and by it killed me. Therefore the law is holy, and the commandment holy and just and good. Has then what is good become death to me? Certainly not! But sin, that it might appear sin, was producing death in me through what is good, so that sin through the commandment might become exceedingly sinful. For we know that the law is spiritual, but I am carnal, sold under sin. For what I am doing, I do not understand. For what I will to do, that I do not practice; but what I hate, that I do. If, then, I do what I will not to do, I agree with the law that it is good. But now, it is no longer I who do it, but sin that dwells in me. For I know that in me (that is, in my flesh) nothing good dwells; for to will is present with me, but how to perform what is good I do not find. For the good that I will to do, I do not do; but the evil I will not to do, that I practice. Now if I do what I will not to do, it is no longer I who do it, but sin that dwells in me. I find then a law, that evil is present with me, the one who wills to do good. For I delight in the law of God according to the inward man. But I see another law in my members, warring against the law of my mind, and bringing me into captivity to the law of sin which is in my members. O wretched man that I am! Who will deliver me from this body of death? I thank God—through Jesus Christ our Lord! So then, with the mind I myself serve the law of God, but with the flesh the law of sin.

Ever since chapter 5 Paul has explained the implications of the doctrine of justification. Through the representative disobedience of Adam, all who are united to him are regarded as sinners and are therefore condemned. Conversely, the representative obedience of the last Adam regards those who are united to Christ as righteous, which is received by faith alone through the sovereign work of God's Spirit (Rom. 5:12–21). Paul dealt with the initial rejection of his doctrine of justification (Rom. 3:20–5:21, esp. 5:21)—namely, should we sin so that God's grace would abound all the more (Rom. 6:1)? In other words, will not Paul's doctrine of justification lead to gross lawlessness? If people receive the forgiveness of all their sins—past, present, and future—will this not incite them to forsake holiness and piety? Paul's quick answer to this objection is no. He spends the entirety of Romans 6 demonstrating two things about justification. First, anyone who has died with Christ has been justified and freed from sin (Rom. 6:7). God's forensic declaration breaks the legal claim and power of sin that once held the believer in its grip (cf. 1 Cor. 15:56). Second, the broader context of the believer's justification is union with Christ. In his union with Christ the believer receives his justification *and* sanctification. He is buried with Christ in baptism and raised to walk in the newness of life (Rom. 6:1–4); the believer is a slave to righteousness and now lives unto God—his members are instruments of righteousness in His hands (Rom. 6:10–23). The believer has been freed from bondage and is now free to serve Christ.

But now in the seventh chapter Paul deals with a second possible objection regarding the law. Our justification frees us from the power of both sin and the law. In this chapter, Paul deals with two chief issues: the believer's freedom from the law and the precise manner in which God employed the law in redemptive history. Paul briefly touched on this second point in Romans 5: "Moreover the law entered that the offense might abound. But where sin abounded, grace abounded much more, so that as sin reigned in death, even so grace might reign through righteousness to eternal life through Jesus Christ our Lord" (Rom. 5:20–21). The question naturally arises, How can the law increase the sin? Is God's law not good? And if it is good, how can it incite sin rather than promote holiness and righteousness? Paul addresses these issues by demonstrating two key points: (1) the believer's freedom from the law (Rom. 7:1–6) and (2) how sin uses the law.[1] Understanding what Paul writes here has significant implications for comprehending how the law functions in the Christian life. In particular, one of Paul's chief points is that the law alone is not a source of holiness or righteousness for the believer. This not only has important consequences for our pursuit of holiness but also sounds a warning to

---

1. My exposition of Romans 7 relies on the views presented in Dennis E. Johnson, "The Function of Romans 7:13–25 in Paul's Argument for the Law's Impotence and the Spirit's Power, and Its Bearing on the Identity of the Schizophrenic 'I,'" in *Resurrection and Eschatology: Theology in Service of the Church*, ed. Lane G. Tipton and Jeffrey C. Waddington (Phillipsburg, N.J.: P&R Publishing, 2008), 3–59; and Moo, *Epistle to the Romans*, 410–67.

preachers who seek to promote the law among their congregations. There is a right and wrong way to employ the law.

Married to Another

All we have to do is look to Hollywood to see how disposable marriage is to our culture. It represents an exaggerated view of the broader culture's attitude toward this sacred bond. Elizabeth Taylor, for example, was married eight times to seven different husbands. Our culture has a very flippant attitude toward one of the most fundamental relationships in all of human society. But in the eyes of God, marriage is an indissoluble bond, regardless of its disposable status to our surrounding culture. There are only three things that can break the bond of marriage: death, infidelity, or abandonment (cf. Matt. 19:1–9; 1 Cor. 7:15). The words of the officiating minister, drawn from Scripture, likely echo in our minds: "Therefore what God has joined together, let not man separate" (Matt. 19:6). Paul was well aware of the seriousness of the marriage bond, as were his readers, and so he used it to illustrate the believer's newfound relationship to Christ (Rom. 7:1–6).

Paul explains that as long as a person is alive, as long as he is in Adam (Rom. 5:17a), he is married to the law. This is Paul's point in invoking Old Testament law regarding marriage: "For the woman who has a husband is bound by the law to her husband as long as he lives. But if the husband dies, she is released from the law of her husband" (Rom. 7:2; cf. Ex. 20:14; Deut. 24:1–4; Hos. 3:3). Paul applies this logic to the believer's newfound relationship to Christ and its implications vis-à-vis the claims of the law: "Therefore, my brethren, you also have become dead to the law through the body of Christ, that you may be married to another—to Him who was raised from the dead, that we should bear fruit to God" (Rom. 7:4). When a believer is in Adam, he is subject to the law's obligation and condemnation on two counts: Adam's sin (Rom. 5:12) and his own personal sin. But once he is united to Christ and declared righteous, the law no longer has any claim on him, because his sins are forgiven—the perfect law-keeping of Christ and His all-sufficient death in suffering the penalty for the broken law have been imputed by faith alone. By virtue of the believer's representative union with Jesus, the believer is dead to the law and now married to another—namely, Christ. Hence, believers are "delivered from the law, having died to what we were held by, so that we should serve in the newness of the Spirit and not in the oldness of the letter" (Rom. 7:6).

In historic and classic Reformed theology, Paul's teaching has been expressed in terms of deliverance from the law as a covenant. The Westminster divines distinguish between the law as a *covenant* versus a *rule*. As a covenant, the law requires perfect, personal, and perpetual obedience in order to receive the verdict of "Righteous!" (WCF 19.1). This is what God required of Adam in the garden of Eden and still requires of anyone outside of Christ (Lev. 18:5; Deut. 6:25; Rom. 2:13). This is what stood behind Christ's counsel to the lawyer who asked what he had to do to inherit eternal life. Jesus asked him what the law stated. The lawyer responded: "You shall love the LORD your God with all your heart, with all your soul, with all your strength, and with all your mind, and 'your neighbor as yourself'" (Luke 10:27; cf. Deut. 6:4–6; Lev. 19:18). Jesus then responded: "You have answered rightly; do this and you will live" (Luke 10:28; cf. Lev. 18:5). The promise of life still stands for the person who flawlessly obeys the law (Rom. 2:13). But for sinners weighed down by Adam's original representative transgression as well as their own sinful actions, perfect obedience to the law is impossible. The grand mountain of perfect obedience stands before the guilty sinner who is unable to make his ascent because of his burden of sin.

God gave Adam a law as a covenant of works by which he and all of his offspring were bound to personal, perfect, and perpetual obedience (WCF 19.1). This same law continued to be the rule of righteousness after Adam's fall, and as such God delivered it to Israel on Mount Sinai in the Ten Commandments, which is also called the moral law (WCF 19.2, 3). The moral law, the confession tells us, forever binds all people to obedience (WCF 19.5), but only believers are "not under the law, as a covenant of works, to be thereby justified, or condemned" (19.6). Christ frees believers, therefore, from the law as a covenant of works because they are no longer married to the law—they have died to the law and its demands because Christ has fully met them. This does not mean, however, that believers have no relationship to the law. The confession explains that for those justified in Christ the law serves as a "rule of life informing them of the will of God, and their duty, it directs and binds them to walk accordingly" (WCF 19.6). Paul will say more about this in chapter 8, but suffice it to say that Christ frees believers from the demands of the law as the condition of their justification.

Law: The Power of Sin

But these statements undoubtedly raise a number of questions—namely, How can a person be free from the law? And how can sin use the law in such a manner that it incites transgression rather than promotes holiness? For many Christians, the law and holiness go hand in hand, so how can Paul seemingly place them at odds? These are the questions that Paul answers in the rest of chapter 7. He rhetorically asks about the nature of the law: "Has then what is good become death to me? Certainly not! But sin, that it might appear sin, was producing death in me through what is good, so that sin through the commandment might become exceedingly sinful" (Rom. 7:13). Paul makes the important point that the law, in and of itself, did not produce sin. The law, according to Paul, is "holy and just and good" (Rom. 7:12). Only through the law do people learn what sin is. As Paul writes, "For I would not have known covetousness unless the law had said, 'You shall not covet'" (Rom. 7:7; cf. Ex. 20:17). So the law is good because it comes from God and reflects His holy and righteous character. "But sin," writes Paul, "taking opportunity by the commandment, produced in me all manner of evil desire. For apart from the law sin was dead" (Rom. 7:8a).

Think of Paul's point in terms of everyday life. All you have to do is stand before a group of children and tell them, "Boys, no matter what you do today, I don't want you to jump into this mud puddle and get dirty. Instead, I'll give you all of these toys, games, and other things for you to use. Just don't jump into the mud puddle." The boys might hold out for a while, but you know as well as I do that given enough time, one or more of the boys will end up covered in mud. Once you tell the child he cannot do something, he becomes preoccupied with the very thing he is supposed to avoid. This is why Paul writes, "For apart from the law sin was dead" (Rom. 7:8b). This is the means by which sin uses the law, and this is how Paul can elsewhere write, "The sting of death is sin, and the strength of sin is the law" (1 Cor. 15:56). Apart from the law sin lies dead and is powerless.

Paul's Autobiography or Israel under the Law?

Thus far, what Paul has written seems straightforward and relatively easy to understand. But another element in this passage that has vexed interpreters for ages has been the identity of the famous "I" of Romans 7. Of whom does Paul write when he states, "I was alive once without the law, but when the commandment came, sin revived and I died" (Rom. 7:9)? Who is in view when Paul writes, "For what I am doing, I do not understand. For what I will to do, that I do not practice; but what I hate, that I do" (Rom. 7:15)? Over the centuries theologians have largely landed on one interpretation with two different versions—namely, Paul writes about his own personal experience; Romans 7 is largely autobiographical. There are two variants of this interpretation. The first holds that this is a reminiscence of Paul's preconversion struggles with his desire to obey the law. Jacob Arminius (1560–1609) notably put this view forward in the late sixteenth century.[2] The second variant contends that Romans 7 presents Paul's postconversion struggles with his desire to obey the law; John Calvin (1509–1564) has argued for this view.[3]

---

2. Jacob Arminius, *Dissertation on the True and Genuine Sense of the Seventh Chapter of the Epistle to the Romans*, in *The Works of James Arminius*, trans. James Nichols and William Nichols (1828; repr., Grand Rapids: Baker, 1996), 2:491–689.

3. Calvin, *Romans and Thessalonians*, 137–55.

Both views have elements in Romans 7 to commend them. For example, Paul states in the previous chapter that Christians have been crucified with Him so that they "should no longer be slaves of sin" (Rom. 6:6), and the person who has died has been justified from sin (Rom. 6:7). Those who have died to sin are "not under law but under grace" (Rom. 6:14). Yet Paul clearly states that apart from the law he was alive, but once the law entered the picture, "sin revived and I died" (Rom. 7:9). Paul also explains, "For we know that the law is spiritual, but I am carnal, sold under sin" (Rom. 7:14). How can one who died to sin and the law and is no longer enslaved to it nevertheless be sold under sin? Is this not evidence that this is a preconversion Paul? But given what Paul writes in Romans 1:18–32 and especially Romans 3:1–14 concerning the universal depravity of humanity, how can an unconverted person struggle with the desire to obey the law? Do they not all hate God (Rom. 3:18)? If there is no fear of God, and by extension His law, then how can an unbeliever struggle with the desire to obey it: "For the good that I will to do, I do not do; but the evil I will not to do, that I practice" (Rom. 7:19)? Both arguments provide strong evidence, which leads me to believe that Paul does not present his personal struggle with the law pre- or post-conversion. Instead, Paul addresses a much larger point. "Is Paul telling his autobiography, pre- or post-conversion?" is the wrong question to ask of the text. What, then, is Paul's point?

As counterintuitive as it might seem, Paul does not reflect solely on his own personal experience, whether pre- or post-conversion. Rather, Paul employs a common first-century rhetorical device. He uses the first-person personal pronoun *I* to refer not to himself but to Israel's collective experience under the law. He also alludes to Adam's struggle under God's command in the garden. This is a literary tactic that Paul elsewhere employs: "For if I build again those things which I destroyed, I make myself a transgressor" (Gal. 2:18). Within its original context, Paul was the last person who would rebuild what he had to rip down in Galatia. He would never advocate justification through works of the law—this was the very thing he opposed. Instead, he uses the first-person pronoun *I* to convey his point—he employs a literary device through the use of the first-person pronoun. Paul does not report autobiographical history. In Romans 7, then, Paul presents Israel as a microcosm of all humanity under the law, whether Adam under God's command in the garden or Israel's life under the Mosaic covenant.

Another consideration is the fact that elsewhere in his epistle Paul has the big picture in view, the grand sweep of redemptive history, not merely the state or condition of individuals. In the opening of Romans, for example, Paul contrasts Christ's ministry according to its two major epochs: His descent from David "according to the flesh" and His declaration to be "the Son of God with power according to the Spirit of holiness" (Rom. 1:4). When Paul contrasts flesh and Spirit, he does not oppose our material bodily existence against our supposed spiritual immaterial existence. Rather, he opposes our existence under the dominion of the first Adam's fallen kingdom, which he characterizes as fleshly, to life under the reign of the last Adam's holy kingdom, which he characterizes as being under the Spirit. The natural man does not receive the things of the kingdom, because they are spiritually discerned (1 Cor. 2:13–14). The works of the flesh—not merely the actions of our bodies but our whole persons under Adam's rule—are "adultery, fornication, uncleanness, lewdness, idolatry, sorcery, hatred, contentions, jealousies, outbursts of wrath, selfish ambitions, dissensions, heresies, envy, murders, drunkenness, revelries, and the like" (Gal. 5:19–21). By contrast, for those under the lordship of Christ, the fruit of the Spirit is "love, joy, peace, longsuffering, kindness, goodness, faithfulness, gentleness, self-control" (Gal. 5:22–23). If you are under Adam, then you are under law, but if you are under Christ, you are under grace (Rom. 6:14–15; cf. John 1:17; Gal. 5:18). This is the theme Paul has in view in Romans 7, not whether the regenerate or unregenerate Paul struggled with following the dictates of the law.

Keeping this theme in view, the first person Paul alludes to is Adam and his struggle with the command of God. Remember, an allusion is imprecise and fast moving—that is, Paul does not dwell on it very long, but his words echo the sin of our first parents: "I was alive once without the law, but when the commandment came, sin revived and I died. And the commandment, which was to bring life, I found to bring death" (Rom. 7:9–10). God told Adam not to eat from the tree lest he suffer the penalty of death (Gen. 2:16–17). Recall that Adam's situation under the command of God anticipated Israel's circumstances under the Mosaic covenant—both Adam and Israel lived under explicitly revealed commands of God (Rom. 5:13–14). Adam received the law and failed to fulfill it. The one tree he was forbidden to eat of became the one thing he could not live without. The forbidden mud puddle called out, and Adam jumped right in.

As the people of Israel stood at the foot of Sinai, they too received the law. They undoubtedly recognized that it was good and holy. What else could it be since it came from God Himself? They knew God spoke the very words of the law (Ex. 20:1–4). Yet as soon as they received the law, they, like Adam, transgressed God's commands (Hos. 6:7). Like the child and the forbidden mud puddle, they leaped right into a violation of the law (Ex. 32:1a). Think of how this recurring pattern unfolded throughout Israel's history—they all knew the goodness of God's law because of its divine origin, but they repeatedly violated it. Israel stood at the bases of Mounts Gerizim and Ebal and swore a self-maledictory oath to follow God's law (Deuteronomy 27–29). Yet Israel failed almost immediately upon its entrance into the Promised Land, evident in Achan's sin (Josh. 7:19–26; 22:20). The repeated pattern in the book of Judges is one of success followed by covenant infidelity from which the people would repent, only to fall back into sin again. Even when Israel was carried into exile in accord with the terms of the Mosaic covenant, and eventually repatriated to the land, they still struggled. The people wept at the reading of the law as they were "gathered… as one man" (Neh. 8:1, 9). Despite their tears and the recognition of the law's goodness, Israel was subsequently unfaithful, evident in God's imposition of a four-hundred-year prophetic drought between Malachi and John the Baptist, which culminated in Israel's ultimate rejection of Christ.

In light of Israel's constant struggle with the law, now consider Paul's statements from Romans 7:

> And the commandment, which was to bring life, I found to bring death. For sin, taking occasion by the commandment, deceived me, and by it killed me. Therefore the law is holy, and the commandment holy and just and good. Has then what is good become death to me? Certainly not! But sin, that it might appear sin, was producing death in me through what is good, so that sin through the commandment might become exceedingly sinful. For we know that the law is spiritual, but I am carnal, sold under sin. For what I am doing, I do not understand. For what I will to do, that I do not practice; but what I hate, that I do. If, then, I do what I will not to do, I agree with the law that it is good. But now, it is no longer I who do it, but sin that dwells in me. For I know that in me (that is, in my flesh) nothing good dwells; for to will is present with me, but how to perform what is good I do not find. For the good that I will to do, I do not do; but the evil I will not to do, that I practice. Now if I do what I will not to do, it is no longer I who do it, but sin that dwells in me. (Rom. 7:10–19)

Paul's rhetorical use of the personal pronoun captures Israel's struggle with the law. Paul even reflects some of this tension and struggle in the earlier portions of Romans. He records how Israel taught others—they relied on the law, boasted in God, and approved what was excellent because they were instructed in it (Rom. 2:17–18). Israel tried to teach others not to steal, but then they stole; they taught others not to commit adultery but then transgressed the very commandment they taught to others. They abhorred idols and then robbed temples. They boasted in the law and then broke it (Rom. 2:21–23).

Living under the law as it was embedded in the Mosaic covenant with all its rules, stipulations, and curses was a burden even for regenerate and justified Israelites such as Moses, Isaiah, or Daniel. As justified believers trusting in the covenant promise of God to send a Messiah—Jesus—to redeem them from their sins, they received a real, genuine, but nevertheless provisional outpouring of the Holy Spirit and were united to Christ. They were freed from the condemnation of the law but were still subject to the Mosaic covenant. When Moses sinned, for example, though he was justified, God barred him from the Promised Land (Num. 20:12; cf. Matt. 17:1–3). When Isaiah stood in the temple as a justified believer, he nevertheless acknowledged that he was a sinner and dwelled among a sinful people who had impure lips and hearts (Isa. 6:5). Isaiah could not think of his salvation divorced from his connection to the rest of the covenant people of Israel; he was corporately bound to them and to the stipulations of the Mosaic covenant. And even Daniel, for whom the Scriptures reserve the highest regard, was still carried into Babylon and cried out to the Lord for His covenant mercies on behalf of the unfaithful people of Israel as they corporately suffered the curses of the Mosaic covenant and lay in an exilic graveyard away from God's presence (Dan. 9:1–19; Ezek. 14:20; 37:1–14).

Justified from the Law

How was Paul and any other Israelite delivered from this love-hate relationship to God's law? How could Israel break free from their "delight in the law of God" in their "inward man" (Rom. 7:22) but at the same time see another law "warring against the law" of their minds, making them captive to "the law of sin" (Rom. 7:23)? Who delivered Paul and every other Israelite who sought freedom from their wretched state under the law (Rom. 7:24)? Paul comes full circle and returns to his boast and theme of the last several chapters: "I thank God—through Jesus Christ our Lord!" (Rom. 7:25). Recall how Paul began this chapter—anyone united to Christ has been delivered from the law and is therefore freed from its power: "Therefore let it be known to you, brethren, that through this Man is preached to you the forgiveness of sins; and by Him everyone who believes is justified from all things from which you could not be justified by the law of Moses" (Acts 13:38–39; cf. Rom. 6:7). In Christ, you are "not under law but under grace" (Rom. 6:14). Indeed, recall how Paul began this chapter: "For when we were in the flesh, the sinful passions which were aroused by the law were at work in our members to bear fruit to death" (Rom. 7:5). "But now"—two words that signal a major shift in redemptive history because of the advent of Christ and the inauguration of the new creation—"we have been delivered from the law, having died to what we were held by, so that we should serve in the newness of the Spirit and not in the oldness of the letter" (Rom. 7:6). Through Christ we have died to the law and have been justified from it.

Paul elsewhere succinctly explains this massive redemptive historical shift when he writes,

> But the Scripture has confined all under sin, that the promise by faith in Jesus Christ might be given to those who believe. But before faith came, we were kept under guard by the law, kept for the faith which would afterward be revealed. Therefore the law was our tutor to bring us to Christ, that we might be justified by faith. But after faith has come, we are no longer under a tutor. For you are all sons of God through faith in Christ Jesus. (Gal. 3:22–26)

Since Romans 5:12–21, Paul has explained the Christian's freedom from sin, which means that a justified Christian has freedom from the law (Romans 7) but will not engage in unchecked antinomian behavior (Romans 6). With the advent of Christ and the outpouring of the Spirit, what was only provisionally present among a very small group of Israelites has now been abundantly poured out on Jew and Gentile (Acts 2; cf. Gal. 3:14). In the language of the Westminster Confession, because of Christ's work and its application by the Holy Spirit, we no longer face the law as a covenant but know it only as a rule.

Significance for the Christian Life

Grasping Paul's point regarding the freedom from the law has the greatest implications for the Christian life. Far too many Christians look at the law of God as the means by which they either save themselves or make themselves holier. This was Israel's fundamental problem: "For they being ignorant of God's righteousness, and seeking to establish their own righteousness, have not submitted to the righteousness of God" (Rom. 10:3). Apart from Christ and His bond-breaking work freeing us from the law as a covenant, whether in Adam's covenant of works or Israel's covenant at Sinai, we are slaves to sin and held captive under its power through the law. Even many well-intentioned Christians fail to realize this and approach the law apart from Christ, thinking, "If I only try harder not to sin, then I'll become more like Jesus." They try to flee from sin by secluding themselves as much as they can from the outside influence of the world, all in the effort to grow in holiness. But the same power of Christ through the gospel that breaks the bonds of sin and the law in our justification is the same power that sanctifies and makes us holier. The only way we grow in our holiness is if we pursue Christ through His appointed means of grace: through Word, sacrament, and prayer.

Where this truth often comes home is in the way many Christian parents raise their children. They tell their children to obey, and they believe that punishing their disobedience will sanctify them. What they do not realize is that this is a miniaturized version of the law—punishing a child does not change a child's heart. Punishment merely teaches the child to fear correction, which can certainly change one's behavior but not implant Christ-driven, Spirit-empowered obedience. The only thing that can change a child's heart is Christ's applied work received by the Spirit through the appointed means of grace. This means that in parenting a wayward child, punishment is certainly necessary and important but is only one part of the process. When you punish your child, ensure that you point him to Christ—encourage him to seek both Christ's forgiveness in prayer and the ability to obey from his union with Christ. Expose your child to the means of grace so that he hears the gospel, which, God willing, then changes his heart.

The same principle extends to preachers. On too many occasions I have heard conservative, well-intended, Bible-believing pastors preach the law of God from the pulpit without ever mentioning the name of Christ. I have been told that such preaching is all in the name of the third, or normative, use of the law—that is, how the law guides the Christian in his daily walk. But any promotion of the law apart from Christ and His gospel is an effort to bring people back under the enslavement of the law—it is an effort to change the role of the law from a rule to a covenant. It tries to move Christians out from under grace and place them back under the law—to turn back the hands on the redemptive-historical clock and treat people as if Christ had never come. Preachers, you must not impose the law as a covenant on your people but rather preach the grace of the gospel. Such Christ-focused preaching empowers your congregation's holiness, transforms them more into the image of Christ, and produces the fruit of the Spirit in the lives of your flock. Your congregation will then, God willing, seek the law as a rule, not as a covenant—they will seek holiness through the Spirit, not in the deadness of the old written code (Rom. 7:6).

Conclusion

Our justification by faith alone in Christ alone frees us from the legal power of sin and the imprisonment to the law. Because of our union with Christ and our concomitant sanctification, Christians will never engage in unchecked lawlessness. Through Christ, the law is no longer a covenant to the believer. Rather, in Christ, he has died to the law, been raised to walk in the newness of life, and has taken his first step into the new heavens and earth. He breathes the air of the new creation by the Spirit's power through Christ's appointed means. In this respect, we must never seek greater holiness through the bare law. Remember Paul's point here: Works-righteousness (using the law as a covenant) is fundamentally incompatible with new creation life in Christ. Rather, we must always seek greater conformity to Christ through our vital, life-giving union with Him. For only in Christ do we find our justification. Only in Christ do we find our sanctification and freedom from sin. Only in Christ is the law transformed from a foe into a friend.

21

God's Dreams Come True

ROMANS 8:1–11

There is therefore now no condemnation to those who are in Christ Jesus, who do not walk according to the flesh, but according to the Spirit. For the law of the Spirit of life in Christ Jesus has made me free from the law of sin and death. For what the law could not do in that it was weak through the flesh, God did by sending His own Son in the likeness of sinful flesh, on account of sin: He condemned sin in the flesh, that the righteous requirement of the law might be fulfilled in us who do not walk according to the flesh but according to the Spirit. For those who live according to the flesh set their minds on the things of the flesh, but those who live according to the Spirit, the things of the Spirit. For to be carnally minded is death, but to be spiritually minded is life and peace. Because the carnal mind is enmity against God; for it is not subject to the law of God, nor indeed can be. So then, those who are in the flesh cannot please God. But you are not in the flesh but in the Spirit, if indeed the Spirit of God dwells in you. Now if anyone does not have the Spirit of Christ, he is not His. And if Christ is in you, the body is dead because of sin, but the Spirit is life because of righteousness. But if the Spirit of Him who raised Jesus from the dead dwells in you, He who raised Christ from the dead will also give life to your mortal bodies through His Spirit who dwells in you.

When we come to the great promises of the Scriptures, we often turn to the images of Christ's return and the final judgment. Yet we unfortunately look at the final judgment as an end-time event. While it is true that the final judgment occurs at the end of the age, we must recognize that there are many other events in the Scriptures that fall into the category of the last days, or eschatology. The prophet Malachi, for example, makes an eschatological promise when he says that Elijah will come before the day of the Lord (Mal. 4:5). We know that God fulfilled this eschatological promise through the ministry of John the Baptist (Matt. 11:14). This, of course, couches the entire ministry of Christ in the category of eschatology. The author of Hebrews tells us as much when he writes, "God, who at various times and in various ways spoke in time past to the fathers by the prophets, has in these *last days* spoken to us by His Son" (Heb. 1:1–2, emphasis added). Therefore, we are now living in the last days.

With this idea in mind we should see the connection between the passage before us and an Old Testament promise about the last days. At first glance, we might not notice that we are reading a passage steeped in eschatology. We read over this passage and our minds most likely drift to the subject of salvation. In other words, we concentrate on issues related to the order of salvation (*ordo salutis*)—justification, sanctification, and glorification—and understandably so. We must not forget, however, to see how this passage is connected with redemptive history (*historia salutis*). Do we recognize that this passage has implications for our doctrines of both salvation and eschatology? In other words, do we realize our doctrine of salvation is ultimately eschatological?

Ezekiel contains passages replete with eschatological promises. In Ezekiel 36:16–32, for example, God promised His people through the prophet that He would sanctify His name (v. 23), gather His people from among the nations (v. 24), sprinkle clean water and cleanse us from all filthiness (v. 25), give us new hearts and spirits (v. 26), place His Holy Spirit within us, and cause us to walk in His statutes (v. 27). These promises constitute the overarching reality that God Himself would deliver His people. These Old Testament promises constitute the foundation of what Paul writes here in the opening verses of chapter 8. Remember, Paul's Bible is the Old Testament; hence, his words have a taproot that reaches deep into the soil of Israel's prophetic past. We must keep these important issues in mind as we explore these opening verses.

Justification Now

We should recall the broader context of Paul's overall argument before we wade into chapter 8. Paul discussed the doctrine of justification in Romans 4:1–5:21 before turning to answer objections—namely, does the believer's justification encourage him to engage in lawless living? Paul addressed the first issue in Romans 6:1–23 by explaining the context in which believers receive their justification—union with Christ. Christ justifies *and* sanctifies those whom He saves. Justified sinners are also sanctified saints because of their life-giving union with Christ. Moreover, their justification from sin means that the legal power of sin, the law, has been broken by the forensic declaration of justification (Rom. 6:7). Paul addressed the second issue in Romans 7:1–25 by explaining that believers are freed from the law as a covenant. Justification, therefore, brings freedom from the legal power of sin (Romans 6) and the law (Romans 7).

On the heels of answering these objections, Paul comes to one of the grand crowning points of Romans here in the opening verse of chapter 8: "There is therefore now no condemnation to those who are in Christ Jesus" (Rom. 8:1). The antonym of *condemnation*, a legal declaration of someone's guilt, is *justification*, so we can restate Paul's point in this manner: "There is therefore now justification to those who are in Christ Jesus." Notice that Paul employs his eschatological word *now* to indicate once again that he has more in view than the believer's individual justification. Paul has been prominently working from his two-Adam / two-age model of redemptive history since Romans 5:12 to argue that Christians no longer live under the ministry of condemnation of the law but rather under the aegis of the last Adam and the outpouring of the Spirit—we live under grace, not law (Rom. 6:14–15; cf. John 1:17). This is Paul's main point here in Romans 8:1—namely, prior to Christ's ministry, Old Testament Israel constantly struggled under the yoke of the Mosaic covenant. They recognized that in this context the law was good; nevertheless, they were unable to fulfill its demands. The good that they wanted to do, they could not carry out. Even though the law was good and holy, as a nation they were "sold under sin" and therefore subject to its condemnation (Rom. 7:14).

But as Paul ends chapter 7, he reaches a pinnacle with the following statement of relief: "O wretched man that I am! Who will deliver me from this body of death? I thank God—through Jesus Christ our Lord!" (Rom. 7:24–25a). Because the believer has died and been raised with Christ, "There is *therefore* now no condemnation to those who are in Christ Jesus" (Rom. 8:1, emphasis added). The believer's union with Christ by faith alone gives him access to the perfect righteousness of Christ, which thereby frees him from the condemnation of the law—the seesaw battle to obey the law ends with the redemption that comes through Christ: "For the law of the Spirit of life in Christ Jesus has made me free from the law of sin and death" (Rom. 8:2).

Deliverance through Christ, Not the Law

Paul succinctly summarizes the points he has made in Romans 5–7 in just two verses: "For what the law could not do in that it was weak through the flesh, God did by sending His own Son in the likeness of sinful flesh, on account of sin: He condemned sin in the flesh, that the righteous requirement of the law might be fulfilled in us who do not walk according to the flesh but according to the Spirit" (Rom. 8:3–4). Christ came to do what sinful humans could not—perfectly fulfill the law, every single jot and tittle, as well as pay the penalty for our violation of the law. Theologians have historically called this twofold obedience the *active* and *passive* obedience of Christ. The active obedience is Christ's perfect law keeping, and the passive (which comes from the Latin word *passio*, "suffering") obedience is Christ's suffering the penalty of the law, which He performed throughout His entire life, not just in His crucifixion. Christ accomplished what we could not do, so that the "righteous requirement of the law might be fulfilled in us" (Rom. 8:4). That is, Christ, the God-man, perfectly fulfilled the law.

Christ's law-keeping is our obedience, and hence the law is "fulfilled in us," in humankind, through Christ's incarnation as a man.[1] Paul has come full circle from Romans 5 and Christ's one act of righteousness that made many people righteous (Rom. 5:17–19). Christ the God-*man* has fulfilled the righteous requirements of the law so that there is *now* no condemnation for those who are in Him.

Life in the Flesh

To contrast the difference between what Christ has accomplished versus the impotence of those still trapped under the dominion of Adam, Paul writes: "For those who live according to the flesh set their minds on the things of the flesh, but those who live according to the Spirit, the things of the Spirit. For to be carnally minded is death, but to be spiritually minded is life and peace. Because the carnal mind is enmity against God; for it is not subject to the law of God, nor indeed can be. So then, those who are in the flesh cannot please God" (Rom. 8:5–8). Anyone still under the federal headship of Adam has a complete inability to meet the righteous requirements of the law. Anyone who is in "the flesh"—that is, still in Adam—cannot please God. Again, recall Paul's contrast between the two worlds:

First Adam	**Last Adam**
flesh	Spirit
sin	righteousness
law	grace
condemnation	justification
death	life
creation	new creation

Anyone in Christ is in the new creation and therefore indwelled by the Holy Spirit. Only those who "live according to the Spirit" can set their minds on the things of the Spirit (Rom. 8:5b).

1. Haldane, *Romans*, 326.

Life in the Spirit

Paul shifts his focus from life in the flesh to what it means to live in the Spirit:

> But you are not in the flesh but in the Spirit, if indeed the Spirit of God dwells in you. Now if anyone does not have the Spirit of Christ, he is not His. And if Christ is in you, the body is dead because of sin, but the Spirit is life because of righteousness. But if the Spirit of Him who raised Jesus from the dead dwells in you, He who raised Christ from the dead will also give life to your mortal bodies through His Spirit who dwells in you. (Rom. 8:9–11)

We cannot have two masters—we cannot be under the dominion of sin and under the dominion the Spirit. We cannot be in Adam and in Christ. We cannot be Christians and atheists. We are under either the dominion of sin or the lordship of Christ. We are either Christians who walk in obedience to the law of God or those who willfully trample God's grace underfoot. We should note why the Holy Spirit indwells us—namely, "because of righteousness" (Rom. 8:10). In other words, it is because of Christ's work—His life, death, and resurrection, His imputed righteousness received by faith alone—that leads to our justification. Our sanctification, the indwelling presence of the Holy Spirit, is predicated on the justification and imputed righteousness of Jesus Christ. Notice the intimacy and irrefragable connection between the work of Christ and the Holy Spirit. To receive justification is to receive sanctification also.

But at this point, we must not forget the Old Testament prophetic background that undergirds what Paul has written here. Ezekiel prophesied that God would cleanse His people from their sin, give them new hearts and a new spirit, and cause them to walk in His statutes—that is, obey them, by giving them His Holy Spirit (Ezek. 36:25–27). Ezekiel looked out on the horizon of redemptive history and saw God's promise from afar and undoubtedly looked to it with anticipation and great longing. But *now* (Paul's verbal flag that the new creation has dawned in Christ) we no longer look forward to such promises but instead bask in the light of their fulfillment through Christ. As Paul writes elsewhere: "Christ has redeemed us from the curse of the law, having become a curse for us (for it is written, 'Cursed is everyone who hangs on a tree'), that the blessing of Abraham might come upon the Gentiles in Christ Jesus, *that we might receive the promise of the Spirit through faith*" (Gal. 3:13–14, emphasis added). The very Spirit who raised Christ from the dead, unleashing the power of the new creation, is the very same Spirit who *now* enables Christians to obey the law of God.

One of the great hopes in all this is that we can see God's faithfulness to His word throughout redemptive history. If we have ever doubted God's promises, we need only look back to the Old Testament to read of things promised and then turn to the New Testament to see those same promises fulfilled. Christ, according to Paul, is the "Amen," the "Yes!" to all God's promises to us. Whenever you find yourself plagued with doubt, look back to the prophetic promises, such as Ezekiel's vision of God's people receiving the Holy Spirit. This means that when it comes to our own sanctification, obedience, and greater conformity to Christ's holy image, we can rest assured that God will complete the good work He has begun in us (Phil. 1:6).

Charles Hodge explains how, as much as sanctification requires our own personal effort, we must recognize that our union with Christ is the source and strength in our battle for personal holiness:

> All that the Scriptures teach concerning the union between the believer and Christ, and of the indwelling of the Holy Spirit, proves the supernatural character of our sanctification. Men do not make themselves holy; their holiness, and their growth in grace, are not due to their own fidelity, or firmness or purpose, or watchfulness and diligence, although all these are required, but to the divine influence by which they are rendered thus faithful, watchful, and diligent, and which produces in them the fruits of righteousness.[2]

---

2. Charles Hodge, *Systematic Theology* (repr., Grand Rapids: Eerdmans, 1991), 3:218.

We may indeed struggle in the midst of our sanctification, but Paul's words here reinforce what he has written in Romans 7: Our growth in holiness does not find its source in the law but in the power of the Holy Spirit, in our union with Christ. Only by the Spirit, not the law, will our minds be set on the things of the Spirit and will our conduct please God. Thanks be to God that He gives us Christ and His Holy Spirit! We need not flounder in our sanctification but rather can soak in the light and breathe in the air of the new heavens and earth, the power of the age to come (Heb. 6:5). Indeed, in the midst of our struggles to grow in grace, we can, in Paul's words, "press on" and forget "those things which are behind" and look "forward to those things which are ahead...toward the goal for the prize of the upward call of God in Christ Jesus" (Phil. 3:12–14).

Conclusion

When we read Romans 8:1–11, we must recognize its connection with the Old Testament. In so doing we will see the implications for our personal salvation as well as for the broader context of redemptive history. We will realize that the eschatological promises of God have come to fruition through the work of Christ and the Holy Spirit, who is now at work in us! Think about these truths through the analogy of a dream: We often dream about the future and what it might be like. In our dreams everything is, of course, perfect—exactly what we would like to see. Well, we find God's dreams for the future in Ezekiel's prophecy. He "dreams" of how the future will be—everything exactly how *He* wants it to be. Do we realize, then, that we are the fulfillment of God's dreams? We are God's dreams come true! What a blessing, then, that God is the dreamer and we are His dreams come true through His covenant faithfulness in Christ and the Holy Spirit. Praise our faithful, covenant-keeping Lord.

22

Our Marvelous Adoption

ROMANS 8:12–17

Therefore, brethren, we are debtors—not to the flesh, to live according to the flesh. For if you live according to the flesh you will die; but if by the Spirit you put to death the deeds of the body, you will live. For as many as are led by the Spirit of God, these are sons of God. For you did not receive the spirit of bondage again to fear, but you received the Spirit of adoption by whom we cry out, "Abba, Father." The Spirit Himself bears witness with our spirit that we are children of God, and if children, then heirs—heirs of God and joint heirs with Christ, if indeed we suffer with Him, that we may also be glorified together.

Man can know God in several ways, the first of which is to know Him as the Creator. We read of this in the first chapter of Romans: "For since the creation of the world His invisible attributes are clearly seen, being understood by the things that are made, even His eternal power and Godhead, so that they are without excuse" (Rom. 1:20). Paul tells us that man knows God, knows that He exists, knows even of some of His attributes, and knows of all of this from the creation. Man knows, therefore, that God created everything. Moreover, this knowledge of God is present not only in creation but also within man himself. God creates human beings in His image and has therefore written His law on their hearts (Rom. 2:14–15). This law, Paul tells us, accuses man when he violates it. This shows us another way that man knows God—as both Creator and Judge. There are, however, two other ways that man can know God.

In his *Institutes of the Christian Religion*, John Calvin, like other theologians of his day, organizes the first of his four books under the title "Of the Knowledge of God the Creator." In book 2, however, he has the title "Of the Knowledge of God the Redeemer." In fact, Calvin scholars have noted that this is a key feature of sixteenth-century Reformed theology: the twofold knowledge of God—as Creator and Redeemer. Calvin, though, notes the following about the relationship between God as Creator and Redeemer: "What he [Paul] denominates the wisdom of God, is this magnificent theater of heaven and earth, which is replete with innumerable miracles, and from the contemplation of which we ought wisely to acquire the knowledge of God. But because we have made so little improvement in this way, he recalls us to the faith of Christ, which is despised by unbelievers on account of its apparent folly."[1] Calvin shows us, as does Paul, that the knowledge of God as Creator cannot save us, and the only way we can know God as Redeemer is in Christ. For only in Christ is there "now no condemnation" for fallen sinners (Rom. 8:1). For those who place their faith in Christ, they know God as Creator, a just Judge, and Redeemer. In the passage before us, however, Paul shows us another way that those who are in Christ know God—namely, as Father.

Life in the Spirit

Crucial to understanding Paul's teaching at this point is remembering what he has covered in the previous verses. This is generally an important rule to follow—always examine the broader context of any statement. But this is especially pertinent in light of the fact that Paul begins Romans 8:12 with *therefore*. This signals that Paul develops a conclusion based on what he has previously written. In this case, he developed the significance of the respective effects of the representative disobedience and obedience of the first and last Adams—condemnation and death versus justification and eternal life (Rom. 5:12–21). Paul then explained that as a consequential

1. Calvin, *Institutes*, 2.6.1.

result, Christians have been freed from sin (Romans 6) and the law as a covenant (Romans 7). He then came full circle to encourage his readers that there is *now* no condemnation for those who are in Christ Jesus because God sent His Son to accomplish what sinful human beings could not—offer His perfect obedience to the law and suffer its penalty on behalf of those who are united to Him by faith. Throughout his epistle Paul has invoked the broader context of the flesh-Spirit antithesis—life under the reigns of the first and last Adams.

Given this context—justification, sanctification, union with Christ, freedom from sin and the law—Paul then writes, "Therefore, brethren, we are debtors—not to the flesh, to live according to the flesh. For if you live according to the flesh you will die; but if by the Spirit you put to death the deeds of the body, you will live" (Rom. 8:12–13). Paul expounds the idea that those who are in Adam will indeed continue in a life of sin, one from which people are unable to extricate themselves. Those, however, who are in Christ have been redeemed from the curse of the law by the imputed righteousness of Christ, and they are indwelt by the Holy Spirit who enables them to please God through their conduct: "For those who live according to the flesh set their minds on the things of the flesh, but those who live according to the Spirit, the things of the Spirit. For to be carnally minded is death, but to be spiritually minded is life and peace" (Rom. 8:5–6). In a sense, Paul comes full circle in Romans 8:12–13 to remind the Roman Christians to whom they are in debt. They must not live as if they are antinomians—how could they live in this manner seeing that Christ redeemed them? Because we have been emancipated from the dominion of sin and death, we must yield our obedience and service to the One who has liberated us. Paul then reminds his audience that if they live by the flesh, they are not in Christ; they are still in Adam and therefore subject to the law's condemnation.

Yet if they live by the Spirit—that is, are justified by faith and have His indwelling presence—they will grow in their sanctification and put to death the deeds of the body. They will live because they are in Christ and have peace with God. Notice how Paul stresses the fact that Christians can and will please God through their conduct—they are not antinomians. They do not, however, do so on their own: There is no works-based justification—or works-based sanctification, for that matter. Only the imputed righteousness of Jesus Christ received by faith alone justifies us from the curse of the law, and the indwelling presence of the Holy Spirit enables us to yield our lives obediently unto our triune Lord.

Sons of God

Paul does not end here but instead says something quite spectacular—something, as you can imagine, that has a great taproot into the soil of the Old Testament: "For as many as are led by the Spirit of God, these are sons of God" (Rom. 8:14). This is an amazing statement when you stop to think about it. Believers united to Christ are not merely creatures, not merely subjects of the King, and certainly not criminals deserving judgment and punishment. Rather, when we approach the Creator, Sustainer, and Judge of the cosmos, we do so as sons; we go to our heavenly Father. This is an idea that goes back to the very beginning, for when God created humanity, He created them in His image, and to bear a person's image means you are related. How often, for example, will you meet two complete strangers but see a resemblance between them and suspect they are related? Adam had a son who bore his image and likeness (Gen. 5:3). This is why Luke calls Adam God's son (Luke 3:38). God created Adam in His own image and likeness (Gen. 1:27). But the fall changed all this: Adam surrendered his kingdom to Satan, sin, and death and placed a great obstacle between God and humanity—we are now His estranged children (cf. Acts 17:29). The only thing that overcomes our covenant infidelity, as Paul has made clear, is Christ's intercessory work—He saves us from our rebellion and enables humanity, once again, to address God as *Father*.

We find this narrative again unfold in the microcosm of Israel's relationship with God. Israel was God's son (Ex. 4:23), but he rebelled—he failed to obey his Father as the law required, which would have ensured long life in the Promised Land (Ex. 20:12). As a result of Israel's repeated rebelliousness, which Paul recounted in Romans 7:12–25, God expelled His rebellious son—just as He cast Adam, His other mutinous son—from the garden of Eden. Israel lay in an exilic graveyard (Ezek. 37:1–14), and God disowned His contumacious son (Hos. 1:9). But in the midst of Israel's stormy relationship with his Father, Yahweh made King David a promise that one of his own descendants, one of his own sons, would rule on his throne: "I will be his Father, and he shall be My son" (2 Sam. 7:14). This son, of course, is Jesus, the One who was "born of the seed of David according to the flesh, and declared to be the Son of God with power according to the Spirit of holiness, by the resurrection from the dead" (Rom. 1:3–4). But given what Paul has written in Romans 5 and 6 concerning our union with Christ, because we are united to Him, whatever is said of Him is said of us. If He is God's Son, then we too are also God's sons. Jesus is the only begotten Son of God (John 3:16), but because the Spirit unites us to Christ by faith, we are adopted into God's family and receive the title of *sons*. Christ uniquely captured this dimension of our redemption when He taught His disciples to pray. They were to begin their prayers in an earth-shattering manner, one quite unprecedented in Christ's day: "Our Father" (Matt. 6:9). Individual Israelites in Christ's day did not address God as *Father*. This would have been too casual and familiar. But this is the precise nature of our relationship with God because of our incorporation into Christ—we now have the intimacy of a father-son relationship with God.

"For you did not receive the spirit of bondage again to fear," writes Paul, "but you received the Spirit of adoption by whom we cry out, 'Abba, Father!'" (Rom. 8:15). Paul expands on the thought of our adoption as sons of God and reminds us that we were not adopted unto bondage—namely, slavery to sin and death, living an antinomian life. On the contrary, we have the Holy Spirit who fills us with a filial love for our heavenly Father—something we are incapable of apart from the effectual calling of the Spirit. When we are unregenerate we ultimately hate God, but when the Holy Spirit effectually calls us we seek God with the heartfelt cry of a loving son. Only believers can call on the judge of the cosmos by the term *Abba*, the intimate Aramaic term for *father*. Only my children, and no others, call me *father*. Every other child on this planet knows me by a less personal and more formal title. We have this type of relationship with our heavenly Father because we are in Christ, indwelt by the Holy Spirit, and adopted as His sons. Although Israel was no longer God's people, the time when Hosea prophesied that the children of Israel would be called "sons of the living God" (Hos. 1:10) is now upon us. We can call out to God: *Abba*, Father!

Our Inheritance

Given our union with Christ, we have an intimate communion with God that rivals the fellowship that Adam and Eve had in the garden. Indeed, as Paul writes: "The Spirit Himself bears witness with our spirit that we are children of God, and if children, then heirs—heirs of God and joint heirs with Christ, if indeed we suffer with Him, that we may also be glorified together" (Rom. 8:16–17). So often people search high and low wanting God to speak directly to them. They look to so-called prophets, the horoscope, or even fortunetellers, but Paul tells us that the Holy Spirit does indeed speak directly to us. He not only speaks through the Word but also testifies to us directly—"You are my son!" Paul further expands on the theme of our union with Christ in connection with the idea of our adoption. Indeed, if we are sons, and Christ is the Son who, according to the author of Hebrews, has been "appointed heir of all things" (Heb. 1:2b), then we as God's sons are also heirs with Christ! If we are heirs with Christ, then all the blessings of the new heavens and earth, but especially the blessing of living eternally in the presence of our triune God, belong to us.

We have an incredible privilege illuminated here before us—we have the privilege of knowing God as Creator, as a just Judge, as our Redeemer in Christ, but also as our Father. In this vein the Westminster Confession offers a succinct summary of what this Father-son relationship entails:

> All those that are justified, God vouchsafeth, in and for his only Son Jesus Christ, to make partakers of the grace of adoption, by which they are taken into the number, and enjoy the liberties and privileges of the children of God, have his name put upon them, receive the Spirit of adoption, have access to the throne of grace with boldness, are enabled to cry, Abba, Father, are pitied, protected, provided for, and chastened by him, as by a father: yet never cast off, but sealed to the day of redemption; and inherit the promises, as heirs of everlasting salvation. (WCF 12)

Because we are God's adopted sons, we share in this wonderful catena of blessings! No longer do we fear the condemnation and curse of the law; no longer do we fear the just sentence of death from the Judge of the cosmos. Rather, because of our redemption in Christ, we now know God as *our* heavenly Father. We have an intimacy with Him unparalleled in redemptive history! Through the ministry of Christ, the barrier was broken down—the veil that once separated the holy presence of God was rent, granting us access into the holy of holies. In fact, the Lord Jesus Christ is making us, as Peter tells us, living stones in the new temple—we are the new Holy of Holies (1 Peter 2:5). This intimacy is conveyed in terms of God's fatherly love for us, His children. This is something that the prophet Hosea foretold (Hos. 1:9–11), and once again, as with Ezekiel's prophecies, we see the eschatological fulfillment of an Old Testament promise—we are the sons of the living God of whom Hosea speaks! We are the ones that can cry out, *Abba*, Father! Moreover, we are not second-class children given only the scraps. We are coheirs with Christ! Much like Mephibosheth, son of Jonathan, son of Saul (2 Sam. 4:4), we are the children of a deposed king (Adam) and are therefore considered enemies of the new King (Jesus). We are God's enemies under the thumb of Satan, under the dominion of sin and death. Yet, like Mephibosheth, we are clothed in the garments worthy of a king and are treated like one of the King's sons: "'As for Mephibosheth,' said the king, 'he shall eat at my table like one of the king's sons'" (2 Sam. 9:11)! God gives us the righteousness of Christ and the kingdom of heaven. Like Mephibosheth, we have been invited to eat at the King's table at the great wedding feast of the Lamb!

Conclusion

Remember to whom we belong—we belong to Christ. We are, consequently, indwelled by the Spirit of the living God. Therefore, we must live not according to the desires of our flesh but in the power of the Holy Spirit. We are sons of the living God and coheirs with Christ. This means we should flee sin because it is wrong and is an offense to God but also because it is beneath our royal dignity. Why would we, who have been raised out of the mire of sin and death, given royal robes and a crown, and given a seat at the King's table, return to roll around in the evil morass from which we were redeemed? Such conduct is incompatible with our royal identity and our union with Christ. If you engage in sin, do not forget who you are, the King's son! Seek the power and strength of your heavenly Father through prayer and His Word. If you struggle and doubt regarding God's goodness and faithfulness, remember that you are the King's son! You were bought with a price—you may flounder and falter, but Christ has not, does not, and will not stumble or fall. Your place is secure, you always have a seat at the King's table, and therefore heaven is yours because of Christ.

23

The Weight of Glory

ROMANS 8:18–25

For I consider that the sufferings of this present time are not worthy to be compared with the glory which shall be revealed in us. For the earnest expectation of the creation eagerly waits for the revealing of the sons of God. For the creation was subjected to futility, not willingly, but because of Him who subjected it in hope; because the creation itself also will be delivered from the bondage of corruption into the glorious liberty of the children of God. For we know that the whole creation groans and labors with birth pangs together until now. Not only that, but we also who have the firstfruits of the Spirit, even we ourselves groan within ourselves, eagerly waiting for the adoption, the redemption of our body. For we were saved in this hope, but hope that is seen is not hope; for why does one still hope for what he sees? But if we hope for what we do not see, we eagerly wait for it with perseverance.

When I was a young boy I nearly drowned. My brother and I were swimming in the ocean when he asked me to help pull him back closer to the beach—a storm recently washed out the shoreline. I thoughtlessly reached out to pull my brother closer to the shore, and he instead pulled me into deeper water. Within seconds both my brother and I were struggling to keep our heads above water, and we began to drown. My brother wanted to stay above water and so he started to crawl on top of me. Now, what is amazing to me to this day is the fact that both my brother and I knew how to swim! Yet somehow the surrounding water, the thought of drowning, and fear put a stranglehold on all rational thought. All we had to do was drop our heads and kick for five to ten feet. Instead, panic set in and we thrashed about, my brother tried to drown me, and we gulped in briny seawater. I think this same type of mentality grips us when faced with the prospects of suffering. Suffering and persecution often have the same effect that the ominous ocean can—it can drive us to panic so that we abandon rationality and begin to thrash about and drown in our own fears. Paul writes about this very issue in the verses before us. He announces that the Christian life, both personal and corporate, is marked by suffering until the consummation of the age, but he also explains why this suffering does not compare to the weight of glory when God places them on the scale.

But the question likely arises, Why does Paul shift gears and descend from the heights of the glories of our redemption only to drop down into the valley of the shadow of death? What about the inauguration of the new creation? What of our union with Christ, our justification, sanctification, adoption, and ultimately our glorification? Given these blessings, should not Paul's discussion move onward and upward? The quick answer to this question, one that Paul will develop throughout the rest of the eighth chapter, is that Christians live straddling the two ages, the old and new creations. Yes, we have been given the right to eternal life (Romans 5) and have been justified from sin (Romans 6) and the law (Romans 7). But we still dwell on this side of glory—we carry about, as Paul elsewhere writes, our "outward man," which is wasting away even though our "inward man is being renewed day by day" (2 Cor. 4:16). Rather than be discouraged by the process of our redemption as we await the consummation of the age, the resurrection of the dead, and our glorification, Paul explains the nature of our sanctification and the Christian life so that "we do not lose heart" and so we ultimately understand that "our light affliction, which is but for a moment, is working for us a far more exceeding and eternal weight of glory" (2 Cor. 4:17).

Our Present Suffering

Paul, probably more so than many of his colleagues, understood the depths of God's self-disclosure in Christ (cf. 2 Peter 3:16). Or in more contemporary terms, Paul knew his theology very well. He knew the depths of our redemption through union with Christ and even caught a glimpse of the future glories (2 Cor. 12:1–4). But Paul was also intimately familiar with the way of the cross and the sufferings of Christ (Col. 1:24). Paul was beaten, whipped, received 195 lashes, was reviled, stoned and left for dead, and shipwrecked three times—he was no stranger to suffering (2 Cor. 11:25–27). As important as his biblical training was, Paul also had a PhD in suffering. So when Paul writes the following, he does not do so from an ivory tower but from his vantage point of following Christ and bearing His cross: "For I consider that the sufferings of this present time are not worthy to be compared with the glory which shall be revealed in us" (Rom. 8:18). Paul wanted his recipients to know that suffering is not inimical or inconsistent with the blessings of their union with Christ and the dawn of the new creation.

Paul tells his recipients that we live in this present evil age, though the age to come, the eschaton, has invaded this present age. He reminds us, though, that while we live in this present age, we will suffer—whether in the struggle of putting to death the deeds of the flesh or persecution for the sake of Christ. Again, Paul keeps us away from an over-realized eschatology—suffering marks this age. Recall what he wrote in the previous verses: "The Spirit Himself bears witness with our spirit that we are children of God, and if children, then heirs—heirs of God and joint heirs with Christ, if indeed we suffer with Him, that we may also be glorified together" (Rom. 8:16–17). But when he compares the suffering of this present age with the weight of glory that will be revealed in us at the consummation, he tells us that there is no comparison. Now remember, Paul was not unfamiliar with great suffering—he was not a cockeyed optimist looking at the world through Pollyanna spectacles—but neither was Paul a theological ostrich, burying his head in the sand waiting for the suffering to pass him by.

Rather, Paul explains the source of his confidence in the verses that follow: "For the earnest expectation of the creation eagerly waits for the revealing of the sons of God" (Rom. 8:19). The whole creation, both inanimate and animate, eagerly awaits the revelation of the sons of God. In other words, at the consummation, we who wage the battle of sanctification, who suffer, will be glorified with Christ. Why does the creation eagerly await the revelation of the sons of God? Paul writes, "For the creation was subjected to futility, not willingly, but because of Him who subjected it in hope; because the creation itself also will be delivered from the bondage of corruption into the glorious liberty of the children of God" (Rom. 8:20–21). Recall the Genesis fall and the curse God placed on the creation as a result of man's sin—"Cursed is the ground for your sake" (Gen. 3:17b). God subjected the creation to this curse in the knowledge that He would one day remove it at the consummation. Paul personifies the creation to make the point that it pines for the removal of the curse and, even more so, for the revelation and glorification of the sons of God. The current disorder and chaos will cease at the consummation. The twisted writhing, however, is not the creation in the throes of death.

Instead, Paul characterizes the creation's chaos and convulsing in a different manner: "For we know that the whole creation groans and labors with birth pangs together until now" (Rom. 8:22). Creation is not on its deathbed but in the maternity ward—it is in the midst of giving birth. Think of it: The earth was originally supposed to be a source of life, but as a result of the fall it was forced to cover the blood of the martyrs and have the dead placed within its bowels. No longer purely a source of life, the earth became an unwilling tomb for the dead. At the consummation of the age, though, the earth will give birth and issue forth the dead at the resurrection. Although the resurrection will be of both the righteous and the unrighteous, it is the resurrection and glorification of the righteous, the people of God, for which the creation longs. The creation, however, is not the only thing that eagerly awaits the consummation of the age. Even more so, Christians also long for the consummation:

"Not only that, but we also who have the firstfruits of the Spirit, even we ourselves groan within ourselves, eagerly waiting for the adoption, the redemption of our body" (Rom. 8:23). Recall that Christ was raised by the power of the Holy Spirit and that the Spirit also raises us from spiritual death to life. Our effectual calling and indwelling are a down payment that lets us know we will be raised from death on the last day—at the consummation of the age. Who would not eagerly look forward to this grand event in which we experience the completion of the fierce battle with sin, the cessation of suffering and persecution, and our vindication?

Paul explains that the end of all things—the consummation, resurrection, and our glorification—is the end goal of our redemption: "For we were saved in this hope, but hope that is seen is not hope; for why does one still hope for what he sees? But if we hope for what we do not see, we eagerly wait for it with perseverance" (Rom. 8:24–25). Paul then concludes this thought with the idea that we are saved by faith pregnant with hope. Hope, of course, is the confidence and expectation of that which we cannot yet see. Here Paul begins to come full circle and return to themes that he raised in the beginning of Romans 5–8. Recall what Paul wrote:

> Therefore, having been justified by faith, we have peace with God through our Lord Jesus Christ, through whom also we have access by faith into this grace in which we stand, and rejoice in hope of the glory of God. And not only that, but we also glory in tribulations, knowing that tribulation produces perseverance; and perseverance, character; and character, hope. Now hope does not disappoint, because the love of God has been poured out in our hearts by the Holy Spirit who was given to us. (Rom. 5:1–5)

The triune God fills us with hope even in the face of awaiting the consummation of the age. We know that we must await our perfection and the creation's liberation until Christ returns. Yet such patience is not pessimism but the height of optimism—we look suffering in the face and do not fear or lose hope, because we rest in the promises of God given in Christ and applied by the Spirit.

Our Suffering in the Light of Eternity

Do we have a better understanding of the weight of glory? When we place our current suffering on the scales, it cannot compare to the glory that will be revealed in us. Think of how painful it is to struggle with the indwelling presence of sin, the infirmities of our mortal bodies, the grief of losing loved ones, persecution—all this pales in comparison to the glory that we will shine forth. This almost seems beyond comprehension. Some, in fact, might think it is a statement loaded with audacity! Who am I to trivialize the suffering of so many for some utopian theory of vindication? Yet this is not my own personal opinion but one that comes from the quill of the apostle Paul in the Word of God. Paul was intimately familiar with suffering, and perhaps it bears repetition so we do not think he was theorizing as if he were a healthy and fit doctor telling a suffering cancer-stricken patient that things will get better and that her pain is not really all that bad:

> Three times I was beaten with rods; once I was stoned; three times I was shipwrecked; a night and a day I have been in the deep; in journeys often, in perils of waters, in perils of robbers, in perils of my own countrymen, in perils of the Gentiles, in perils in the city, in perils in the wilderness, in perils in the sea, in perils among false brethren; in weariness and toil, in sleeplessness often, in hunger and thirst, in fastings often, in cold and nakedness. (2 Cor. 11:25–27)

Paul could take all this suffering and tribulation and still say that it was not worthy to be compared with the glory that would be revealed in him: "Eye has not seen, nor ear heard, Nor have entered into the heart of man The things which God has prepared for those who love Him" (1 Cor. 2:9). We must realize that the glory of which Paul speaks is not a generic glory but the glory of Christ that will be revealed in us. We follow in the footsteps of our Savior—just as He endured humiliation and suffering, so too we must do likewise.

Moreover, just as He was glorified, we too will be glorified: "As was the man of dust, so also are those who are made of dust; and as is the heavenly Man, so also are those who are heavenly. And as we have borne the image of the man of dust, we shall also bear the image of the heavenly Man" (1 Cor. 15:48–49).

Do you recognize, then, that you will emanate the glory of Christ? This is the glory that drove Isaiah to cry out with a self-maledictory oath in the temple, and the glory that frightened James and John, and turned Peter into a babbling fool! We will possess this glory by virtue of our union with Christ and our glorification! All our sufferings will fade in our minds in the light of this glory. We must recognize that this glory is not simply a consummated eschatological reality. Remember, beloved, we are being conformed into the image of Christ at this very moment. Remember that Christ shone forth His preincarnate glory in His crucifixion as well as in His glorification (John 17:1–5). So we too shine forth the glory of Christ in our own Christlike humiliation now, as we will brilliantly shine it forth in our glorification:

> For it is the God who commanded light to shine out of darkness, who has shone in our hearts to give the light of the knowledge of the glory of God in the face of Jesus Christ. But we have this treasure in earthen vessels, that the excellence of the power may be of God and not of us. We are hard-pressed on every side, yet not crushed; we are perplexed, but not in despair; persecuted, but not forsaken; struck down, but not destroyed—always carrying about in the body the dying of the Lord Jesus, that the life of Jesus also may be manifested in our body. For we who live are always delivered to death for Jesus' sake, that the life of Jesus also may be manifested in our mortal flesh. (2 Cor. 4:6–11)

Let us not lose hope in the face of our current sufferings; as the famous hymn "Who Are These like Stars Appearing" states,

> Who are these of dazzling brightness,
> These in God's own truth arrayed,

Clad in robes of purest whiteness,
Robes whose luster ne'er shall fade,
Ne'er be touched by time's rude hand?
Whence come all this glorious band?

These are they who have contended
For their Savior's honor long,
Wrestling on till life was ended,
Foll'wing not the sinful throng;
These, who well the fight sustained,
Triumph through the Lamb have gained.

These are they whose hearts were riven,
Sore with woe and anguish tried,
Who in prayer full oft have striven
With the God they glorified;
Now, their painful conflict o'er,
God has bid them weep no more.

Our redemption in Christ, the consummation of the age, the resurrection, and our glorification should be cause to give us great hope in the face of our present suffering.

Conclusion

So, then, how do we live? Will we allow the knowledge of our current sufferings to strangle our hope in Christ? Will we allow our suffering to drown out our knowledge of who Christ is, what He has done, and our union with Him? Will we let fear rob our lungs of the air of the new creation? Will we panic and forget that the very Spirit of the living God indwells us and will transform our lowly bodies? When my brother and I slipped beneath the ocean, I thought I would die. As a child I never opened my eyes under water because it irritated them. On that day as I went under, my eyes were wide open, and I will never forget what I saw: a man wearing a pair of white pants running through the water and coming straight for my brother and me. That man was my father—he pulled us out and saved our lives that day. If you find yourself drowning in your fears, open the eyes of your faith and look to the One who saved you—Jesus Christ, the One who entered the miry depths of death so that you might have eternal life. Pray and cry out to Him that He would strengthen your faith, give you peace in the midst of the storm, and assuage your fear-stricken heart. Remember, "Therefore we do not lose heart. Even though our outward man is perishing, yet the inward man is being renewed day by day. For our light affliction, which is but for a moment, is working for us a far more exceeding and eternal weight of glory, while we do not look at the things which are seen, but at the things which are not seen. For the things which are seen are temporary, but the things which are not seen are eternal" (2 Cor. 4:16–18).

24

The Spirit and Prayer

ROMANS 8:26–27

Likewise the Spirit also helps in our weaknesses. For we do not know what we should pray for as we ought, but the Spirit Himself makes intercession for us with groanings which cannot be uttered. Now He who searches the hearts knows what the mind of the Spirit is, because He makes intercession for the saints according to the will of God.

One of the most devastating things that a person can suffer is isolation. I have seen news stories in which prisoners started a hunger strike to protest their long-term incarceration in isolation. These particular prisoners spent twenty-three hours a day in solitary confinement. Even the most hardened criminals long for communication with others. Silence in the midst of solitude can become a thunderous, deafening, psychological roar to our minds. The same is true, I believe, for people caught in the midst of suffering. Sick people like to have visitors so they do not feel as though they are all alone. When you lay in your bed in pain all alone for days on end, familiar surroundings can become a strange, lonely place. For these and other reasons, I think Paul discusses prayer and our connection to the Spirit as they relate to the church's present suffering. In the midst of our suffering, Paul wants the church to know that we are not alone. But prayer, we must realize, is not a monologue—a person confusedly muttering to himself in a pain-induced stupor. Prayer is a genuine dialogue between the living God and His children. In the midst of our suffering, then, Paul shows us the importance of the work of the Spirit and prayer. These are important truths, of course, that significantly factor in our sanctification.

The Comforter

Recall that Paul addressed believers' suffering even though they are united to Christ, have been justified, adopted, and are being conformed to His image in their sanctification. Yes, we have entered the new heavens and earth through our union with Christ, but we still live with a foot, if you will, planted in the present evil age. We are being renewed day to day according to our inner man, but all the while our outer man is wasting away (2 Cor. 4:16). In the midst of the Christian life in which we live torn between the ages, Paul encourages his recipients to pray: "Likewise the Spirit also helps in our weaknesses. For we do not know what we should pray for as we ought, but the Spirit Himself makes intercession for us with groanings which cannot be uttered" (Rom. 8:26). In the midst of our suffering, whether the battle we wage is against the indwelling presence of sin, persecution, or trials, the Holy Spirit of God "helps in our weakness."

In the second half of the verse, Paul elaborates one of the ways the Holy Spirit brings us strength—He intercedes on our behalf in our prayers. So often we do not know how to pray when we are in the midst of suffering, or we pray thinking that what we ask is in accord with the will of God when it is not. The Holy Spirit intercedes on our behalf in our prayers so that even when we do not know how to pray, or even pray for the wrong things, our prayers are still effective. C. S. Lewis (1898–1963) captures the heart of the Spirit's intercession in our prayers: "Take not, oh Lord, our literal sense. Lord, in thy great, unbroken speech our limping metaphor translate."[1] This means that the genuine heartfelt prayers of God's people are never ineffective, though we must remember that God can answer our prayers in three ways: yes, no, and wait. Nevertheless,

1. C. S. Lewis, *Poems*, ed. Walter Hooper (New York: Harcourt Brace Jovanovich, 1965), 129.

we need not fear that in our absence of knowing what to say or ask, God will turn a deaf ear to our cries. What a blessing this is! Not only does Christ continually intercede in the court of heaven on our behalf, but the Holy Spirit also tends to our needs in the "theater of our own hearts."[2] And if we lack the words to say to God in prayer, we can always turn to His own words. As P. T. Forsyth (1848–1921) explains:

> We must use the Bible as an original; for, indeed, the Bible is the most copious spring of prayer, and of power, and of range. If we learn to pray from the Bible, and avoid a mere *cento* [scraps] of its phrases, we shall cultivate in our prayer the large humane note of a universal gospel. Let us nurse our prayer on our *study* of our Bible; and let us, therefore, not be too afraid of *theological* prayer.[3]

The Word of God is the best schoolroom, in which we can learn the grammar and language of prayer.

According to God's Will

Paul explains that we have the wonderful blessing of the Spirit's intercession in our prayers, so our minds might naturally ponder, Does this mean I can ask for anything that I want and the Father will grant my request because the Spirit has made my prayer effectual? The answer to this question comes in the following verse: "Now He who searches the hearts knows what the mind of the Spirit is, because He makes intercession for the saints according to the will of God" (Rom. 8:27). The Spirit always intercedes for us when we pray, but He always does so according to God's will, not our own. Take, for example, the apostle Paul's prayers. He repeatedly prayed that the Lord would remove his thorn in the flesh. The Spirit interceded on his behalf in accordance with the will of God. Christ replied to Paul: "My grace is sufficient for you, for My strength

2. Murray, *Epistle to the Romans*, 311.

3. P. T. Forsyth, *The Soul of Prayer* (1916; repr., Vancouver: Regent College Publishing, 1995), 90–91.

is made perfect in weakness" (2 Cor. 12:9). So, yes, prayer is "an offering up of our desires unto God," as the Westminster Shorter Catechism tells us. But it also states, like Paul, that our desires must be "agreeable to his will" (Q. 98).

At first glance this might seem to release all the air out of the prayer balloon. After all, if one of the points of prayer is to tell God *our* concerns, needs, and desires, how personally beneficial and fulfilling can it be if God always gets His way? In one sense the sentiment, though misguided, is perfectly understandable until we take a few points into consideration. First, God "searches hearts," which means that He knows us better than we know ourselves. As the psalmist writes, "O LORD, You have searched me and known me. You know my sitting down and my rising up; You understand my thought afar off. You comprehend my path and my lying down, And are acquainted with all my ways. For there is not a word on my tongue, But behold, O LORD, You know it altogether" (Ps. 139:1–4). If God knows us intimately, better than we know ourselves, then who else knows what we need most? We might think, like Paul, that we need to be freed from a personal affliction, but God knows better.

Second, to assume that we know better than God, the Creator of the cosmos, One whose wisdom, knowledge, power, and righteousness far exceeds our own, is folly and arrogance. While we can certainly lay our desires before the Lord in prayer, we must be prepared to have our desires conformed to God's will, to Christ Himself. In this respect, we must recognize that prayer is the arena in which God conforms us to His will and desire, not where we mold God's will into our own desires. We do not pray to change God's mind but pray so He will change ours.

The Spirit, Prayer, and Sanctification

Our suffering is the crucible of our sanctification, and our prayers are one of the means by which God sees us through. Suffering places us in the cauldron, and God applies the sanctifying heat of His Holy Spirit so that in prayer He burns away the dross of our lives, leaving only the purity of Christ's image. God does not give His Holy Spirit to make our lives easier. Rather, He gives us His Spirit to conform us to Christ's image. In other words, God is more concerned about revealing Christ's glory in us than our ease of life. Ultimately the Spirit works to form the life of Christ in us! So many Christians think that once we receive the grace of God in our justification, it is then our responsibility to be more like Christ. We must try harder, read our Bibles more, or set up rules for ourselves to improve our sanctification. This is not at all the case. One seventeenth-century Puritan theologian, Walter Marshall (1628–1680), explains our sanctification in this manner:

> The great mystery in the way of sanctification, is, the glorious manner of our fellowship with Christ, in receiving a holy frame of heart from him. It is by our being in Christ, and having Christ himself in us; and that not merely by his universal preference as he is God, but by such a close union, as that we are one spirit and one flesh with him; which is a privilege peculiar to those that are truly sanctified. I may well call this a mystical union, because the Apostle calleth it a great mystery, in an epistle full of mysteries.[4]

Our sanctification, then, does not lie simply in our own intensified effort but rather in our union with the resurrected Christ.

When Paul discusses the bond between Christ and His church, he likens it to the marital union: "'For this reason a man shall leave his father and mother and be joined to his wife, and the two shall become one flesh.' This is a great mystery, but I speak concerning Christ and the church" (Eph. 5:31–32; cf. Gen. 2:24). That Paul identifies marriage as a *mystery*, something once hidden and now revealed, means that marriage foreshadows the relationship between Christ and His body, the church. Husband and wife cannot produce the fruit of offspring unless they unite and become one flesh. Likewise, we cannot produce holiness and sanctification unless we

---

4. Walter Marshall, *The Gospel Mystery of Sanctification* (1692; repr., Grand Rapids: Reformation Heritage Books, 1999), 28–29.

are united to Christ. To change metaphors, only the life-giving sap from Jesus, the vine, can cause the fruit of holiness to grow on the branches (John 15:1–10). We must, therefore, draw nigh unto Christ through the means of grace in order to be sanctified, in order to be conformed to His image and to produce the fruit of holiness. This is what Paul presents here—unless we draw nigh unto Christ in prayer we will falter in our sanctification. In the midst of our sufferings the Holy Spirit intercedes for us when we cry out in prayer, and He answers them according to the will of the Father. And what is the will of the Father? To conform us to the image of Christ. But there is also a larger aspect to the Spirit's work.

The Spirit, the Church, and Sanctification

Although the eschatological age has invaded this present evil age, the times in which we live are nonetheless marked by suffering, persecution, and trial. When Paul points us to prayer, he teaches us not only that it is vital for our sanctification but that the church will indeed suffer. Along these lines Paul makes a seemingly audacious claim: "I now rejoice in my sufferings for you, and fill up in my flesh what is lacking in the afflictions of Christ, for the sake of His body, which is the church" (Col. 1:24). How is it possible that there is something lacking in the afflictions of Christ? Does not Scripture uniformly teach the sufficiency of the satisfaction and obedience of Christ? The answer, of course, is a resounding yes! Christ's intercessory work is abundantly all-sufficient. Paul's statement teaches us that what is insufficient is the suffering related to Christ's body, the church. Paul does not address the topic of Christ's satisfaction but the life of sanctification. Christ, the head of the body, suffered once (1 Peter 3:18) and has made satisfaction for our sins. But His body, the church, must now suffer. Our suffering is not for the satisfaction of sins—it is not propitiatory. Our suffering is not connected to our justification but rather to our sanctification. We must be conformed to Christ's image—we must bear our cross and follow Him.

Just as Christ's humiliation preceded His glorification, so too we must travel the *via dolorosa*, the way of the cross, prior to our glorification—both individually and corporately. This is why Paul tells us that we suffer now, in this present evil age: "For I consider that the sufferings of this present time are not worthy to be compared with the glory which shall be revealed in us" (Rom. 8:18). The church must fill up what is lacking in the afflictions of Christ until the consummation of the age. We see, though, from the verses before us that we are not alone in the midst of our suffering—the Holy Spirit is present, interceding on our behalf when we pray. We know the eschaton has dawned, but we also know that we must live in this present evil age, a period of suffering for the body of Christ until His return. We also know, however, that we are not orphans (John 14:18). In the midst of our suffering, we can call out to *our* heavenly Father. And when we ask for bread, He will not give us a stone or a serpent:

> For everyone who asks receives, and he who seeks finds, and to him who knocks it will be opened. Or what man is there among you who, if his son asks for bread, will give him a stone? Or if he asks for a fish, will he give him a serpent? If you then, being evil, know how to give good gifts to your children, how much more will your Father who is in heaven give good things to those who ask Him! (Matt. 7:8–11)

Conclusion

When we contemplate the work of the Holy Spirit, we must remember that He is present in our lives to bring us strength when we are weak and to conform us to the image of Christ. We are not orphans living without hope in this present evil age. Rather, we are sons of the living God, coheirs with Christ, living by the power of the age to come, with the indwelling presence of the Holy Spirit, eagerly awaiting the consummation of the age, the judgment of the powers of this present evil age, and the revelation of the sons of God—the glorification of the body of Christ! In the midst of your sufferings, never forget: You are not alone! You have the Spirit, who indwells you and intercedes for you when you do not know how to pray, and you are joined to the body of Christ, the church. You are not alone. Cry out, therefore, to God in prayer—join together with your fellow saints and pray to the one, true, living God to give you strength when you are weak. In a word, pray!

25

The Golden Chain

ROMANS 8:28–30

And we know that all things work together for good to those who love God, to those who are the called according to His purpose. For whom He foreknew, He also predestined to be conformed to the image of His Son, that He might be the firstborn among many brethren. Moreover whom He predestined, these He also called; whom He called, these He also justified; and whom He justified, these He also glorified.

In military training, one of the tools that drill sergeants employ is psychological uncertainty. Many would-be soldiers have the necessary physical strength and stamina to complete the training but not the psychological conviction. If a person does not know when his physical suffering will end, he might likely quit. Drill sergeants will, for example, tell their trainees to run ten miles, return to the barracks and get showered, get dressed, and line up in formation. Most think their hard work is over, but they are mistaken because the drill instructor will tell them to get their fresh uniforms soaking wet and go run ten more miles. Just when the trainees think they are done, they start more physical exercise. Not knowing when the merry-go-round will stop can be psychologically defeating, and for this reason trainees quit.

This example has parallels, I believe, with the point Paul addresses here in Romans 8:28–30. Paul has addressed the reality that Christians live torn between the ages: between this present evil age and the age to come. By virtue of their union with Christ they have entered the new creation, been justified, been adopted as sons of God, and begun the process of sanctification. But given that we still live in this world and since Christ has not yet returned, we find our outer man wasting away even though our inner man is being renewed day by day (2 Cor. 4:16). This means that the church will suffer in the present time, but as Paul has explained, we are not alone. In Romans 8:18–25 Paul told his recipients that when our present suffering is placed on the scales with the future glory that will be revealed in us, there is no comparison. The weight of glory far exceeds any suffering we might presently endure. In Romans 8:26–27 Paul also reminds us that we are not alone in the midst of our suffering. God has given us His Holy Spirit to intercede for us in prayer, which is the crucible in which He further conforms us to the image of Christ.

Here Paul adds another element to bring further comfort to suffering Christians. Unlike military training that leaves the end of the pain of training a mystery, Paul explains that even though Christians suffer, they will undoubtedly reach their final destination. How and why? Unlike military training in which a person's success largely depends on personal effort, our salvation hinges solely on God. Paul makes this point through what theologians have historically called *the golden chain*, or *the order of salvation*. One seventeenth-century Puritan theologian, George Downame (c. 1563–1634), explains the order of salvation in the following manner:

> It has been the received opinion, and usual practice of all *Orthodox* Divines, to hold and set down in this order the degrees of salvation, which are wrought in this life, viz. Our vocation, justification, sanctification. And that in order of nature vocation, (wherein justifying faith is begotten) goes before justification; and that justification, wherein we are made just before God by imputation of Christ's righteousness, goes before sanctification: wherein we, being already justified from the guilt of sin, and redeemed from the hand of our spiritual enemies, and

> reconciled unto God, receive grace to worship him in holiness and righteousness before him.[1]

Downame ultimately preserves the apostle's main point in Romans 8:28–30; namely, if you begin the journey, you will complete it. You will complete it not because of your strength or fidelity but because of God's faithfulness and the unbreakable links of His golden chain of salvation.

Providence and Suffering

One of the more common responses to suffering is to think that God has somehow forgotten or abandoned us. The Bible records a number of such responses from various saints, both in the Old and New Testaments. The prophet Habakkuk cried out to the Lord to heal Israel from her sins but was despondent when God told him that judgment, not healing, would fall upon the nation (Habakkuk 1–2). John the Baptist faithfully ministered and lived an austere life, all in the hopes that God would return, save the righteous, and judge the wicked. He was stunned to discover that he would be the one to baptize the Messiah and likely awestruck when the Spirit descended on Jesus like a dove and God spoke from heaven, "This is My beloved Son, in whom I am well pleased" (Matt. 3:17). But I suspect he was crushed when Jesus walked off into the wilderness rather than bringing salvation and judgment against Israel's brood of vipers (Matt. 3:7), and his feelings of abandonment undoubtedly intensified when he was later imprisoned by Herod (Matt. 11:1–3). I suspect that John's disciples were especially disheartened when he was beheaded (Matt. 14:1–12). There was no immediate redemption, no judgment of the wicked—only suffering and death.

As aware as Paul was of such suffering, no doubt from personal experience in his own life, he was also equally aware of another important truth: "And we know that all things work together for

---

1. George Downame, "An Appendix to the Treatise of the Certainty of Salvation," in *The Covenant of Grace: or An Exposition upon Luke 1.73, 74, 75* (London: Ralph Smith, 1647), 281–82, modernized spelling.

good to those who love God, to those who are the called according to His purpose" (Rom. 8:28). The first thing to note is that "all things work together for good" only and exclusively for those who "love God." This truth does not apply to those who hate God (e.g., Rom. 1:18–3:19). Only those in union with Christ (Rom. 5:12–6:4) have the ability to love God. This undoubtedly strikes a nerve in the average unbeliever because it sounds undemocratic. After all, should not everyone have equal access to God? And if all have equal access to Him, then should they not also have equal benefits? This mentality is enshrined in the ideological founding of our nation—all men are created equal. But here is the truth: We do not live in a democracy. God is the sole monarch of the entire cosmos, and as Paul makes abundantly clear, we are all, Jew and Gentile, universally sinful (Rom. 3:10–18; 5:12–14). All deserve judgment, so it is a wonder that God should save anyone.

God's people can rest assured that, despite the apparent chaos in the world or their own personal tumult, He makes all things work together for good for those who love Him and are called according to His purpose. In His providence, God sovereignly controls all history. As the Westminster Confession informs us, God ordains whatsoever comes to pass (WCF 3.1). We are not, then, tossed to and fro by the supposed random circumstances of life, hoping that God can somehow pick up the pieces and make something of our shattered lives. Rather, as difficult as it may seem, every event in our lives, even our tragedies, are by design for our good, and most importantly, His glory.

God's Eternal Love

Regardless of what happens in this life, there are several undeniable and irrefutable certainties, which Paul begins to list: "For whom He foreknew, He also predestined to be conformed to the image of His Son, that He might be the firstborn among many brethren" (Rom. 8:29). Paul begins with the love of God, which at first glance is not immediately apparent. Readers likely see Paul's term *foreknew* and assume that the apostle means that God looked into the future, saw the people that would love Him, and then predestined or chose them. God ratified the human being's choice of God. Stated simply, God says: "Oh? You chose me? Ok, then I'll choose you." But we must remember that Paul's Bible is his Old Testament. And in the Old Testament, to *know* someone is to love them. This usage of the term appears in the earliest portions of the Old Testament: "Now Adam knew Eve his wife" (Gen. 4:1). Adam did not merely cognitively recognize his wife—he was physically united to his wife, an expression of his love for her. The prophet Hosea speaks in this same manner in his description of God's love for Israel: "Yet I am the LORD your God Ever since the land of Egypt, And you shall know no God but Me; For there is no savior besides Me. I *knew* you in the wilderness, In the land of great drought" (Hos. 13:4–5, emphasis added). Likewise, the prophet Amos states: "You only have I *known* of all the families of the earth" (Amos 3:2, emphasis added). So when Paul says, "those whom He foreknew," he actually means for those whom God "foreloved" He also predestined.[2] Paul elsewhere states this same truth in a slightly different way: "In love, having predestined us to adoption as sons by Jesus Christ to Himself, according to the good pleasure of His will" (Eph. 1:4c–5). God's electing love was not to an indefinite or uncertain end but rather purposeful—to the end goal of conformity to the image of Christ so that He would be the first among many brothers. As Paul has written earlier, the chief purpose of our suffering is conformity to Christ.

The Unbreakable Chain

How does God carry out His plan to conform Christians to the image of Christ? Paul unveils his golden chain of salvation: "Moreover whom He predestined, these He also called; whom He called, these He also justified; and whom He justified, these He also glorified" (Rom. 8:30). Although we struggle with sin in the midst of our sanctification, though we suffer persecution or trial, we will never

2. Murray, *Epistle to the Romans*, 317.

be abandoned. Paul uses an ancient Greek rhetorical device called a *sorites* (pronounced “sore-ee-tees”), which was also known as a heap, pile, stair step, or chain argument. The idea in a *sorites* is that each link in the chain logically presupposes and rests on the previous link. Romans 8:30 is not the only place where Paul uses such an argument. There are two other *sorites* in Romans, the first of which occurs in chapter 5:

> And not only that, but we also glory in *tribulations*, knowing that *tribulation* produces *perseverance*; and *perseverance*, *character*; and *character*, hope. Now hope does not disappoint, because the love of God has been poured out in our hearts by the Holy Spirit who was given to us. (Rom. 5:3–5, emphasis added)

Notice that in each step in Paul’s argument the predicate becomes the subject in the next clause, and as such, is repeated until he arrives at his goal: Tribulation (2x) → Perseverance (2x) → Character (2x) = Hope. Each step of the argument presupposes the previous step. The second *sorites* appears in chapter 10:

> How then shall they call on Him in whom they have not *believed*? And how shall they *believe* in Him of whom they have not *heard*? And how shall they *hear* without a *preacher*? And how shall they *preach* unless they are sent?” (Rom. 10:14–15a, emphasis added)

Once again the chain pattern appears: believe (2x) → hear (2x) → preach (2x) = sent. Remove any one link and the argument collapses: If there is no one to preach, then no one will hear, and if no one hears, then no one will believe. Paul employs this same kind of chain argument here in Romans 8:29–30:

> For whom He foreknew, He also *predestined* to be conformed to the image of His Son, that He might be the firstborn among many brethren. Moreover whom He *predestined*, these He also *called*; whom He *called*, these He also *justified*; and whom He *justified*, these He also glorified. (emphasis added)

The same pattern emerges: predestined (2x) → called (2x) → justified (2x) = glorified. What is Paul's point? And why does he employ this chain argument?

Paul sets forth this chain argument and what theologians have called the *order of salvation* to make several crucial points. First, our final destination is an absolute certainty—we *will* be conformed to Christ's image—we will be glorified. Paul conveys this certainty by using aorist verbs in the Greek. He uses this verbal aspect not to convey the idea that these things have already occurred in the past but to express the absolute certainty of our redemption. Absolutely nothing will impede our salvation. Second, this golden chain is unbreakable. Remove any single link and the whole argument collapses: How can one have faith and thereby be justified if he is not effectually called by the Holy Spirit? How can a person be justified and given the irrevocable right to eternal life and not also be glorified (Rom. 5:21)? How can the Spirit effectually call someone unless God first sets His love on him and predestines him?

Third—and this is so important given Paul's overall discussion regarding sanctification and suffering—our salvation does not hinge on our sanctification (Eph. 2:8–9). In other words, we will undoubtedly be sanctified because of our union with Christ. Paul makes this abundantly clear (e.g. Rom. 6:1–4; Eph. 2:10). People, however, sometimes think that if they have setbacks, moral failings, and struggle with besetting sins that they can somehow jeopardize their standing before God. They believe that God will revoke their right to eternal life and overturn the verdict of their justification. This thought likely crosses the minds of some suffering Christians. How many of us, for example, have become Job's friends when we have seen others suffer or perhaps even said the same things in our own hearts: "Am I suffering because I have sinned? Is God punishing me? Have I lost my salvation?" Paul's answer to these questions is a resounding no! Christians have been predestined, called, justified, and glorified! Martin Luther reflects on the hope that Christians can harvest from the bountiful blessings Paul enumerates in Romans 8:29–30:

> When, therefore, your sin and unworthiness assail you and the thought occurs to you that you are not elected by God, that the number of the elect is small but the mass of the godless large, and you are frightened at the terrible instances of divine wrath and judgment, then do not argue at length why God does this or that as He does and why He does not act differently even though He is well able to do so. Nor venture to explore the depth of divine election with your reason. Otherwise you will certainly go wrong. You will either despair or become reckless. Rather hold to the promise of the Gospel. This will teach you that Christ, God's Son, came into the world in order to bless all the nations on earth, that is, to redeem them from sin and death, to justify and save them.... When you treat of election in this way (as St. Paul, so constantly does), it is comforting beyond measure."[3]

Nothing can break this golden chain, because our union with Christ undergirds it, one that begins with God's predestined love for us in Christ. In a word, Paul's message is "He who has begun a good work in you will complete it until the day of Jesus Christ" no matter what happens (Phil. 1:6).

Conclusion

All this should make our hearts swell with hope, assurance, and faith in any situation that we face. Whether we believe the events in our lives to be good or bad, they are all ultimately good because God uses them to conform us to the image of Christ. Moreover, it should point us to our source of hope in the midst of life—Jesus Christ. Along these lines Geerhardus Vos writes:

> The Christian can hope perfectly. He is the only [one] who can hope perfectly for that which is to be brought to him. For him not to have his face set forward and upward would be an anomaly, sickliness, and decadence. To have it set upward and forward is life and health and strength. The air of the world to

---

3. Luther, *What Luther Says*, 1:457, no. 1351.

> come is the vital atmosphere which he delights to breathe and outside of which he feels depressed and languid.[4]

Vos's point is that in the midst of everything, we must live and breathe the air of the age to come. We must live and breathe with our sight firmly fixed on Christ who has saved us, justified us, inaugurated the age to come, and sent the Holy Spirit to sanctify us and conform us to His image as we live in the twilight of this present evil age. We should therefore eagerly await the consummation of the age when we will be glorified and our sanctification is completed. This is the air that we must breathe—this is the great unbreakable golden chain of our redemption! In the midst of trial, if we breathe only the poison air of this present evil age we will inevitably lose hope and lose sight of Christ. Like Peter who took his eyes off of Christ as he walked on the storm-tossed sea, we will sink into the depths of fear and hopelessness. Rather, keep your eyes firmly fixed on Christ, the Author and Finisher of your faith.

---

4. Geerhardus Vos, *Grace and Glory: Sermons Preached in the Chapel of Princeton Theological Seminary* (Edinburgh: Banner of Truth, 1994), 143.

26

The Love of God in Christ

ROMANS 8:31–39

What then shall we say to these things? If God is for us, who can be against us? He who did not spare His own Son, but delivered Him up for us all, how shall He not with Him also freely give us all things? Who shall bring a charge against God's elect? It is God who justifies. Who is he who condemns? It is Christ who died, and furthermore is also risen, who is even at the right hand of God, who also makes intercession for us. Who shall separate us from the love of Christ? Shall tribulation, or distress, or persecution, or famine, or nakedness, or peril, or sword? As it is written: "For Your sake we are killed all day long; We are accounted as sheep for the slaughter." Yet in all these things we are more than conquerors through Him who loved us. For I am persuaded that neither death nor life, nor angels nor principalities nor powers, nor things present nor things to come, nor height nor depth, nor any other created thing, shall be able to separate us from the love of God which is in Christ Jesus our Lord.

Paul was well aware that he and the Roman Christians were not the first to suffer in redemptive history. Many godly saints throughout the ages had suffered and cried out to the Lord. Most famous among the prayers of Scripture are the cries of the psalmist. For this reason Paul looks back on Psalm 44 in the passage of Scripture before us. In its original context the psalmist lamented the fact that the surrounding nations were oppressing Israel—they had God's people under their collective thumb. Despite their suffering, the psalmist did not look to his own might or power but to the Lord—God's faithful children were filled with praise: "For I will not trust in my bow, Nor shall my sword save me. But You have saved us from our enemies, And have put to shame those who hated us. In God we boast all day long, And praise Your name forever" (Ps. 44:6–8). But this did not blind the psalmist to his difficult circumstances. He did not gloss over Israel's suffering: "You make us a reproach to our neighbors, A scorn and a derision to those all around us. You make us a byword among the nations, A shaking of the head among the peoples. My dishonor is continually before me, And the shame of my face has covered me, Because of the voice of him who reproaches and reviles, Because of the enemy and the avenger" (Ps. 44:13–16). Nevertheless, in the face of Israel's suffering and apparent abandonment by God, the psalmist looked back to God's mighty saving acts with the hope that He would once again deliver Israel from her foes: "We have heard with our ears, O God, Our fathers have told us, The deeds You did in their days, In days of old: You drove out the nations with Your hand, But them You planted; You afflicted the peoples, and cast them out" (Ps. 44:1–2). Given God's faithfulness in the past, and in spite of his present suffering, the psalmist nevertheless cries out: "Yet for Your sake we are killed all day long; We are accounted as sheep for the slaughter" (Ps. 44:22).

Paul takes the psalmist's theme and uses it in a similar fashion here in the closing verses of chapter 8. Like the psalmist, Paul recounted the mighty saving acts of Christ (e.g., Rom. 3:23–26; 4:25; 5:12–21; 8:1). Just as the psalmist recounted and remembered the great exodus from Egypt and subsequent conquest of the Promised Land, so too Paul communicated our great exodus out from under the dominion of Satan, sin, and death. Jesus Christ led us out of bondage from sin and death; He has justified us and imputed His perfect righteousness to us. Moreover, Paul told us that we have the indwelling presence of the Holy Spirit—a fulfillment of the great eschatological promises of the Old Testament prophets. We also live at the dawn of the eschatological age because Christ has been raised from the dead, which signals that the resurrection has begun.

We now await the conclusion of this present evil age and the consummation of the kingdom of God.

Yet, as we also know, despite these victorious events, things do not have the appearance of success. God's people still struggle with sin; they are still persecuted and suffer trials. How is this compatible with the ideas of victory and conquest associated with the work of Christ? Well, as we have seen in the previous sections, this conforms with the ministry of Christ by virtue of the fact that the body of Christ must suffer, just as Christ suffered, before we are glorified and freed from sin, persecution, and suffering. We must not lose sight, however, of the fact that even in the midst of God-ordained trials and suffering, He has poured out His love on us through the redemption of Christ. Let us see how we receive the unbounded love of God through Christ and see why the apostle Paul would say that we are killed all day long and are counted as sheep for the slaughter.

The Source of Our Confidence

Ever since the beginning of chapter 5 Paul has explained the significance and implications of our justification by faith alone and its connections to sanctification, union with Christ, and freedom from sin and the law. Recall that he began chapter 5 with themes that reappear here at the end of chapter 8:

> Therefore, having been justified by faith, we have peace with God through our Lord Jesus Christ, through whom also we have access by faith into this grace in which we stand, and rejoice in hope of the glory of God. And not only that, but we also glory in tribulations, knowing that tribulation produces perseverance; and perseverance, character; and character, hope. Now hope does not disappoint, because the love of God has been poured out in our hearts by the Holy Spirit who was given to us. (Rom. 5:1–5)

What Paul only briefly develops in Romans 5:1–5 he explains with greater attention here. He writes with great confidence: "What then shall we say to these things? If God is for us, who can be against us?" (Rom. 8:31). Given everything that we have read in Romans 3:20–8:30, what should our response be? Should we be filled with hope or fear? Yes, our foes and suffering are great—death is a powerful and destructive enemy. But He who is with us is greater than he who is in the world. The Creator of heaven and earth has poured out His love on us in Christ in great abundance. With words that evoke Abraham's sacrifice of Isaac (Gen. 22:16), Paul describes the Father's love for us: "He who did not spare His own Son, but delivered Him up for us all, how shall He not with Him also freely give us all things?" (Rom. 8:32). Paul reminds us that if God did not spare His only Son but delivered Him to the agony and ignominy of the cross, then of course He will not hesitate to bring about our glorification. We must not divorce the doctrines that we considered in Romans 8:28–30 (effectual calling, justification, sanctification, glorification, providence, predestination, Christology, and eschatology) from the very real sacrifice and gift of love that it constitutes. Too often people talk about these truths in rather dry and technical terms and forget the reality, costliness, and love that stands behind them all.

Just as Paul started chapter 5 with the consequential peace that we have with God as the consequence of our justification, he raises this same hope again. But this time Paul focuses our attention not on God but on our enemies. All too often the enemies of the church, including Satan, accuse the saints of unrighteousness. Think back, for example, to the vision of Zechariah the prophet when Joshua the high priest stood before the Lord wearing excrement-stained garments. The words of *Satan*, the Accuser, undoubtedly rang loud in his ears—"He's unworthy! Look at his sinfulness—he is wicked!" Yet the Lord rebuked Satan and turned not to condemn Joshua but to justify him—to declare him righteous. He told the messenger of the Lord to take away Joshua's filthy garments and to give him a holy and pure robe. Even Zechariah the prophet entered the excitement and cried out for the court attendants to place a clean turban on Joshua's head. The Lord told Joshua He had removed his sin from him, and the divine donation of clean garments signified the imputation of righteousness (Zech. 3:1–5). If God declared Joshua righteous, why would he fear any of the false accusations of Satan or the world? As Paul writes, "Who shall bring a charge against God's elect? It is God who justifies. Who is he who condemns? It is Christ who died, and furthermore is also risen, who is even at the right hand of God, who also makes intercession for us" (Rom. 8:33–34). The same confidence that filled Joshua's heart undoubtedly filled Paul's. Think of Stephen. He was falsely accused and condemned by Israel's religious leaders—the highest judicial and theological court in all the land. Yet as he was being stoned, the heavens opened and he saw Christ *standing* at the right hand of the Father interceding on his behalf (Acts 7:55; cf. Ps. 110:1). Stephen may have been condemned by men, but his justified status before God's throne gave him courage unto death, for he knew his life was in the hands of His Savior, Christ.

Stephen knew in his heart the truths that Paul places before us. He knew that *nothing* could separate him from God's love in Christ: "Who shall separate us from the love of Christ? Shall tribulation, or distress, or persecution, or famine, or nakedness, or peril, or sword?" (Rom. 8:35). My father told me of a time when he was out on the open ocean in a small twelve-foot boat with a tiny outboard motor. He and his friend decided to make a run to a nearby island. They made the first leg of the trip just fine, but on the return leg things got scary. He said the swells got so big that they chugged up one side of the swell and then descended the other side. It was an ominous sight, he said, to look around him and see nothing but a massive wall of water surrounding his insignificant boat. I think this is the way we often look at the trials in our lives—they appear so big that they are all we see, and they seemingly surround us on all sides to the point that we think that God has somehow abandoned us. But Paul's point is that God has gone to such great lengths to save us that He will unquestionably allow *nothing* to get in the way of His love in Christ for us—absolutely nothing.

Carrying Our Crosses

At this point Paul now quotes Psalm 44:22 to emphasize his willingness to suffer on account of Christ, which should also be our own attitude: "As it is written: 'For Your sake we are killed all day long; We are accounted as sheep for the slaughter'" (Rom. 8:36). Paul was not a masochist—he did not enjoy pain. Rather, because he was united to Christ, he was equipped by God and therefore willing to do whatever God set before him, even if this meant suffering. As John Calvin explains, Paul

> affirms that the condition of the Church in all ages is here portrayed. Thus, then, we ought to regard it as a settled point, that a state of continual warfare in bearing the cross is enjoined upon us by divine appointment. Sometimes, it is true, a truce or respite may be granted us; for God has compassion upon our infirmity: but although the sword of persecution is not always unsheathed against us, yet, as we are members of Christ, it behooves us always to be ready to bear the cross with him.[1]

Ours is the way of the cross—we follow in the footsteps of Christ. As Jesus Himself said, "If anyone desires to come after Me, let him deny himself, and take up his cross, and follow Me" (Matt. 16:24).

Sadly, I think for many in the church, and definitely for those outside it, the cross is a symbol of defeat, ignominy, and weakness. How absurd, after all, that God would come to suffer and die at the hands of His own rebellious people! Yet we must realize that God's wisdom and ways are very different from the world's ways. The world believes that strength can be revealed only in might and power. If a nation wants to flex its muscles, it will put on a parade of military might with a stream of soldiers, tanks, rockets, and planes going by in solemn procession. The town sheriff in old western movies always carried his six-shooter on his hip to show any potential

1. John Calvin, *Commentary on Psalms 36–92*, Calvin Translation Society (repr., Grand Rapids: Baker, 1991), 170–71.

criminals that he was in the business of dispensing lead, not hugs. God does not work this way—God chooses to show His strength in weakness, not power.

Paul elsewhere writes, "We preach Christ crucified, to the Jews a stumbling block and to the Greeks foolishness, but to those who are called, both Jews and Greeks, Christ the power of God and the wisdom of God. Because the foolishness of God is wiser than men, and the weakness of God is stronger than men" (1 Cor. 1:23–25). God did not demonstrate His power through clenched fists but with open hands so that nails could be driven through them. Christ's enemies certainly thought they had won, but in reality, through the weakness, shame, and suffering of the cross, Christ conquered Satan, sin, and death. Moreover, the cross is the means by which Christ rules in the midst of His enemies—He applies the power of the cross through the Spirit to the hearts of rebels to bring them into submission to His kingly rule.

Therefore, if we are united to Christ, then He will manifest His life in ours—His sufferings in our sufferings—but like Christ, our sufferings will eventually give way to resurrection and ultimately victory. We will have victory, of course, not because of our own strength and wisdom but because of Christ's victory. Hence, for these reasons Paul confidently writes: "For I am persuaded that neither death nor life, nor angels nor principalities nor powers, nor things present nor things to come, nor height nor depth, nor any other created thing, shall be able to separate us from the love of God which is in Christ Jesus our Lord" (Rom. 8:38–39). Far from a symbol of defeat, our sufferings embody the way of the cross through which God manifests His power in our weakness. Far from merely enduring and surviving in the midst of our trials, we actually *conquer*. Hence, no matter what, neither earthly nor heavenly powers of any sort will separate us from the love of God in Christ!

Godly Responses to Trials

Hopefully now we can understand why Paul would write that we are counted as sheep for the slaughter. Paul lived in the knowledge of Christ's great condescension—that God the Father gave him a costly gift in Christ the Son. That is, while we were sinners Christ died for us (Rom. 5:8). What a tremendous outpouring of love! Octavius Winslow (1808–1878) makes a penetrating observation regarding the depths of God's love for us in Christ:

> As of yet, how many of us stand but upon the shore of this ocean! How little do we know experimentally, of the love of Christ in our souls, dislodging slavish fear, a bondage spirit, unbelieving doubt, and so enlarging our hearts that we may run the way of the Lord's commandments. Bring your heart with its profoundest emptiness, its most startling discovery of sin, its lowest frame, its deepest sorrow, and sink it into the depths of the Savior's love. That infinite sea will flow over all, erase all, absorb all, and your soul shall swim and sport amid its gentle waves, exclaiming in your joy and transport, "Oh the depths!" The Lord direct your heart into the love of God!—just as it is, hard, cold, fickle, sinful, sad, and sorrowful. Christ's love touching your hard heart, will dissolve it; touching your cold heart, will warm it; touching your sinful heart, will purify it; touching your sorrowful heart, will soothe it; touching your wandering heart, will draw it back to Jesus. Only bring your heart to Christ's love. Believe in its existence, its reality, its fullness, and its freeness.[2]

We must desperately cling to this grand and majestic love and seek to give it to others. Only Christ's love and His indwelling presence can enable us to say we are ready to be counted as sheep for the slaughter. I suspect that this is one of the more difficult parts of the Christian life and our sanctification.

All too often we think our suffering is the result of sin or that somehow God has failed to consider all the details of our particular case. When we discover that we, or a loved one, has been stricken by serious illness, is our first response one of joy? Is our first thought "Thank you Lord, for You have counted me worthy to manifest your

2. Winslow, *Sympathy of Christ*, 166–67.

power and might through my weakness. When I am weak, You are strong. Thank You for deeming me worthy to manifest the sufferings of Your Son in my life. Strengthen me that I would be faithful and not forget that You continually love me"? I suspect this is not our first thought, but by God's grace we should all hope and pray that it would be. In other circumstances, such as being wrongly accused of sin or error, our usual first reaction is to demand vindication. We want everyone to know the righteousness of our cause. On the one hand, this is perfectly understandable, but this impulse can become deadly to our sanctification. Our quest for vindication can become an idol to self rather than a manifestation of the cross of Christ.

Conclusion

No matter how things might appear, we should never forget that the Father has poured out His love on us in Christ and that He uses every event, even our trials and sufferings, to conform us to the image of His Son. So, then, live in the knowledge of Christ's wonderful love for you. Remember that the new heavens and earth have dawned, but we are still being conformed to the image of Christ in the midst of this present evil age. As you walk through the valley of the shadow of death, look to the heavens to where you are seated with Christ, and breathe in the life-giving air of the new creation. Immerse yourself in Christ's love, draw nigh unto Him, and encourage those around you to seek His love. Share the message of His love with others—we who have been loved so much should desire to love others as much as we can (Heb. 10:24–25; 1 John 4:9–12). As we continue on our pilgrim journey to the new Jerusalem, remember that in all our sufferings and trials we are more than conquerors and that *nothing* will separate us from God's love in Christ.

27

The Preface to Predestination

ROMANS 9:1–5

I tell the truth in Christ, I am not lying, my conscience also bearing me witness in the Holy Spirit, that I have great sorrow and continual grief in my heart. For I could wish that I myself were accursed from Christ for my brethren, my countrymen according to the flesh, who are Israelites, to whom pertain the adoption, the glory, the covenants, the giving of the law, the service of God, and the promises; of whom are the fathers and from whom, according to the flesh, Christ came, who is over all, the eternally blessed God. Amen.

If one passage of Scripture has famously been the location of many pitched theological battles, it is Romans 9. In this chapter Paul sets forth the doctrine of predestination, which the Westminster Larger Catechism defines as the "eternal and immutable decree, out of his mere love, for the praise of his glorious grace, to be manifested in due time, [God] hath elected some angels to glory; and in Christ hath chosen some men to eternal life" (A. 13). One of the passages that the Westminster divines cite in support of their definition is Romans 9:17–18, 21–22. I think it is only natural that statements such as "Jacob I have loved, but Esau I have hated" (Rom. 9:13) draw us into Paul's argument with rapt attention, or perhaps even utter horror. How can God, after all, love some and hate others? But I suspect that one of the things people do all too frequently is ignore or pass by the first five verses of this famous passage of Scripture. In the same way that we skip the preface in a book to get to the meat, we miss important and crucial details.

The overall impression we might have is that Paul has just scaled the heights of glory in Romans 8 by discussing the unsurpassed love of God in Christ for His people, but then, all of a sudden, he has too quickly, and with little explanation, changed theological topics. But if we pay careful attention to what Paul has written, his transition to predestination makes perfect sense. Paul has significantly challenged the common Jewish conception of how God saves people. Many Israelites in Paul's day believed they would be saved because of their circumcision and observance of the law. Paul, however, told his readers that no flesh would be justified in God's sight by works of the law (Rom. 3:20). Moreover, circumcision was not the means of their salvation but rather a sign and seal of righteousness received by faith alone (Rom. 4:11). Paul's point from the very outset of the epistle is that the gospel is first for the Jew and then the Greek (Rom. 1:17) and that anyone who believes in Jesus by faith alone, Jew or Greek, will be justified (Rom. 3:20–5:21).

These statements and arguments undoubtedly had many Jews asking, "But what about God's promises to Israel? What about His promises to Abraham, Isaac, and Jacob?" If Gentiles are on equal footing with Jews, then has God forgotten His people? These questions give Paul reason to discuss the doctrine of election. But vital to this doctrine are the words that precede his explanation. Paul is in no way calculating, cold, or indifferent. Paul's earnest desire was to see his brothers in the flesh saved by Christ, but he also recognized that their salvation was ultimately not up to him. He had to bow before his sovereign Lord and recognize himself as the creature and God as the Creator.

Paul's Anguished Heart

When we consider the depths of God's love that Paul recounts in the previous chapter, especially the idea that we are more than conquerors through Christ and that nothing can separate us from God's love in His Son (Rom. 8:37–39), I suspect that Paul was both thrilled and anguished. He was thrilled because of the incomparable love of God, of which he was a recipient—Saul the persecutor of the church was now Paul the apostle, whose heart was set afire with zeal to serve Christ. But he was also likely filled with anguish because he knew that so many of his fellow Israelites hated God and were separated from Christ. Like a beggar at a sumptuous meal, he was desperate to tell other beggars where they too could find refreshment, rest, and food for their weak and wearied souls.

Paul's agony surfaces in the way he begins this ninth chapter: "I tell the truth in Christ, I am not lying, my conscience also bearing me witness in the Holy Spirit" (Rom. 9:1). Paul starts with a threefold emphasis on the veracity of his testimony. In the Hebrew language you signal the superlative by repeating the key word. The prophet Isaiah, for example, did not say God is the *holiest* but that He is "holy, holy, holy" (Isa. 6:3). The seraphim repeated the word to denote the superlative. Christ offered a similar verbal pattern when He told His disciples "For assuredly, I say to you" (Matt. 5:18) when He wanted to emphasize the veracity or importance of His teaching. Note, then, Paul's threefold emphasis: (1) "I tell the truth in Christ," (2) "I am not lying," (3) "my conscience also bearing me witness in the Holy Spirit." What Paul writes is the absolute, unvarnished truth.

What did Paul want his readers to know? Paul wanted them to know of his heart's anguish: "That I have great sorrow and continual grief in my heart. For I could wish that I myself were accursed from Christ for my brethren, my countrymen according to the flesh" (Rom. 9:2–3). Paul likely felt the need to emphasize the truthfulness of what he wrote for two reasons. First, anyone who had been beaten, mistreated, and reviled like Paul by his fellow countrymen would have good reason to dislike or even hate his brothers (cf. 2 Cor. 11:23–25). It may, therefore, have come as a surprise to Paul's recipients that he had great sorrow and anguish in his heart for his fellow Jews. Paul embodied the life of Christ, who told His disciples that they had to love their enemies (Matt. 5:43–48). Paul loved his persecutors.

Second, Paul had to emphasize the veracity of his statements because of the depth of his love for his fellow countrymen—he was willing to be cut off, cursed, and even damned for the sake of his brothers. In other words, Paul was willing to trade places with his unbelieving brothers, were that possible, so that they could be saved. Few of us have attained such a level of sanctification—our hearts break, we shed tears, and we grieve for the lost, but seldom, I suspect, are we willing to trade places with them, especially with those who have persecuted us. Instead, most Christians think that their persecutors will get what they deserve—judgment. But not Paul, who, like Moses, was willing to be blotted out of the Book of Life for the sake of Israel (Ex. 32:32–33).

Now, before we proceed, Paul's words are of the utmost importance as we consider what follows in the ninth chapter. These words should resonate in our hearts because it demonstrates the character of a true theologian. As he pondered and meditated on the doctrine of election, he did not approach it as if he were looking at the bottom line in a ledger—looking at the elect and the non-elect as if they were mere numbers on a page, beans to be counted. So often discussions, and sadly arguments, about election devolve into cold and abstract pontifications rather than heartrending meditations on the sovereignty of God in the salvation and judgment of living and breathing *people*. For Paul, election was far from abstract—he was about to unfold matters pertaining to salvation and damnation, heaven and hell.

Israel's Great Privilege

I believe Paul's concern for his countrymen was intensified because of their great privileged state. As Paul commented earlier in his letter, "For as many as have sinned without law [Torah] will also perish without law [Torah], and as many as have sinned in the law [Torah] will be judged by the law [Torah]" (Rom. 2:12). In other words, Israel was privileged in comparison with the Gentile nations because God gave them the law, the Torah. But God did not merely give Israel the Torah. On the contrary, "[My brethren] who are Israelites, to whom pertain the adoption, the glory, the covenants, the giving of the law, the service of God, and the promises; of whom are the fathers and from whom, according to the flesh, Christ came, who is over all, the eternally blessed God. Amen" (Rom. 9:4–5). Paul lists blessing upon blessing to demonstrate Israel's great privilege. God formally adopted Israel when He told Moses to demand of Pharaoh, "Israel is My son, My firstborn. So I say to you, let My son go that he may serve Me" (Ex. 4:22–23). Israel beheld the glory of the Lord in their deliverance from Egypt (Ex. 15:6) as He led them by the pillar of fire by night and cloud by day (Ex. 13:21–22) and in His glory-cloud presence as He descended on the tabernacle and later the temple to dwell in Israel's midst (1 Chron. 7:1–2). The Gentiles knew nothing of these blessings. Israel alone was privileged to be in covenant with God, which was manifest in the covenant promises God made to Abraham, Isaac, Jacob, Moses, and David in the various administrations of the one covenant of grace. They alone received God's written law on tablets of stone, and they alone basked in the glory of the one true living God as they worshipped Him.

But as great as all these blessings were, the pinnacle of Israel's privilege is that they were the one race out of the entire earth given the honor of manifesting the one true living God according to the flesh: "Christ came, who is over all, the eternally blessed God. Amen" (Rom. 9:5). Paul's statement stuns on several fronts. First, he specifically identifies the one true God with the God of Israel. Second, he identifies Jesus Christ (e.g., Rom. 1:1) as "God," one of the New Testament's many affirmations of Christ's deity. But third, this is a striking admission for Paul, a Jew, to make. Given the general Jewish reception of Christ, Paul was definitely swimming against the tide of public opinion. Recall that the Jews rejected Jesus and preferred the kingship of Caesar to Christ (John 19:15). Yet this crucified brigand was the very man whom Paul upheld as God in the flesh—indeed, God over all! This undoubtedly filled Paul's heart with praise and agony—the one true God had come in the flesh, and came to Israel, but Israel rejected Him! Paul was very much aware of the idea that with great privilege comes tremendous responsibility. Correlatively, the reception of the supreme and exclusive revelation of God in Christ means great benefits (salvation) and awful consequences (damnation). And as Paul looked over his countrymen and saw their rejection of Christ, his heart filled with sorrow.

A Heart for the Lost

In light of these opening verses in the ninth chapter, I hope we now have a better appreciation for their significance in the overall flow of Paul's letter. More often than not we likely pass by these verses and jump straight to Romans 9:13, "Jacob I have loved, but Esau I have hated." Yet Paul shows us so many important things here that we dare not pass them by. First, do we see the Christlike heart of the apostle Paul in these verses? How many of us would willingly stand in the breach for those who had so vehemently and violently persecuted us? I daresay few, if any of us, would truly be able to say this. Does this not show us what our attitudes should be toward the lost and perishing? Do our hearts yearn and ache for the lost? Does it break our hearts to see people rebel against Christ?

Second, do we realize the gravity of the subject of predestination? So many commentators try to argue that Paul does not speak of the predestination of individuals but rather of nations. Jacob, they argue, signifies the people of God as a corporate entity—Paul therefore argues for predestination to service rather than salvation. Would Paul, however, be so distraught and willing to be cursed if he were talking only about predestination to service? Paul knows that salvation and damnation rest in the balance—those who reject Christ, God incarnate, are damned to hell. These are indeed weighty matters.

Third, do we see how genealogical descent and birth within the visible covenant community does not guarantee one's salvation? Paul lists the exalted nature of the Jews as the recipients of God's revelatory and providential favor, yet this did not guarantee their salvation. Just because you are born within the church does not mean that you are automatically saved. Salvation is not by works, circumcision, baptism, genealogical descent, or mere association with the church. Salvation is by faith alone in Christ alone by grace alone. Judas is certainly evidence of this—he sat at the feet of Christ for three years and still was not saved; he was a son of perdition (John 17:12).

This is an important truth that Paul will explain in the verses that follow, but we should certainly begin to meditate on these issues as Paul raises them here.

Conclusion

All these things should cause us to reflect on our attitudes toward the electing grace of God. Do we recognize our status as fellow beggars who have been graciously invited to the great wedding feast of the Lamb? Do we recognize that even our wedding garments, the imputed righteousness of Christ, are not our own? We may possess them, but we do not own them. Ours is an alien righteousness graciously imputed to us by faith alone. Do our hearts yearn to see those who are lost become saved? Do we take pride in our holiness and our ability to obey God when it is not something in which we can or should boast? Our holiness and righteousness is not our own—it is the gift of God. Do we rest on our laurels because we associate with the people of God or because we regularly attend church? Do we place an unbiblical confidence in our baptism? Do we seek shelter from the coming wrath of God under the blood of the Lamb? Paul's words should certainly echo in our hearts and minds as we reflect on these important questions. Or, in the words of Isaac Watts's famous hymn "How Sweet and Awesome Is the Place,"

> While all our hearts and all our songs
> Join to admire the feast,
> Each of us cries, with thankful tongue,
> "Lord, why was I a guest?"
>
> "Why was I made to hear your voice
> And enter while there's room,
> When thousands make a wretched choice,
> And rather starve than come?"
>
> 'Twas the same love that spread the feast
> That sweetly drew us in;
> Else we had still refused to taste,
> And perished in our sin.

Pity the nations, O our God,
Constrain the earth to come;
Send your victorious Word abroad,
And bring the strangers home.

We long to see your churches full,
That all the chosen race
May with one voice and heart and soul,
Sing your redeeming grace.

28

Jacob and Esau

ROMANS 9:6–13

But it is not that the word of God has taken no effect. For they are not all Israel who are of Israel, nor are they all children because they are the seed of Abraham; but, "In Isaac your seed shall be called." That is, those who are the children of the flesh, these are not the children of God; but the children of the promise are counted as the seed. For this is the word of promise: "At this time I will come and Sarah shall have a son." And not only this, but when Rebecca also had conceived by one man, even by our father Isaac (for the children not yet being born, nor having done any good or evil, that the purpose of God according to election might stand, not of works but of Him who calls), it was said to her, "The older shall serve the younger." As it is written, "Jacob I have loved, but Esau I have hated."

The doctrine of predestination is one of those scriptural truths that can be difficult to understand and embrace. I can remember struggling with the sovereignty of God in salvation until a valued friend told me to read and reread the ninth chapter of Romans until I surrendered my claim on my salvation. I finally surrendered and recognized that God is sovereign and I am not; He is the Creator and I am but a mere creature. In the words of Martin Luther, "Following the order of this Epistle: first be concerned about Christ and the gospel, in order to recognize your sin and His grace; then fight against your sins.... Adam must first be quite dead before a man is able to bear this subject and to drink this strong wine. Watch that you do not drink wine while you are still an infant. Every doctrine has its limit, time, and age."[1] In other words, we must pray for spiritual maturity as we contemplate the truth of God's sovereign election in salvation.

Romans 9:1–5 gave a glimpse into Paul's heart—his sorrow and anguish for his fellow brothers in the flesh, his fellow Israelites. Paul mourned over their great privileges—the covenants, promises, adoption, glory, and the Scriptures—but yet they still rejected the Christ, who is God over all. The natural question is, If Israel has not embraced the Messiah, then has God failed to keep His word? Is God unfaithful to His promises? The quick answer to this question is no! God's word has not failed. Paul, however, does explain why every rank-and-file Israelite has not embraced Christ. He explains how God defines Israel—the lines fall where God decides by His sovereign will, not along lines of genealogical descent or human decisions. God defines Israel by His promise. Such a truth certainly reminds us of our place. All too often we treat God as if He were the accused and we are the judge and jury. But this passage tells us that we are the creature and He is the Creator; He is the judge, and we are in the dock.

Not by Genes

After Paul's expressed sorrow over Israel's rejection of Christ, he immediately explains that God's word has not failed: "But it is not that the word of God has taken no effect. For they are not all Israel who are of Israel, nor are they all children because they are the seed of Abraham; but, 'In Isaac your seed shall be called'" (Rom. 9:6–7). God's word accomplishes His purposes and goals. Paul's contemporaries undoubtedly thought that their physical descent, their DNA, constituted the ground of their acceptability before God. When the Pharisees, for example, challenged Christ's claim that He was the Son of God, they told Him that Abraham was their father (John 8:39). Yes, the Jews, the physical descendants of Abraham, received the covenant promises of God. Nevertheless, Paul has already informed

---

1. Luther, *What Luther Says*, 1:455–56, no. 1347.

his recipients that God does not save by genealogical descent: "For he is not a Jew who is one outwardly, nor is circumcision that which is outward in the flesh; but he is a Jew who is one inwardly; and circumcision is that of the heart, in the Spirit, not in the letter; whose praise is not from men but from God" (Rom. 2:28–29). Just because one physically descends from Abraham, or was circumcised in the flesh of his foreskin, does not make him a *true* Jew or a *true* Israelite. As Paul elsewhere writes, "Therefore know that only those who are of faith are sons of Abraham" (Gal. 3:7).

Within the immediate context, Paul quotes Genesis 21:12 to make his point: "In Isaac your seed shall be called" (Rom. 9:7). This is not a reference to Isaac's physical descent, as some might quickly assume, but rather the faith that Abraham had in God's promise to give him offspring. Recall that Abraham and Sarah were as good as dead, but God promised Abraham that he would have an heir from his own body (Gen. 15:1–6; Rom. 4:17–22). This event is prima facie evidence that God kept His promises and that His word is effectual—He promised Abraham a son, and He delivered. Yet Abraham's son did not originate exclusively from natural means but through God's promise. This event also reveals that God's promise, not physical descent, is all-determinative in establishing who belongs to Israel. The presence or absence of faith in Christ defines who belongs to Israel, and as such, true Jews and true Israelites arise from every tribe, tongue, and nation, including from among the physical descendants of Abraham. God has not forgotten His covenant promises. Rather, many Israelites have misunderstood His word and devalued the significance of His promises. In the verses that follow, Paul further expands on the nature of God's promise: "That is, those who are the children of the flesh, these are not the children of God; but the children of the promise are counted as the seed. For this is the word of promise: 'At this time I will come and Sarah shall have a son'" (Rom. 9:8–9). Faith, not DNA, defines who belongs to Israel.

God's Purpose

Even still, some looked at Isaac's situation and naturally assumed that surely he was one of God's people. But Isaac had a half brother, Ishmael, who was excluded from God's covenant promise (Gen. 17:18–21). Ishmael was not the child of the promise—he was not a pure Israelite, because he was born of Hagar, Sarah's handmaiden. So Paul takes the next step of the patriarchal history and briefly examines the events surrounding the birth of Isaac's sons, Jacob and Esau: "And not only this, but when Rebecca also had conceived by one man, even by our father Isaac (for the children not yet being born, nor having done any good or evil, that the purpose of God according to election might stand, not of works but of Him who calls), it was said to her, 'The older shall serve the younger.' As it is written, 'Jacob I have loved, but Esau I have hated'" (Rom. 9:10–13). To demonstrate that God's purposes prevail over man's desires, Paul notes that God did not consider Jacob and Esau's future actions in His decision to choose one over the other, as Paul clearly states, "for the children not yet being born, nor having done any good or evil." Moreover, one element that makes his point especially powerful is that Jacob and Esau were children of the same father and mother—even twins, born on the same day. Despite Jacob and Esau's sharing the same parents, and even womb, God decided to choose one over the other. He even went against Israelite practice that the firstborn son was to be the heir, the one who would receive the double portion of the inheritance (Deut. 21:17). Rather than follow expected Israelite custom, God told Isaac that the older, Esau, would serve the younger, Jacob. All this revealed God's purpose of election.

Paul also picks up on a theme that he previously developed, especially as it relates to the doctrine of justification. Throughout chapters 3–4 Paul made a steady drumbeat that our works have nothing to do with our justification: "Therefore by the deeds of the law no flesh will be justified in His sight, for by the law is the knowledge of sin" (Rom. 3:20; 3:27–28; 4:2, 4, 6). He also mentioned the fact that our salvation finds its genesis in God's love and sovereign choice: "Moreover whom He predestined, these He also called; whom He called, these He also justified; and whom He justified, these He also glorified" (Rom. 8:30). Hence Paul reiterates this point here when he says that God's purpose in election is first and foremost, not our desires: "That the purpose of God according to election might stand, not of works but of Him who calls" (Rom. 9:11). As we will see in the sections to follow, God's chief purpose is to magnify and glorify His name, which He does in the salvation of His chosen people and in the judgment of the wicked. So even with these two children, both of whom were physically descended from Abraham, God chose one over the other, the younger over the older, apart from any consideration of works.

Paul quotes from the prophet Malachi to punctuate his argument: "Jacob I have loved, but Esau I have hated" (Rom. 9:13; Mal. 1:2–3). As brief as Paul's quotation is, there is a profound point embedded in these nine words (seven in the Greek text). Paul presents twins born from the same father and both raised under the umbrella of God's covenant promises to Abraham and Isaac. But as we know from the patriarchal history, Esau forsook his birthright and interest in the covenant and Jacob received the blessing of the firstborn, the blessings of God's covenant promises. Only by God's sovereign election did Jacob, a deceiver and a conniver, receive God's covenant blessings. By contrast, even though Esau physically descended from Isaac, the Scriptures characterize him very differently—he was "a fornicator" and "profane," someone who sold his interest in God's covenant promises for "one morsel of food" (Heb. 12:16). Esau was not only profane, cut off from God's covenant by virtue of his own sinful disinterest, but he also gave birth to an entire people, the Edomites, who were cut off from God's covenant promises and who would eventually fall under God's righteous judgment (Gen. 27:39–40; Jer. 49:8–10; Obad. 8–9, 18–19; Mal. 1:1–4). Before the foundation of the world, God set His love on Jacob and chose him so that he would be called, justified, and glorified. By contrast, God did not set His love on Esau. With God there is no middle ground—God is not indifferent toward people. He either loves or hates them. And by *hate* we should recognize that God's hatred is holy and pure, unlike our own sinful manifestations of hatred.

Our Need for Humility

Paul displays God's awesome attributes and shows how He has fulfilled His covenant promise to Abraham—His word never wavered. I think it is fair to say, however, that His promise has differed from the sinful expectations of Paul's fellow Jews. God is sovereign in salvation—God saves by His sovereign dispensation of saving grace and nothing else. If we read these statements in the broader context of Paul's epistle, we also know from Romans 1:18–3:19 that all people, Jew and Gentile, deserve to fall under God's wrath and judgment. The miracle is that God chooses to save anyone. When all humanity rightfully falls under God's just wrath, the amazing thing is that He showers some of Adam's fallen children with His love. God's election, remember, is not an intellectual choice—He does choose, He makes a decision, but it is one driven and motivated by love. As Paul writes elsewhere, "in love, having predestined us to adoption as sons by Jesus Christ to Himself" (Eph. 1:4c–5). And as we know from Romans 8:38–39, God sets His love on us before the foundation of the world and never takes it away: "For I am persuaded that neither death nor life, nor angels nor principalities nor powers, nor things present nor things to come, nor height nor depth, nor any other created thing, shall be able to separate us from the love of God which is in Christ Jesus our Lord" (Rom. 8:38–39). God's promises, therefore, and His word, are effectual! They do not fail.

These truths should cause us to fear the Lord—not in the sense of a servile fear but in the sense of awe and reverence. Indeed, how many of us forget that God is not only a God of love but also of wrath and justice. If the God we worship has no wrath or justice, if the God we worship does not exercise His righteous justice against sinful man, then we do not worship the God of Scripture but an idol of our imagination. We must not be afraid to declare the full counsel of God, the bad news, God's judgment on unbelief and rebellion, and the good news, the mercy for those who are in Christ.

Paul makes this very point at the outset of Romans: "For in it the righteousness of God is revealed from faith to faith; as it is written, 'The just shall live by faith.' For the wrath of God is revealed from heaven against all ungodliness and unrighteousness of men, who suppress the truth in unrighteousness" (Rom. 1:17–18).

Upon further reflection on these truths, we should recognize our need for great humility. Paul has struck a deathblow to the idea that man can save himself. The Jews could not and cannot save themselves by their works, observing the law, circumcision, or by genealogical descent. This of course means that we cannot save ourselves either. If we intellectually recognize these truths, especially in the Reformed community, then why do our ranks swell with prideful people? We, of all people, we who cling to the truth of election, the sovereignty of God in salvation, should be the humblest group within the church at large. If we recognize that God has saved us by His sovereign will and not because there is anything attractive about us, then our boasting should be in Christ alone: "For who makes you differ from another? And what do you have that you did not receive? Now if you did indeed receive it, why do you boast as if you had not received it?" (1 Cor. 4:7).

Conclusion

This passage should cause us to reflect on God's faithfulness throughout the ages and learn to evaluate it by His word and not our sinful expectations. Though we were outside of the covenant, God has reached down and saved us—He has made us children of Abraham. In the words of Augustus Toplady's (1740–1778) hymn "How Vast the Benefits Divine:"

> How vast the benefits divine
> Which we in Christ possess!
> We are redeemed from guilt and shame
> And called to holiness.
> But not for works which we have done,
> Or shall hereafter do,

Hath God decreed on sinful men
Salvation to bestow.

The glory, Lord, from first to last,
Is due to thee alone;
Aught to ourselves we dare not take,
Or rob thee of thy crown.
Our glorious Surety undertook
To satisfy for man,
And grace was given us in him
Before the world began.

This is thy will, that in thy love
We ever should abide;
That earth and hell should not prevail
To turn thy word aside.
Not one of all the chosen race
But shall to heav'n attain,
Partake on earth the purposed grace
And then with Jesus reign.

29

The Righteousness of God

ROMANS 9:14–18

What shall we say then? Is there unrighteousness with God? Certainly not! For He says to Moses, "I will have mercy on whomever I will have mercy, and I will have compassion on whomever I will have compassion." So then it is not of him who wills, nor of him who runs, but of God who shows mercy. For the Scripture says to the Pharaoh, "For this very purpose I have raised you up, that I may show My power in you, and that My name may be declared in all the earth." Therefore He has mercy on whom He wills, and whom He wills He hardens.

In our democratic culture people constantly seek fairness in every aspect of life. When people go to buy a car, they want a fair deal. When they pay taxes, they want to make sure they have to pay only their fair share. And certainly when anything has a direct influence on their lives, they want to make sure that people treat them fairly. This mentality also impacts humanity's beliefs about God and salvation. One of the most common ideas that we find in the church is that God gives everyone a chance to accept or reject Him. This is, after all, the fairest way to go about it. But such opinions are not confined to our own day. You can only imagine that Paul's fellow Jews had significant questions when he told them that salvation was based on God's purpose in election and not on their genealogical descent or their adherence to the law. The most pressing question was likely, How can that be fair? But such a question belies a backward opinion about the relative places of God and man. If sinful man accuses God of injustice, the roles have been reversed.

How can a sinful person see clearly enough to decide whether our holy and perfectly upright God has been unfair? So at this stage in Paul's explanation of predestination, he addresses the question of the apparent inequity in God's sovereignty in salvation.

But before we proceed, it is important that we note a few things about our investigation of predestination. John Calvin has famously noted that predestination "is truly a labyrinth from which the mind of man is wholly incapable of extricating itself." As we discover this truth, we become curious and boldly rush into places where only fools dare to tread. We impetuously plunge headlong into the depths of God's mind and quickly find ourselves blinded by His brilliance and glory. This experience elicits two diametrically opposed responses: People either engage in unwarranted and sinful speculation about predestination or they recognize that they must stay firmly fixed on God's revelation, His Word. This is Calvin's counsel:

> Since the Holy Spirit has taught us nothing but what it is to our interest to know, this knowledge will undoubtedly be useful to us, provided we shall confine it to the Word of God. Let this, therefore, be our sacred rule, not to seek to know anything about it except what Scripture teaches us. Where the Lord closes His holy mouth, let us also stop our minds from going on further. Since, however, these foolish questions will come naturally to us, being what we are, let us hear from Paul how they are to be met.[1]

As we proceed, therefore, we need to stay closely affixed to Scripture so that we do not wander off the path. In so doing, we will see that Paul not only exonerates God from any wrongdoing but shows that God is unchanging in His ways. Paul reaches back to the Old Testament and Israel's exodus from Egypt to show why He chooses some and rejects others.

1. Calvin, *Romans and Thessalonians*, 202–3.

Is God Unrighteous?

Paul grabs the proverbial bull by the horns and asks the question, "What shall we say then? Is there unrighteousness with God? Certainly not!" (Rom. 9:14). As quickly as he poses the question he sweeps it away with his famous, "Certainly not!" How could that possibly be? How could God, in whom there is no shadow of turning, be unrighteous or unfair in His treatment of fallen, sinful people? Why should God save anyone? If God were to deal justly with sinners, He would condemn them all. But instead, He mercifully saves many out of Adam's fallen, sinful children. Even then, I suspect that some of Paul's fellow Jews recognized this fact but would have objected to Paul's arguments because he precluded all reference and consideration of works: "(for the children not yet being born, nor having done any good or evil, that the purpose of God according to election might stand, not of works but of Him who calls), it was said to her, 'The older shall serve the younger.' As it is written, 'Jacob I have loved, but Esau I have hated'" (Rom. 9:11–13). The knee-jerk response to Paul's argument—indeed, even to this day—is "That's not fair!" This is why Paul asks if there is any unrighteousness with God, to which he responds with a resounding and emphatic "Certainly not!"

Paul's emphatic dismissal of the charge of unrighteousness is certainly understandable, but what we might expect is his appeal to the Old Testament to support his point. On the heels of the accusation of unrighteousness with God, Paul sets forth exhibit A, quoting Exodus 33:19, in his defense of God's righteousness: "For He says to Moses, 'I will have mercy on whomever I will have mercy, and I will have compassion on whomever I will have compassion'" (Rom. 9:15). Why does Paul quote this verse from Exodus? As with any statement from Scripture, the broader context provides vital information for proper comprehension. Right before God said, "I will have compassion on whom I will have compassion," Moses asked him a question: "Please, show me Your glory" (Ex. 33:18). Moses was one of the very few people in redemptive history who was privileged to converse directly with God. The Lord responded to Moses's question: "I will make all My goodness pass before you, and I will proclaim the name of the LORD before you. I will be gracious to whom I will be gracious, and I will have compassion on whom I will have compassion" (Ex. 33:19). At first glance, the Lord's response might not make sense. God's actions after Moses's request seem understandable—God cloistered Moses in the cleft of a rock and allowed him to see His "back" (Ex. 33:22–23). This is the same glory that illuminated Moses's face and made him glow long after he descended from atop Sinai (Ex. 34:29–35). This all makes sense. So how does God's announcement fit Moses's question? And more specifically, how does this response fit with Paul's argument in his defense of God's righteousness?

God's glory is manifest in the brilliance that emanates from His presence, such that it made Moses's face light up with the reflective glory of God. But God also reveals His glory in His activity, both in salvation and condemnation. We must recognize, worship, and herald all God's attributes: His omnipotence, holiness, omniscience, love, *and* justice. In other words, if we worship God only for His love and ignore His justice, then we do not worship the one, true, living God but an idol of our own fabrication. Hence, when Moses asked to see God's glory, not only did he bask in the brilliance of God's presence but he also heard God declare, "I will be gracious to whom I will be gracious, and I will have compassion on whom I will have compassion" (Ex. 33:19). God shows His glory in revealing His sovereign will concerning the objects of His mercy and love as well as the objects of His perfect and holy justice and wrath. God shows unmerited mercy and grace to the elect and gives the non-elect His just wrath.

Paul drills down into the events of the exodus to elaborate on the theme of God's glory in His sovereign dispensation of mercy and justice. Paul writes: "For the Scripture says to the Pharaoh, 'For this very purpose I have raised you up, that I may show My power in you, and that My name may be declared in all the earth.' Therefore He has mercy on whom He wills, and whom He wills He hardens" (Rom. 9:17–18). Paul appeals to God's interaction with Pharaoh to explain the purpose of His display of justice and wrath. God raised Pharaoh so that He could demonstrate and reveal His justice against sin and disbelief. Moreover, by demonstrating His justice and wrath against Pharaoh and the Egyptians, He also displayed His mercy through the deliverance of His people. The former serves as the contrasting background for the latter.

But we must understand the nature of how God hardened Pharaoh's heart. Remember, Paul emphatically denies that there is any unrighteousness in God. We can therefore safely rule out the idea that God directly created evil in Pharaoh's heart the same way He creates holiness in the heart of the elect. So, then, how did God harden Pharaoh's heart? God hardens the hearts of the non-elect by removing His hand of restraint—the hand that keeps people from plunging headlong into wickedness. This is the way Paul describes God's judgment against the unbelief of the wicked: "Professing to be wise, they became fools, and changed the glory of the incorruptible God into an image made like corruptible man—and birds and four-footed animals and creeping things. Therefore *God also gave them up* to uncleanness, in the lusts of their hearts, to dishonor their bodies among themselves" (Rom. 1:22–24, emphasis added). When God removes His hand of restraint, people plunge headlong into wickedness. This is a sovereign act of God's justice against the non-elect.

Remembering Our Place

Do we see the attitude that Paul refutes? How is it possible that Paul's recipients could accuse God of unrighteousness in His dealings with the Jews and with humanity in general? C. S. Lewis (1898–1963) best captures the attitude Paul refuted:

> The ancient man approached God (or even the gods) as the accused person approaches his judge. For the modern man the roles are reversed. Man is the judge: God is in the dock. Man is quite a kindly judge: if God should have a reasonable defense for being the god who permits war, poverty and disease, he is ready to listen to it. The trial may even end in God's

> acquittal. But the important thing is that Man is on the Bench and God in the Dock.[2]

This is certainly the attitude many bring to God both here in Romans 9 as well as any time that the doctrine of election is discussed. Theologians attempt to soften Paul's words by claiming that God gives everyone the ability to believe so that it places the onus of rejection on man, not God. It sounds very democratic and fair, does it not, that God gives each person the opportunity to choose or reject Christ? Yet, if this were the case, if God truly did give everyone the ability to believe, then why would Paul answer the charge that God is unrighteous in His dealings with man? After all, what would be more equitable? If a man rejects God, then it is totally his own doing—God gives everyone the same chance, right?

No! If this were the true state of affairs, then why would Paul refute the charge of injustice on the part of God? Indeed, God decides, not man. Moreover, if Adam, living in a perfect world and having no sin nature, did not choose God, then what makes us think that we, with a sin nature in a fallen world, can fare any better? There are others who are precisely the type of individuals that Lewis describes. I watched a documentary where various religious scholars rejected the idea that God would or could ordain the terrorist attacks of 9/11. Some alluded to the Reformed belief in the sovereignty of God, which is biblical doctrine, and said that they could not and would not worship such a God. Now, if this is the attitude toward the sovereignty of God in providence, imagine the vehemence that would be leveled against God for His sovereign choice in the salvation and damnation of men.

Man fails to consider his place before God. Recall what Paul said about sinful man: No one seeks God, not one—all hate God (Rom. 3:10–18). After reading passages that describe man's condition, we must affirm with Calvin that humanity is utterly sinful: "Let us hold this, then, as an undoubted truth, which no opposition can

---

2. C. S. Lewis, "God in the Dock," in *God in the Dock: Essays on Theology and Ethics*, ed. Walter Hooper (Grand Rapids: Eerdmans, 1970), 244.

ever shake—that the mind of man is so completely alienated from the righteousness of God, that it conceives, desires, and undertakes every thing that is impious, perverse, based, impure, and flagitious; that his heart is so thoroughly infected by the poison of sin, that it cannot produce any thing but what is corrupt."[3] God is under no obligation to save anyone—especially considering the fact that man is so sinful and rebellious against Him. If God were fair, He could justly condemn the entire human race. Yet do we recognize that God has not been fair or just with us but has poured out His mercy on us? So, then, far from predestination being injustice on God's part, it is a demonstration of His glorious mercy and love. This is why when Moses asked to see God's glory He told him, "I will have mercy on whomever I will have mercy, and I will have compassion on whomever I will have compassion" (Rom. 9:15). Predestination is a manifestation of God's glory because it demonstrates all His attributes—His love and wrath, His mercy and justice.

Conclusion

We must ask ourselves, What type of attitude do we bring before God as we approach His throne? Do we approach with blasphemy in our hearts by thinking that He is unrighteous in His dealings with us? Or do we approach His throne in utter humility, recognizing that we have received His immeasurable love in Christ Jesus even though we deserved His just condemnation? Remember that there is no shelter save the embassy of peace—Jesus Christ. Our works will amount to nothing for salvation—they will only add to our condemnation if we try to bring them forward rather than the perfect righteousness of Jesus Christ. And we know that we can bring forth the righteousness of Jesus Christ only if God has sovereignly chosen to give it to us. Is God unrighteous in doing this? Absolutely not! He is gracious in His dispensation of love and just in His administration of justice—herein lies the glory of our marvelous God.

---

3. Calvin, *Institutes*, 2.5.19.

30

The Potter and the Clay

ROMANS 9:19–26

You will say to me then, "Why does He still find fault? For who has resisted His will?" But indeed, O man, who are you to reply against God? Will the thing formed say to him who formed it, "Why have you made me like this?" Does not the potter have power over the clay, from the same lump to make one vessel for honor and another for dishonor? What if God, wanting to show His wrath and to make His power known, endured with much longsuffering the vessels of wrath prepared for destruction, and that He might make known the riches of His glory on the vessels of mercy, which He had prepared beforehand for glory, even us whom He called, not of the Jews only, but also of the Gentiles? As He says also in Hosea: "I will call them My people, who were not My people, And her beloved, who was not beloved." "And it shall come to pass in the place where it was said to them, 'You are not My people,' There they shall be called sons of the living God."

Over the centuries countless parents and their children have participated in an ongoing tug-of-war. Children want to do something but their parents have other ideas. The children and parents negotiate, bicker, and verbally joust back and forth. At some point the parent finally pulls rank. When the exasperated child complains, "Why can't I go to the party?" the parent responds, "Because I said so. My house, my rules. When you become the head of your own household, then you can make the rules." Regardless of the culture or even the context, we inherently know the concept that the king, boss, or parent has the right to set and make the rules—to do as he sees fit. This pattern exists in the world and ultimately reflects the very nature of God: He is the sovereign King over the cosmos, and we are subject to His rule. In a word, He is the Creator and we are creatures. The problem is, as sinful human beings, we tend to forget this all-important truth.

It should come as no surprise, then, that Paul would still answer objections to the idea of God's sovereignty in salvation. In the previous sections, Paul swept away several erroneous ideas, such as the misconception that God bases our salvation on genealogical descent or good works. He has also rejected the idea that there is any injustice in God's sovereign decisions in salvation, to choose some and reject others. Here in this portion of Romans 9 Paul addresses another objection—namely, if God chooses and enables people to believe, how can He still find fault and condemn people for their unbelief? Once again Paul answers this objection and appeals to the Old Testament to make his case. At the heart of Paul's message is the idea that we are creatures and God is the Creator.

Who Can Resist His Will?

Recall that Paul made a few statements that would undoubtedly draw questions and criticism: "For the Scripture says to the Pharaoh, 'For this very purpose I have raised you up, that I may show My power in you, and that My name may be declared in all the earth.' Therefore He has mercy on whom He wills, and whom He wills He hardens" (Rom. 9:17–18). If God has mercy on whomever He wills and hardens whomever He wills, then, "Why does He still find fault? For who has resisted His will?" (Rom. 9:19). At this point we approach the inner recesses of God's wisdom and encounter mysteries God has not revealed. If we liken the relationship between God's sovereignty and man's responsibility to an envelope, we can define its edges, size, and the type of paper from which it is made. We cannot, however, open the envelope and curiously examine its contents, which remain a mystery. Paul clearly affirms God's sovereignty in salvation, but he also affirms man's responsibility for his actions. God chose Jacob and rejected Esau, yet Esau was responsible for his own sinful actions.

We must always affirm divine sovereignty and human responsibility. If we deny either we create a monster. If we deny God's sovereignty we disregard the clear teaching of Scripture and, worse, posit an absolutely unthinkable scenario, one in which God is not in control of the world around us. If we deny God's sovereignty, then we cannot affirm with Paul that God makes all things work for good for those who are called according to His purpose (Rom. 8:28). But if we deny man's responsibility, we make God the author of sin, as He alone is responsible for all of man's actions, both good and evil. This too is an unacceptable conclusion. We must accept, therefore, the reality of God's sovereignty and man's responsibility. One of the most powerful biblical microcosms of the conundrum of divine sovereignty and human responsibility appears in Christ's crucifixion. Christ was crucified, the apostle Peter tells us, by the "determined purpose and foreknowledge of God." Yet God's definite plan was in no way exculpatory, because Peter still tells his countrymen that they "have taken [Jesus] by lawless hands, have crucified, and put to death" the Lord of glory (Acts 2:23). Peter never tries to explain how God is sovereign and sinners are responsible—he simply affirms the existence and reality of these two truths.

Who Are You, O Man?

Paul takes the same approach as Peter when he writes, "But indeed, O man, who are you to reply against God?" (Rom. 9:20a). Paul does not engage in a sophisticated theological or philosophical argument to explain this conundrum. He simply rebukes his interrogator for failing to recognize that God is the Creator and man is but a creature. Who are we as mere creatures to question God? Paul's response reminds me of the foolhardy claim of the philosopher Friedrich Nietzsche (1844–1900), who once said that God is dead.[1] Who

---

1. Friedrich Nietzsche, "The Madman," in *The Gay Science*, ed. Walter Kaufmann (1882, 1887; repr., New York: Vintage, 1974), § 125 (pp. 181–82).

is Nietzsche, a microscopic imp, to tell God Almighty, who spoke worlds into existence, that He is dead? To make his point, Paul draws on the prophetic Old Testament metaphor of the potter and the clay. God, as the potter, has the right to form His clay into whatever types of pots that He wants to make. If He wants to create some pots for worthy purposes, argues Paul, then it is His prerogative. If He wants to create some pots for dishonorable purposes, again, it is His right as the potter. Paul elaborates this point in the verses that follow: "What if God, wanting to show His wrath and to make His power known, endured with much longsuffering the vessels of wrath prepared for destruction, and that He might make known the riches of His glory on the vessels of mercy, which He had prepared beforehand for glory, even us whom He called, not of the Jews only, but also of the Gentiles?" (Rom. 9:22–24). Paul explains that God prepares certain vessels for His wrath. Paul does *not* say that God makes the non-elect evil. Rather, He gives them over to their sinfulness and removes His hand of restraint. This is not only an immediate outpouring of God's wrath, as we saw from Romans 1; God also will pour out His wrath on them in the day of judgment.

Yet Paul also explains that God pours out the riches of His glory on His vessels of mercy. It is important that we understand, once again, that God's wrath is one of His attributes—we cannot worship God and believe He is not a God of wrath. If we do, then we do not worship God but rather an idol. Also, notice what purpose the non-elect serve—they make God's power known to His vessels of mercy. In other words, recipients of God's mercy have a greater appreciation of who God is. The elect know God is mighty and holy—His wrath against the wicked instills a healthy reverence and awe for our covenant Lord. It also shows us from what we have been saved. Contrary to popular belief, we are not saved from the devil—rather, God saves us from His wrath. Paul comes full circle at this point to show that God fulfills the promises He made to Abraham. Remember that Paul was defending the idea that God has been faithful to His people. Moreover, God promised to Abraham that in his seed "all the nations of the earth shall be blessed"

(Gen. 22:18b; cf. Matt. 28:19a). This is why Paul says that God called His people "not of the Jews only, but also of the Gentiles" (Rom. 9:24). Indeed, God reveals all His attributes—both His mercy and justice, His love and His wrath—throughout all the earth. He sovereignly dispenses His mercy on His people, the descendants of Abraham, children of the promise, those who place their faith in Christ—both Jew and Gentile alike.

Paul then uses a quote from the prophet Hosea to substantiate that this has been God's plan all along: "As He says also in Hosea: 'I will call them My people, who were not My people, And her beloved, who was not beloved.' 'And it shall come to pass in the place where it was said to them, 'You are not My people,' There they shall be called sons of the living God'" (Rom. 9:25–26). In its original context, Hosea told the Israelites that God rejected them because of their refusal to worship Him. They were a nation of idolaters. God used the prophet's marriage to Gomer and the birth of their children to prophesy what would happen to the Israelites. Through the living parable of Hosea's life and his marriage to his adulterous wife, symbolic for Israel's idolatrous ways, God told the prophet to call his daughter, "Lo-Ruhamah," which literally means "no mercy" (Hos. 1:6). When the prophet's adulterous wife had another child, God informed the prophet that he was to name the child, "Lo-Ammi," which literally means "Not my people" (Hos. 1:10). Blessedly, this was not the last word of the Lord to the prophet. Paul quotes the verse from Hosea to remind his Jewish recipients that God never promised to base election on racial descent but rather on His sovereign choice: "And I will have mercy on her who had not obtained mercy; Then I will say to those who were not My people, 'You are My people!' And they shall say, 'You are my God!'" (Hos. 2:23). It was God's intention from the very beginning to bless the nations through Abraham, and Hosea reiterates this point. Paul's move is both humble and at the same time deft. Rather than attempt to delve into the mystery of divine sovereignty and human responsibility, he rests firmly on the mercies that God dispenses in Christ.

Proclaiming and Living These Truths

This passage should cause us to bow in reverence and awe before our mighty covenant Lord. So often when people, even Christians, hear of the sovereignty of God in salvation they recoil, protest, and either rebuff what the preacher says on the grounds that he has misinterpreted the passage, or simply reject what Paul writes. I once had a fellow seminarian tell me that Paul was an ordinary man just like any other and was mistaken about his views on God's sovereignty. My friend understood what Paul was saying but chose to dismiss it as the erroneous personal opinions of a mere man rather than accept it as the authoritative revelation of God through His chosen apostle. Those who might say that Paul is wrong quarrel not with the apostle but with God Himself.

Along these lines Charles Spurgeon (1834–1892) notes how quickly man kicks against the goads when it comes to God's sovereignty in salvation. Christians find the sovereignty of God a great comfort and source of assurance when they encounter trials and adversity—they rest assured in the knowledge that Christ rules over all creation and that no one can challenge His authority or remove Him from His throne. "On the other hand," writes Spurgeon,

> there is no doctrine more hated by worldlings, no truth of which they have made such a football, as the great, stupendous, but yet most certain doctrine of the Sovereignty of the infinite Jehovah. Men will allow God to be everywhere except on His throne. They will allow Him to be in His workshop to fashion worlds and make stars. They will allow Him to be in His almonry to dispense His alms and bestow His bounties. They will allow Him to sustain the earth and bear up the pillars thereof, or light the lamps of heaven, or rule the waves of the ever-moving ocean; but when God ascends His throne, his creatures then gnash their teeth. And we proclaim an enthroned God, and His right to do as He wills with His own, to dispose of His creatures as He thinks well, without consulting them in the matter; then it is that we are hissed and execrated, and then it is that men turn a deaf ear to us, for God

> on His throne is not the God they love. But it is God upon the throne that we love to preach. It is God upon His throne whom we trust.[2]

The question we must ask is, Are we going to kick against the goads or are we going to stop, drop on our faces, and worship our faithful covenant God? If we kick against the goads, then we are the proverbial beggar with a stick.

We want God's mercy, but we want it on our own terms rather than His. That God showers us in His undeserved mercy should silence our clamoring. Indeed, this is the same God throughout all redemptive history—God exhibits His wrath on His enemies so that His people recognize the righteous judgment from which they have been saved. This is the constant refrain, for example, in Israel's reflections on their exodus redemption. When the Israelites offered their song of praise, they worshipped God for His judgment against Pharaoh and Egypt, for casting them into the sea (Ex. 15:1–4). The psalmist echoes this song of praise in his own meditations on God's mercy and judgment: "To Him who divided the Red Sea in two, For His mercy endures forever; And made Israel pass through the midst of it, For His mercy endures forever; But overthrew Pharaoh and his army in the Red Sea, For His mercy endures forever" (Ps. 136:13–15). This is essentially the same song that the people of God sing as they dwell before His throne; indeed, it is the same song that we will sing on the last day: "They sing the song of Moses, the servant of God, and the song of the Lamb, saying: 'Great and marvelous are Your works, Lord God Almighty! Just and true are Your ways, O King of the saints! Who shall not fear You, O Lord, and glorify Your name? For You alone are holy. For all nations shall come and worship before You, For Your judgments have been manifested'" (Rev. 15:3–4).

We are not the arbiters of whether God is just or unjust. God is the judge of His own character and reveals in His Word that He

---

2. Charles Spurgeon, "Sermon on Matthew 20:15," as cited in A. W. Pink, *The Attributes of God* (Mulberry, Ind.: Sovereign Grace Publishers, 2002), 32–33.

is righteous, holy, and just in all His ways. Paul does not encourage us, therefore, to assume the bench in the divine courtroom but rather to remain in the seat of the accused and to revel in the fact that God has declared us righteous on the basis of an alien righteousness—that we have been delivered from His just condemnation by His own intervention. God interposed the obedience and blood of His own Son so that we could be His children and receive His mercy. When we look over at His just rejection and punishment of the non-elect, our position should not be one of criticism or doubt but rather worship, praise, and thanksgiving. We can clearly see the judgment from which we have been delivered. We will praise God because we will remember that the eternal punishment that falls on the non-elect has been borne on the shoulders of Jesus Christ, our Savior. When Jesus drank the bitter cup of God's wrath, He did so on our behalf. And in case we think that God is stingy with His mercy and that the number of the elect will be few, remember the words of the prophet Hosea: "Yet the number of the children of Israel shall be as the sand of the sea, which cannot be measured or numbered; and it shall come to pass in the place where it was said to them, 'You are not My people,' there it shall be said to them, 'You are sons of the living God'" (Hos. 1:10).

Conclusion

What more is there to say? We must recognize God's mighty sovereignty. Bask in the wonderful love God has poured out on us in Christ Jesus our Lord. Remember that God has saved us from His wrath by sending His only begotten Son to suffer the curse on our behalf. We must resist the urge to remake God in our own image and try to hide attributes that we fear. We can no more tame God than we can domesticate a wild lion. Rather than try to domesticate God, we must rest in His mercy, submit to His sovereignty, pray for humility, and herald His gospel far and wide. We must recognize that He is the potter and we are the clay, and rejoice that He has condescended to make us vessels for honorable use—for proclaiming and sharing His glory.

31

The Stumbling Stone

ROMANS 9:27–33

Isaiah also cries out concerning Israel: "Though the number of the children of Israel be as the sand of the sea, The remnant will be saved. For He will finish the work and cut it short in righteousness, Because the LORD will make a short work upon the earth." And as Isaiah said before: "Unless the LORD of Sabaoth had left us a seed, We would have become like Sodom, And we would have been made like Gomorrah." What shall we say then? That Gentiles, who did not pursue righteousness, have attained to righteousness, even the righteousness of faith; but Israel, pursuing the law of righteousness, has not attained to the law of righteousness. Why? Because they did not seek it by faith, but as it were, by the works of the law. For they stumbled at that stumbling stone. As it is written: "Behold, I lay in Zion a stumbling stone and rock of offense, And whoever believes on Him will not be put to shame."

Here in the ninth chapter Paul continues to demonstrate God's faithfulness to the covenant promises He made to Abraham and the great promises made through Jeremiah and Ezekiel regarding the salvation of the Gentiles. The Jews to whom Paul wrote might have thought that God abandoned His promises by saving Gentiles instead of Jews. This, however, was not the case. The Gentiles do not replace the Jews but from the beginning have been included with them in God's plan of salvation. Paul has labored to show in this ninth chapter that God has been faithful to His covenant promises. Paul shows that God promised to save the "children of the promise," those who trust in Christ by faith, not simply Abraham's physical descendants. He demonstrated this point by the example of Jacob and Esau—twin Israelite boys from the same parents, yet God sovereignly chose one over the other. The sovereign choice of God defines the people of God, not race, descent, or works (Rom. 9:6–8, 24–26). Naturally, Paul had to deal with common objections, such as accusations that God was unrighteous and that no one could resist His will if He was sovereign in these matters. Paul rebuffed these accusations and answered questions by appealing to the Old Testament—Moses's desire to see God's glory, His judgment against Pharaoh, and prophetic imagery of God as the potter and His creation as the clay as well as quotations from Hosea the prophet. Here in this portion of Romans 9 Paul cites Isaiah the prophet to seal his argument and prove God's faithfulness to His covenant promises, which he contrasts with Israel's faithlessness—their failed attempt to bypass God's covenant promises and establish their salvation by their own efforts. If such a path was doomed to failure for Paul's fellow countrymen, then we know our own efforts to secure salvation by our own works will equally fail.

Isaiah's Indictment

Paul opens this section of the ninth chapter with a quotation from Isaiah the prophet: "Isaiah also cries out concerning Israel: 'Though the number of the children of Israel be as the sand of the sea, The remnant will be saved. For He will finish the work and cut it short in righteousness, Because the LORD will make a short work upon the earth.' And as Isaiah said before: 'Unless the LORD of Sabaoth had left us a seed, We would have become like Sodom, And we would have been made like Gomorrah'" (Rom. 9:27–29). Paul quotes Isaiah 10:22–23, which comes from the context of a proclamation of judgment against Israel. God was going to punish them by using the Assyrians, a pagan Gentile nation, as a rod of judgment in His hand. The prophet acknowledges that Israel's numbers were great, as abundant as the "sand of the sea," a common biblical phrase for a great number. But despite Israel's numbers, God would save only a remnant from judgment. Paul employs this quotation to demonstrate that God never intended to save every rank-and-file physical descendant of Abraham—that is, the number of the elect, those predestined to salvation, is not coextensive with Abraham's biological children. Again, recall Paul's affirmations of God's righteousness throughout this chapter—God is righteous in all His dealings with sinful man, whether in salvation or damnation.

Paul's contemporaries undoubtedly rejected Paul's characterization of them. Christ's encounters with the self-righteous Pharisees confirm this, not to mention Paul's own pre-Christian self-estimation—namely, that with respect to the law, he was blameless (Phil. 3:6). Paul's personal experience and firsthand knowledge confirmed in his mind the necessity to quote Isaiah 1:9, which says that apart from God's mercy Israel would have become like Sodom and Gomorrah. In fact, at one point in Israel's history, this type of wickedness did occur in Israel. Recall when a Levite wandered into the territory of Benjamin, the hill country of Ephraim, and he took shelter in the home of one of the local residents. That night the men of the city surrounded the home, and like the wicked inhabitants of Sodom and Gomorrah, demanded that the local resident turn over his guest so they could rape him. The local man instead sent out his concubine, who was then raped and left for dead. The Levite dismembered her and sent twelve pieces to all the tribes of Israel to incite outrage against the wickedness that had occurred (Judg. 19:17–30). Israel was not immune to great wickedness; the only way they could cease from such evil was by the outpouring of God's sovereign grace, not their own moral efforts.

By Faith, Not by Works

Paul identifies Israel's chief problem in the verses that follow: "What shall we say then? That Gentiles, who did not pursue righteousness, have attained to righteousness, even the righteousness of faith; but Israel, pursuing the law of righteousness, has not attained to the law of righteousness. Why? Because they did not seek it by faith, but as it were, by the works of the law. For they stumbled at that stumbling stone. As it is written: 'Behold, I lay in Zion a stumbling stone and rock of offense, And whoever believes on Him will not be put to shame'" (Rom. 9:30–33). He posits the main thrust of his argument thus far by essentially asking, What are we to make of all this? What are we to make of the fact that the Gentiles, who were not covenanted with God, have obtained righteousness, and the Jews, who were covenanted with Him, have not? Paul explains that the Jews did not pursue the righteousness of God by faith but rather by works. This has been one of the core elements of Paul's epistle from the outset: "For in it [the gospel] the righteousness of God is revealed from faith to faith; as it is written, 'The just shall live by faith'" (Rom. 1:17).

Paul addresses this point in the next section, but we should certainly take note of it now: "For they being ignorant of God's righteousness, and seeking to establish their own righteousness, have not submitted to the righteousness of God" (Rom. 10:3). The Jews sought to secure God's favor through their works, which is impossible to do for several reasons, but most notably because it leaves grounds for boasting. Such boasting rubs completely against the grain of Scripture but certainly against the points that Paul has raised in the ninth chapter. Human boasting derogates God's purpose in salvation, which is to bring glory to His name and reveal His righteousness, not ours. As Paul elsewhere writes: "For by grace you have been saved through faith, and that not of yourselves; it is the gift of God, not of works, lest anyone should boast" (Eph. 2:8–9). Paul's fellow countrymen were supposed to rely not on their own adherence to the law but on Christ's. This is why Paul quotes Isaiah 8:14—Christ was and is "a stumbling stone and rock of offense" (Rom. 9:33).

The Whole Counsel of God

Among the many points we can note, there are at least two that deserve our attention: (1) Paul does not withdraw from preaching the whole counsel of God, and (2) he intently focuses on Christ. As plainly evident as these two points are, they are principles that the church historically has eschewed. First, note how Paul does not withdraw from preaching the whole counsel of God. The ninth chapter of Romans is Paul's response to various questions about God's fidelity to His covenant promises. I think few preachers today would respond in this manner. Why would a minister want unnecessarily to offend? Why would he want to challenge the prevailing notions of how God saves sinners? Why would Paul say that God chose Jacob over Esau apart from any consideration of their works? How is this fair? Why would he reject any and all claims about the necessity of our good works as prerequisites for our salvation? Paul does not backpedal but stands firm on the gospel and its sovereign foundation—predestination, God's sovereign and loving choice. He does not heed appeals to the lowest common denominator such as "Let's just preach Jesus" or cries of "Deeds, not creeds!" Nor does he back down because of the controversial nature of predestination.

Today the church desperately needs Paul's staunch commitment to divine revelation and the whole counsel of God. The church urgently needs preachers who herald the whole counsel of God. Preaching the whole counsel of God, even the doctrine of predestination, was the motivating factor behind the sixteenth-century Reformation. The Reformers, like John Calvin (1509–1564), Martin Luther (1483–1546), Heinrich Bullinger (1504–1575), or Zacharias Ursinus (1534–1583), were unafraid to proclaim the unfettered gospel of Christ. We must remember that we cannot improve on the Word of God, nor should we try to soften the so-called rough edges off the gospel, such as predestination. If we do this, we remove its cause for stumbling and its source of offense.

Such a commitment removes the gospel from the realm of entertainment and moral therapy, where much of the church places it, and recognizes it as the power of God unto salvation. If we try to soften its edges and remove its perceived offensive elements and present it in the trappings and accoutrements of entertainment, then we will neutralize our preaching. Nineteenth-century Danish philosopher Søren Kierkegaard (1813–1855) tells the parable of a clown in a theater that entertained his audience. This clown, however, noticed a fire in the back of the theater and began to yell out, "Smoke! Fire! Get out of the building!" But the people only responded with uproarious laughter because they thought the clown's frantic warning was part of his performance.[1] If we come into the church singing, dancing, and juggling, wearing the jester's garb, we will undoubtedly win a large audience and elicit laughter and admiration. But the moment we shift gears and warn people of the righteous and holy wrath against works-righteousness and idolatry, our audience (rather than sinners under God's condemnation) will fail to take us seriously—they will fail to distinguish between entertainment and truth. Judgment becomes rhetorical flare and hyperbole, and grace is an empty word rather than the very foundation for redemption. Christ becomes our friend and helper rather than our Redeemer and Savior. We must, therefore, preach the gospel in all its glory and never shrink back or mute any of its truths whether out of reticence, temerity, or the desire to entertain.

Second, we must maintain a radically Christ-centered approach to the gospel. This is another area in which the church historically falters. Many within the church, even those considered to be stalwarts for the gospel, have compromised on the necessity and exclusivity of Christ as the only Savior for humanity. Billy Graham (1918–2018), for example, once said the following:

> [The body of Christ will be made up of] all the Christian groups around the world, outside the Christian groups. I think that everybody that loves or knows Christ, whether they are conscious of it or not, they are members of the body of Christ. And I don't think that we are going to see a great sweeping revival that will turn the whole world to Christ at any time. I think James answered that—the Apostle James in the first Council of Jerusalem—when he said that God's purpose for this age is to call out a people for his name. And that is what he is doing today. He is calling people out of the world for his name, whether they come from the Muslim world, or the

1. Søren Kierkegaard, *Either / Or, Part I* (Princeton, N.J.: Princeton University Press, 1987), 30.

> Buddhist world or the non-believing world, they are members of the Body of Christ because they have been called by God. They may not know the name of Jesus but they know in their hearts that they need something they do not have, and they turn to the only light they have, and I think that they are saved and they are going to be with us in heaven.[2]

Despite his humble demeanor and well-intentioned disposition, such a statement clashes with the clear teaching of Scripture.

Graham tells the Muslim and Buddhist that it does not matter what they think—they are Christians. You are called and therefore saved. But remember what Paul sets forth in this chapter and its roots in the previous chapter: "For whom He foreknew, He also predestined to be conformed to the image of His Son, that He might be the firstborn among many brethren. Moreover whom He predestined, these He also called; whom He called, these He also justified; and whom He justified, these He also glorified" (Rom. 8:29–30). God grounds His call in His sovereign election, and He connects this sovereign election to His Son, Jesus Christ. Paul elsewhere writes that we were chosen "in [Christ] before the foundation of the world" (Eph. 1:4). God reveals His righteousness in the gospel, and it comes solely through the work of Christ: "For what the law could not do in that it was weak through the flesh, God did by sending His own Son in the likeness of sinful flesh, on account of sin: He condemned sin in the flesh, that the righteous requirement of the law might be fulfilled in us who do not walk according to the flesh but according to the Spirit" (Rom. 8:3–4).

Why would Paul say that faith in Christ is necessary if it was not? We cannot remove Christ from the gospel—if we do, we no longer have the gospel. Christ is not one of many options to heaven in a pantheon of deities—He is the only way, and we must place our faith in Him alone! This is why the Reformation lifted high the

---

2. Billy Graham, "Radio Interview with Robert Schuller," as quoted in Iain Murray, *Evangelicalism Divided: A Record of Crucial Change in the Years 1950–2000* (Edinburgh: Banner of Truth, 2000), 73–74.

banners of the *solas*—salvation is by grace alone through faith alone in Christ alone to the glory of God alone—*sola gratia*, *sola fide*, *solus Christus*, and *soli Deo gloria*!

Conclusion

We must faithfully preach and teach the whole counsel of God—we must never deviate from the truth of Scripture. We must never yield to the temptation to remove the block of stumbling, or cave to the impulse to entertain for the sake of acceptance. We must preach the block of stumbling and the stone of offense—we must preach Christ and Him crucified. Moreover, we must remember, as Paul has told us, "whoever believes on Him will not be put to shame" (Rom. 9:33).

32

Christ—The End of the Law

ROMANS 10:1–13

Brethren, my heart's desire and prayer to God for Israel is that they may be saved. For I bear them witness that they have a zeal for God, but not according to knowledge. For they being ignorant of God's righteousness, and seeking to establish their own righteousness, have not submitted to the righteousness of God. For Christ is the end of the law for righteousness to everyone who believes. For Moses writes about the righteousness which is of the law, "The man who does those things shall live by them." But the righteousness of faith speaks in this way, "Do not say in your heart, 'Who will ascend into heaven?'" (that is, to bring Christ down from above) or, "'Who will descend into the abyss?'" (that is, to bring Christ up from the dead). But what does it say? "The word is near you, in your mouth and in your heart" (that is, the word of faith which we preach): that if you confess with your mouth the Lord Jesus and believe in your heart that God has raised Him from the dead, you will be saved. For with the heart one believes unto righteousness, and with the mouth confession is made unto salvation. For the Scripture says, "Whoever believes on Him will not be put to shame." For there is no distinction between Jew and Greek, for the same Lord over all is rich to all who call upon Him. For "whoever calls on the name of the Lord *shall be saved."*

I recall reading a story about a man who fell asleep on his airline flight. The plane's landing did not jostle him awake, so he kept on sleeping. The plane's crew and the cleaning staff, however, failed to see this passenger dozing in his seat. They completed their work, locked the plane, and went home. When the man awoke he was stunned to discover that he was alone inside a locked airplane unable to get out. He had to call his wife to call the airport authorities to let him off. My interest in this story has little to do with who was at fault for leaving the sleeping man on the plane and more with the passenger who failed to realize that the plane had arrived at its destination. The journey was complete. Many of Paul's contemporaries failed to recognize that Israel's time with the Mosaic covenant was complete. With the advent of Christ, they failed to realize that the end of the law as a covenant had dawned on them. Like the man slumbering on the parked airplane, Paul's fellow Jews were fast asleep in their theological darkness—they failed to realize that Christ was the end of the law. But this slumbering attitude toward the law was not possessed solely by Paul's contemporaries. Old Testament Israel suffered from the same malady.

When the Israelites were on the verge of entering the Promised Land, Moses renewed the covenant with the people in Deuteronomy 29; he set before them covenant blessings and curses. Even though God delivered them from Egypt and performed many signs and wonders, He did not give them eyes to see the ultimate significance of these great acts: "You have seen all that the LORD did before your eyes in the land of Egypt, to Pharaoh and to all his servants and to all his land—the great trials which your eyes have seen, the signs, and those great wonders" (Deut. 29:2b–4). For this reason, Moses anticipated that Israel would be unfaithful to the covenant and would be carried off into captivity. Yet there would be a time when God would bring His people out of captivity—He would circumcise their hearts and enable His people to love Him:

> Now it shall come to pass, when all these things come upon you, the blessing and the curse which I have set before you, and you call them to mind among all the nations where the LORD your God drives you, and you return to the LORD your God and obey His voice, according to all that I command you today, you and your children, with all your heart and with all your soul, that the LORD your God will bring you back from

> captivity, and have compassion on you, and gather you again from all the nations where the LORD your God has scattered you. If any of you are driven out to the farthest parts under heaven, from there the LORD your God will gather you, and from there He will bring you. Then the LORD your God will bring you to the land which your fathers possessed, and you shall possess it. He will prosper you and multiply you more than your fathers. And the LORD your God will circumcise your heart and the heart of your descendants, to love the LORD your God with all your heart and with all your soul, that you may live. (Deut. 30:1–6)

God promised to do this through other prophets as well. Similar promises appear in the prophets Jeremiah and Ezekiel. Jeremiah prophesied of a time when God would make a new covenant with the house of Israel and Judah, one quite different from the covenant that He made with Israel, which they broke. God would write His law on their minds and hearts; He would be their God and they would be His people (Jer. 31:31–33). Likewise the prophet Ezekiel foretold of a time when God would gather His people from among the nations, the disparate ends of the earth from where they had been driven into exile, and would sprinkle them with clean water, place a new spirit within them, and cause them to walk in His statutes. Then, and only then, would Israel dwell in God's presence (Ezek. 36:24–28).

Over the course of the last several chapters Paul has shown that these great prophecies have begun to be fulfilled through the ministry of Christ, which signaled the in-breaking of the new heavens and earth into this present evil age. Now, just as Moses stood before the people and exhorted them to be faithful to the Lord and His covenant, so Paul stands before the people of God and gives them the same exhortation. This exhortation, however, is illuminated by the greater revelatory light of Christ. Paul shows how Israel failed to believe the gospel of Christ and, by connection, his recipients' need to believe in this same gospel. Paul comes full circle by returning to the manner in which God justifies people: either by perfect obedience to the law or by faith in the perfect work of Christ. Or, in Paul's words, the righteousness of the law versus the righteousness of God that comes only through the gospel.

Christ the End of the Law

Paul opens this chapter by expressing his desire that his countrymen would be saved (Rom. 10:1), which echoes the sorrow and anguish he revealed at the beginning of chapter 9 (vv. 1–5). Keep in mind that Paul expounded the doctrine of predestination—he knows that salvation is ultimately up to God's sovereign choice. Nevertheless, this does not govern his attitude toward those who appear to reject the gospel. John Murray rightly notes:

> God has mercy on whom he wills and whom he wills he hardens. Some are vessels for wrath, others for mercy. And ultimate destiny is envisioned in destruction and glory. But this differentiation is God's action and prerogative, not man's. And, because so, our attitude to men is not to be governed by God's secret counsel concerning them. It is this lesson and the distinction involved that are so eloquently inscribed on the apostle's passion for the salvation of his kinsmen. We violate the order of human thought and trespass the boundary between God's prerogative and man's when the truth of God's sovereign counsel constrains despair or abandonment of concern for the eternal interests of men.[1]

Murray's point is well taken. While we must firmly believe in God's sovereign choice in salvation, we must not misunderstand predestination and allow ourselves to become reticent when it comes to our evangelism or preaching.

But whatever sympathy Paul had for his fellow countrymen, he in no way soft-pedaled the nature of their problem. The worst thing a doctor can do is misdiagnose a condition or fail to inform his patient of the true nature of his illness. So many preachers and

1. Murray, *Epistle to the Romans*, 47.

Christians want to soften the blow of the law's condemnation—they do not want to offend nonbelievers for fear that they will lose their audience. But as a fellow colleague once told me, "You can't turn a light off if it's already off." So Paul drills down into the specific nature of Israel's problem: "For I bear them witness that they have a zeal for God, but not according to knowledge. For they being ignorant of God's righteousness, and seeking to establish their own righteousness, have not submitted to the righteousness of God" (Rom. 10:2–3). Paul explains that he knows his countrymen have a zeal for God, yet zeal alone is insufficient. Good intentions pave the way to hell—they accomplish nothing. A person can be zealous for many different things. Take Paul, for example. When he was unconverted, his zeal led him to persecute the church. After Paul's conversion, God used his zeal to build the church. Zeal is helpful only when it breathes the air of truth.

Now, to be sure, when Paul states that the Jews have not sought God "according to knowledge" (Rom. 10:2), we must realize that he is not simply talking about information or data. Rather, we must define *knowledge* in a scriptural manner. Fear of the Lord is the beginning of knowledge (Prov. 1:7). The Jews were, therefore, ignorant of God's righteousness—the imputed righteousness of Christ and God's righteousness in His judgment against sin. The Jews did not fear God's righteous judgment and seek out Christ's righteousness. Rather, they sought to create their own righteousness (Deut. 6:25). They believed they could make a full-frontal assault on the law of God and walk away victorious—that they could merit justification through their own obedience. But they failed to understand that such a path was impassable. The key Israelite failure was not a defective understanding of the law. They rightly understood the function of the law—namely, "not the hearers of the law are just in the sight of God, but the doers of the law will be justified" (Rom. 2:13). Paul's countrymen understood how the law functions: obedience merits justification. Instead, they had defective doctrines of man, sin, Christ, and salvation.

Remember, the law is holy and good (Rom. 7:12). But sinful human beings are incapable of meeting the law's demand for perfect obedience. Hence, if anyone desires to be justified before the divine bar, he must rely on an alien righteousness, the righteousness of another—Christ. This is why Paul writes, "For Christ is the end of the law for righteousness to everyone who believes" (Rom. 10:4). Christ fulfills the demands of the law perfectly by being obedient to every jot and tittle, every single command, in word, thought, and deed. Moreover, He also offers His own life in sacrifice to pay the penalty for the elect's violation of the law. In this manner Christ is the end of the law—He vicariously fulfills the law and bears its curse for anyone who believes in Him.

Salvation by Works versus by Faith

To prove that Christ is the end of the law, Paul explains the antithesis between works and faith in the doctrine of salvation. He first explains the relationship between obedience, righteousness, and the law: "For Moses writes about the righteousness which is of the law, 'The man who does those things shall live by them'" (Rom. 10:5; cf. Lev. 18:5). Some commentators mistakenly think that Paul assumes the erroneous position of his theological opponents to demonstrate its falsehood. In their minds, Paul would never say that a person can obey the law and secure God's favor. But remember, Paul's opponents have a correct understanding of the law in the sense that if you perfectly obey, you will be declared righteous. That Paul has this scriptural principle in view is evident because he specifically states, "For Moses writes...." In other words, he correctly quotes Moses and not an erroneous understanding of the law. Paul quotes Leviticus 18:5—a man can be righteous *if* he obeys the law—I must stress the word *if*. The problem is, of course, that the Jews could not fulfill the obligations of the law—Romans 2:1–3:19 makes this clear.

Conversely, Paul reintroduces the righteousness that comes by faith: "But the righteousness of faith speaks in this way, 'Do not say in your heart, "Who will ascend into heaven?"' (that is, to bring

Christ down from above) or, '"Who will descend into the abyss?" (that is, to bring Christ up from the dead)'" (Rom. 10:6–7). Paul's beginning verse 6 with the word *but* indicates that he marks a stark contrast between what he has written in verse 5 and what follows in verse 6. If the righteousness of the law requires obedience, or doing, then by contrast, the righteousness by faith requires belief. You *do* the law and *believe* the gospel. To highlight this point, Paul demonstrates the antithesis between faith and works by quoting Deuteronomy 30:12–14 here in Romans 10:6–8. A man convicted of his sin and his inability to save himself by his own works will *not* say, "I can ascend into heaven by my own works, by my own obedience to the law." This nullifies the work of Christ. If man were capable of saving himself, then why would Christ's work on his behalf be necessary? This is why Paul says, "that is, to bring Christ down." Likewise, a man convicted of his sin and his inability to save himself by his own works will *not* say, "I can conquer death by my own good works." That too would nullify the work of Christ, because who but Christ alone can raise himself from the dead?

Now, we should not miss Paul's implied point here in this two-fold explanation—namely, rising to heaven or conquering death. Notice how these aspects of the law—earning one's salvation and negating the effects of the fall—are connected to the person and work of Christ, not with the abilities of the individual believer! This is why Paul states, "For Christ is the end of the law for righteousness to everyone who believes" (Rom. 10:4). The work of Christ—His life, death, and resurrection—can be received only by *faith*, not by works. Faith and works are mutually exclusive paths to justification and salvation. Choose one and you automatically forfeit the other. Paul's unquestioned preference—indeed, one of the chief points of his whole epistle—is that salvation is by faith alone in Christ alone (Rom. 1:17).

Paul makes this point once again in the following verses: "But what does it say? 'The word is near you, in your mouth and in your heart' (that is, the word of faith which we preach): that if you confess with your mouth the Lord Jesus and believe in your heart that God has raised Him from the dead, you will be saved" (Rom. 10:8–9). Paul explains the nature of salvation in specific detail; what he implied in the previous verses he now explicitly states. Salvation is not an effort to merit God's favor. Rather, as Paul tells us, salvation is near us, in our mouths and hearts. It is not by works but by faith in Christ—this is why Paul says that if you confess with your mouth and believe in your heart in the work of Christ, you will be saved.

Instructive is the fact that Paul continues to quote from Deuteronomy 30:12–14, which were the prophetic words Moses preached to Israel as they were perched on the border of the Promised Land. The same gospel that God announced to Abraham was the same gospel Moses preached to Israel. Just because God had given them the law did not nullify His covenant promises to Abraham. As Paul elsewhere writes, "And this I say, that the law, which was four hundred and thirty years later, cannot annul the covenant that was confirmed before by God in Christ, that it should make the promise of no effect. For if the inheritance is of the law, it is no longer of promise; but God gave it to Abraham by promise" (Gal. 3:17–18). Salvation in a sin-fallen world has always been by God's grace alone through faith alone in Christ alone.

Paul never wavers on this point. He therefore writes, "For with the heart one believes unto righteousness, and with the mouth confession is made unto salvation" (Rom. 10:10). Note the close connection between justification and salvation, evident by Paul's use of a synonymous parallelism (where he repeats the same idea with slightly different words in two separate phrases). If you believe in Jesus alone for salvation, you are justified—declared righteous. And if you truly confess faith in the gospel and the saving work of Christ alone, you are saved (cf. Rom. 5:21). Paul's intention is not to slight the other elements of our redemption—our sanctification, adoption, perseverance, and glorification. Rather, he simply highlights that when a person believes in Jesus he irrevocably receives right and title to eternal life. Given our union with Christ, we certainly receive all the benefits of salvation. But at this point, Paul specifically dwells on the source of our right standing before God, not the other benefits of redemption.

Hence Paul's point is clear: The righteousness of God (Rom. 1:17) comes by faith alone, not by our efforts to obey the law, which is what Paul's fellow Jews were trying to do (Rom. 10:3). In a sense, Paul comes full circle to ideas and doctrines he set out in his thesis statement from Romans 1:17, which signals that he is on the verge of completing his main arguments and preparing to engage other subjects: "For the Scripture says, 'Whoever believes on Him will not be put to shame.' For there is no distinction between Jew and Greek, for the same Lord over all is rich to all who call upon Him. For 'whoever calls on the name of the LORD shall be saved'" (Rom. 10:11–13). The gospel reveals the righteousness of God and is the power of God unto salvation, first for the Jew and then for the Greek. For in the gospel God reveals His righteousness only to those who believe, from faith to faith. Therefore, whoever believes in Christ will never be put to shame. To seal his argument, Paul quotes Joel 2:32, which speaks of the outpouring of the Spirit and the salvation that comes from Yahweh. Anyone who calls on Yahweh in the flesh, Jesus, will be saved.

Conclusion

As we reflect on Paul's words, we should never forget the utter antithesis that exists between faith and works in justification. If we choose, as Israel did, to seek salvation by the law, then we stand before an insurmountable obstacle. The law is holy, perfect, and good, and for the one who perfectly obeys it, there is eternal life. This was a possibility for Adam in the garden in his unfallen state, but it is impossible for fallen, sinful humanity. This is a fundamental point that Paul's countrymen failed to grasp. They rightly understood how the law functions but grossly misunderstood their inability to fulfill it. This is why Paul trumpeted the glorious truth that Christ is the end of the law for all who believe and that whoever calls on Him will never be put to shame. Call, therefore, on the name of the Lord if you have not yet done so. Only Christ has perfectly met the demands of the law. If you have already called on Christ by faith alone, then pray that your heavenly Father will enable you to continue to trust in Christ—that you would forsake all temptations to return under the law for your justification. Instead, rest in the completed work of Christ and recognize that you are not only justified but saved. And if you are saved, then you are being sanctified. And if you are being sanctified, it means that you will, without doubt, ultimately be glorified. Rejoice in the righteousness of God that comes through the gospel of His Son, Jesus Christ!

33

Preaching Good News

ROMANS 10:14–21

How then shall they call on Him in whom they have not believed? And how shall they believe in Him of whom they have not heard? And how shall they hear without a preacher? And how shall they preach unless they are sent? As it is written: "How beautiful are the feet of those who preach the gospel of peace, Who bring glad tidings of good things!" But they have not all obeyed the gospel. For Isaiah says, "LORD, who has believed our report?" So then faith comes by hearing, and hearing by the word of God. But I say, have they not heard? Yes indeed: "Their sound has gone out to all the earth, And their words to the ends of the world." But I say, did Israel not know? First Moses says: "I will provoke you to jealousy by those who are not a nation, I will move you to anger by a foolish nation." But Isaiah is very bold and says: "I was found by those who did not seek Me; I was made manifest to those who did not ask for Me." But to Israel he says: "All day long I have stretched out My hands To a disobedient and contrary people."

Isaiah 52 tells of a time when Israel was oppressed by the Egyptians and the Assyrians. Israel was also rife with idolatry. Under such circumstances the faithful might lose hope and fear that God had forgotten them. To assuage the hearts of His faithful remnant, God revealed a future when things would be different, when heralds would proclaim good news among the nations:

> How beautiful upon the mountains Are the feet of him who brings good news, Who proclaims peace, Who brings glad tidings of good things, Who proclaims salvation, Who says

> to Zion, "Your God reigns!" Your watchmen shall lift up their voices, With their voices they shall sing together; For they shall see eye to eye When the LORD brings back Zion. Break forth into joy, sing together, You waste places of Jerusalem! For the LORD has comforted His people, He has redeemed Jerusalem. (Isa. 52:7–9)

Paul declares the fulfillment of another ancient prophecy. It has arrived with the ministry of Jesus Christ—the eschatological age has broken into this present evil age. With the life, death, and resurrection of Christ the last days have burst onto the stage of redemptive history, and we now await one last piece of the puzzle—Christ's return. But the period of the last days does not mean that God's people merely sit by and watch the show. Rather, if you knew that a wrecking ball was soon to crash into a condemned home still inhabited by people, you would undoubtedly warn the residents of the impending danger. The same can be said about the present judgment on the world (Rom. 1:18–32) and the only means of escaping it, the gospel (Rom. 1:17). The last days are upon us, which means we must tell the lost and dying world of the impending judgment to come. While this scenario might sound like the proverbial fool wearing a sandwich board warning of the end of the world, the truth is that God has called His people to the *foolish* task of preaching the gospel—to publish the inaugurated reign of Christ and the comfort He brings to His people.

The Need for Preachers

In the previous section (Rom. 10:1–13) Paul emphasized that salvation and justification come through faith in Christ and that anyone who calls on the name of the Lord will be saved. This naturally leads to the following questions: "How then shall they call on Him in whom they have not believed? And how shall they believe in Him of whom they have not heard? And how shall they hear without a preacher? And how shall they preach unless they are sent? As it is written: 'How beautiful are the feet of those who preach the gospel of peace, Who bring glad tidings of good things!'" (Rom. 10:14–15).

Plain and simple, the only way people will believe in the gospel is if someone preaches the good news. Keep in mind, this is the same apostle who affirmed divine sovereignty in salvation (Rom. 9:1–31). Yes, God ordains the ends—namely, the salvation and damnation of whomsoever He chooses—but He also ordains the means by which He accomplishes His will (cf. WCF 3.1). As an illustration of this point, consider how God ordained that I would have a bowl of cereal this morning for breakfast. The cereal did not magically appear in my stomach, the end goal of God's decree. Rather, God ordained the means and the ends: that I would get up, go downstairs to my kitchen, get a bowl, fill it with cereal, pour milk on it, get a spoon, and politely shovel it into my mouth. This is the same relationship between election and salvation—God ordains the ends (salvation) as well as the means (preaching). Therefore, far from the decree of election making evangelism and preaching superfluous, it ensures their success.

In words from J. I. Packer's important little book, *Evangelism and the Sovereignty of God*, "Far from inhibiting evangelism, faith in the sovereignty of God's government and grace is the only thing that can sustain it, for it is the only thing that can give us the resilience that we need if we are to evangelize boldly and persistently, and not to be daunted by temporary setbacks."[1] Preachers can proclaim God's Word boldly knowing that they will see fruit. God's sovereignty does not undermine preaching in the least but undergirds and empowers it. Like the messenger who runs back to the city to inform its inhabitants that their armies have been successful in battle, preachers herald the good news that Yahweh has come in the flesh and conquered sin and death. Anyone who brought such good news would undoubtedly have beautiful feet! They carry the message of Christ's victory and the salvation that comes through His gospel. These runners do not shuffle along, barely able to keep themselves upright—they do not carry a message of defeat and

1. J. I. Packer, *Evangelism and the Sovereignty of God* (Downers Grove, Ill.: InterVarsity Press, 1991), 10.

death. Their footfall is firm, their legs briskly kick up dust, and their lungs are full of strength because hope carries them along and they are eager to tell others about God's victory. Paul quotes Isaiah 52:7 to prove that God fulfills His covenant promises and to instruct the church to preach the good news of the gospel. Preachers and every member of the church can rest in God's sovereignty and approach the lost with the message of the gospel.

To the Ends of the Earth

But to what extent should the church herald the gospel of Christ? Paul turns to matters pertaining to this in Romans 10:16–17: "But they have not all obeyed the gospel. For Isaiah says, 'LORD, who has believed our report?' So then faith comes by hearing, and hearing by the word of God." Paul recognizes that all who hear the gospel do not automatically believe. Behind the preaching of the gospel lies God's sovereign election: "Jacob I have loved, but Esau I have hated" (Rom. 9:13). And, for this reason, Paul says, "they have not all obeyed the gospel." He then quotes Isaiah 53:1 to show that Israel has historically rejected the gospel. They rejected the message in Isaiah's day and in Paul's. But Paul continues to remind us that the gospel must be preached regardless. Why? Because faith comes by hearing, and hearing by the Word of God. The only way people will believe is if they hear, and the only way people will hear the gospel is if someone preaches it.

This means that if the nations are to have any hope of embracing Christ, then naturally, the gospel must go out to the whole world: "But I say, have they not heard? Yes indeed: 'Their sound has gone out to all the earth, And their words to the ends of the world'" (Rom. 10:18). Paul posits the rhetorical question that maybe the Jews have not heard the gospel. On the contrary, the Jews have heard the gospel. Paul applies the words of Psalm 19:4 and the universality of the proclamation of general revelation to the preaching of the gospel. The gospel has gone throughout the world—the Jews cannot claim ignorance of it. Indeed, as Paul writes in Romans 4, Abraham knew the gospel, and so did Israel as Moses preached it to them at the border of Canaan: "But I say, did Israel not know? First Moses says: 'I will provoke you to jealousy by those who are not a nation, I will move you to anger by a foolish nation.' But Isaiah is very bold and says: 'I was found by those who did not seek Me; I was made manifest to those who did not ask for Me.' But to Israel he says: 'All day long I have stretched out My hands to a disobedient and contrary people'" (Rom. 10:19–21). Paul asks the basic question, How did Israel know?

The Jews knew that they would ultimately reject the gospel because Moses told them they would. Recall Paul's quotations from Deuteronomy 30 in the previous section (Rom. 10:1–13). He also quotes Deuteronomy 32:21 to remind his Jewish readers that they would reject the gospel and God would therefore give it to the Gentiles. What, however, would happen to the Jews? Moses states that God would provoke Israel to jealousy by giving the gospel to the Gentiles. Paul quotes yet another Old Testament Scripture (Isa. 65:1) to substantiate his claim that God told the Jews He would give His gospel to the Gentiles. Paul reiterates the point that he made at the beginning of the chapter, that the Jews have a zeal but not according to knowledge.

The Church's Task

As we reflect on the import of this passage, we should note how the dawning eschatological day gives prominence to the preaching of the gospel. The church must preach the gospel to the nations. This does not mean that every layperson is supposed to take up the task of preaching. Paul says that the gospel requires preachers, so the church must send them. I argue, as others typically do in the Reformed community, that Christ connects gospel preaching to the Great Commission (Matt. 28:18–20). Christ gave the commission to the apostles, which they in turn passed to preachers (Eph. 4:11–14). The church must see that its preachers carry out this task. Yes, God sovereignly predestines, but He has also ordained that the church accomplish this goal through preaching the gospel.

Hence, preachers must herald the gospel of peace—they must not adulterate or compromise the gospel in this task. Along these lines, a well-known twentieth-century political theorist, Albert Jay Nock (1870–1945), once observed an important aspect of Isaiah's preaching ministry in his popular essay "Isaiah's Job":

> If, say, you are a preacher, you wish to attract as large a congregation as you can, which means an appeal to the masses, and this in turn means adapting the terms of your message to the order of intellect and character that the masses exhibit.... But as we see on all sides, in the realization of these several desires the prophetic message is so heavily adulterated with trivialities in every instance that its effect on the masses is merely to harden them in their sins; and meanwhile the Remnant, aware of this adulteration and of the desires that prompt it, turn their backs on the prophet and will have nothing to do with him or his message.[2]

The preacher must be fully committed to preaching the undiluted gospel. This was Paul's ethos, and certainly the pattern that appears in the prophet Isaiah. In many respects we can say that Paul was Isaiah's New Testament counterpart. In preaching the pure gospel of Christ, the preacher, like Isaiah and Paul, can know that his message will accomplish God's intended purpose. Nock writes, "The other certainty which the prophet of the Remnant may always have is that the Remnant will find him. He may rely on that with absolute assurance. They will find him without his doing anything about it; in fact, if he tries to do anything about it, he is pretty sure to put them off."[3] Preach a substitute or weakened message, and God's elect will not hear. They will not hear the voice of their Shepherd calling but the voice of a charlatan.

Paul was aware of this given his firm conviction and knowledge of God's sovereign predestinating will. Not only must preachers

2. Albert Jay Nock, "Isaiah's Job," *The Atlantic Monthly* 157 (1936): 641–50, esp. 645.

3. Nock, "Isaiah's Job," 645.

stand firm on the gospel, but the church must support faithful preachers and reject those who do not preach it. While preachers are responsible for what they preach, churches are also responsible for doctrinal decline. While many believe that doctrinal demise comes through liberal seminaries that train liberal ministers, the ultimate onus lies on the churches. When their minister substitutes the gospel for pop psychology, or he simply denies it, the church must reject their minister. This passage, however, also shows us another dimension about the nature of preaching the gospel.

We live in an age in which people measure success in terms of numbers. This is not the way that the Bible measures success. God does not always intend to have the gospel save—it is sometimes a tool of judgment. Or, in this case, God used the gospel and its reception among the Gentiles to provoke the Jews to jealousy. As Paul writes elsewhere, the preaching of the gospel is the aroma of life for those who are being saved and the aroma of death for those who are perishing (2 Cor. 2:14–16). So, then, we may never see droves of people converted by the preaching of the gospel, but this does not mean that our preaching has been unsuccessful. Was Isaiah unsuccessful in his ministry? No. Was Elijah unsuccessful in his ministry since a remnant of only seven thousand out of millions of Israelites was chosen? No. Was Christ unsuccessful in His preaching because the Jews preferred Barabbas instead of Him? No. Was Paul unsuccessful because only some of the Jews in Rome embraced Christ? No. In fact, Paul's own supposed failures caused him to look back on Isaiah's prophecies, which assured him that he was doing the right thing. When Paul preached about the kingdom of God from the Law and the Prophets, some Jews were persuaded, while others walked away in disbelief, which caused Paul to say:

> So when they did not agree among themselves, they departed after Paul had said one word: "The Holy Spirit spoke rightly through Isaiah the prophet to our fathers, saying, 'Go to this people and say: "Hearing you will hear, and shall not understand; And seeing you will see, and not perceive; For the hearts of this people have grown dull. Their ears are hard of hearing,

> And their eyes they have closed, Lest they should see with their eyes and hear with their ears, Lest they should understand with their hearts and turn, So that I should heal them."' Therefore let it be known to you that the salvation of God has been sent to the Gentiles, and they will hear it!" (Acts 28:25–28)

Therefore, we should not be discouraged by the appearance of meager results. Rather, we must be faithful to ensure that ministers faithfully preach the gospel. We can intercede in prayer on their behalf, financially contribute to the ministry of the church, pray for missionaries in the field, and even support seminarians preparing for ordained ministry. There are many ways to ensure the church proclaims the gospel of Christ.

Conclusion

We must realize the awesome realities that transpire each and every Sunday that we gather for worship and hear the gospel. We participate in the fulfillment of great eschatological prophecies, whether as one who preaches or as one who sits under the preaching of the gospel. Isaiah prophesied that there would be a great day when this would happen, and indeed we are living in that day. The psalmist prophesied of a day when the Messiah would be enthroned and would rule the nations with a rod of iron (Ps. 2:8–9). Indeed, that day has come. The rod of iron by which Christ rules is the gospel—the preached Word of God, which is living and powerful, sharper than any two-edged sword (Heb. 4:12). Cling to the gospel, therefore, for it is the announcement of peace and salvation to all who place their faith in Christ. Implore others to heed the preaching of the gospel, for we should, like Paul, desire to see our brethren saved. And rest assured that the sovereign power of God stands behind the preaching of the gospel of Christ. If we preach, people will be saved.

34

God's Ways

ROMANS 11:1-10

I say then, has God cast away His people? Certainly not! For I also am an Israelite, of the seed of Abraham, of the tribe of Benjamin. God has not cast away His people whom He foreknew. Or do you not know what the Scripture says of Elijah, how he pleads with God against Israel, saying, "LORD, they have killed Your prophets and torn down Your altars, and I alone am left, and they seek my life"? But what does the divine response say to him? "I have reserved for Myself seven thousand men who have not bowed the knee to Baal." Even so then, at this present time there is a remnant according to the election of grace. And if by grace, then it is no longer of works; otherwise grace is no longer grace. But if it is of works, it is no longer grace; otherwise work is no longer work. What then? Israel has not obtained what it seeks; but the elect have obtained it, and the rest were blinded. Just as it is written: "God has given them a spirit of stupor, Eyes that they should not see And ears that they should not hear, To this very day." And David says: "Let their table become a snare and a trap, A stumbling block and a recompense to them. Let their eyes be darkened, so that they do not see, And bow down their back always."

My mother tells a story about a family vacation she took in which her parents, sister, and brother drove from San Francisco to Los Angeles. Along the way my grandfather pulled into a service station to gas up the car. My grandmother, aunt, and mother all exited the car so they could freshen up. My grandfather did the same, but before he walked away from the car he checked on my uncle, a young ten-year-old boy who was fast asleep in the back of the station wagon. When everyone returned to the car they shut the doors and drove off. About an hour later my aunt noticed that my uncle was not in the car and asked, "Where's John?" My grandfather turned around and gasped! My uncle was not in the car. It turns out that while everyone was out of the car, my uncle woke up and walked barefoot into the service station just as the rest of the family got in the car and drove away. My grandfather immediately turned the car around and sped back to the gas station.

What was my uncle doing? He was sitting in front of a gas pump, patiently waiting, with his chin propped on his folded hands. He got in the car, and everyone asked, "John! Weren't you scared?" My uncle smiled and calmly replied, "Nah…I knew you guys would come back for me." My uncle was assured of the love of his family and that they would never forget him or purposefully leave him behind. Stated more succinctly, though my uncle was a child, he was secure in the love and faithfulness of his father. This trust between father and child was something that some of Paul's audience failed to possess. Given what Paul has written in his epistle, they thought they had been left behind, forgotten by God. Had God utterly abandoned Israel? What about the biological descendants of Abraham? Did not God promise that they would be saved? Paul turns his attention to this particular issue in the effort to show God's faithfulness to the Jewish people. He wanted to restore peace in their hearts so they would know they had not been left behind. We must listen to the apostle's answer to this question and then think about its implications for the church in our own day. We must rest in the faithfulness of our covenant Lord to care for and provide for His children.

Has God Forgotten His People?

Paul opens the eleventh chapter of his epistle with the following question and answer: "I say then, has God cast away His people? Certainly not!" (Rom. 11:1a). After reading Romans 9–10 some of Paul's fellow Jews might have thought that God utterly cast off the biological descendants of Abraham. Paul rejects this erroneous conclusion and points to himself as living proof that God still has a place for Abraham's biological sons: "For I also am an Israelite, of the seed of Abraham, of the tribe of Benjamin" (Rom. 11:1b). Paul is a Hebrew of Hebrews and proof that God did not forget Abraham's physical descendants. To buttress his point Paul digs beyond his own personal salvation and appeals to the Old Testament ministry of Elijah the prophet: "God has not cast away His people whom He foreknew. Or do you not know what the Scripture says of Elijah, how he pleads with God against Israel?" (Rom. 11:2). Paul again explains that God *foreknew*—that is, He loved Israel before the foundation of the world. Evidence of His love appears in the fact that, though Israel forsook their covenant Lord, God nevertheless preserved a remnant. Elijah looked on his own seemingly grim circumstances and cried out to the Lord, fearing that he alone was left: "'LORD, they have killed Your prophets and torn down Your altars, and I alone am left, and they seek my life.' But what does the divine response say to him? 'I have reserved for Myself seven thousand men who have not bowed the knee to Baal'" (Rom. 11:3–4; 1 Kings 19:18). Even during Israel's darkest days, times when idolatry and wickedness flowed like water in the streets, God still preserved a faithful remnant for Himself. What is especially interesting in his appeal to Elijah's cry is Paul's addition to his quotation of 1 Kings 19:18: "Yet I have reserved [for Myself] seven thousand in Israel." Paul authoritatively and under divine inspiration adds the words *for Myself* to indicate that God personally ensured that there would be a remnant. This proves Paul's point that God has never completely rejected His people.

Paul uses this remnant idea and applies it to his present context in the face of Israel's large-scale rejection of Christ: "Even so then, at this present time there is a remnant according to the election of grace. And if by grace, then it is no longer of works; otherwise grace is no longer grace. But if it is of works, it is no longer grace; otherwise work is no longer work" (Rom. 11:5–6). Even though things appeared grim for Israel, Paul was confident that God had faithfully preserved a remnant for Himself just as He did in Elijah's day. But Paul again reiterates the works-faith antithesis to remind his readers that the remnant exists because of God's grace, not works. Paul does not want his fellow Jews to think mistakenly that they might be saved due to their ancestral connection to Abraham or adherence to the law. God saves the remnant the same way He saves the Gentiles—by grace alone through faith alone in Christ alone. Grace and works, in Paul's mind, are antithetical in justification. That is, if we try to secure redemption by our works, then salvation is not by grace. But if God saves us by His grace, then He excludes our works. "Otherwise," as Paul writes, "grace is no longer grace." Paul's point can be stated simply: Either you save yourself or Christ saves you. There is no middle ground, no theological or moral alchemy that can somehow produce the gold of salvation. Hence, God saves the ethnic Jewish remnant and Gentiles by His grace, not by their adherence to the law.

God's Inscrutable Judgment

Paul now summarizes his argument. He transitions from his presented evidence, his own identity as a saved Jew and the remnant in Elijah's day, with a quick question and answer: "What then? Israel has not obtained what it seeks; but the elect have obtained it, and the rest were blinded" (Rom. 11:7). All of Paul's argumentation and presented evidence leads him to the conclusion that ethnic Israel, those who crucified Christ, did not obtain the righteousness they were seeking, but this does not mean that every Israelite therefore failed to receive God's covenant promises. Recall Paul's earlier words: "For they being ignorant of God's righteousness, and seeking to establish their own righteousness, have not submitted to the righteousness of God" (Rom. 10:3; cf. 9:31–32). In other words, there were some who rejected the righteousness of God whereas other Israelites did receive the righteousness of God. God gave some grace and hardened others. In this respect, we must recognize how God defines Israel—He does include the biological children of Abraham among His elect, but they receive God's grace by virtue of His sovereign election, not their Abrahamic DNA. Recall Paul's words: "But it is not that the word of God has taken no effect. For they are not all Israel who are of Israel, nor are they all children because they are the seed of Abraham" (Rom. 9:6–7).

This might have been a stunning statement to some of Paul's Jewish readers, but he was standing on firm Old Testament ground: "Just as it is written: 'God has given them a spirit of stupor, Eyes that they should not see And ears that they should not hear, To this very day.' And David says: 'Let their table become a snare and a trap, A stumbling block and a recompense to them. Let their eyes be darkened, so that they do not see, And bow down their back always'" (Rom. 11:8–10). The elect remnant received God's mercy, but the rest of ethnic Israel has been hardened. As offensive as these things might sound, such is the inscrutable judgment of our holy and righteous God, and Paul unflinchingly presents these truths. Once again note the conundrum of divine sovereignty and human responsibility. Paul shows us that Israel's bountiful table—their adoption, glory, covenants, reception of the law, service to God, promises, patriarchs, and ultimately the line of the Messiah (Rom. 9:4–5)—has become a curse rather than a blessing. This munificent table has become a snare and a trap to them.

God's Mercy on Israel

We might think Paul's message fits the description that Mark Twain (1835–1910) gives of a church service through the eyes of Tom Sawyer: "The minister gave out his text and droned along monotonously through an argument that was so prosy that many a head by and by began to nod—and yet it was an argument that dealt in limitless fire and brimstone and thinned the predestined elect down to a company so small as to be hardly worth the saving."[1] As we read the text, we might think that Paul whittles the company of the elect to such a small number that hardly a person will be left. After all, it hardly

---

1. Mark Twain, *The Adventures of Tom Sawyer* (1876; repr., London: CRW Publishing, 2004), 48.

seems encouraging that God would spare only seven thousand out of an entire nation in Elijah's day. Hence it is perhaps initially difficult to see how Paul's application of Elijah's circumstances to his own situation would be helpful. Moreover, why would God use His special revelation as a tool of judgment rather than blessing? There are, I believe, two answers to these questions.

First, God must and will exhibit all His attributes—His justice and mercy, His love and His wrath. He will reveal His attributes in a manner befitting His glory. As Isaiah the prophet writes, "I am the LORD; that is My name; And My glory I will not give to another" (Isa. 42:8). God is, therefore, righteous to judge the wicked and merciful to grant clemency to those who do not deserve it. He dispenses His judgment and mercy in a manner appropriate to His glory, not man's. This pattern dominates the warp and woof of redemptive history. When God delivered Israel from Pharaoh and the furnace of Egypt, they were weak and hotly pursued by Egypt's armies, yet God delivered them in a manner that only He could do—He sent plagues and parted the Red Sea. He raised up Pharaoh to demonstrate His power before His people (Rom. 9:17). When the Philistines harried Israel and Goliath taunted them, God brought a shepherd boy, the unlikeliest of heroes, to dispatch Israel's foe. David wore no armor and slew the giant with a stone. This once again manifested Israel's weakness and God's glory and strength (1 Sam. 17:46–47). When Israel entered the Promised Land, God did not allow them to defeat Jericho through superior might but through the foolishness of marching around the fortified city (Josh. 6:16). And when Gideon gathered his army to battle the Midianites, God whittled his army of thousands to a mere handful of three hundred (Judg. 7:2). Why does God therefore reduce the number of saved Jews to a remnant? So that He receives the glory for the salvation of His people. If He did not do this, man's prideful heart would quickly rise to usurp God's honor. Sinful man would try to push and claw his way into the spotlight so that he would receive the credit and glory.

The second answer to these questions comes from Paul himself: "But I say, did Israel not know? First Moses says: 'I will provoke you to jealousy by those who are not a nation, I will move you to anger by a foolish nation'" (Rom. 10:19). God uses the hardening of Israel as a means to draw the remnant to Himself. We might think that there is a better way to accomplish the salvation of the remnant, but this is where we must withdraw to the outer courts of God's revelation and say in all humility: "The secret things belong to the LORD our God, but those things which are revealed belong to us and to our children forever" (Deut. 29:29). Indeed, Paul cries out at the end of this chapter: "Oh, the depth of the riches both of the wisdom and knowledge of God! How unsearchable are His judgments and His ways past finding out! 'For who has known the mind of the LORD? Or who has become His counselor?' 'Or who has first given to Him And it shall be repaid to him?' For of Him and through Him and to Him are all things, to whom be glory forever. Amen." (Rom. 11:33–36). Rather than raise accusations of unfairness or inequity, our response should instead be humble adoration and praise as we bow before our mighty and sovereign Lord.

The truths of God's inscrutable wisdom and His sovereign mercy, however, should lead us to another thought. John Calvin writes:

> Let this truth remain fixed in our hearts, that the Church, which may not appear as anything to our sight, is nourished by the secret providence of God. Let us also remember that those who calculate the number of the elect by the measure of their own senses are acting in folly and arrogance, for God has a way, accessible to Himself but concealed from us, by which He wonderfully preserves His elect, even when all seems lost.[2]

We must remember not to judge the success of the church only by sight—rather, we must judge it by faith. In other words, we must not judge the success of the gospel by what our eyes see. We may think that the church is small and that few are being saved, but

2. Calvin, *Romans and Thessalonians*, 240.

God is at work. The gates of hell will not prevail against the kingdom of God (Matt. 16:18). Like the small mustard seed, the church is imperceptibly growing and will one day fill the entire creation (Matt. 13:31–32; cf. Revelation 21–22). Although only a remnant of Israel belongs to Christ, we must not think that the company of the elect has been whittled down to a number hardly worth saving.

The blood of the Lamb is powerful and mighty to save, and He is saving an innumerable host of sinners. The Scriptures tell us that from one man, Abraham (think of the mustard seed), "were born as many as the stars of the sky in multitude—innumerable as the sand which is by the seashore" (think of the mustard tree) (Heb. 11:12). Moreover, when we look at John's heavenly vision, we undoubtedly know that Christ will save an innumerable host from every tribe, tongue, and nation (Rev. 5:9–13). God is not miserly with His mercy—perish the thought! Instead, even though the church appears small and persecuted, under the proverbial thumb of the world, like Israel in Egypt, she continues to grow: "But the more they afflicted them, the more they multiplied and grew" (Ex. 1:12). Indeed, it could very well be that we are in the infancy of the church and that countless millions have yet to be saved. In other words, the lesson for the church that we can glean from God's dealings with the remnant of Israel is that He is faithful to His word and will save all His people. Nothing will get in God's way. Hence, we must not lose hope but instead pray that God will buoy our flagging spirits so that we will trust Him despite what our eyes might see. Our job as the church is to ensure that all the nations, including the Jews, hear the message of the gospel. Our mission is to carry the gospel to the ends of the earth by whatever biblical means we have at our disposal.

Conclusion

We must heed Paul's warning to the unbelieving Jews—it applies equally to us. Paul has reminded his recipients of the dangers of trying to bring works before God's throne. We must never forget this. Paul has reminded his recipients of God's faithfulness to His promises—namely, to save the children of Abraham—both Jew and

Gentile alike. Paul has reminded his recipients of the need to bow before God's sovereign dispensation of grace—He is righteous in His judgment and wrath and in His dispensation of mercy and love. Remember that God has ordained redemptive history in this manner so that His saving mercies in Christ receive the glory and honor they deserve.

35

Pride Goes before the Fall

ROMANS 11:11–24

I say then, have they stumbled that they should fall? Certainly not! But through their fall, to provoke them to jealousy, salvation has come to the Gentiles. Now if their fall is riches for the world, and their failure riches for the Gentiles, how much more their fullness! For I speak to you Gentiles; inasmuch as I am an apostle to the Gentiles, I magnify my ministry, if by any means I may provoke to jealousy those who are my flesh and save some of them. For if their being cast away is the reconciling of the world, what will their acceptance be but life from the dead? For if the firstfruit is holy, the lump is also holy; and if the root is holy, so are the branches. And if some of the branches were broken off, and you, being a wild olive tree, were grafted in among them, and with them became a partaker of the root and fatness of the olive tree, do not boast against the branches. But if you do boast, remember that you do not support the root, but the root supports you. You will say then, "Branches were broken off that I might be grafted in." Well said. Because of unbelief they were broken off, and you stand by faith. Do not be haughty, but fear. For if God did not spare the natural branches, He may not spare you either. Therefore consider the goodness and severity of God: on those who fell, severity; but toward you, goodness, if you continue in His goodness. Otherwise you also will be cut off. And they also, if they do not continue in unbelief, will be grafted in, for God is able to graft them in again. For if you were cut out of the olive tree which is wild by nature, and were grafted contrary to nature into a cultivated olive tree, how much more will these, who are natural branches, be grafted into their own olive tree?

Pride is a cancer that manifests it ugliness in unlikely places. If we were to find someone of meager financial origins, raise him from poverty, give him every conceivable luxury, and refuse him nothing, I suspect that such a person would be easily tempted by pride in a very short amount of time. In one sense this is a story we all know. How many times have we watched celebrities rise from the nadir of obscurity to ascend to the zenith of fame? In many of these rags-to-riches stories we easily perceive the star's change in character and personality. The humble and quiet person becomes the obnoxious superstar. I think that many of the celebrity meltdowns we watch in the media come about because pride takes root in their heart and they refuse to listen to anyone but their own twisted counsel. As far removed as celebrity meltdowns might seem, Paul unpacks a similar pattern here in this portion of Romans 11.

Paul continues to defend and explain God's covenant faithfulness to Abraham and his offspring, the children of the promise (Rom. 9:7–8). He explained that one's ethnic ties do not automatically save him. Rather, God's sovereign choice is the deciding factor. Paul drove this point home by the statement "Jacob I have loved, but Esau have I hated" (Rom. 9:13). God rejected Esau, a biological descendant of Abraham. Paul, however, did not want his recipients to think that God forgot Abraham's biological offspring. Yes, God cast off the nation of Israel as His people, but He has not cast off every single Jew. Recall that Paul brought himself forward as evidence that God had not totally cast off the Jews (Rom. 11:1). Moreover, he explained that there was still a remnant of ethnic Israelites that God was drawing to Himself (Rom. 11:5). In this section of Romans 11 Paul describes the manner by which God presently saves the remnant of ethnic Israel. But he also warns the Gentiles who have been grafted into the people of God not to allow the seed of pride to grow in their hearts. Like the person lifted from obscurity to fame, the Gentiles were aliens and strangers to the covenants and promises of God but were now drawn into the people of God. The grace of God, therefore, should never be the basis for boasting in ourselves but rather the occasion and ground for boasting in the Lord.

Provoking Abraham's Descendants

The New Testament presents the nearly complete rejection of Christ by His own people. The cry of "we have no king but Caesar" (John 19:15) likely echoed in the minds of the apostles as they remembered the mournful events surrounding Christ's arrest and crucifixion. Such sentiment undoubtedly echoed in Paul's mind as he meditated on his countrymen's rejection of Christ (Rom. 9:1–5). But Paul wanted both Jews and Gentiles to understand something of God's mysterious ways and the end-goal of ethnic Israel's judicial hardening. Paul writes, "I say then, have they stumbled that they should fall? Certainly not! But through their fall, to provoke them to jealousy, salvation has come to the Gentiles. Now if their fall is riches for the world, and their failure riches for the Gentiles, how much more their fullness!" (Rom. 11:11–12).

God's plan in His judicial hardening of Abraham's biological descendants was ultimately to save a remnant. As Abraham's biological children rejected the gospel and Christ, the gospel would make further incursions among the Gentiles. Imagine the waves of the ocean rebounding off a sea wall—as the waves come in they rebound off the sea wall and head back out. As Abraham's biological descendants rejected the gospel, the waves of God's grace would rebound and land in the midst of the Gentiles. Think, for example, what occurred on the heels of the Jewish rejection and crucifixion of Jesus—Pentecost! People from the nations were gathered, heard the gospel, repented, believed, and were baptized (Acts 2). The wave of God's grace rebounded off the wall of Jewish rejection and landed on the Gentiles gathered in Jerusalem.

But as anyone who lives along the coast knows, eventually the ocean will destroy objects that stand in the midst of the surf. The waves take their toll and the sea wall, as impenetrable as it might seem, eventually crumbles. This occurs with the waves of God's grace. As the waves of God's grace landed on the Gentiles and saved them, this made the Jews jealous! As Gentiles were saved, God's grace rebounded back to the Jews and began to destroy the wall of opposition. John Calvin explains this principle well when he writes: "As envy rouses a wife who has been rejected by her husband through her own fault to strive to be reconciled, so now it may be, he says, that the Jews, having seen the Gentiles put in their place, may be touched with grief at their rejection, and seek after reconciliation."[1] Think again about the events of Pentecost—what occurred on the heels of the salvation of thousands of Gentiles? I suspect that some fail to notice, but Luke records that a number of Jews embraced the gospel: Aquila and Priscilla (Acts 18:2), Apollos (Acts 18:24), and of course, most famously, Saul of Tarsus (Acts 9)!

This back-and-forth wave motion of God's grace between Jew and Gentile was the means by which He was accomplishing the salvation of both the elect Gentiles and the Jewish remnant. This was one of the driving factors in Paul's own ministry among the Gentiles: "For I speak to you Gentiles; inasmuch as I am an apostle to the Gentiles, I magnify my ministry, if by any means I may provoke to jealousy those who are my flesh and save some of them" (Rom. 11:13–14). Paul wanted to see more Gentiles receive Christ so that more of the Jewish remnant would be saved. Moreover, Paul marveled that if their rejection of the gospel meant the salvation of thousands upon thousands of Gentiles, the complete salvation of the Jewish remnant would mean something even more wonderful. "For if their being cast away is the reconciling of the world," writes, Paul, "what will their acceptance be but life from the dead?" (Rom. 11:15).

The Holy Root

Paul argues for the legitimacy of the present salvation and inclusion of the Jewish remnant on the basis of God's covenant promises to Abraham, Isaac, and Jacob. He illustrates his point with two common analogies: "For if the firstfruit is holy, the lump is also holy; and if the root is holy, so are the branches" (Rom. 11:16). Paul appeals to the analogy of the firstfruits, a reference to the first and very best part of the harvest that was sacrificed to God (Num. 15:17–21). The firstfruits signaled not only that the harvest was ready to be brought

1. Calvin, *Romans and Thessalonians*, 246–47.

in but that there was more like the firstfruits waiting in the fields. So, if the firstfruits are holy and set apart, so is the rest of the harvest. If the firstfruits of the offered dough are holy, so is the rest of the batch. The firstfruit is representative of the whole. In this case, the firstfruits to which Paul refers are the patriarchs—Abraham, Isaac, and Jacob—the fathers of Israel and of the Jews. So Paul, mixing his metaphors (combining the images of firstfruits and the rest of the batch of dough with a tree and its roots), explains that if Abraham, Isaac, and Jacob are the holy firstfruits or root of the tree, then there are branches that are holy as well; that is, there are Jews who belong to the remnant that are holy.

Beware of Pride

Paul now elaborates this analogy and brings a word of warning to the Roman Gentiles who received his epistle. Remember that the congregation at Rome was made up of both Jews and Gentiles. Moreover, there was likely strife between the two groups, which Paul now addresses in the verses that follow:

> And if some of the branches were broken off, and you, being a wild olive tree, were grafted in among them, and with them became a partaker of the root and fatness of the olive tree, do not boast against the branches. But if you do boast, remember that you do not support the root, but the root supports you. You will say then, "Branches were broken off that I might be grafted in." Well said. Because of unbelief they were broken off, and you stand by faith. Do not be haughty, but fear. For if God did not spare the natural branches, He may not spare you either. (Rom. 11:17–21)

The likely scenario at Rome was that Gentile Christians were boasting about their salvation. They knew of the large-scale Jewish rejection of Christ and the gospel and bragged about the fact that they were included in God's covenant despite the fact that they were once aliens and strangers. Like the humble country boy who skyrockets to fame, the fast-moving cancer of pride swelled in Gentile hearts.

But Paul wanted both Jew and Gentile to understand the wave pattern of God's grace. The Jews needed to recognize how God's grace worked so that they would know that God had not forgotten them—He was still faithful to His promises to Abraham, Isaac, and Jacob. The Gentiles, however, needed to grasp the nature of the movement of God's grace so that they would not become prideful and arrogant. They needed to know that they were originally wild branches, pagans, those with whom no God-fearing Jew would even deign to share a meal. But God nevertheless grafted them into the holy people of God. Moreover, they were grafted in by God's grace through faith, not by their own inherent superiority or worthiness. A Jewish root also supported these Gentiles—the promises God gave to Abraham, Isaac, and Jacob. So, contrary to Gentile misperceptions, they had not taken over the house of Abraham. Rather, they were guests in Abraham's house, and Paul wanted them to remember this. Therefore, he warns his Gentile recipients at Rome about the dangers of pride:

> Therefore consider the goodness and severity of God: on those who fell, severity; but toward you, goodness, if you continue in His goodness. Otherwise you also will be cut off. And they also, if they do not continue in unbelief, will be grafted in, for God is able to graft them in again. For if you were cut out of the olive tree which is wild by nature, and were grafted contrary to nature into a cultivated olive tree, how much more will these, who are natural branches, be grafted into their own olive tree? (Rom. 11:22–24)

Remember the old saying: "Pride goes before the fall." In this case, Paul wanted the Roman Gentile Christians to recognize that they were saved by grace, not by works. As such, salvation by God's grace precluded all grounds for boasting and pride. If they boasted in their own self-worth, works, or supposed superiority, they would reveal that they were not truly united to Christ and would be broken off the tree. Recall Christ's words to his disciples: "If anyone does not abide in Me, he is cast out as a branch and is withered; and they gather them and throw them into the fire, and they are burned" (John 15:6). Rather than sink into a pit of pride, the Gentile Christians at Rome are encouraged to meditate on the mercy and grace of God. Not only this, he implicitly gives the Gentile Christians something for which to pray—that the Jews would be regrafted onto the tree.

Heeding Paul's Counsel

How many of us read through the Old Testament and portions of the New and shake our heads in bewilderment at the foolishness of the Jews. Think about it: The Jews were delivered in a miraculous and mighty demonstration of God's power—He divided the Red Sea! They saw God judge the Egyptians with the ten great plagues leading to the condemnation, judgment, and execution of the firstborn. Despite this they quickly fell headlong into idolatry and worshiped the golden calf. We shake our heads in disbelief because of how quickly they departed from God—they were and are a proud and stiff-necked people (Ex. 32:9). How many of us read the clashes between Christ and the Pharisees and, again, shake our heads in disapproval and bafflement? How can they, the most knowledgeable teachers in all Israel, fail to recognize the Messiah?

Yet we must not miss Paul's point here—namely, pride of this nature is characteristic not only of the Jews. We are equally prone to such a spiritual cancer as well. Paul makes this very point in his first epistle to the Corinthians when he writes about Israel's idolatry and sexual immorality. We are supposed to learn from their sins lest we fall into the same pattern of rebellion (1 Cor. 10:10–11). Notice that Paul gives Gentiles as well as the church at Corinth the same warning: Beware—pride goes before the fall. On this point, Calvin offers helpful counsel:

> This is a most powerful argument for repressing all overconfidence. We should never think of the rejection of the Jews without being struck with dread and terror. The one thing

> which caused their ruin was their despising of the divine judgment through their negligent disregard of the dignity which they had obtained. They were not spared, though they were natural branches. What then will become of us who are wild and alien branches, if we become excessively insolent? But this reflection leads us to distrust ourselves, and makes us cling with greater boldness and tenacity to the goodness of God.[2]

Our prayer should be that Christ would preserve us from pride and enable us to recognize that but for the grace of God, we too would reject Christ.

Conclusion

This should be a warning to us, that we would soberly examine ourselves. When we survey the wondrous cross on which the Prince of Glory died, pray that our richest gain we would count but loss, and pour contempt on all our pride. Yes, we have been grafted into the olive tree in the place of ethnic Jews who scorned Christ, but forbid it Lord that we should boast, save in the death of Christ our God.

---

2. Calvin, *Romans and Thessalonians*, 251.

36

All Israel Will Be Saved

ROMANS 11:25–36

For I do not desire, brethren, that you should be ignorant of this mystery, lest you should be wise in your own opinion, that blindness in part has happened to Israel until the fullness of the Gentiles has come in. And so all Israel will be saved, as it is written: "The Deliverer will come out of Zion, And He will turn away ungodliness from Jacob; For this is My covenant with them, When I take away their sins." Concerning the gospel they are enemies for your sake, but concerning the election they are beloved for the sake of the fathers. For the gifts and the calling of God are irrevocable. For as you were once disobedient to God, yet have now obtained mercy through their disobedience, even so these also have now been disobedient, that through the mercy shown you they also may obtain mercy. For God has committed them all to disobedience, that He might have mercy on all. Oh, the depth of the riches both of the wisdom and knowledge of God! How unsearchable are His judgments and His ways past finding out! "For who has known the mind of the Lord? Or who has become His counselor?" "Or who has first given to Him And it shall be repaid to him?" For of Him and through Him and to Him are all things, to whom be glory forever. Amen.

Too many of us compartmentalize our lives: "Work does not mingle with my home life, and my recreation does not mix with work. My religious beliefs and practices remain at church on Sunday but certainly do not affect my home or work life. The same goes for my politics—religion and politics do not mix!" Yet as common as these sentiments might be, the reality is that the way we understand

Scripture informs the way we live. Take, for instance, the dispensationalist Christians who convinced President Harry S. Truman that the United States had to support Jews in their efforts to create their own state in 1948. Theology drove U.S. foreign policy.[1] A similar pattern has unfolded in more recent years. I recall reading about a number of well-known dispensationalist pastors who were invited to Egypt, where they participated in a forum of Christian and Islamic scholars to understand why the U.S. government supported Israel. They told their Islamic hosts that Israel was God's chosen people, which meant the United States had to support the nation-state of Israel. Yet we must recognize that the salvation of Israel of which Paul writes here in Romans 11:25–32 does not entail the redemption of what we now know as the nation-state Israel, the geopolitical entity. Rather, Paul has something very different in mind when he writes "all Israel will be saved." If what Paul writes here has any connection to the rest of his epistle, then the manner of Israel's salvation will dictate how we, the church, go about the important task of evangelizing the nations of the world. Far from entering geopolitics, the church's primary concern must be about evangelism of all the nations, including even the Jewish people.

The Revealed Mystery

Paul begins this section of chapter 11 by expressing his desire that his recipients understand the mystery of redemption: "For I do not desire, brethren, that you should be ignorant of this mystery, lest you should be wise in your own opinion, that blindness in part has happened to Israel until the fullness of the Gentiles has come in" (Rom. 11:25). This statement rests on his earlier argument in Romans 11:17–24 and the wave pattern that exists between the Jews and the Gentiles. As God calls the Jews and they reject the gospel, like ocean waves bouncing off a sea wall, the gospel rebounds off of the Jews and saves the Gentiles. But as Gentiles are saved, the wave

1. See, e.g., Aaron William Stone, "Dispensationalism and United States Foreign Policy with Israel" (M.A. thesis, University of Texas at Arlington, 2008).

bounces back and falls on the Jews, which brings about the redemption of the elect remnant. Paul does not want his recipients to be ignorant of this *mystery*—that is, something that was once hidden but is now revealed (cf. Rom. 16:25–26). In this case, the people of God were ignorant of how God would redeem the Jewish remnant and Gentiles. But now Paul has authoritatively revealed how God saves Jew and Gentile.

Paul describes the wave motion of the Jews' hardening and the Gentiles' salvation, which results in the elect Jews' jealousy and eventual salvation. Paul explains, "And so all Israel will be saved, as it is written: 'The Deliverer will come out of Zion, And He will turn away ungodliness from Jacob; For this is My covenant with them, When I take away their sins'" (Rom. 11:26–27). When Paul says "all Israel will be saved," he does not mean that every rank-and-file Israelite will be redeemed, nor does he mean that at some point immediately before the return of Christ there will be a mass conversion of the Jewish people. There are several factors that point in a very different direction.[2]

We must not automatically assume that just because Paul invokes the term *Israel* that he has only the biological descendants of Abraham in mind. First, notice Romans 11:12 in which Paul speaks of the "fullness" or "full inclusion" (ESV), the *pleroma*, of the Jews. Paul uses the word *fullness* (*pleroma*) in connection with the Gentiles in verse 25. The "fullness of the Gentiles" does not refer to a mass Gentile conversion. It simply means the full company of the elect Gentiles. Therefore, the "fullness" of the Jews (v. 12) does not refer to a mass conversion. Rather, *fullness* refers to the full number, or the number of the elect, in this case of both Jews and Gentiles.

Second, remember how Paul applied categories to Gentiles that once referred exclusively to the Jews. Regarding circumcision, for example, Paul applies this to both Jew and Gentile at Philippi: "For we are the circumcision, who worship God in the Spirit, rejoice

2. For what follows, see O. Palmer Robertson, *The Israel of God: Yesterday, Today, and Tomorrow* (Phillipsburg, N.J.: P&R Publishing, 2000), 167–93.

in Christ Jesus" (Phil. 3:3). Those who possess God-given faith in Christ are, according to Paul, the true "sons of Abraham" (Gal. 3:7). Earlier in Romans Paul similarly explains what it means to be truly a Jew: "For he is not a Jew who is one outwardly, nor is circumcision that which is outward in the flesh; but he is a Jew who is one inwardly; and circumcision is that of the heart, in the Spirit, not in the letter; whose praise is not from men but from God" (Rom. 2:28–29). But most importantly, especially as it pertains to Paul's use of the term *Israel*, Paul defined the term to include Gentiles. Recall what Paul wrote in Romans 9: "Nor are they all children because they are the seed of Abraham; but, 'In Isaac your seed shall be called.' That is, those who are the children of the flesh, these are not the children of God; but the children of the promise are counted as the seed" (Rom. 9:7–8). Paul reoriented his countrymen's understanding of who truly constituted Israel—it was ultimately defined by God's election and His promise, not solely descent from Abraham. This is why Paul could close his epistle to the Galatians, a largely Gentile group of churches, by addressing them as "the Israel of God" (Gal. 6:16).

Third, to argue that Paul is saying "all ethnic Israel will be saved" or that there will be a mass conversion of the Jewish people does not fit the flow of his argument. Does it make sense for Paul to talk of a "remnant" of Jews (Rom. 11:5) and then say, "all ethnic Israel will be saved"? I believe the answer is no. A thin reading of the English adverb *so* in Romans 11:26 has fostered this misinterpretation: "And *so* all Israel will be saved" (emphasis mine). The English leaves the reader thinking that Paul merely states that all Israel will be saved, when Paul's underlying Greek (*kai houtos*) conveys the idea that the wave motion is the manner by which God will save all Israel. Note the ESV's translation of this verse: "And in this way [*kai houtos*] all Israel will be saved." In other words, Paul is saying by way of summary that this wave motion of God's grace that goes back and forth between the Jews and Gentiles will save all Israel: the elect, the children of the promise, both Jew and Gentile.

To support this affirmation, Paul conflates two Old Testament passages, Isaiah 59:20–21 and Jeremiah 31:34. These are passages that both prophets state in connection with the redemption of God's people—the elect. Paul reaffirms God's covenant promise by quoting these two verses, which incidentally do not apply only to ethnic Jews but to all God's people. This is why Paul says "this is My covenant with them, When I take away their sins" (Rom. 11:27). And with whom has God made this covenant? With the descendants of Abraham: "And I will establish My covenant between Me and you and your descendants after you in their generations, for an everlasting covenant, to be God to you and your descendants after you" (Gen. 17:7). And who are the descendants of Abraham? "Only those who are of faith are sons of Abraham," writes Paul (Gal. 3:7). Therefore Paul states that all Israel, both Jew and Gentile, will be saved.

Irrevocable Promises

At this point some might ask, "Why does he disclose the rebounding wave pattern that moves back and forth between the Jews and Gentiles?" Paul was disinterested in speculation or peering into the mysteries of God for the sake of bald curiosity. Rather, he wanted to remind the Gentile Christians at Rome of their place within the household of God as former aliens and strangers to the covenants of God. By understanding their place, they would be equipped to fend off the temptation of pride over and against the Jews. Therefore Paul writes, "Concerning the gospel they are enemies for your sake, but concerning the election they are beloved for the sake of the fathers. For the gifts and the calling of God are irrevocable" (Rom. 11:28–29). Paul was no stranger to the persecution by his fellow Jews—he bore the scars on his body as the sign of his intimate knowledge of their animosity toward Christ, His gospel, and His church. So Paul acknowledges this fact to his Gentile audience when he states that the Jews "are enemies for your sake." But to fend off pride, indifference, or hatred toward their "enemies," Paul wanted the Gentile Christians to see the bigger picture. The Jewish people were still beloved of God because of His love for Abraham,

Isaac, and Jacob—God's promises to them were irrevocable. He promised Abraham a multitude of offspring, one that included both Gentiles *and* Jews.

Paul called his Gentile brothers and sisters to look on the Jews with kindness, love, and compassion. He did not want them looking on the Jews with contempt or pride. He reminded them of their own recalcitrance and hatred of Christ and how God saved them: "For as you were once disobedient to God, yet have now obtained mercy through their disobedience, even so these also have now been disobedient, that through the mercy shown you they also may obtain mercy" (Rom. 11:30–31). Paul once again reiterates the saving purposes of God—the manner in which He will save "all Israel." Paul restates the idea of the wave motion that will bring about the salvation of the elect—both Jew and Gentile. He reminds the Gentiles not to swell with pride but rather to realize that God has not rejected the Jews in toto. He tells the Gentiles that God committed ethnic Jews to disobedience in order to save the Gentiles *and* elect Jews.

The Mind of the Lord

We should take a step back, pause, and think about the grandeur of this text. Too often, we take the truths of the gospel for granted. Moreover, like the disciples in the garden of Gethsemane, our minds may grow weary as we try to follow Paul's argumentation. Our spirit is willing, but our flesh is weak. Nevertheless, we must brush away the mental cobwebs and meditate on Paul's words. Think of it: the wrath and judgment of God has fallen on the nation of Israel for their rejection of the Messiah (1 Thess. 2:14–16). God's wrath has been poured out on them, which was manifest in the destruction of Jerusalem in AD 70. This is why, as Paul says, we must contemplate both the goodness that has been poured out on us and the severity of the judgment that has come on the nation of Israel (Rom. 11:22). Yet we should also contemplate the depths of the wisdom and mercy of God, the reason for Paul's spontaneous doxology at the end of the chapter.

Think about the wonderful nature of God's saving purposes—namely, that God has taken the two, Jew and Gentile, and through the obedience and satisfaction of Christ has broken down the wall of division and created one body, one man. Christ came and preached peace to those who were far off, the Gentiles, and to those who were near, the Jews. As a result, the pagan Gentiles who once walked in darkness are no longer strangers and aliens but fellow citizens with the saints and members of the household of God (Eph. 2:11–22)! Notice that Paul tells us that the *one* new man (Eph. 2:15), the *one* olive tree with natural (Rom. 11:17) and wild olive branches, the strangers and foreigners to the covenant (Eph. 2:19), the *one* spiritual temple (Eph. 2:21) is being built "on the foundation of the apostles and prophets, Jesus Christ Himself being the chief cornerstone" (Eph. 2:20).

This has been God's plan from the beginning, and Paul has revealed the manner by which God executes His plan. He draws both Jew and Gentile to Himself through this constant wave of His grace until the consummation of the age. This is the mystery Paul wants his Gentile recipients to know. We too should not be ignorant of this mystery. Therefore, when Paul writes, "In this way all Israel will be saved" (Rom. 11:26 ESV), what should our response be? Undoubtedly, we should join the apostle in praise and adoration of our merciful and loving God: "Oh, the depth of the riches both of the wisdom and knowledge of God! How unsearchable are His judgments and His ways past finding out! 'For who has known the mind of the LORD? Or who has become His counselor?' 'Or who has first given to Him And it shall be repaid to him?' For of Him and through Him and to Him are all things, to whom be glory forever. Amen" (Rom. 11:33–36).

Paul builds his doxological song with two quotations from the Old Testament. The first comes from Isaiah 40:13, which speaks of God's might and wisdom in the manner in which He will save His people. God promised His people that there would be a second exodus, but this time they would be delivered from Babylon. God eventually raised Cyrus to open the doors to the Promised Land and allow God's people to return to the land flowing with milk and honey, but this was merely a provisional or typical exodus—there was still a greater exodus to come, led by one greater than Moses: Jesus. That Paul quotes Isaiah 40:13, "For who has known the mind of the LORD? Or who has become His counselor?" indicates that God honors His word and keeps His promises. Paul's words here are not merely praise but ultimately a crowning jewel on his overall argument. He draws from Isaiah's praise of God's wisdom in Israel's salvation to prove his own argument regarding the salvation of the remnant and at the same time adorn his point with doxological diamonds.

Paul draws his second quotation from Job 41:11, which comes from God's famous reply to Job's complaint:

> Can you draw out Leviathan with a hook, Or snare his tongue with a line which you lower? Can you put a reed through his nose, Or pierce his jaw with a hook? Will he make many supplications to you? Will he speak softly to you? Will he make a covenant with you? Will you take him as a servant forever? Will you play with him as with a bird, Or will you leash him for your maidens? Will your companions make a banquet of him? Will they apportion him among the merchants? Can you fill his skin with harpoons, Or his head with fishing spears? Lay your hand on him; Remember the battle—Never do it again! Indeed, any hope of overcoming him is false; Shall one not be overwhelmed at the sight of him? No one is so fierce that he would dare stir him up. Who then is able to stand against Me? Who has preceded Me, that I should pay him? Everything under heaven is Mine. (Job 41:1–11)

Paul draws from God's response to Job to remind his readers of the grandeur of God's wisdom. Even in our own day there are still many things about creation that we do not understand, and likely never will. As scientifically and technologically advanced as we are, we still have many unanswered questions about the world. If this is so, then we should bow before God's wisdom and power as Luther counsels; we must constantly meditate on and study God's Word to learn true wisdom: "We can find the wisdom of God nowhere but in His Word. Whoever loves and values it and constantly studies it is not only a doctor enlightened by God and an approved man superior to all worldly-wise and learned people but a judge of all the wisdom and teaching of devils and men."[3]

Praise should certainly fill our hearts, but as I intimated in the introduction, Paul's words have implications for how we view things such as our evangelism and politics, particularly our view of the Middle East. I think that many Christians of Gentile origin, which probably constitutes the lion's share of the church, look on the Jewish people with a degree of indifference. Yet should our hearts not break and should we not grieve with the apostle Paul? Recall Paul's mournful words that began his arguments in Romans 9–11: "I have great sorrow and continual grief in my heart. For I could wish that I myself were accursed from Christ for my brethren, my countrymen according to the flesh" (Rom. 9:2–3). We should grieve with Paul that so many Jewish people have scorned Christ. We should pray with Paul that God would redeem the Jewish remnant. We should engage in conversations about the gospel with our Jewish friends, neighbors, and coworkers. Ask them what they think about the Messiah. Ask them what they believe about the Old Testament Scriptures. Such simple questions can likely lead to broader discussions about Christianity. We should encourage our churches to investigate and participate in missions to the nation of Israel so that the gospel would go forth in the land where Christ once walked, where God's temple once stood, and where Christ was crucified and raised from the dead.

But one of the dangers we must avoid is using Paul's words about his love for his fellow Jews and the salvation of the remnant as a battering ram for our Middle Eastern foreign policy. Praying for the salvation of the Jewish remnant is one thing; unwavering support for the twenty-first-century geopolitical entity we call Israel is entirely another. We carry our support, love, and compassion for the Jewish remnant through prayer and the sword of the Spirit,

3. Luther, *What Luther Says*, 3:1455, no. 4695.

the gospel, not through military weaponry and opposition to terror states in the region. How many Arabic Christians, for example, have died at the hands of Israeli weapons? These Arabic Christians are part of the true Israel, children of the promise, sons of Abraham because they have faith in Christ. These Arabic Christians have become citizens of the commonwealth of the Israel of God through their union with Christ, the head of His body, the church. In our blind support of geopolitical Israel, how many Arabic Christians have we unwittingly subjected to pain, suffering, and even death? Our desire to draw straight lines from our theology to our politics sometimes yields disastrous consequences because we have failed to understand correctly the Scriptures. Our heavenly citizenship must drive our chief allegiances, not our political convictions. Rather than blindly support one nation over another, we should be circumspect and give our first allegiance to our fellow brothers and sisters in Christ no matter where they live, whether in our own country or in places we designate as terror states. We should pray, therefore, for the church, wherever it exists, and pray for wisdom for our political leaders that they would act with prudence and equity (1 Tim. 2:1–2).

Conclusion

As we contemplate Paul's challenging and weighty words, we should rejoice that we have been grafted onto the tree and have been united to Christ. We who were once aliens and strangers are now fellow citizens of the commonwealth of Israel and the household of God. We should pray for humility; pray for the conversion of the Jewish remnant; pray that the gospel would go forth; and, as Gentiles come to Christ, which creates jealousy among the Jewish remnant, pray that all Israel would be saved. As we behold the glorious plan of redemption unfolding before our very eyes, we should join with Paul in words of praise: "Oh, the depth of the riches both of the wisdom and knowledge of God! How unsearchable are His judgments and His ways past finding out! 'For who has known the mind of the LORD? Or who has become His counselor?' 'Or who has first given to Him And it shall be repaid to him?' For of Him and through Him and to Him are all things, to whom be glory forever. Amen" (Rom. 11:33–36). Or in the words of a recent hymn,

> Give praise to God who reigns above
> For perfect knowledge, wisdom, love;
> His judgments are divine, devout,
> His paths beyond all tracing out.
>
> No one can counsel God all-wise,
> Or truths unveil to His sharp eyes;
> He marks our paths behind, before;
> He is our steadfast counselor.
>
> Nothing exists that God might need
> For all things good from Him proceed.
> We praise Him as our Lord, and yet
> We never place God in our debt.
>
> Creation, life, salvation too,
> And all things else both good and true,
> Come from and through our God always,
> And fill our hearts with grateful praise.
>
> Come, lift your voice to heaven's high throne,
> And glory give to God alone![4]

---

4. James Montgomery Boice, "Give Praise to God," in *Hymns for a Modern Reformation*, ed. James Montgomery Boice and Paul Jones (Philadelphia: Tenth Presbyterian Church, 2000), 9.

37

The Eschatological Priesthood

ROMANS 12:1–2

I beseech you therefore, brethren, by the mercies of God, that you present your bodies a living sacrifice, holy, acceptable to God, which is your reasonable service. And do not be conformed to this world, but be transformed by the renewing of your mind, that you may prove what is that good and acceptable and perfect will of God.

Early in our Lord's ministry He encountered the doubting and censorious Pharisees, who demanded a miraculous sign that Jesus was the Christ, the Messiah. To this challenge Jesus responded that He would destroy the temple and raise it up in three days (John 2:19–21). John parenthetically explains that Jesus was not speaking of destroying and raising the Herodian temple, though indeed it would be destroyed in AD 70. Rather, Christ was talking about raising the great eschatological temple—the temple of which many of the prophets spoke that God would build in the last days (Amos 9:11; Hag. 2:6–9). These Old Testament prophecies envision the great eschatological temple—ideal, perfect in every way. This temple is the final dwelling place of the triune Lord that Christ said He would raise in three days. Indeed, the apostle Paul tells us that Christ is the very foundation, the chief cornerstone of the new temple (Eph. 2:20–22). Paul addresses his recipients from this broader Old Testament outlook.

Paul has labored since the beginning of his epistle to explain the glory of God in the gospel. He recounted man's sinfulness and depravity culminating in the familiar verse "For all have sinned and fall short of the glory of God" (Rom. 3:23). God, however, intervened on man's behalf through the work of Jesus Christ—His life lived in perfect obedience to the law; His death for those who deserve it; and His resurrection, Christ's justification and prophetic declaration of our own resurrection. When the Holy Spirit sovereignly grants an individual the ability to believe, that person exercises faith in Christ and trusts in His work to save him. And because we have been buried with Christ through baptism and raised to walk in the newness of life, Christians are supposed to be markedly different from unbelievers.

At this point in Paul's letter to Rome, he has turned a corner. In Romans 1–11 Paul set forth who the Roman Christians are in Christ, and now from chapters 12–16 he tells them how they must live. In more technical terms, indicatives dominate Romans 1–11, which explain the Christian's state, identity, and union with Christ. Imperatives dominate Romans 12–16: what Christians must do in light of who they are in Christ. As important as it is to distinguish indicatives and imperatives, we must never separate them. Nor must we think that Paul has left the saving power of the gospel behind in his rearview mirror now that he discusses matters pertaining to Christian conduct. On the contrary, the gospel is as important for entry into the Christian life as it is throughout the entire journey. Hence, we must consider Christian conduct in light of who we are in Christ, which Paul couches in terms of the ministry of the eschatological priesthood—the priests of God's final temple.

Our Reasonable Service

Paul begins chapter 12 with the word *therefore*, which means that everything heretofore informs the conclusion that he makes. In other words, everything that follows in chapter 12 presupposes chapters 1–11. Paul writes: "I beseech you therefore, brethren, by the mercies of God, that you present your bodies a living sacrifice, holy, acceptable to God, which is your reasonable service" (Rom. 12:1). How should Christians act? How should they live? Paul couches his call to action in the language of the Old Testament—the temple priestly duties. Paul tells Christians to present their bodies as living sacrifices. Why does Paul use this language? He has used it not because it is quaint, intriguing, or useful literary imagery but because of everything else that the New Testament teaches us regarding our union with Christ. When we are united to Christ we are incorporated into the great eschatological temple. We are, as Peter and Paul remind us, living stones and the temple of the living God (1 Cor. 3:16; 1 Peter 2:5). Notice, though, that we are not only the temple, the edifice, the building; we are also "a holy priesthood," according to Peter.

What were priests supposed to do in the Old Testament? One of their functions was to offer sacrifices, and this is why Peter says we are "a holy priesthood, to offer up spiritual sacrifices acceptable to God through Jesus Christ." Notice how closely Peter's description follows Paul's exhortation: "Present your bodies a living sacrifice, holy, acceptable to God" (Rom. 12:1). We must present our bodies —our whole being, will, actions, affections, members—to God as *holy* sacrifices, as those that are acceptable to God. The presentation of our lives must be *holy*. What, however, does it mean to present a holy sacrifice? Well, as Paul has explained earlier, we must not give our lives over to sin (Rom. 6:11–13). We are to use our members as instruments of righteousness. It is in this manner that we are acceptable to God—when we seek righteousness. This, of course, is one of the prime exhortations of our Lord: "But seek first the kingdom of God and His righteousness, and all these things shall be added to you" (Matt. 6:33). Living our lives as acceptable, holy, living sacrifices unto God, in light of our redemption, is certainly our "reasonable service" (*logiken laterian*). Paul employs the same Greek terminology found in passages dealing with Israel's priestly service to God in the Passover celebration (Ex. 12:25–26; 13:5; Josh. 22:27; 1 Chron. 28:13 LXX). But in the Old Testament, the priests offered sacrificial animals—they did not offer themselves in sacrifice to the Lord. How, then, can we offer ourselves as living sacrifices?

Living Sacrifices

Paul explains how Christians offer their bodies as living sacrifices in the following verse: "And do not be conformed to this world, but be transformed by the renewing of your mind, that you may prove what is that good and acceptable and perfect will of God" (Rom. 12:2). Paul tells his recipients not to "be conformed to this world." Why is this so? This world, as Paul elsewhere reminds us, belongs to this "present evil age" (Gal. 1:4). What are the marks of this present evil age and its thinking? The world exchanged the truth for a lie; darkened its heart; became foolish; and worshiped birds, animals, and creeping things (Rom. 1:21–23). For these reasons, and others, the New Testament tells us that this world is passing away, coming to nothing, and will fall under God's judgment (1 John 2:17; 1 Cor. 2:6; 7:31). Like the world around Noah's ark that God judged beneath the floodwaters, He will flood the earth beneath the fiery outpouring and baptism of the Holy Spirit (2 Peter 3:1–7). If the world therefore presses and conforms us to its mold, then God will sweep us away in His judgment because we live contrary to His will.

Rather than engage in worldly, sinful conduct, Paul states that we must be transformed by the renewing of our minds. What, however, transforms our minds? Do we have to try hard to be different? Do we have to search high and low for some secret hidden knowledge known only to a few? Can we find a method through self-help books and pop psychology? Remember the indicatives from Romans 1–11: The gospel is the power of God unto salvation, first for the Jew, then for the Greek (Rom. 1:16–17). Only through revealing the mystery of the gospel and the transformative work of the Spirit does God change and conform us to His will, to the image of His holy and righteous Son, Jesus Christ. The more we think and meditate on and draw near to the teaching of the gospel—the revealed will of God—and His law, the more He will conform us to the image of Christ. The more we worship God in Spirit and truth—that is, in the power of the Holy Spirit and according to the revealed truth of God, Jesus Christ—the more He will transform and renew our minds. We will become more like the God we worship.

But this does not mean that the renewing of our minds is purely an intellectual process. As Charles Hodge (1797–1878) explains, "While Christians should remember that the service which they are called upon to render is a rational service, pertaining to the soul, they should not suppose that it consists merely in the secret exercises of the heart. The whole man and the whole life must be actively and constantly devoted to God."[1] Christ's meditation on His Father's will led to action—He humbled Himself and was obedient to Him to the point of death, even death on the cross (Phil. 2:5–11). When we are more like Christ, therefore, we are obedient, which pleases the Father, and demonstrate "what is good and acceptable and perfect."

Who and Where We Are

When we contemplate Paul's exhortation we should recognize the two major ways these short verses impact us. First, we must understand the significance of our union with Christ. Because we have been joined to Christ by faith, we must recognize who we are—sons of the living God, those who have been raised from death to walk in the newness of life. Are our actions, thoughts, decisions, and behavior dissonant or consonant with our calling and union with Christ? Up until this point, Paul has dealt generally with the issue of how our conduct should be consonant with our calling. What exactly does holy living look like? Paul will show us in the subsequent verses and chapters to come. But the point still stands: Are we being conformed to the patterns of the present evil age or are we renewing our thinking according to God's pattern—namely, Christ?

Second, we must acknowledge our identity as priests in God's final temple, the body of Christ. The people of God no longer go to a physical temple under the Levitical priesthood, offering animal sacrifices. Those who worship Christ in Spirit and truth are

---

1. Hodge, *Romans*, 394.

the temple. We approach the Father not by the blood of bulls and goats but by the blood of the spotless Lamb of God. We no longer offer animals but instead offer our lives as living sacrifices. Those who look for a physical temple to be rebuilt in Israel miss out on the fact that *they* are the final temple. We are also, as Peter writes, the eschatological priesthood—a holy priesthood and royal nation to the one true, living God (1 Peter 2:5). If we stop and ask what guide the Old Testament priests used to govern their conduct in the temple, we would quickly recognize that they used God's revelation, His law. They were, without a doubt, experts in God's law. This is the very function that Nehemiah, for example, served when the Israelites returned to the Promised Land under the Cyrus-decreed exodus from Babylon. Nehemiah read from the law and gave the sense so that the people understood it (Neh. 8:8).

This means that each one of us as a priest has a responsibility to study diligently the Word of God so that we know what is good, acceptable, and pleasing to Him. We must meditate, as the psalmist writes, on the law of God: "My hands also I will lift up to Your commandments, Which I love, And I will meditate on Your statutes" (Ps. 119:48). All too often Christians misunderstand the earlier portions of Romans and mistakenly think they have been completely and utterly freed from the law. Remember, we have been freed from the law as a covenant, but in Christ God gives us the law as a rule (WCF 19.6; WLC 97). Moreover, as the Westminster Confession states, the moral law's function as a rule in the Christian life is in no way contrary to the grace of the gospel; it sweetly complies with it, but only because the Spirit of Christ subdues and enables us to obey God freely and cheerfully (WCF 19.7). In our sanctification, the law is not our enemy but our friend because Christ has fulfilled it on our behalf.

This means that pastors must set the law of God before their congregations to instruct them and "give them the sense" so they understand what conduct is good, acceptable, and pleasing to the Lord. Too many pastors preach poor and inadequate substitutes and rob their sheep of the vital Word-nutrition they so desperately need.

But when pastors preach the law, they must also do so in concert with the gospel. Preaching bald imperatives apart from the indicatives of the gospel makes the law a covenant, not a rule. Sadly, I have heard orthodox pastors preach the law without ever mentioning the gospel or the name of Christ, all under the guise of preaching the law as a rule. Never approach the law apart from Christ, for apart from Him you will find only the covenant of works, that which demands perfect, personal, and perpetual obedience. Only through the perfect, personal, and perpetual obedience of Christ imputed by faith alone can we approach the law as a friend. Pastors, when you preach the law, preach Christ and Him crucified!

But life as a living sacrifice ultimately means that we focus our entire lives to the service of Christ and His church. All too often we gear our lives around many other things—careers, hobbies, sports, and the like. We gain reputations of devotion to these things. People know where they can find us on the weekend—at work, on the golf course, or in the garage. On the one hand, we do not commit sin when we engage in such things, but on the other hand, how much thought and time do we give these activities in comparison with our service to the church? Do we have a reputation of tireless service to the church or for other things? If Paul's words mean anything, above all else, we should desire to serve Christ and His church—this must be the focus of our energy, work, and life. If Christ is not our top priority, then we should pray that He would grant us the proper perspective so that we would pursue the life of discipleship—life as a living sacrifice.

Conclusion

In light of who we are in Christ, what type of priest will you be? What type of sacrifices will you bring? Pray that you will be a faithful priest, seeking conformity to the image of Christ, not conformity to the patterns of this passing present evil age. Sons of the living God, live out your royal identity so that you can prove what is good and acceptable in the sight of God. This is your reasonable service.

38

Living Sacrifices

ROMANS 12:3–8

For I say, through the grace given to me, to everyone who is among you, not to think of himself more highly than he ought to think, but to think soberly, as God has dealt to each one a measure of faith. For as we have many members in one body, but all the members do not have the same function, so we, being many, are one body in Christ, and individually members of one another. Having then gifts differing according to the grace that is given to us, let us use them: if prophecy, let us prophesy in proportion to our faith; or ministry, let us use it in our ministering; he who teaches, in teaching; he who exhorts, in exhortation; he who gives, with liberality; he who leads, with diligence; he who shows mercy, with cheerfulness.

One of the most common mantras in the church is that people must all be alike. From one vantage point, this is true. We should all, for example, confess the same faith, believe the same scriptural doctrines, and practice biblical piety. But this is not the type of uniformity that most have in mind. Rather, there is a tendency within the church in which people believe that if we all profess and practice the same faith, then everyone should be engaged in the same activities. If I, for example, believe that Christians should be involved in politics, then I will lobby, convince, persuade, and perhaps even pressure my fellow Christians to do the same. But what if there is someone else in the church who believes that working at a local Christian pregnancy crisis center is more important and thus lobbies, convinces, persuades, and pressures his fellow Christians to do the same? Multiply this pattern by ten or twenty, and soon there are different competing agendas circulating within the church. This type of uniformity is appealing but is ultimately unscriptural. Why? Because such a pattern, as well intended as it might be, assumes that everyone has the same gifts, abilities, and God-given interests. This is not at all how the Scriptures explain the nature of the church's varied callings.

When we come to this portion of Romans we must remember the question that we posed in the previous section. Recall that we reached a major turning point in Paul's epistle to the Romans. Chapters 1–11 explain redemption through the work of Christ and the Spirit. Paul explained how the prophecies of the Old Testament have been inaugurated in the ministry of Christ and that God is raising His people to walk in the newness of life—to walk obediently to His revealed will (Rom. 6:4–5). Just as we have been united to Christ to walk in the newness of life, we have also been incorporated into the final temple. We are both the temple and a holy priesthood (1 Peter 2:5). As priests in God's temple made from living stones, we are called to offer worship and service to our covenant Lord: "I beseech you therefore, brethren, by the mercies of God, that you present your bodies a living sacrifice, holy, acceptable to God, which is your reasonable service. And do not be conformed to this world, but be transformed by the renewing of your mind, that you may prove what is that good and acceptable and perfect will of God" (Rom. 12:1–2).

In other words, in light of our union with Christ, incorporation into the temple, and holy priesthood, we are living sacrifices. Note, we are not living sacrifices in an effort to redeem ourselves. Rather, we are living sacrifices by God's grace, trusting in Christ for our salvation—we are living sacrifices by God's design and out of thankfulness (Eph. 2:8–9). As the Heidelberg Catechism explains in question 86,

> Q. We have been delivered from our misery by God's grace alone through Christ and not because we have earned it: why then must we still do good?

> A. To be sure, Christ has redeemed us by his blood. But we do good because Christ by his Spirit is also renewing us to be like himself, so that in all our living we may show that we are thankful to God for all he has done for us, and so that he may be praised through us. And we do good so that we may be assured of our faith by its fruits, and so that by our godly living our neighbors may be won over to Christ.

Christ redeems us, and so our response to this redemption should be manifest in the fruit of our union with Christ, which is also an expression of our gratitude.

Based on all this I posed a question in the previous section: What does a living sacrifice look like? What does it look like when an individual walks "in the newness of life" (Rom. 6:1–4)? Paul spends the rest of his epistle demonstrating what it means to be a living sacrifice—what the holy priesthood, the final temple, the body of Christ looks like in action. In this passage before us he first explains how God has equipped individuals in the church to serve Him and the body of Christ. But God does not democratically distribute spiritual gifts to the church. He uniquely gifts people within the church so that they can serve in different ways. Paul shows how the body of Christ is united in redemption but diverse in the ways they serve Him.

A Foundation of Humility

Before Paul describes the diversified nature of gifts that Christ distributes to the church, he establishes a necessary foundation for the church—humility: "For I say, through the grace given to me, to everyone who is among you, not to think of himself more highly than he ought to think, but to think soberly, as God has dealt to each one a measure of faith" (Rom. 12:3). Ever since the fall, humans have had a proclivity toward pride. Just as Paul had to warn the Gentiles about pride (Rom. 11:1–6), he reminds the whole congregation in Rome not to think too highly of themselves regarding their God-given gifts. Paul models humility for his recipients. In other words, Paul recognizes that his own calling as an apostle is by God's grace—it is a gift from God. The recognition of grace, the foundation of our existence in the church, is the basis from which we must soberly examine God's gifts. In other words, apart from our union with Christ, we are nothing—Christ is everything and has given to us everything that we are or ever will be. Therefore, we must not think highly of ourselves.

Why is this the case? Must we grovel in dust and ashes and never have a positive self-image? Not at all. We can have a positive self-image, but it is important that we recognize the proper way to see ourselves. Our self-image must not start and begin by looking in the mirror, where we make ourselves the measure of all things. Rather, we must behold ourselves in the mirror of Christ and His Word. In so doing, He becomes the measure by which we esteem others and ourselves. We can have a positive self-image not because of who we are or what we have done but because God loved and sent His Son to die for us—Christ sacrificially gave Himself for us. When we look in the mirror of Christ, we see a precious lamb, one for whom Christ gave His very own life. But we have been individually redeemed to be part of Christ's body, the church. This means that the whole church is filled with precious lambs, which is why we ought not to think too highly of ourselves but rather esteem others as more important.

One Body

Paul writes, "For as we have many members in one body, but all the members do not have the same function, so we, being many, are one body in Christ, and individually members of one another" (Rom. 12:4–5). One way to look at the relationship of the individual to the rest of the church is that each living stone in Christ's final temple is unique, both in terms of personality and in terms of God's gifts. We must not, therefore, think of each stone as being the same, like perfectly shaped blocks. Instead, we must think of each living stone of the final temple as unique, specifically designed by Christ to fit into a precise location. Like unique pieces of a jigsaw puzzle, each piece has a specific place but contributes to presenting one unified picture. If you try to put a piece in the incorrect place, the picture gets distorted and you might even damage the puzzle. Moreover, no one piece of the puzzle can think it is more important than another, because every piece of the puzzle works together to present one picture. Separately, they cannot function. In this case, Paul explains that Christ gives each person within His body a unique function, but despite the different gifts, abilities, and functions, they all must work together for the mutual benefit of one another, the church.

We must recognize that we are all part of the body of Christ. When a person receives God's gifts, there is no place for pride. God has not given these gifts to the individual but to the corporate body—the church. Notice that the divinely gifted person is a member of "one body." Moreover, no one person can exalt himself over other members of the body, because we are all connected to one another. As Paul says, we are "individually members of one another." For a person to exalt himself over another person is like a person bragging against himself. It is like a person saying, "I am better than myself." Such a statement is absurd at face value. Paul's statements parallel those he wrote to the Corinthians. The hand, for example, cannot say to the foot, "I am more important than you because you are not a hand" (1 Cor. 12:4–31). The gifts of God all function together as part of Christ's body. Moreover, God gives His gifts not for personal gain but for the edification of the body and the exaltation of Christ. Now, what gifts has God given to the church?

Different Gifts

Paul writes of the pluriform gifts God has given to the church: "Having then gifts differing according to the grace that is given to us, let us use them: if prophecy, let us prophesy in proportion to our faith; or ministry, let us use it in our ministering; he who teaches, in teaching; he who exhorts, in exhortation; he who gives, with liberality; he who leads, with diligence; he who shows mercy, with cheerfulness" (Rom. 12:6–8). He lists seven distinct gifts of the Spirit, though this list is not comprehensive. Now, before we examine each of the gifts, we must first recognize two factors.

First, as is evident from our passage, not all believers receive the same gifts of the Spirit. There is a difference between the gifts and fruits of the Spirit. Every Christian should manifest the fruit of the Spirit: love, joy, peace, patience, kindness, goodness, faithfulness, gentleness, and self-control (Gal. 5:22–24). The *fruit* of the Spirit is universal in the church. The *gifts* of the Spirit, on the other hand, are particular and sovereignly given to specific individuals in the church, not to everyone. On this point note that Paul states in Romans 12:3 that God has "dealt to each one a measure of faith." While it is true that all of us to some extent should exhibit these characteristics generally, there are those members of the body of Christ that have been especially gifted in one or more of these areas. In other words, some members of the body of Christ do not receive any of the gifts of the Spirit, while others may receive one or more. Second, the Holy Spirit no longer distributes some of the gifts that Paul lists here and in other places (e.g., 1 Cor. 12:8–10; Eph. 4:11–12). For example, in 1 Corinthians 12:28 Paul lists the apostolic office as a gift of the Spirit, yet few would argue there are still apostles in our midst, claims of the papacy notwithstanding. Now, then, what gifts does Paul list?

Prophecy

The first gift is that of prophecy. Paul exhorts the one with the gift of prophecy to "prophesy in proportion to our faith"; in other words, be faithful to the gift that God has given and prophesy the revelation that God has given. Men and women (Joel 2:28; Luke 2:36; Acts 21:10) exercised the gift of prophecy. Prophecy is authoritative divine revelation. There was a need for prophets in the Old and New Testaments because the word of God had not been completely inscripturated. Christians possessed only the Old Testament—the apostles had yet to write the New Testament. The Holy Spirit no longer gives the gift of prophecy. We know this from what Paul has written about the church's foundation, which is "built on the foundation of the apostles and prophets" (Eph. 2:20a). The apostles and prophets all died in the first century, which marked the completion of the church's revelational foundation. Just as the apostles have died off, so too have the prophets. The gift of prophecy in the apostolic period, however, was a crucial and necessary gift in the construction of the foundation of the church. Even with this gift, though, it was not used for private boasting but for the edification of the church: "But he who prophesies speaks edification and exhortation and comfort to men" (1 Cor. 14:3). But just because the gift of prophecy has ceased does not mean that it is entirely irrelevant.

The gift of prophecy echoes into our own day through the prophetic Scriptures, and any time a minister preaches the Word, he expounds the prophetic Word of God. The ability to preach, which is a gift of God (Eph. 4:11–12), is not universally dispensed in the church. Hence, those who have received the gift of preaching, which is concomitant with the gift of being an elder (1 Tim. 3:1–7; 5:17), need to recognize that their gift has not been given for self-exaltation but for the church's edification. Preachers, when you mount the pulpit, do you desire to glorify God and edify His saints? If your desire is to impress people with your oratory and knowledge, then you fail to grasp Paul's point. You are not more important than the rest of the body. Just because you stand before the congregation does not mean you are more valuable than the person who sits in the pew. Consider others more important than yourself. Do you seek to meet the needs of your congregation through your preaching?

Service

The next gift Paul mentions is service. The typical understanding is that everyone in the church can exercise this gift. After all, it is "ministry." Anyone can minister, right? Well, we must always be sensitive to the context and the meaning of words. In this particular case the Greek states *eite diakonian en te diakonia*. In other words, Paul uses the Greek root word for *deacon*—this most likely refers to the deaconate of the church. Paul includes the deaconate because the tendency might be to think that the administration of material goods is unspiritual. Yet God has called deacons to care for the physical needs of the church. In ancient Israel the priests served

God in His temple. Recall from the previous section that Paul employs terms from the Old Testament when he tells his recipients that offering their bodies as living sacrifices is their "reasonable service" (Rom. 12:1). In this respect, the Levites served their covenant Lord. In fact, in the Greek translation of the Old Testament, we read that deacons served Artaxerxes: "Then the king's deacons said, 'Let the beautiful young virgins be sought for the king'" (Est. 2:2; my translation, based on LXX). The Levites attended both to the King and to His temple. Deacons are the Old Testament Levitical counterpart—those who serve the King and care for His temple, the church. Deacons serve King Jesus by caring for His body. Like the Levites who tended to the physical needs of the temple (trimming the lamps, providing oil, baking bread, and offering sacrifices), the deacons of the church tend to the physical needs of the eschatological temple, the church. Deacons, therefore, serve the body of Christ. Tend to the physical needs of Christ's body! Are there people struggling with their finances? Provide them with assistance. Are there widows who need help maintaining their homes? Repair their roofs. Do saints suffer from illness? Visit them in the hospital and care for their physical well-being.

Teaching and Exhortation

Paul lists the gifts of teaching and exhortation, which are certainly but not exclusively under the purview of ordained ministers. Paul tells Titus, for example, that older women in the church who have the gift of teaching should exhort younger women: "Older women likewise, that they be reverent in behavior, not slanderers, not given to much wine, teachers of good things" (Titus 2:3). Moreover, while prophecy was given only to New Testament prophets, teaching is not a revelatory gift. Rather, teaching is a gift that imparts understanding of already revealed prophecy, and exhortation is the encouragement to follow and obey God's Word. Now, while there are other people in the church who may receive the gifts of teaching and exhortation, the universal exercise of these gifts is given to ordained ministers alone. In other words, while a woman may have the gift of teaching, Paul clearly tells us that women are not to exercise authority over men: "I do not permit a woman to teach or to have authority over a man" (1 Tim. 2:12). Only ordained men may teach, exhort, and exercise authority *over* a congregation, whereas women and other teachers may teach *within* a congregation under the oversight of the elders. There are plenty of opportunities and occasions for non-ordained people to exercise the gift of teaching, whether as older women teach younger women, people teach in the church's Sunday school, or parents instruct their children. Christ equips His body so that we can know His will. If we fail to exercise this gift, then we impede the church's comprehension of God's Word. To borrow and adapt Paul's argument regarding the necessity of preaching, "How will they obey if they do not understand? And how will they understand unless someone teaches them? And how will someone teach unless they exercise their gift of teaching?"

Giving

The next gift is that of giving (Rom. 12:8). Paul does not say that only some people in the church should give of their money and resources. Everyone should give his time and money to the church; otherwise, how can the church carry out its God-given mission to preach the gospel? The whole body of Christ should give, but there are also some individuals who have the ability to give abundantly, over and above what people might expect. In simple terms, God gives certain people great wealth. Contrary to popular belief, great wealth is not a sin but a God-given platform for generosity—not simply a generic philanthropy but rather to support the mission and ministry of the church. All too often people put themselves first and the church second, third, or perhaps even last. When we come into wealth, is our first thought personal gain? Do we start looking at new cars, houses, clothes, jewelry, or the latest tech gadget? Could it be that God has given us the extra money or wealth so we can give it to the church? Rather than a new car, what about giving the money to fund a new church plant, to assist with the salary of a missionary, or to see to the physical needs of God's people?

Giving to the church, however, should not be restricted to money. There might be some who have slender financial means but plenty of time on their hands. They might not be able to offer large sums of money, but they can volunteer to serve the church in a variety of ways—from the ordinary, such as mowing the grass or painting walls, to the extraordinary, such as incessant prayer on behalf of God's people. Regardless of what one gives to the church, we should note the attitude marking those who give: "So let each one give as he purposes in his heart, not grudgingly or of necessity; for God loves a cheerful giver" (2 Cor. 9:7). When we give, it should be done cheerfully and humbly, not with a begrudging or prideful attitude.

Leading

The next gift Paul mentions is leading or ruling. This is not a generic reference applicable to anyone in the church but is specifically for the elders of the church. One of the biggest trends in the church these days is male abdication of their God-given responsibility to lead the church. It seems that within the last century one denomination after another has opened ordained leadership to women. There are many denominations that now have female pastors and ruling elders. To be sure, Christ has given an authority structure in the church, one where men are supposed to lead (1 Cor. 14:34; 1 Tim. 2:12; 3:1–7). They are supposed to lead not because they are somehow better than women but because God has given some men this task. God-given male leadership appears in the microcosm of marriage. Just as Christ is the head of the church, so the husband is the head of the wife (Eph. 5:22–24). We cannot invert the parallel between Christ/church and husband/wife: that as the church is the head of Christ, so the wife is the head of the husband. Yet, sadly, just as many men abdicate their husbandly leadership duties, many men also abdicate their responsibility to lead the church. I believe that if men exercised their gifts to lead Christ's church, and did so in a Christlike manner, laying down their lives for the sheep, women would rarely seek ordained office. The presence of ordained women is sometimes not so much a failing on the part of women but rather a failure on the part of men in the church both in their teaching and lack of doing. Just as Eve ate of the forbidden fruit first but Adam was held accountable, many men in the church who have abdicated their God-given roles will be held accountable for the fact that women lead the church. Therefore, those who have been given the gift of the office of elder should rule the church well—as Christ Himself.

Acts of Mercy

The last gift is that of mercy (Rom. 12:8). The exhortation is cheerfully to render mercy. Often acts of mercy are disagreeable or difficult and are done in a begrudging or perfunctory manner. Who, for example, wants to help a dying person? All too often many Christians die all alone in hospitals because they have no family and few want to linger around the specter of death. I can remember praying for a man who was in a catatonic state—he was at death's door. There was a disgusting odor in the room because the man was dying. In all honesty, it is difficult to maintain a cheerful attitude under such circumstances, but this is precisely the disposition for which Paul calls. In difficult circumstances we might grit our teeth and grin and bear the ugliness of life, but such actions are not infused with the gospel of Christ. Only Christ through His Spirit enables us to engage in acts of mercy with cheerful hearts. This does not mean that we turn a blind eye to the difficulties of life and sing campfire songs while people around us suffer and die. Rather, we count it a privilege to exercise mercy toward Christ's body, the church, because when we exhibit mercy to our fellow brothers and sisters in the Lord we administer this mercy to Christ Himself: "Assuredly, I say to you, inasmuch as you did not do it to one of the least of these, you did not do it to Me" (Matt. 25:45). It should be a joy to serve Christ, not a chore.

Christ the Center

Now, a common reaction in many churches after reading a passage like this is for people to wonder what spiritual gift they have received. Churches break out spiritual gift inventory tests and then eagerly await the results. This, however, is a misguided approach to the gifts of the Spirit and is not Paul's point. Notice who is central to this passage. God engrafts us into the body of Christ by His grace, and God has equipped the body by His Spirit to carry out its mission. We make disciples of the nations and serve as living sacrifices. We are living sacrifices when the church proves what is the good, acceptable, and pleasing will of the Father. Just as Christ was obedient to the will of the Father unto death, so we must seek to please our heavenly Father. The Father, however, has equipped us for this task by providing Christ's body with gifts: prophesy (though now this has ceased), ministry, teaching, exhorting, giving, leading, and mercy.

When we think of the gifts of the Spirit, then, our first step should be to meditate on the grace of God in Christ and how the Father has lavishly equipped us. Second, when it comes to the question of whether we have these gifts, we should not resort to spiritual gift inventory tests or introspection. Chances are the people who possess these gifts are already exercising them. And, in the case of elders and deacons, God makes it plainly evident to both the individual and church which men have been gifted. Third, and last, we should recognize who embodies all these gifts—Jesus Christ. Is it any wonder that the body should resemble its head? Is it any wonder that Paul's exhortation to be living sacrifices manifests the characteristics and qualities of Christ? The more we are renewed by the transformation of our minds by the revealed gospel of Christ, the more we will be conformed into His image, both corporately and individually.

Conclusion

In the end, seek conformity to the image of Christ. Use your gifts for the greater edification of the body of Christ. Boast not in yourself but in Christ. Be a living sacrifice to the honor and glory of Christ.

39

A Portrait of Christ

ROMANS 12:9–16

Let love be without hypocrisy. Abhor what is evil. Cling to what is good. Be kindly affectionate to one another with brotherly love, in honor giving preference to one another; not lagging in diligence, fervent in spirit, serving the Lord; rejoicing in hope, patient in tribulation, continuing steadfastly in prayer; distributing to the needs of the saints, given to hospitality. Bless those who persecute you; bless and do not curse. Rejoice with those who rejoice, and weep with those who weep. Be of the same mind toward one another. Do not set your mind on high things, but associate with the humble. Do not be wise in your own opinion.

When people imagine the kingdom of God, I believe they often have grandiose ideas—visions where Christian ideals prevail in society: Christian politicians enacting Christian policies, Christian actors creating Christian movies, and Christian artists making Christian art. People think of the kingdom of God in terms of cultural conquest. I think words from the film version of *The Hobbit*, however, give a better understanding of how Christians make an impact in the world: "Saruman believes that it is only great power that can hold evil in check. That is not what I have found. I have found that it is the small things, everyday deeds from ordinary folk, that keeps the darkness at bay. Simple acts of kindness and love."[1] This statement aptly captures the way that Christ manifests His kingdom in

1. *The Hobbit: An Unexpected Journey*, directed by Peter Jackson (Burbank: Warner Brothers, 2012).

seemingly very mundane and ordinary ways—exercising patience, blessing people who persecute you, weeping with those who mourn, and holding fast to what is good. As ordinary as these things may seem, when we take a closer look at how sinful and twisted the world is, we realize how special they are. But as we reflect on what Paul writes in this portion of Romans 12, we must not forget the source of all these things—namely, Christ. Paul paints a portrait in which he shows the Roman Christians that they should manifest Christ in the way they treat one another. In a word, the church should be a place dominated by the presence of Christ that is manifest through action, good works, and chiefly love. In the previous section (Rom. 12:3–8), Paul began with characteristics that church leaders should exhibit: service, prophecy, and teaching, for example. But in this section, he reflects on characteristics that should appear in the body of Christ at large—namely, love, honor, zeal, patience, prayer, rejoicing, weeping, humility, and living in harmony. When we take all these elements together, we realize that Paul informs his recipients that Jesus Christ in word *and deed* should be manifest among them.

Love One Another

"Let love be without hypocrisy," writes Paul. "Abhor what is evil. Cling to what is good. Be kindly affectionate to one another with brotherly love, in honor giving preference to one another" (Rom. 12:9–10). For Christians, love must be genuine, empty of pretense and hypocrisy. We cannot say that we love Christ and at the same time love what is evil. It may sound strange, but do we love enough to hate evil? A love for Christ, of course, must lead toward a love for His body. How can we love the Head, Jesus Christ, and not love His body, the church? For this reason Paul exhorts the Roman Christians to "be kindly affectionate to one another with brotherly love" (Rom. 12:10a). Moreover, rather than seek praise and honor for ourselves, we should bestow these on others. What type of attitude should mark the believer's love? Paul writes, "Not lagging in diligence, fervent in spirit, serving the Lord" (Rom. 12:11). Paul urges his recipients to serve the Lord zealously. In other words, the

Christian should not only rebuff evil but also actively pursue that which is good—namely, serving the Lord.

What else should mark the character of the church? Paul writes, "Rejoicing in hope, patient in tribulation, continuing steadfastly in prayer" (Rom. 12:12). We should rejoice in hope, and our hope should be focused on the future: "For we were saved in this hope, but hope that is seen is not hope; for why does one still hope for what he sees?" (Rom. 8:24). In other words, we should eagerly look forward to the return of Christ. Remember, our attitude about the present must not be bound by what we see but rather shaped by what we do not see: "And do not be conformed to this world, but be transformed by the renewing of your mind" (Rom. 12:2a). What we see in this world is passing away—it is coming to an end. That is why we must be patient in tribulation and steadfast in prayer. This does not mean that we simply *endure* tribulation, as if we were waiting in a doctor's office. Rather, we live out our calling—we seek conformity to the image of Christ: "Yes, and all who desire to live godly in Christ Jesus will suffer persecution" (2 Tim. 3:12). Moreover, where do we receive the strength to persevere in the midst of trials but through the means of grace, in this case, prayer? This does not mean, however, that we eke out a deluded existence with our hopes set on a mythical utopia. We are not to be so heavenly minded that we are of no earthly good.

On the contrary, Paul continues his exhortation in Romans 12:13: The church is supposed to contribute "to the needs of the saints, given to hospitality." In the midst of waiting for Christ's return, as we spend time in prayer and look to the horizon for Christ, we care for the needs of the church. We should care not only for its spiritual needs but for its physical needs as well. Again, something as simple as a cup of cold water, says Christ, is an act of mercy not only to a fellow Christian but ultimately for Christ Himself. Paul elucidates this by stating that hospitality is a means of seeing to the needs of the saints, something echoed by the book of Hebrews: "Do not forget to entertain strangers, for by so doing some have unwittingly entertained angels" (Heb. 13:2). Paul himself was the personal recipient of this type of hospitality: He rejoices elsewhere that Onesiphorus sought Paul, found him, and provided for his needs, even when he was in jail (2 Tim. 1:16–18). We must not forget the needs of our fellow brothers and sisters in Christ.

But our attention must not exclusively fall on the body of Christ. Paul tells his recipients: "Bless those who persecute you; bless and do not curse" (Rom. 12:14). We must love both those who are easy to love, like our brothers and sisters in Christ, and also our enemies. Paul does not simply refer to those who are indifferent to the church but rather to those who actively hate it. Once again, when we do this, we are not living up to a moral ideal but are manifesting the image of Christ. When we love our enemies we manifest the same type of love Christ has shown us, because He loved us despite our hatred for Him. Whether we demonstrate our love for those inside or outside the church, we can "rejoice with those who rejoice, and weep with those who weep. Be of the same mind toward one another. Do not set your mind on high things, but associate with the humble. Do not be wise in your own opinion" (Rom. 12:15–16). Note how Paul demonstrates the interconnectedness of the body of Christ—not simply in theory but in practice as well. Remember that Paul said that we are one body in Christ and individually members of one another (Rom. 12:5). We are connected to one another as the body of Christ, but notice how this works in life. Do we rejoice and mourn alike with our fellow members of the church? If one portion of our body is wounded, certainly the rest of our body knows about it. Simply ask what happens when a person has a toothache. It should be the same for the church. It is easy to rejoice with others, but it is difficult to mourn with others. John Calvin writes on this point: "The nature of true love is such that each one prefers to grieve with his brother than to look from a distance on his grief through fastidiousness or unwillingness to act. In short, therefore, we should adapt ourselves to one another as far as possible, and whatever our circumstances may be, each should enter into the feelings of the other, whether to sorrow with him in adversity or to rejoice in prosperity."[2]

---

2. Calvin, *Romans and Thessalonians*, 274.

Additionally, Paul re-emphasizes the need for the body of Christ to be humble. We know that this must have been (and continues to be) a problem in the body. Once again, this is not an exhortation to high-minded ideals; this is Paul's instruction to be conformed to the image of Christ:

> Let nothing be done through selfish ambition or conceit, but in lowliness of mind let each esteem others better than himself. Let each of you look out not only for his own interests, but also for the interests of others. Let this mind be in you which was also in Christ Jesus, who, being in the form of God, did not consider it robbery to be equal with God, but made Himself of no reputation, taking the form of a bondservant, and coming in the likeness of men. And being found in appearance as a man, He humbled Himself and became obedient to the point of death, even the death of the cross. (Phil. 2:3–8)

Christ was humility incarnate; He descended from the greatest heights and served others. If this is true of the Head, then the same humility must mark His body, the church.

Christ in You

So what does all this mean? What is Paul's point? What does the body of Christ look like when it lives sacrificially? Paul described how a Christian is supposed to live, what it means to "walk in the newness of life" (Rom. 6:4). Paul described what it means to be a slave of righteousness (Rom. 6:18). He demonstrated what it means to walk according to the Spirit (Rom. 8:4). Paul explained what it means to be more than conquerors, though we are accounted as sheep for the slaughter (Rom. 8:36–37). Paul explained that the body of Christ clings to what is good and hates what is evil. He elsewhere writes, "Finally, brethren, whatever things are true, whatever things are noble, whatever things are just, whatever things are pure, whatever things are lovely, whatever things are of good report, if there is any virtue and if there is anything praiseworthy—meditate on these things" (Phil. 4:8). Yet the body does not hate those who are evil. Instead, we must love our enemies, even those who persecute us. This is, of course, what Christ did with His enemies. As He was in the depth of His suffering, undoubtedly in excruciating pain, He nevertheless beseeched His Father to have mercy on those who persecuted Him: "Father, forgive them, for they do not know what they do" (Luke 23:34). As a body, our love should never be hypocritical, one where we shower someone with verbal blessings and then scour them in verbal carping the moment they leave. Christ did not simply say He loved His bride—He laid His life down for her (Eph. 5:25). Christ's words and actions were inseparably bound in a holy union of love and integrity.

When the church is in the midst of tribulation, Paul does not advise her to look for the rapture, nor does he tell us that tribulation will come to an end before Christ's return. Rather, he tells the church to seek the means of grace—fervent prayer. This is, of course, what our Lord did in the midst of His trials in the garden of Gethsemane. He sought His heavenly Father in prayer. Moreover, though Christ certainly had the right to assert His status as King of kings, Creator of the cosmos, and Lord of lords, He nevertheless humbled Himself to the point of death on the cross. Certainly, there is no place for pride in the corporate body given Christ's humility. Everything in this passage shows us that it is the Father's design to make His people, His children, into the image of Christ.

Conclusion

Paul's words describe what it means to be a living sacrifice—how the church manifests the image of Christ. We, as a body, as the church, are supposed to be a portrait of Christ to the world. Reflect on the person and work of Christ and recognize that He should be manifest in us, because, like Christ, we are now sons of the living God. As sons of the living God we must seek the power of Christ and His gospel, which is the only means by which we can be a living sacrifice. In the end, present your body as a living sacrifice, holy and acceptable to God, which is your reasonable service.

40

Conquering Evil through Love

ROMANS 12:17–21

Repay no one evil for evil. Have regard for good things in the sight of all men. If it is possible, as much as depends on you, live peaceably with all men. Beloved, do not avenge yourselves, but rather give place to wrath; for it is written, "Vengeance is Mine, I will repay," says the Lord. Therefore "If your enemy is hungry, feed him; If he is thirsty, give him a drink; For in so doing you will heap coals of fire on his head." Do not be overcome by evil, but overcome evil with good.

Among the many mysterious passages of the Old Testament we find the taunting song of Lamech: "Then Lamech said to his wives: 'Adah and Zillah, hear my voice; Wives of Lamech, listen to my speech! For I have killed a man for wounding me, Even a young man for hurting me. If Cain shall be avenged sevenfold, Then Lamech seventy-sevenfold'" (Gen. 4:23–24). A vengeful spirit inhabits Lamech's song. Indeed, the Hebrew says that "a boy" hurt him, and for this minor infraction Lamech killed him. In fact, Lamech sets a high price of retribution—he goes far beyond an eye for an eye and a tooth for a tooth, and instead opts for a seventy-sevenfold degree of retribution. Sinful people seem ever intent on raising the bar for retribution for the slightest infractions—in the eyes of many in the world, might makes right.

This type of mentality has certainly surfaced in countless dictatorships and kingdoms across the span of history. Ruthless kings lead and rule with might, retribution, and fear. But Christ, the King of kings, taught His disciples the antithesis of Lamech's song of retribution: "Then Peter came to Him and said, 'Lord, how often shall my brother sin against me, and I forgive him? Up to seven times?' Jesus said to him, 'I do not say to you, up to seven times, but up to seventy times seven'" (Matt. 18:21–22). There is a total antithesis in the two lines—the line of Cain seeks revenge up to seventy-seven times whereas the line of Abel, ultimately the line of the Messiah, offers forgiveness up to seventy times seven. Sons of the living God demonstrate love in the face of evil. The ethics of the kingdom no longer rotate around the principle of an eye for an eye but rather in turning the other cheek. Hence Paul explains to the church what it means to be a living sacrifice before our enemies, even those who hate, persecute, and do harm to the church. Rather than the clenched fist, power, and fear, Paul arms the church with weapons of a different order: love, patience, and the gospel of Christ.

Repay Evil with Good

Up to this point Paul has largely dealt with intrachurch relations—how Christians were supposed to treat one another. Paul touched on dealing with outsiders when he exhorted them to bless those who persecuted them, and not to curse them, as tempting as such a response might be (Rom. 12:14). Step into the shoes of a godly Christian who is persecuted by a reprehensible and wicked criminal—would not justice be best served by swift and deadly retribution? For Christians, vengeance and retribution are completely off the menu, and Paul orders an entirely different course of action: "Repay no one evil for evil. Have regard for good things in the sight of all men" (Rom. 12:17). Paul exhorts his recipients to reject a spirit of retaliation. A common misconception is that this is a new command and that in the Old Testament the *lex talionis*, or law of retribution, an eye for an eye, ruled the day. Yet this is not the case—we serve the God of Abraham, Isaac, and Jacob in whom there is no shadow of turning. Therefore it should be no surprise that we read: "Do not say, 'I will recompense evil'; Wait for the LORD, and He will save you" (Prov. 20:22). Even in the Old

Testament God instructed His people to exercise mercy and show love to one's enemies: "If you meet your enemy's ox or his donkey going astray, you shall surely bring it back to him again. If you see the donkey of one who hates you lying under its burden, and you would refrain from helping it, you shall surely help him with it" (Ex. 23:4–5). Rather than distribute vengeance like the surrounding pagan Gentiles, they were supposed to show one another love: "You shall not take vengeance, nor bear any grudge against the children of your people, but you shall love your neighbor as yourself: I am the LORD" (Lev. 19:18). Remember, the gospel is the same in both the Old and New Testaments. But what has changed with the advent of Christ is that the love for one's enemy, formerly referring only to a fellow Israelite, is now supposed to extend to the nations, those who were once Israel's pagan enemies. God's covenant mercies were supposed to extend even to those outside of the covenant. Paul's exhortation, therefore, is that Christians must not resort to revenge but must seek good things in the sight of all men.

Live Peaceably with All

Paul does not give us a naked command. He goes on to explain why Christians, as living sacrifices, must never resort to vengeance: "If it is possible, as much as depends on you, live peaceably with all men" (Rom. 12:18). First, as always, there are positive and negative aspects of exhortations and commands. To many in the church, living life according to the revealed will of God is a list of dos and don'ts. Yes, there are certainly those things that a Christian must never do, such as carry out revenge. That is the negative aspect of the revealed will of God—the "do not." There are, however, positive aspects to God's commands. On this principle, the Westminster Larger Catechism explains, "That as, where a duty is commanded, the contrary sin is forbidden; and, where a sin is forbidden, the contrary duty is commanded: so, where a promise is annexed, the contrary threatening is included; and, where a threatening is annexed, the contrary promise is included" (Q. 99.4). We should not seek revenge. But positively, we must live at peace with all men as much as possible. That means that even if we receive evil from someone, if possible, we should return good. Now, this does not mean that Christians should compromise the truth or the gospel for the sake of peace. May it never be! On the contrary, Paul says "If it is possible," not "At all costs." Why must the Christian, negatively, not seek revenge and, positively, live in peace with all men?

The answers appear in Romans 12:19: "Beloved, do not avenge yourselves, but rather give place to wrath; for it is written, 'Vengeance is Mine, I will repay,' says the Lord." We must leave room for God to act. Paul elsewhere tells the church that we must not descend into sinful anger: "Be angry, and do not sin": do not let the sun go down on your wrath, nor give place to the devil" (Eph. 4:26–27). To allow anger to degenerate into vengeance subverts God's intended order. He alone has the divine prerogative to exercise vengeance, not we. Paul also does not address the wrath of the state, something he treats in the following section (Rom. 13:1–7). Rather, Paul speaks of God's wrath. For this reason Paul quotes Deuteronomy 32:35. Again, notice how Paul roots his exhortation against vengeance in the Old Testament; it does not arise *de novo* from the New Testament. Why must the believer never give in to vengeance? Because the believer knows that God will rectify all wrongs at the final judgment. It is not up to us to wield a sword of vengeance—this is the right of God alone. Only a perfectly holy and righteous God has the ability to wield the sword of vengeance in such a way that sin never enters the picture. Even as redeemed sinners indwelt by the presence of the Holy Spirit, we still have the ability to fall into sin, to let righteous judgment slip into unrighteous vengeance. Under such circumstances, give all your suffered wrongs to the Lord. We therefore do not wield the sword of vengeance but rather the sword of the Spirit, one that dispenses mercy to sinners, and if they refuse to repent, then God brings judgment through His Word (Heb. 4:12). This means we should not wield the sword of the Spirit out of a desire to heap condemnation on our enemies but rather to bless them. Remember what Paul has written about those who persecute us—we must bless and not curse them

(Rom. 12:14). We must therefore pray that God would save those who dispense evil to us, knowing that if they do not repent He will judge them for their evil.

Love Your Enemies

Paul then gives his recipients instructions in this regard: "Therefore 'If your enemy is hungry, feed him; If he is thirsty, give him a drink; For in so doing you will heap coals of fire on his head'" (Rom. 12:20). Paul cites Proverbs 25:22 as an exhortation of how to treat our enemies. Keep in mind, this is not simply an exhortation to give our enemies food and drink but rather to assist our enemy in whatever way we can. We do not assist our enemy in his evil, but if we see him suffering or in need, then we must clothe, feed, and assist him. At the close of the Second World War, for example, one chaplain tells of when Japanese forces captured numerous Allied soldiers.[1] The captured soldiers spent a number of years in a prisoner of war camp where they endured difficult living conditions and torture from their captors. As the end of the war neared, a number of wounded Japanese soldiers wandered through the jungle and found themselves at the prisoner of war camp. Initially the Allied prisoners were commanded not to render aid to the enemy, but the Christian soldiers decided to do otherwise. They responded that they did not see an enemy, a persecutor, but rather human beings created in the image of God, those who were hungry, thirsty, and in need of care. So these Christians rendered care to their enemies. In a word, we must love those who hate us. But how does kindness to our enemies translate into heaping coals of fire on their heads? The metaphor is always negative, indicative of God's judgment (e.g., Ps. 140:10). Does this mean that we should be kind because it is really a way to exercise vengeance? No. Rather, either our enemy will see the love of Christ in our action and it will be instrumental in his conversion, or it will be further grounds for God's judgment against him. Our job is to love, and God ultimately decides whether

1. Emerst Gordon, *To End All Wars* (Grand Rapids: Zondervan, 2002).

our love will be the occasion for His mercy or the ground for His holy vengeance. This is why Paul concludes with the aphorism in Romans 12:21: "Do not be overcome by evil, but overcome evil with good."

Manifesting the Love of Christ to All

Now, the tendency in reading this passage is to forget the overall context of Paul's exhortation. Paul does not give moralistic Polly-anna commands—"Be nice to others and they'll be nice to you." Rather, the context is conformity to the image of Christ—believers as living sacrifices. The context flows from the basis of an acute awareness of the inaugurated eschaton and the imminent consummation of the age. When Paul instructs us to bless our enemies or lavish them with acts of love and kindness, we ultimately manifest the love of God we have received. At this point Paul's teaching echoes Christ's:

> You have heard that it was said, "You shall love your neighbor and hate your enemy." But I say to you, love your enemies, bless those who curse you, do good to those who hate you, and pray for those who spitefully use you and persecute you, that you may be sons of your Father in heaven; for He makes His sun rise on the evil and on the good, and sends rain on the just and on the unjust. For if you love those who love you, what reward have you? Do not even the tax collectors do the same? And if you greet your brethren only, what do you do more than others? Do not even the tax collectors do so? Therefore you shall be perfect, just as your Father in heaven is perfect. (Matt. 5:43–48)

Remember your own condition and how the Bible describes you prior to your conversion. When you were without strength and the enemy of God, Christ died for you—He reconciled you to God through His death and saved you by His life (Rom. 5:6, 10). God demonstrated His love to His enemies, and it was costly—the sacrifice of His Son. How do we communicate this demonstration of God's love? We demonstrate it not only by wielding the sword of the gospel but also by living our lives to the glory of God. Are we faithful to Christ? Do we seek conformity to His image? Are we living sacrifices? Notice that Paul does not diminish the costliness of serving Christ. He describes those who oppose the church as "enemies" and as those who "persecute," who perpetrate evil.

It is indeed sacrificial to love in the face of evil, but we must do this because we are sons of the living God: "When He was reviled, did not revile in return; when He suffered, He did not threaten, but committed Himself to Him who judges righteously" (1 Peter 2:23). Christ knew that He was bringing redemption to His persecutors, to those whom God chose to show His mercy, such as Paul himself, and that He was also bringing judgment to those who refused to repent. Christ was aware of His calling, the inaugurated eschaton, the eschatological judgment—indeed, He embodied a living sacrifice. Well, if we are to be conformed to Christ's image, then we too must be living sacrifices, even in the face of evil. Ours is not a hopeless endeavor—ours is a hopeful calling. God calls us to conquer evil with good—the good of giving a Christlike gospel love to our enemies so that we might participate in the salvation of some.

Conclusion

So, then, what does it mean to be a living sacrifice in the face of our enemies? It means that we, as a corporate body, must love our enemies rather than exercise vengeance. Retribution and final justice belong to God Almighty. Who knows, God may use our love as an instrument in His hands for the conversion of our enemies. Or He may use our love as further grounds for their condemnation: "Although we ought not to pray to God to avenge our enemies, but should pray for their conversion, so that they may become our friends, yet if they continue in their wickedness, the same thing will happen to them as will happen to all the others who despise God."[2] No matter what, we should pray and bless our enemies, not curse or

2. Calvin, *Romans and Thessalonians*, 278.

repay their evil with evil. The same love of Christ we received when we were God's enemies is the same love we show to others. We love our enemies in the hope that they too will embrace Christ so that they may escape God's coming wrath. We love because we have been loved. Therefore, overcome evil with good.

41

Living Sacrifices and the Government

ROMANS 13:1–7

Let every soul be subject to the governing authorities. For there is no authority except from God, and the authorities that exist are appointed by God. Therefore whoever resists the authority resists the ordinance of God, and those who resist will bring judgment on themselves. For rulers are not a terror to good works, but to evil. Do you want to be unafraid of the authority? Do what is good, and you will have praise from the same. For he is God's minister to you for good. But if you do evil, be afraid; for he does not bear the sword in vain; for he is God's minister, an avenger to execute wrath on him who practices evil. Therefore you must be subject, not only because of wrath but also for conscience' sake. For because of this you also pay taxes, for they are God's ministers attending continually to this very thing. Render therefore to all their due: taxes to whom taxes are due, customs to whom customs, fear to whom fear, honor to whom honor.

The swinging pendulum on an old-fashioned clock best illustrates human tendencies when it comes to learning new truths or correcting perceived errors. A person who has gained too much weight over the holidays might decide to eliminate all desserts and sweets to ensure that he can see the proper numbers on the scale reappear. During the holidays the pendulum was high on one side, where the person was eating whatever treats were put before him, and now the pendulum has swung high to the other side where he refuses sugar in all perceivable forms. The swing of the pendulum is not restricted to the mundane circumstances of our lives but can also infect our theological thinking. The Christians in the church at Rome undoubtedly rejoiced in the blessings of the inaugurated new creation. They rejoiced at the thought that they were now seated with Christ in the heavenly places because of Christ's resurrection and ascension (cf. Rom. 1:3–4; Eph. 1:19–23). They likely felt as if they had been freed from obligation to all earthly and temporal authority because they were now under the reign of Christ. Unlike the Jews who shouted out, "We have no king but Caesar!" the Roman Christians likely wanted to shout out the antithesis, "We have no king but Christ!" The pendulum had swung hard in the opposite direction from where it previously rested.

Paul, however, wanted the Christians at Rome to ensure that the pendulum would not swing too far to one side. In other words, as true as it is that Christ has inaugurated the new heavens and earth, this does not mean believers are free from the authority of the civil government. Just because Christians have been freed from the law as a covenant does not mean they can ignore all earthly authorities. Paul therefore addresses the question of how Christians, as living sacrifices, are supposed to relate to the civil government. In a word, Christians are supposed to be the best citizens because they are united to Christ.

Submitting to Governing Authority

Before we look at Paul's opening two verses of the chapter, we should recall the overall context of these statements. First, remember that Paul explains what it means not to be conformed to this world but to be transformed by the renewing of our minds (Rom. 12:1). Paul shows us what it means to be a living sacrifice (Rom. 12:2). He explained how we are to be conformed to the image of Christ, a living sacrifice, a part of the final temple. Paul addresses the issues of how we as living sacrifices relate to one another individually as the body of Christ (Rom. 12:3–13), to our enemies (Rom. 12:14–21), and to the civil government (Rom. 13:1–7). This is the scriptural context in which we find this passage, but we must also consider its historical context.

Recall that the Jews had many questions regarding the rights of Roman government.[1] The Jews asked Jesus, for example, whether it was lawful to pay taxes to Caesar (Matt. 22:17). During this time revolutionary movements wanted to throw off the bonds of their Roman overlords. Around the time of Christ a man by the name of Theudas led four hundred men in armed rebellion against the Roman authorities before he and others were killed (Acts 5:36–37). In addition to this the Roman government enacted unjust laws, such as the expulsion of Jews from Rome (Acts 18:2). This type of law likely caused suffering for many Christians because the Roman authorities failed to distinguish between Jews and Christians. They believed Christians were merely a Jewish sect.

Yet what counsel does Paul give to the congregation at Rome, the church that lived in the capitol city and heart of the Roman Empire? Paul writes: "Let every soul be subject to the governing authorities. For there is no authority except from God, and the authorities that exist are appointed by God. Therefore whoever resists the authority resists the ordinance of God, and those who resist will bring judgment on themselves" (Rom. 13:1–2). The Christians in Rome were supposed to submit to the Roman government. Why? Because God establishes all institutional authority. We are citizens of the kingdom of Christ, the visible church, but we nonetheless live in this world. Christians hold a dual citizenship in two realms—of Christ's kingdom and of our local civil authorities, which are God's servants. While we live in both realms, we have an obligation to submit to the authority of both. And we must recognize that both serve and have different functions. The visible church "is the kingdom of the Lord Jesus Christ" and has been given "the ministry, oracles, and ordinances of God, for the gathering and perfecting of the saints" (WCF 25.2–3). By contrast, the civil authorities are under God, "the supreme Lord and King of all the world" and have been instituted for "the public good" and have therefore been "armed...with the power of the sword" (WCF 23.1).

1. Murray, *Epistle to the Romans*, 146.

In other words, the church (kingdom of Christ) is an institution of special, or saving, grace, and the state is an institution of common, or preserving, grace.

We cannot mistakenly believe that we are not subject to the authority of civil governments just because Christ has come. Moreover, we should not argue that had Paul known of the later injustices that the Roman government would commit under Emperor Nero, he would have changed his tune. Paul was well aware of the injustices committed by the Roman government; the unjust crucifixion of Christ was chief among them. We must not think, however, that we owe blind allegiance to the civil authorities. Rather, our ultimate allegiance is to Christ, and when the civil authorities and their laws contradict the revealed will of God, we have an obligation to obey God rather than man (Acts 5:29). But even then, this does not give Christians license to disobey the lawful ordinances of the government. If we resist the government without warrant, Paul clearly states we will suffer the consequences.

Our Responsibilities

How does Paul flesh out the details of how Christians must respect civil government? Paul gets fairly specific in the following verses: "For rulers are not a terror to good works, but to evil. Do you want to be unafraid of the authority? Do what is good, and you will have praise from the same. For he is God's minister to you for good. But if you do evil, be afraid; for he does not bear the sword in vain; for he is God's minister, an avenger to execute wrath on him who practices evil" (Rom. 13:3–4). Civil government is not necessarily inimical to the calling of a Christian. Just because we have dual citizenship, with our ultimate allegiance to Christ, does not mean that our calling to be living sacrifices is hindered. On the contrary, government is typically not a terror to good works. I say *typically* because in the event that a government does become a hindrance to good works, then we have an obligation to obey God rather than man. Paul does not address every single case here; he merely establishes a general principle.

What is Paul's point? If you follow Christ and pursue what is good, you have no reason to fear the sword of the state. Do what is evil, and you have reason to fear the sword of the state. The state does not bear the eschatological sword of judgment, but it does bear the sword of temporal judgment—which is a manifestation of God's wrath. Notice that the government is God's *diakonos*, or servant, to execute temporal judgment on evildoers. Moreover, while the use of the sword does not necessarily mean that the government punishes those who do evil with death for every crime, the use of the sword can entail the punishment of death. For these reasons Paul writes: "Therefore you must be subject, not only because of wrath but also for conscience' sake" (Rom. 13:5).

As a living sacrifice the Christian is supposed to be a model citizen rather than one who rejects or rebels against the authority of the state. To what areas does the authority of the state extend? Paul explains: "For because of this you also pay taxes, for they are God's ministers attending continually to this very thing. Render therefore to all their due: taxes to whom taxes are due, customs to whom customs, fear to whom fear, honor to whom honor" (Rom. 13:6–7). Paul gives several examples of what it means to be subject to the authority of the civil government:

- Paying taxes: The government needs financial support to carry out the tasks of ruling—the punishment of evil. In Paul's world taxes included those directly collected from individuals as well as property and poll taxes, although Roman citizens were exempt from these taxes.
- Customs: This refers to taxes levied on goods, which included indirect taxes, sales tax, and tolls. Roman citizens were required to pay these taxes.
- Fear and honor: All Christians must give respect to the civil authorities.[2]

2. Schreiner, *Romans*, 686–87.

These three elements—taxes, customs, and fear—are not merely the demands of the governing authorities but ultimately commands from God. They are incumbent on all Christians.

Being Christlike toward Government

This passage of Scripture has important implications for the way we are to pursue our calling as living sacrifices and to ensure that we are not conformed to the world. Paul has shown us that Christians must submit themselves to the authority of civil government, even though it is a common grace institution. Yes, civil government will be done away with at the consummation of the age, but we still owe our obedience, respect, and honor to government because God Himself ordains it. Even corrupt governments maintain civil order in their countries. Think, for example, of Daniel's time in Babylon. Daniel served in the Babylonian government, an institution that conquered Israel, razed the temple of God, and took the Israelites into exile and captivity. Daniel embodied Paul's counsel that we find here in Romans 13:1–7. However, when Darius's laws required idolatry, then, and only then, did Daniel refuse to obey the king. Daniel, of course, was willing to suffer the consequences of his rebellion and spent a night in the lions' den as a result. Blessedly, God delivered Daniel from his punishment (Daniel 6). All this presses the question and perhaps makes us a bit uncomfortable in the process: Do we submit to the governing authorities? Does our submission to the government reflect the world's conduct or our union with Christ?

Does our tax return reflect the word *honor*? Or do we indirectly steal from the government? Do we believe that the government is in the hands of the wrong political party, which therefore entitles us to cheat the government out of legitimate tax revenue we owe? Does our behavior reflect one of fear, respect, and honor for the government? Or does it reflect one of grumbling, murmuring under the breath, insults, and arrogance? Do we join in the chorus of political rancor and the culture of insult, disrespect, and even unlawful protest? Christ was not hindered in His earthly ministry and therefore had no reason to fear the civil government. However, even when the civil government unjustly persecuted our Lord and put Him to death, He never once murmured, insulted, or was disrespectful to the governing authorities. Are we living sacrifices in this regard? Are we like Christ? Are we sons of the living God? In this respect Robert Haldane (1764–1842) notes what ideally should distinguish the believer's from the unbeliever's obedience to the state:

> Men in general obey the laws from fear of punishment of transgression; and if there was no punishment, they would transgress every law which thwarted their inclinations. But this must not be the case with Christians.... Christians are to obey from a conscientious regard to the authority of God thus interposed. This is the motive which, above every other, ought to actuate them; and it is exhibited by the apostle as the grand consideration by which he terminates his injunctions of obedience to civil government. This is the foundation of true loyalty.[3]

In other words, is our obedience to the state driven by a fear of punishment or by our union with Christ and our desire to honor God, the source of all authority in the world?

On the other hand, do we assign the government too great a place in our understanding of life as a living sacrifice? It is important that we see where Paul sets the limits for the civil government. Notice that Paul does not assign the responsibilities of the church to the civil government. God, for example, did not assign the punishment of Cain, or his protection from vengeance, to the covenant community, the church. Nor does Paul say that the state is supposed to perform the duties of the church (Gen. 4:14–16). God has given the church, not the state, the responsibility of preaching, teaching, and propagating the gospel. The civil government has the sole task of maintaining the peace and punishing evildoers. Civil governments are God's servants to this end—the punishment of the wicked. The state bears the sword of steel and the church the sword of the Spirit, the Word.

3. Haldane, *Romans*, 584.

So, then, why do so many within the church think that political reform or the enactment of legislation will change our nation's spiritual climate? Or why do so many within the church advocate political activism? A common grace institution can *never* bring true spiritual reform. Why do Christians believe there is more power in the sword of the state rather than the sword of the Spirit? Paul's whole point is that the church wields the sword of the Spirit, which it uses to bring the nations into submission—they bend the knee in repentance and confess Christ or they hear the gospel to their condemnation. The church should never think that the sword of the state is more powerful than the sword of the Spirit.

Conclusion

The world around us engages in all sorts of rebellious behavior against their governments. People are verbally disrespectful, financially evasive, and even resort to violent protest and armed conflict. Such conduct is antithetical to how Christians are supposed to act. As those who have been united to Christ, we are to conduct ourselves as living sacrifices. We are most certainly citizens of the kingdom of Christ, but we also live under the authority of the civil government. Our salvation in Christ is no excuse for disobedience, even to unjust governments. Our prayer should be that, rather than be swept up by the conduct of the unbelieving world, we would heed Paul's divinely inspired Christ-shaped counsel. Daniel lived in Babylon and embodied the principles Paul sets forth. In the words of the children's hymn, we should "dare to be a Daniel" toward the governing authorities.

42

All You Need Is Love?

ROMANS 13:8–14

Owe no one anything except to love one another, for he who loves another has fulfilled the law. For the commandments, "You shall not commit adultery," "You shall not murder," "You shall not steal," "You shall not bear false witness," "You shall not covet," and if there is any other commandment, are all summed up in this saying, namely, "You shall love your neighbor as yourself." Love does no harm to a neighbor; therefore love is the fulfillment of the law. And do this, knowing the time, that now it is high time to awake out of sleep; for now our salvation is nearer than when we first believed. The night is far spent, the day is at hand. Therefore let us cast off the works of darkness, and let us put on the armor of light. Let us walk properly, as in the day, not in revelry and drunkenness, not in lewdness and lust, not in strife and envy. But put on the Lord Jesus Christ, and make no provision for the flesh, to fulfill its lusts.

The very first live worldwide satellite broadcast was the Beatles' song, "All You Need Is Love." The Beatles recorded the song in the Abbey Road studios on June 25, 1967, with a host of celebrities in attendance. John Lennon's intention was to write a song that could be understood by the whole world. In fact, the members of the studio audience had signs reading, "All you need is love" in various languages. Subsequently, this song was declared the anthem of the "Summer of Love." This venture, of course, was set against the backdrop of the Vietnam War. The message was clear—the world needs a good dose of love, then everything from poverty to war to famine will disappear. Now, the question we must ask is, Are the Beatles right? Stated simply, no. Why is this the case? In this passage of Scripture Paul exhorts the Christians in Rome to love all people, but there is a distinct difference between Paul's exhortation and the Beatles' well-intentioned but nevertheless trite song. The difference is between a human-centered love and one that flows from Christ.

Love One Another

When we come to this portion of chapter 13, Paul continues to make his rounds through the groups of people and institutions with whom Christians must relate. In chapter 12 he exhorted the Christians at Rome not to be conformed to the pattern of this world but to be transformed by the renewing of their minds (Rom. 12:1–2). In the subsequent verses he outlined the Christian's relationships to the body of Christ, fellow believers (Rom. 12:3–8); enemies of the body of Christ, those who persecute the church (Rom. 12:9–21); and the civil government (Rom. 13:1–7). And now Paul explains what it means to be a living sacrifice with the world at large—namely, with those whom we call our "neighbors." Paul writes:

> Owe no one anything except to love one another, for he who loves another has fulfilled the law. For the commandments, "You shall not commit adultery," "You shall not murder," "You shall not steal," "You shall not bear false witness," "You shall not covet," and if there is any other commandment, are all summed up in this saying, namely, "You shall love your neighbor as yourself." (Rom. 13:8–10)

The first exhortation that Paul gives us is that we "owe no one anything except to love one another" (v. 8). This is not a blanket prohibition against borrowing money, because the Bible tells us in several places that borrowing money is an allowable practice (cf. Ex. 22:25; Ps. 37:26; Matt. 5:42). Rather, Paul plays off a phrase that appears in the Old Testament where the wicked borrows and does not repay his debt (Ps. 37:21a). In other words, if you borrow, do not be as the wicked and not pay your debt. Do not leave outstanding debt.

The only thing that should fall into the category of debt is love. As Robert Haldane (1764–1842) observes, "Love is here beautifully represented as a debt that is never paid. It is a debt that ever remains due. Christians ought not only to love one another continually, but to abound in love more and more. The more they pay this debt, the richer will they be in the thing that is paid."[1] In general, this exhortation covers all three previously mentioned groups of people: the church, those who persecute the church, and the civil government. We must demonstrate love to all. How do we demonstrate love to all with whom we come into contact? Paul reminds his recipients that they can do this by means of the law, the Ten Commandments, which serve as a rule for the Christian life. Paul invokes the commandments prohibiting adultery, murder, theft, false witness, and coveting.

Why does he quote the law? Luther explains: "Just as the lofty Song of Solomon has been called a song above all songs, so should the Ten Commandments be called a teaching above all teachings. From them we know the will of God, what God commands of us, and our shortcomings."[2] Paul therefore quotes commands from the second table of the law to support his claim and show his recipients how they were supposed to love all people. Indeed, as he says, these are essentially all a demonstration of love toward others, and for this reason it is a fulfillment of the law of God. Thus Paul quotes the aphorism, "Love your neighbor as yourself." Now, why must the believer love his neighbor? Well, of course, because it is our calling as sons of God, as living sacrifices. However, Paul explains in the verses that follow why Christians must live in this manner.

The Armor of Light

We must pursue our calling as living sacrifices, in this particular case demonstrating the love of Christ to all men, because the end of the

---

1. Haldane, *Romans*, 588.

2. Martin Luther, *Off the Record with Martin Luther: An Original Translation of the Table Talks*, trans. Charles Daudert (Kalamazoo, Mich.: Hansa-Hewlett Publishing, 2009), §6288 (p. 379).

age is soon upon us. This is why Paul writes, "And do this, knowing the time, that now it is high time to awake out of sleep; for now our salvation is nearer than when we first believed. The night is far spent, the day is at hand. Therefore let us cast off the works of darkness, and let us put on the armor of light" (Rom. 13:11–12). With the passing of each calendar day, we move closer to Christ's return. Paul uses the language of night and day to convey the proximity of the return of Christ. Much of the night—namely, this present evil age (Gal. 1:4)—has passed by and the day, the consummation of the age, is soon upon us. For this reason Paul urges the Roman Christians to cast off the works of darkness, the pursuits of the flesh, and to put on the armor of light. What does this mean?

We see an answer in the last two verses of chapter 13: "Let us walk properly, as in the day, not in revelry and drunkenness, not in lewdness and lust, not in strife and envy. But put on the Lord Jesus Christ, and make no provision for the flesh, to fulfill its lusts" (Rom. 13:13–14). Paul comes full circle in this exhortation from where he started back in Romans 6. He reminded his recipients that they were baptized into Christ, raised to walk in the newness of life; therefore, they were to leave their old sinful ways behind (Rom. 6:3–5). We are sons of the living God raised to walk in righteousness and holiness, not sin and darkness. Although we live in the midst of this present evil age, we are part of the new creation, part of the coming day, a taste of the eschatological consummation of the age. If righteousness marks the age to come, then we display that righteousness in the way we live now: we love the body of Christ and our enemies, we obey the civil government, and we love our neighbors as ourselves. Why? Because we have been made in the image of Christ. We therefore do not pursue the desires of the flesh—we do not surrender our freedom wrought by Christ to return to the dominion of sin and death. We do not live as though we belong to this present evil age. Rather, we live our lives as living sacrifices, sons of the living God, image bearers of Christ, inhabitants of the age to come.

Different Kinds of Love

Given all that Paul has written, we should ask, What is the difference between Paul's exhortation to love our neighbors and the Beatles' song? Hopefully the differences are clearly evident. First, any time man tries to exhort others to love one another, it usually occurs apart from Christ. Paul's exhortation to demonstrate love cannot be separated from our position in Christ, the fact that we bear His image. The connections between Christ and love, therefore, show us that the chief goal in love is God's glory. God's demonstration of love toward a fallen world, and more specifically His chosen people, comes to us through Christ. So, then, is love all we need? No, it is not. We need the love of God that comes to us through Christ. We need the love of God that replaces our hearts of stone with hearts of flesh, which truly enables us to love others.

Any time man tries to exhort others to love one another it is also usually divorced from eschatology. Notice how Paul's exhortation has an eschatological frame of reference. Think about the various eschatological aspects of Paul's exhortation to love. Recall that God's raising His people from death to life is a fulfillment of the great prophecies of Jeremiah (31:33) and Ezekiel (36:24–27). This effusion of love into the world, whether expressed within the covenant community or without to the world at large, is as a result of the Lord's placing His law in our minds, writing it on our hearts, and causing us to walk in His statutes. Paul knows he can exhort Christians to live out the law—that is, to demonstrate love to others—because of the fulfillment of these prophecies. Paul's exhortation is of a totally different nature than that of the unbelieving world, unlike that of the Beatles.

Paul can exhort the church to love because we bear the image of Christ! We have been raised, like Ezekiel's valley of dry bones, to walk in the newness of life—to fulfill the obligations of the law. Moreover, notice that when the world exhorts people to love one another, it is devoid of any reference to the consummation of the age, the second coming of Christ, and the final judgment. There will come a time when Christ will separate the righteous from the wicked.

Those who fulfill the obligations of the law through imputation of the righteousness of Christ and the sanctifying power of the Holy Spirit will enjoy dwelling eternally in the presence of our triune Lord. Those who bring forth an empty, Christless love (essentially their own works) and their own pretended righteousness will be judged by our righteous and holy God—they will suffer eternally in hell.

Conclusion

Paul shows us, then, that we need more than just "love." We need the redemption that comes by grace alone through Christ alone, which we receive through faith alone. We must live out our calling to fulfill the obligations of the law and love all with whom we come into contact. We must demonstrate love that is irrefragably connected to the person and work of Christ and eschatology—namely, His imminent return. When we do this, we tell a lost and dying world of the love of God that has been poured out on us, miserable sinners. We bring glory to God by fulfilling the obligations of the law—an existence as a living sacrifice, an aroma that is pleasing to our Lord. And we live out our hope for the future return of Christ by giving the world a foretaste of the consummation of the age—glimmers of a time when righteousness will eclipse the evil of night. Therefore, in the knowledge of our redemption in Christ and His imminent return, love with zeal to the glory of our triune Lord.

43

The Strong and the Weak

ROMANS 14:1–12

Receive one who is weak in the faith, but not to disputes over doubtful things. For one believes he may eat all things, but he who is weak eats only vegetables. Let not him who eats despise him who does not eat, and let not him who does not eat judge him who eats; for God has received him. Who are you to judge another's servant? To his own master he stands or falls. Indeed, he will be made to stand, for God is able to make him stand. One person esteems one day above another; another esteems every day alike. Let each be fully convinced in his own mind. He who observes the day, observes it to the Lord; and he who does not observe the day, to the Lord he does not observe it. He who eats, eats to the Lord, for he gives God thanks; and he who does not eat, to the Lord he does not eat, and gives God thanks. For none of us lives to himself, and no one dies to himself. For if we live, we live to the Lord; and if we die, we die to the Lord. Therefore, whether we live or die, we are the Lord's. For to this end Christ died and rose and lived again, that He might be Lord of both the dead and the living. But why do you judge your brother? Or why do you show contempt for your brother? For we shall all stand before the judgment seat of Christ. For it is written: "As I live, says the L*ORD*, *Every knee shall bow to Me, And every tongue shall confess to God." So then each of us shall give account of himself to God.*

When a person learns about the gospel, I suspect the knowledge is overwhelming. People realize they have been saved from condemnation and given right to eternal life—indeed, even given the title of coheir with Christ. Such blessings are almost surreal. Soon after embracing Christ and making a profession of faith, people then begin to learn more about the Scriptures and basic doctrine—they might study the Westminster Shorter Catechism or Heidelberg Catechism, for example. But as sublime and wonderful as all the doctrine is, new Christians soon find themselves living their faith in the mundane day in, day out circumstances of life. And sooner than later they might find themselves embroiled in disagreement or debate—not over some of the greatest and grandest doctrines of Scripture, such as justification or the inerrancy of Scripture, but about something as ordinary as food.

As odd as it may seem, the Christians to whom Paul wrote engaged in disagreement over the type of food they were eating and the specific days that certain members of the church considered special. As commonplace as life can seem, and as silly as it might be to argue about food, Paul wanted his recipients to understand that their ordinary lives were still connected to their extraordinary salvation. Even though disagreements were over something as simple as food, the seemingly mundane issues with which the Roman Christians struggled were connected to important and fundamental doctrines, such as justification and Christian liberty—our freedom from the extrabiblical and contrabiblical commandments of men (WCF 20.1–4). Both of these doctrines were also connected to the ethical and moral imperative that Paul gave to his recipients to be kind and love one another (Rom. 12:10). Even though there was strife over seemingly mundane and trivial things, weightier matters were at stake. It should also come as no surprise that Paul's counsel, and the issues at stake for his first-century recipients, are still relevant in our own day. Heeding Paul's counsel, therefore, is vital for the life and doctrine of the church today.

The Weak and Strong

Paul begins chapter 14 by addressing the conflict that existed between those he labeled the *weak* and *strong*. Paul writes: "Receive one who is weak in the faith, but not to disputes over doubtful things. For one believes he may eat all things, but he who is weak eats only vegetables. Let not him who eats despise him who does not eat, and let not him who does not eat judge him who eats; for God has received him" (Rom. 14:1–3). From what we can gather, there was a group within the Roman congregation that believed consuming meat was sinful, so they ate only vegetables—Paul labeled these Christians as *weak*. Paul does not explain why these Christians thought eating meat was sinful. It does not appear, for example, that they objected to eating meat on the same grounds as the Corinthians, who scrupled over consuming meat that was offered in pagan sacrifice (1 Cor. 8:1–9). In one sense, it is unimportant as to why these Christians scrupled over eating meat, but what is important is that Paul says they were weak *in faith* (Rom. 14:1). In other words, they struggled to accept the clear teaching of Scripture that all food, vegetables and animals, were made by God and therefore were good and legitimate for consumption (1 Tim. 4:4). Moreover, God lifted the ban on eating unclean foods (Acts 10:11–16), which meant that meat of all kinds was back on the menu, so to speak. Another group in the church, however, had no problem eating meat. Paul labels this group the *strong* because they had a robust faith that enabled them to eat both meat and vegetables.

Gentiles likely had few, if any, scruples about food—this is an opinion that Gentiles possess in our own day. But imagine sitting down for a fellowship meal at church and all of a sudden someone opened a bottle of wine and began to drink a glass with his meal. Someone would probably object to the idea of drinking alcohol at a church social function. Some might even consider such actions sinful. This scenario, perhaps, gives us a window into the conflict at Rome. There were those who were genuinely conscience-stricken over the consumption of meat and therefore could not do so. Others had no such scruples. How does Paul counsel these two groups to interact?

Notice that Paul does not berate those who had weak faith. He does not tell them "Toughen up!" Neither does Paul tell these weaker brothers simply to accept the fact that they are wrong and to ignore their stronger brothers. Paul instead teases out the implications of what it means to love one another—to consider the needs of others more important than our own (Rom. 12:10; cf. Phil. 2:3). He instructs the stronger brothers to receive and accept the scruples of their weaker brethren. This means that the strong are not to push or ridicule their weaker brethren but instead are to respect them. Based on what grounds does Paul exhort the strong? On the grounds that God Himself has received the weaker brother into the body of Christ. If God Himself has received the weaker brother, then who is the stronger brother to refuse to accept him?

Now, it is important to note that scruples cover what Paul says are "doubtful things" (Rom. 14:1). In other words, we are not talking about cardinal doctrines of the faith but rather debatable matters. But even if we disagree over doubtful things, we must remember with whom we debate and disagree—with someone bought and redeemed by the precious blood of Christ: "Who are you to judge another's servant? To his own master he stands or falls. Indeed, he will be made to stand, for God is able to make him stand" (Rom. 14:4). We must all recognize that we serve Christ, and it is contrary to the grace we have received to pass stricter judgment than God Himself has passed over someone who has been justified, declared righteous in the sight of God, and justified from the law (Rom. 6:7). The church, whether weak or strong in faith, belongs to Him. All faith, whether weak or strong, is the gift of God (Eph. 2:8–10). And for this reason Paul says that both those who are strong and look down on those who are weak *and* those who are weak who judge the liberty of the strong have no authority. True love will exercise kindness to those who are weak in their faith, and true love will show deference to those who are strong in theirs.

Living unto God

Paul expands these basic principles and addresses the issue of the observation of special days: "One person esteems one day above another; another esteems every day alike. Let each be fully convinced in his own mind. He who observes the day, observes it to the Lord; and he who does not observe the day, to the Lord he does not observe it. He who eats, eats to the Lord, for he gives God thanks;

and he who does not eat, to the Lord he does not eat, and gives God thanks" (Rom. 14:5–6). The days Paul references were probably Old Testament feast days. There were likely those within the Roman congregation who believed they should still celebrate them whereas others refused because they were no longer required in the wake of Christ's ministry (cf. Col. 2:16–17). Once again Paul instructs his recipients to love one another, not for the strong to crush the weak with a theological hammer. Rather, they were supposed to respect one another's convictions. The "weak," for example, observed specific days and abstained from meat to honor the Lord and give thanks to Him. Likewise, the stronger brother did not observe festival days to the Lord and also consumed his meat and gave thanks to God (Rom. 14:6). Paul exhorted both groups to recognize that they both sought to serve, honor, and thank God in their conduct and, therefore, even though they disagreed as to how best to do this, they were supposed to love one another regardless.

Paul did not advocate relativism or doctrinal indifference, as he clearly indicates that there was one group who was *weak* in faith and another that was *strong*. I think Paul would eventually want the weaker brothers to strengthen their faith and become like the strong. But as is often the case in the church, the strong want the weak to embrace the truth immediately. To put this in cooking terms, strong Christians want their weaker brother to mature in doctrine quickly, like using a microwave, but the truth of the matter is that God has people develop gradually, simmering like Crock-Pots. In other words, our timetable for doctrinal maturity is sometimes different from God's. This is one of the most challenging aspects of ministry for pastors, for example, or even parents. Pastors want their congregants immediately to grasp, embrace, and live out the truth they preach from the pulpits, but they are often crushed and discouraged to discover that people in their churches take weeks, months, years, or even longer to grasp and live the truth. The same holds true for parents of children—they inculcate them in the gospel and catechisms and expose them to the means of grace and expect to see results. But sometimes progress is slow going. It is one thing to expect immediate action when congregants are engaged in open sin, and entirely another for them to grow in their understanding of Scripture such that their weak faith becomes strong.

Whether as pastors, parents, the weak, or the strong, the congregation at Rome was to understand the ground on which they all stood: "For none of us lives to himself, and no one dies to himself. For if we live, we live to the Lord; and if we die, we die to the Lord. Therefore, whether we live or die, we are the Lord's" (Rom. 14:7–8). If all in the church have been purchased and redeemed by Christ, then they all, weak or strong, belong to and serve Him. As Paul writes: "For to this end Christ died and rose and lived again, that He might be Lord of both the dead and the living" (Rom. 14:9). In the business world, or even in the military, an authority structure or chain of command governs the organization. If someone has a problem with another, he can take the complaint to his superior, boss, or commanding officer. Paul's point is similar—he was telling both the weak and the strong to recognize that Christ is Lord of both, and as such, both are precious in His sight and beyond rebuke when it pertained to doubtful things. In this respect Christ is the foundation both for their love for another as well as their mutual respect and acceptance of their convictions. Paul does not embrace pragmatism, saying, "Let's just get along so we don't waste our time arguing." Nor does he counsel theological warfare: "I'm right and you're wrong, so you need to embrace the truth or suffer the consequences." And neither does Paul advise theological tyranny of the weaker brother: "You have to do whatever I say because it violates my conscience." Rather, Paul grounds their conduct and mutual respect for one another in Christ.

In his effort to exhort them to a mutual love for one another, Paul reminds his recipients that they all must give an account: "But why do you judge your brother? Or why do you show contempt for your brother? For we shall all stand before the judgment seat of Christ. For it is written: 'As I live, says the LORD, Every knee shall bow to Me, And every tongue shall confess to God.' So then each of us shall give account of himself to God" (Rom. 14:10–12).

Paul rebukes the church at Rome because, in their effort to live out their lives concerning doubtful things, they engaged in censorious behavior—they harshly judged one another. Paul applies this indictment against both groups. The weak, for example, likely looked down on the strong for consuming meat. And the strong likely looked down on the weak for failing to eat meat. Contempt is a two-way street, and Paul wanted his recipients to stay off it and take an entirely different route. In all matters of the Christian life, whether in explicit matters of doctrine or over doubtful things, Paul reminded his recipients that all of them would stand before the judgment seat of Christ and account for their actions. If this is the case, then whether weak or strong, both groups were supposed to worry about their own conduct rather than engage in the judgment of others, something that was the strict purview of Christ alone.

The Weak and the Strong Today

Now, when we come to a passage such as this, the reaction is for us to take the principles that Paul gives and immediately apply them to our present context. Questions abound regarding the consumption of alcohol, Christmas and the church calendar, listening to music, and the like. I think our desire often falls into the very attitudes that Paul rebukes in these verses. I speak of the attitude of censoriousness, or the tendency to censure or be highly critical of others. The strong wants to prove to his weaker brother that he can listen to music or consume alcohol. The weak, on the other hand, wants to find some justification for his chosen practices. While determining practices of the Christian life is relevant for this passage, we should not pass by the main focus of Paul's admonition and instruction—namely, Christ.

Notice that both the weak and strong brothers in the congregation of Rome have completely forgotten Christ's place in the church. Whether the strong showing contempt for the weak, or the weak judging the strong, they have completely forgotten the place of Christ in the church as her Lord, her Master. Many in the church claim to know the significance of the resurrection, for example, but fail to demonstrate that knowledge in action. They give lip service to the resurrection of Christ and its concomitant result—namely, His lordship over the church. The one who consumes alcohol, for example, looks down on the one who does not consume it. The one who does not consume alcohol judges the one who consumes it. This two-way censoriousness is not the pleasing aroma of a living sacrifice. As a living sacrifice, a believer rightly recognizes the lordship of Christ over the church because of His life, death, and resurrection. For the believer who questions the practices of another brother, he must leave the judgment of his brother to Christ. He must not play the role of the Holy Spirit but allow Christ this exclusive place of honor and right. In like manner, the believer who questions the weakness of faith in another brother must also leave the judgment of his brother to Christ.

Notice also how inaugurated eschatology plays a part in all this. Because of Christ's resurrection, an eschatological event, He reigns and rules over the church right now. Do we demonstrate the knowledge of the lordship of Christ and the inaugurated eschaton in our day-to-day interaction with our fellow brothers and sisters in Christ? Let us not forget to see Christ in this passage. But what of the principles that Paul gives the Roman Christians? While Paul is not finished spelling out all the principles connected with the weak and strong conscience, it is important that we rightly recognize the limitations of this issue. We must remember that Paul addresses the subject of doubtful things. In other words, Paul can tolerate a diversity of practices on matters such as food and drink because these practices "do not violate any biblical or moral norm, as long as they are motivated by the glory of God."[1]

We may not scruple over what God explicitly or implicitly commands in His Word nor show contempt for the commands of God. For the strong, just because a brother with a weak conscience has objections to your attendance of a movie does not mean that he is wrong. Likewise, for the weak, just because your brother attends a movie does not automatically mean that it is sinful. Another such

1. Schreiner, *Romans*, 720.

example comes from the celebration of Christmas. I know of some Christians who refuse to celebrate Christmas because it is not found in Scripture; there are many others, however, who do celebrate the holiday. Both, I know, carry out their convictions from a desire to honor and please God. But regardless of their convictions, they should never judge one another. The one who does not celebrate Christmas should not pass judgment over the one who does, and vice versa. Over such issues we should have a principled "live and let live" approach. Additionally, when it comes to either consuming or not consuming, whatever it may be, do we first and foremost examine our own behavior and thought processes for sin? Or are we too concerned with the behavior of our brother or sister to give any attention to our own practices? We should examine ourselves and ask whether we are not placing enough faith in God, barring ourselves from what He has declared as good or consuming God's good creation in a sinful manner.

Martin Luther offers a helpful illustration of how we should live in the church with one another:

> When it happens that two goats meet upon a narrow footbridge over the water, how should they behave? They can't back up, nor can they go around each other, because the bridge is too narrow. Should they charge each other, they would both fall in the water and drown. What should they do? Nature has given them such traits, that one submits to the other and lets the other go over it, and that way both remain uninjured. That is what a person should do in regards to another, and let him walk over him, rather than quarrel, squabble and fight with him.[2]

In other words, conflict is not the best way to resolve disagreements in the church when it comes to doubtful things. At a minimum, we should give way to our weaker brother, but such actions, remember, are not compromise but ultimately an expression of love.

---

2. Luther, *Off the Record with Martin Luther*, §6963 (pp. 163–64).

Conclusion

It is important to see that our freedom from sin and death and the just condemnation of God has been bought for us by the life, death, and resurrection of Christ. Christ has earned His seat of authority as Lord and King of the church. We, therefore, have no right to usurp His God-appointed authority and place as Lord and King when we censoriously pass judgment on our fellow brother in Christ, whether weak or strong. Whenever we have the temptation to judge another censoriously, let us remember to leave that responsibility to Christ. Let us repent of that critical spirit and turn our attention to our own actions and ask whether they are sinful. Recognize that Christ is our King and we are His servants.

44

Destroying God's Work?

ROMANS 14:13–23

Therefore let us not judge one another anymore, but rather resolve this, not to put a stumbling block or a cause to fall in our brother's way. I know and am convinced by the Lord Jesus that there is nothing unclean of itself; but to him who considers anything to be unclean, to him it is unclean. Yet if your brother is grieved because of your food, you are no longer walking in love. Do not destroy with your food the one for whom Christ died. Therefore do not let your good be spoken of as evil; for the kingdom of God is not eating and drinking, but righteousness and peace and joy in the Holy Spirit. For he who serves Christ in these things is acceptable to God and approved by men. Therefore let us pursue the things which make for peace and the things by which one may edify another. Do not destroy the work of God for the sake of food. All things indeed are pure, but it is evil for the man who eats with offense. It is good neither to eat meat nor drink wine nor do anything by which your brother stumbles or is offended or is made weak. Do you have faith? Have it to yourself before God. Happy is he who does not condemn himself in what he approves. But he who doubts is condemned if he eats, because he does not eat from faith; for whatever is not from faith is sin.

Imagine how long it must have taken Michelangelo to paint the ceiling of the Sistine Chapel. How many hours did Michelangelo lay on his back, crane his neck, raise his arms in the air until they ached with pain? When he placed the final touches on his masterpiece, how enraged would he have been if someone climbed a ladder and began to whitewash his work? We would certainly think poorly of the person who would thoughtlessly paint over one of the greatest works of art the world has ever seen. While the analogy is imperfect, Paul has a similar scenario in mind as he continues to explain why the Roman Christians were supposed to love rather than judge one another. In the previous section (Rom. 14:1–12) Paul exhorted the weak and the strong to respect one another's convictions. Each one in the church was not to judge censoriously but rather to leave the evaluation of one another's practices to Christ. There was a group of people within the congregation who scrupled over the consumption of meat. Their scruple, however, was not over cardinal doctrines or the commands of God but over doubtful matters. Paul's instruction was that the strong should not look down on his weaker brother and that likewise the weak should not judge his stronger brother. In the portion of Scripture before us, Paul continues his explanation on this matter of scruples and gives an exhortation primarily to the stronger brother. There is an implicit rebuke to the weaker brother as well, albeit a gentle one. As with the previous passage, Paul does not center on the matters of food and drink, but on Christ. As we focus on Christ, our goal is to edify the church, not tear it down. Building up the body of Christ is what it means to be a living sacrifice.

Love and Do Not Judge

In the previous section Paul counseled his recipients that they were not supposed to judge one another, because all, strong or weak, would eventually appear before Christ's throne and would have to account for their conduct. Based on what he has written in Romans 14:1–12, Paul comes to a conclusion in the verses that follow: "Therefore let us not judge one another anymore, but rather resolve this, not to put a stumbling block or a cause to fall in our brother's way. I know and am convinced by the Lord Jesus that there is nothing unclean of itself; but to him who considers anything to be unclean, to him it is unclean" (Rom. 14:13–14). Not only are Christians not supposed to judge one another, but Paul now adds another element to his counsel—namely, they should not erect a stumbling block. Chances are this counsel is for the stronger brother. If the weaker brother had scruples concerning the consumption of meat, for example, then the stronger brother was not supposed to flaunt his stronger faith—he was not supposed to taunt the weaker brother and cajole him into doing things that troubled his conscience. As wonderful as our Christian liberty is—that is, our freedom from the condemnation of the law and the unbiblical and extrabiblical commandments of men—this does not mean that we are free to exercise it irresponsibly. The Westminster Confession explains that our Christian liberty is not given so that we may practice any sin or cherish any lust (WCF 20.3). Someone, for example, may have the liberty to consume alcohol, but if he exercises this liberty around someone who struggles with alcoholism, he acts irresponsibly. His actions very well might be the occasion for his weaker brother to fall into sin. Or, as you exercise your Christian liberty to consume alcohol and chide a weaker brother for his failure to do likewise, you might encourage him to imbibe out of fear rather than faith.

Paul expands on these ideas by informing his recipients that nothing is inherently unclean, whether meat, food, or drink. This is why Christians can legitimately eat all things. As we saw in the previous section, the weaker brother had scruples over consuming meat because his *faith* was weak, not because meat is somehow tainted or evil. God has declared all things are clean, yet the weaker brother had reservations in accepting that declaration. A small snapshot of this pattern appears in Peter's rooftop vision, when God commanded Peter to rise, kill, and eat. Peter responded with disbelief, "Not so, Lord! For I have never eaten anything common or unclean" (Acts 10:14). When the God of heaven and earth tells you to rise, kill, and eat, who are you to respond with disbelief and question the suitability of the dinner menu? But at the same time, Paul stipulates that for the one who believes that certain things are unclean, they are unclean for him. On a related note, the fact that Paul invokes the *clean* and *unclean* categories of Old Testament dietary food laws indicates that this group of weaker brothers in the Roman church were likely Jewish converts who struggled with eating foods that were formerly unclean. To put things in our own terms, even though lobster and shrimp were now on the menu by God's sovereign decree, some were still reluctant to attend the local Gentile lobster boil.

Now how can Paul say that if a person believes something is unclean, it is? Does not the decree of God trump the mistaken and erroneously informed conscience of the weaker brother? Is this some sort of ethical relativism? No, Paul will eventually explain in the verses that follow how all Christians are supposed to approach this matter—they must approach all things in faith. At this point, however, Paul presses the point that love is absolutely necessary: "Yet if your brother is grieved because of your food, you are no longer walking in love. Do not destroy with your food the one for whom Christ died" (Rom. 14:15). Paul reminds the strong of the dictates of love. Although the strong have every right to consume all things, if their actions cause their weaker brothers to stumble, then they no longer exhibit love toward their weaker brother. The stronger brother, the one who should know better given his stronger faith, fails to be a living sacrifice. As correct as the stronger brother might be in his consumption of meat, if he grieves his weaker brother, then he has failed to live in love; he has failed to consider the needs of others more important than his own (Phil. 2:3). In this case, it does not appear, then, that the weaker brothers were somehow trying to force their convictions on the strong but that they genuinely struggled with eating meat.

Paul once again appeals to Christ as the bedrock on which Christians base their conduct. Paul does not offer pragmatism, feigned kindness, or grin-and-bear it sanctification. He appeals to the resurrection of Christ and His lordship over the church as the grounds for both the strong and weak to respect one another's convictions—it was not their place to judge one another. Likewise, Paul appeals to the stronger brother on the grounds of the sacrifice of Christ. If Christ was willing to lay down His life for the sake of the weaker brother, then should not the stronger brother be willing to exercise his Christian liberty carefully or even give up his consumption of meat? As Robert Haldane observes: "If Christ died for the weak brother, how unlike Christ is this strong believer, who will do what he knows will destroy his brother, if he follow his example without having his knowledge! The love of Christ in giving His life for this brother, and the indifference with respect to him which is manifested by the person who should thus abuse his liberty, are here set in strong contrast."[1] Changing one's dining menu seems like a small price to pay in comparison to the sacrifice of Christ. He does not invoke the specific language, but note that the idea of being a living sacrifice appears here as Paul exhorts the stronger brothers to sacrifice their choice of food for the sake of their weaker brothers.

All too often Christians, especially in Reformed churches, value orthodoxy at the expense of orthopraxy; in simpler words, doctrinal precision trumps love. People can talk about justification, the order of salvation, Christology, and the history of doctrine with the greatest precision and zeal, but when asked to exercise their Christian liberty with caution and love, they balk. They protest and claim their freedom is being restricted rather than consider how they might be wounding or even destroying God's work in their fellow brothers and sisters. Like the ignorant person who mounts the ladder to whitewash the Sistine Chapel, with a few careless brush strokes they wound the conscience of their weaker brother with little to no thought that they have damaged one of God's masterpieces. This is why Paul reminds the strong of the larger picture: "Therefore do not let your good be spoken of as evil; for the kingdom of God is not eating and drinking, but righteousness and peace and joy in the Holy Spirit" (Rom. 14:16–17). While food is certainly part of God's good creation and a blessing, the pursuit of righteousness, peace, and joy takes precedence over the dinner menu. Paul did not want God's good creation, food, to become the occasion of evil—namely, destroying God's work.

I think, however, that the strong in Paul's day, and we can add the strong today, believe that they will somehow miss out on their Christian liberty and the things to which they are entitled if they surrender them to their weaker brothers. They are afraid of being

1. Haldane, *Romans*, 603.

robbed or cheated out of the things they want. Yet Paul's words here echo Christ's own counsel regarding worries about food and clothing: "But seek first the kingdom of God and His righteousness, and all these things shall be added to you" (Matt. 6:33). In other words, if we seek Christ's kingdom and righteousness, then all these other things will fall into place—we will see them in their proper place and relation to the greater good of protecting the weaker brother. We will not fear being cheated but rather recognize our revised menu selection as the smallest of sacrifices for the sake of edifying the church. In this respect Paul urges the strong to serve Christ unto the building up of the church: "For he who serves Christ in these things is acceptable to God and approved by men. Therefore let us pursue the things which make for peace and the things by which one may edify another" (Rom. 14:18–19).

Living by Faith in All Things

Paul brings the reality and weight of our conduct within the purview of the church when he reminds the strong of the potential impact of their irresponsible exercise of Christian liberty: "For he who serves Christ in these things is acceptable to God and approved by men. Therefore let us pursue the things which make for peace and the things by which one may edify another" (Rom. 14:18–19). As lawful as it is to eat meat, to eat in an irresponsible and unloving manner could possibly destroy God's work. This is not to say that someone could somehow cause another person to lose his salvation, to reverse God's sovereign decree of election. Rather, Paul wants to minimize the damage that could be done, even permanently within the scope of this life, to a fellow brother or sister who stumbles over the conduct of another. Think, for example, of the newly converted Christian who struggles with alcoholism but sees the strong Christian freely exercising his liberty to consume alcohol. Even though he might lack the confidence or faith, he might imbibe because he sees the stronger brother doing so, and in the process, in a moment, irreversibly change his life for the worse.

That is why Paul reiterates the points that he made before—namely, that all things are pure, but to the believer who thinks it is impure, he should not consume it. This does not mean that conscience, however erroneously informed it might be, always trumps scriptural doctrine. Rather, Paul makes the point that Christians must live by faith in all things. If the weaker brother does not believe that all meat is good, then he fails to trust that God has declared all food clean and therefore good. If he proceeds to eat what he believes is impure, then in his conscience he mistakenly believes that he sins. In his heart, the weaker brother not only fails to take God at His word but also engages in what he believes is sinful. Hence Paul writes: "But he who doubts is condemned if he eats, because he does not eat from faith; for whatever is not from faith is sin" (Rom. 14:23). Doubt is never a foundation for the Christian life.

Paul largely directs his exhortation in this portion of Romans to the stronger brothers. But we must not pass by Paul's implicit exhortation to the weak. Yes, Paul has told the weak not to violate conscience, for whatever is not of faith is sin. But he has also said that all things, meat and wine, are clean and pure (Rom. 14:14, 20). We must realize it is sinful to call God's good gifts unclean, impure, or evil. To do so is blasphemous. We must realize that the weakness is with *our faith*, not with God's good creation. Moreover, while it is true that the strong must love the weak and exercise their liberty with caution and discretion, we must ask ourselves, are we truly grieved? Does our brother's conduct truly injure our conscience? Too often I believe what flies under the banner of a wounded conscience is really someone's attempt at meddling. The weak must place their unswerving faith in God.

Nevertheless, Paul tells the stronger brother, "It is good neither to eat meat nor drink wine nor do anything by which your brother stumbles or is offended or is made weak" (Rom. 14:21). In other words, life in the church is not one of isolation and disconnection, with each person doing as he pleases. Life in the church is lived in community and connection with one another. To borrow Paul's analogy from 1 Corinthians 12, the church is a body, and what any one part does affects the whole. So the strong were supposed to exercise their Christian liberty with love and care for the rest of the body of Christ. They were not supposed to assume that everyone was like them, strong in their faith. Hence Paul writes, "Do you have faith? Have it to yourself before God. Happy is he who does not condemn himself in what he approves" (Rom. 14:22). Paul informs the strong that if they have a robust faith, one that allowed them to eat without scruples, then it was something that they could share with God—it was not something they were supposed to bandy about or boast in, or a perch from which they could cast scorn on their weaker brothers. Paul told the strong to exercise their faith and liberty with discretion, but most importantly, with love.

Putting Life in Perspective

We must recognize that everything Paul has written in chapter 14 is not ultimately about food and drink. Rather, the point of the passage is the redemptive work of Christ and the kingdom of God. This passage is ultimately about what our justification and sanctification free us to do—they free us to love, to be living sacrifices. When a believer, who is supposed to be a living sacrifice, cannot show enough love to his weaker brother, he forgets the costly sacrifice of Christ. The degree to which we demonstrate love to our weaker brothers and sisters shows how much we understand and appreciate Christ's costly sacrifice. Ultimately, when we demonstrate love to our weaker brother, we demonstrate love to Christ Himself. So, then, how well do we comprehend the sacrifice of Christ? If we understand it well, we will have no qualms about the careful exercise of our Christian liberty. It is *nothing* to sacrifice the consumption of food or drink for the edification of the church.

The other major focal point of this passage, as I said, is the kingdom of God. Notice how Paul contrasts the two options for the strong in their treatment of the weak: (1) he instructs the strong not to destroy the weak (Rom. 14:15; cf. v. 20) and (2) he encourages the strong to pursue peace and the edification of the church (Rom. 14:19). Paul poses the antithetical choices between destroying or edifying the church. When Paul says that the kingdom of God is not in eating and drinking, it is in connection with these two choices. In other words, will we work to build the kingdom of God or destroy it? If we truly realize that Christ has inaugurated the eschaton and He is in the process of building the final temple made of us, living stones, we will do everything we can to construct the temple. If we are truly heavenly minded, then we will not mind sacrificing food or drink for the sake of the advancement of the kingdom of God.

Conclusion

Once again, we must not lose the centrality of Christ and His kingdom in this passage of Scripture. If we come here looking for vindication for our consumption or avoidance of food or drink, then we have entirely missed Paul's point. Seek first His kingdom, and all these things will be added unto you. Love Christ's body, both weak and strong, in the same way that Christ has loved you.

45

Zeal for God's House

ROMANS 15:1–6

We then who are strong ought to bear with the scruples of the weak, and not to please ourselves. Let each of us please his neighbor for his good, leading to edification. For even Christ did not please Himself; but as it is written, "The reproaches of those who reproached You fell on Me." For whatever things were written before were written for our learning, that we through the patience and comfort of the Scriptures might have hope. Now may the God of patience and comfort grant you to be like-minded toward one another, according to Christ Jesus, that you may with one mind and one mouth glorify the God and Father of our Lord Jesus Christ.

Most within the church desire unity—that everyone would zealously believe the same things about God, live in the same manner, and pursue the same goals. Within the confessional Reformed community there is a greater degree of cohesion than in the church at large due to the fact that its churches adhere to confessions, such as the Westminster Standards or Three Forms of Unity. Generally speaking, confessional documents unify Reformed churches in their beliefs about cardinal doctrines of the Christian faith. We confess the Westminster Standards and believe they are a summary of the teachings of Scripture. The same can be said for the churches who confess the Three Forms of Unity. While there is a degree of cohesion in our doctrinal belief about God, there is a lack of cohesion when it comes to opinions about the way we should live. There are a host of differing opinions regarding issues as diverse as education, relationships (how to find a spouse), alcohol, and parenting, for example.

Within the confessional Reformed community there are subcultures organized around each of the various positions on these subjects. A common mind-set is a desire to achieve unity around specific distinctives. In other words, "We're the Reformed home school church—you are welcome if you agree with us on this particular distinctive." The sentiment is "We will have peace, harmony, and unity as a body so long as we can agree to unite on this one distinctive, which is ________." You fill in the blank with the respective conviction. If you disagree with this distinctive, then you may want to find another subcommunity where you will be more comfortable. The message is that you must conform to our understanding and way of life. Now, the question we must ask ourselves is, What is the basis of unity within the body of Christ? Is the foundation of unity within the body found in a distinct belief about a particular practice or in something else? This is the issue that Paul addresses in the passage before us. We can pursue our answer through three questions: First, what is the basis of unity within the church? Second, what is the mark of a person who understands this basis? Third, who is the source of unity within the church? But we must first deal with the burden of the strong and Paul's prayer for the church at Rome before we can answer these three questions.

The Burden of the Strong

With great faith comes great responsibility. If faith is a gift from God and He distributes it according to His will and He sovereignly determines the degree of its strength in each person, then He gives the strong in the church greater faith for a reason. Some might too easily forget this and believe that their strong faith comes from their own efforts—their own study of Scripture and attention to the means of grace. True, our faith will grow when we meditate on God's Word and make use of the means of grace, but this activity is much like the church planting of Paul and the apostles: We water and plant, but God gives the increase (1 Cor. 3:6).

If this is the case, then God gives the strong greater faith not for their own personal benefit but for the mutual benefit of the church: "We then who are strong ought to bear with the scruples of the weak, and not to please ourselves. Let each of us please his neighbor for his good, leading to edification" (Rom. 15:1–2). God has given the strong great faith so that they can carry the weak. Once again, notice how the theme of living sacrifices surfaces. Christ, who was strong, became weak so that He might save us, who were weak (1 Cor. 1:27). As Paul wrote earlier in his epistle, "For when we were still without strength, in due time Christ died for the ungodly" (Rom. 5:6). It seems more than likely that Paul employs the language of *strong* and *weak* to remind his recipients that the life of Christ was supposed to be manifest in them—the strong were supposed to lay down their lives for the weak. The overall goal is not a nebulous, altruistic moral ethic but rather the edification of the church.

What Paul stated implicitly, he makes explicit in the following verse: "For even Christ did not please Himself; but as it is written, 'The reproaches of those who reproached You fell on Me'" (Rom. 15:3). Paul points to Christ, who did not seek His own interests but sought the interests of others, in this case our redemption. Paul employs a quotation from Psalm 69:9, and the first part of the verse shows us why Paul quotes it: "Because zeal for Your house has eaten me up" (Ps. 69:9a). In other words, it was Christ's zeal for God's house, which we now know is His body, that He was willing to undergo humiliation. Along these lines Calvin writes: "He had burned with such passion for the glory of God, and was seized by such a desire to advance His kingdom, that he forgot himself and was absorbed in this one thought."[1] Paul's point is that if zeal truly consumes the strong, then they will be more than willing to care for their weaker brothers.

1. Calvin, *Romans and Thessalonians*, 304.

Paul's Prayer

Paul instructed his recipients by pointing them to Christ and the Word, but he did not simply convey information—he did not merely supply data for their consumption. Rather, as a good shepherd and pastor, Paul prayed for the church in Rome so that they would embody the truths he set forth: "Now may the God of patience and comfort grant you to be like-minded toward one another, according to Christ Jesus, that you may with one mind and one mouth glorify the God and Father of our Lord Jesus Christ" (Rom. 15:5–6). All too often pastors are willing to preach, but do they pray fervently for their congregations? Paul knew of the importance and power of prayer and so, as these verses indicate, he prayed for God's intercession regarding the church's lack of unity. He relied not on his ability to persuade but on Christ's power to save and transform the church. Paul, in essence, called on the triune God to enable the church in Rome to walk in the newness of life, set aside their selfish ways, and present themselves as living sacrifices. This transformation would be abundantly evident in the sacrificial love that the strong showed for the weak.

The fact that Paul committed the church into God's hands shows that his zeal was ultimately rooted in his union with Christ. Paul prayed that the Christians in Rome would "be like-minded toward one another" (Rom. 15:5). This is not to say that they would agree on everything—this is certainly clear from the surrounding context. There were those who thought that they should not eat meat or drink wine, and then there were those who consumed such things. They were not to debate and argue over food and drink but to pursue the righteousness of the kingdom of God. Rather, the like-mindedness comes in pursuing the edification of the body of Christ—building up the final temple. Their unity comes in spite of their differences of opinion. It comes in the strong bearing up the scruples of the weak, the weak growing in their faith, and in both groups refusing to judge one another censoriously. The ultimate goal of Paul's prayer is that God would conform the Roman Christians to the image of Christ. For what purpose does our conforming to the image of Christ serve? To glorify our heavenly Father. On this point Calvin writes: "There is no reason, therefore, for anyone to boast that he will glorify God in his own way, for God sets so high a store on the unity of His servants that He will not allow His glory to be sounded amid discord and controversy."[2]

The Basis of Our Unity

Recall the three questions that we set out to answer at the beginning of this section: (1) What is the basis of unity within the church? (2) What marks a person who understands the true basis of unity? (3) Who is the source of unity within the church?

What Is the Basis of Unity within the Body of Christ?

Christ once again rests at the heart of this passage. So often we get tangled in issues and try to determine who has the right to believe or do something, such as debates over food and drink, and we thus fail to see Christ. While we may not debate food and drink, there are other issues that cloud the church's vision. Once again, we are all familiar with the questions surrounding schooling, relationships, and child rearing. Regardless of what Christians might think about these issues, we must never attempt to build unity around these distinctives—it is the fool's errand. It would be akin to the strong in Rome saying, "We will build unity on the consumption of meat." Unity is not built on debatable distinctives. Unity is built only on Jesus Christ *in spite* of our distinctives. The church will *never* achieve any semblance of unity unless it is centered on Jesus Christ.

What Marks a Person Who Understands the True Basis of Unity?

Zeal for the church's edification will consume the person who truly understands the basis of the church's unity. The one who is zealous for the house of God will unhesitatingly forgo the consumption of any food or drink or the advocacy of any distinctive for the sake of the weaker brother. The stronger brother will not pursue his own selfish interests but will instead sacrifice them to God, not in the

2. Calvin, *Romans and Thessalonians*, 306.

name of self-deprecation but out of a desire for conformity to the image of Christ. Just as Christ sacrificed Himself for the church, so we must be willing to sacrifice our desires for the church.

Who Is the Source of Unity within the Body of Christ?

We must finally recognize that no degree of unity will result in rallying around distinctives. Nor does unity result if we all purpose to sacrifice our desires. That is the pursuit of sanctification through the power of the flesh, not the Spirit (Rom. 8:5). We must live according to the Spirit and pursue unity in His power. To whom did Paul cry to bring about unity within the church? To God! Yes, he appealed to the Christians at Rome, but he ultimately cried out to God in prayer for unity. Paul knew that only the power of God working in us by the presence of His Holy Spirit brings unity. Paul lived in the power of the Spirit. How do we ensure that we pursue unity in the same way? Well, Paul shows us two things. First, he drew nigh unto God in prayer—a means of grace. Second, he drew nigh unto God through His Word, exhorting both the Roman Christians and us to do likewise. Only our triune God can bring unity to the church. Moreover, if we bear the image of Christ, we will participate in that divinely wrought unity. One of God's tools, His chisel, if you will, is the Word of God, which conforms us to the image of Christ as the Sculptor removes all our excesses until only the perfect sculpture remains.

Conclusion

So then, who is the basis of unity within the church? Jesus Christ. What is the mark of a person who understands this basis? A zeal for the house of God, the church, the final temple. Who is the source of unity within the body of Christ? The triune God alone through His appointed means of grace: Word, sacraments, and prayer. Pursue unity through Jesus Christ. Pray that Christ would give you a sacrificial zeal for the church. Pursue greater conformity to the image of Christ by drawing nigh unto God through the means of grace. May we do all these things to the glory of God—Father, Son, and Holy Spirit.

46

The Chief End of the Church

ROMANS 15:7–13

Therefore receive one another, just as Christ also received us, to the glory of God. Now I say that Jesus Christ has become a servant to the circumcision for the truth of God, to confirm the promises made to the fathers, and that the Gentiles might glorify God for His mercy, as it is written: "For this reason I will confess to You among the Gentiles, And sing to Your name." And again he says: "Rejoice, O Gentiles, with His people!" And again: "Praise the Lord*, all you Gentiles! Laud Him, all you peoples!" And again, Isaiah says: "There shall be a root of Jesse; And He who shall rise to reign over the Gentiles, In Him the Gentiles shall hope." Now may the God of hope fill you with all joy and peace in believing, that you may abound in hope by the power of the Holy Spirit.*

"What is the chief end of man? Man's chief end is to glorify God, and to enjoy him forever," or so goes the familiar first question and answer to the Westminster Shorter Catechism. This is a question that, regardless of a person's church affiliation, anyone should be able to affirm. Yet it is a truth that we often fail to translate into the corporate life of the church. At the core of this catechism question is the chief reason for the church—namely, worship. This is something of which many in the church have lost sight. There are many, for example, who think that the purpose of the church is everything except worship. This type of trend often shows up in the most mundane of places, like our mailboxes. I once received a church's advertising flier that offered the following benefits: relevant teaching; comfortable ambiance; worship, music, video, and lighting that would "blow you away"; and refreshments during the worship service. The brochure stated: "We're committed to helping you live life successfully by offering support classes with themes on Finances, Marriage, Weight Loss, Parenting, Financial Planning, and more." I flipped the brochure over several times, carefully scanning and rereading, looking for something that might indicate that people who attended the church were there primarily to worship and glorify God. Yet I found only the so-called benefits of membership.

As much as we might think that the church in our own day suffers from self-centeredness, we should realize that the church in Rome struggled with the same problems. Recall from the outset of chapter 14 that Paul has dealt with the conflicts between the weak and the strong, which boils down to the question of whether the Roman Christians were going to be self- or Christ-centered. In a word, Paul's recipients forgot that their chief end was to glorify God—to worship Him. This is why Paul exhorted them to pursue the high calling of being a living sacrifice. And while being a living sacrifice has a horizontal dimension (that is, serving and showing love to one another), there is undoubtedly a vertical dimension as well—serving and showing love to our triune God. Paul, therefore, continues his counsel to these two warring factions and points them to a number of Old Testament passages of Scripture to show them that the chief end of the church is to glorify God and enjoy Him forever—to worship Him. Paul's counsel, as you can well imagine, continues to be relevant in our own day. Indeed, the church at large needs constant reminders to pursue its chief end.

Christlike Love

In the apex of his exhortation to the strong and the weak, Paul makes another Christ-focused appeal. Paul writes, "Therefore receive one another, just as Christ also received us, to the glory of God" (Rom. 15:7). He appeals to his recipients to love one another as Christ has loved them. Remember, Paul grounds his imperative (to love one another) in the indicatives (who they are in Christ). In this case, Paul does not merely exhort his recipients to imitate Jesus.

Rather, he wants them to draw on the power of the Holy Spirit, their union with Christ, to love one another. Paul then appeals to the specific nature of Christ's ministry, which likely further reveals the identity of the strong and the weak: "Now I say that Jesus Christ has become a servant to the circumcision for the truth of God, to confirm the promises made to the fathers, and that the Gentiles might glorify God for His mercy" (Rom. 15:8–9a). The fact that he points to Christ's ministry to "the circumcision," the Jews, indicates that Paul wanted the strong (likely Gentiles) to serve the weak (likely Jews who scrupled over matters pertaining to diet and the Old Testament festival days). By His ministry to His fellow Jews, Christ was able to serve both Jew and Gentile. Again, Paul exhorts the strong to become weak in the same way that Christ redeemed the weak (Rom. 5:6–10). Moreover, Christ confirmed "the promises made to the fathers" (Rom. 15:8). In other words, as Paul argued (Rom. 11), God did not abandon His covenant promises to Abraham. God was saving the biological descendants with Paul as the chief example of His covenant faithfulness.

The Goal of Worship

Christ became weak to save the weak so they could worship and praise God. This was God's intention from the outset—to redeem a people for Himself so that they would glorify Him. To prove this point Paul offers a catena of quotations from the Old Testament: "As it is written, 'For this reason I will confess to You among the Gentiles, And sing to Your name.' And again he says: 'Rejoice, O Gentiles, with His people!' And again: 'Praise the LORD, all you Gentiles! Laud Him, all you peoples!' And again, Isaiah says: 'There shall be a root of Jesse; And He who shall rise to reign over the Gentiles, In Him the Gentiles shall hope'" (Rom. 15:9b–12). Paul gives a chain of four quotations from the Old Testament: 2 Samuel 22:50 (Ps. 18:49), Deuteronomy 32:43, Psalm 117:1, and Isaiah 11:10. Paul marshals these quotations to substantiate the fact that it was God's intention from the outset to save Gentiles so that they would praise, worship, and glorify Him. Including the Gentiles was never a back-up plan. Paul draws each of these quotations from across the Old Testament, whether in the Pentateuch, the Writings, or the Prophets, the three major subdivisions of the Hebrew Bible. Paul's main point here is that Christ saved the Jews to glorify God and also saved the Gentiles to this same end.

Notice the common thread that runs through all four quotations. Not only do they speak of the salvation of the Gentiles, but they speak of the Gentiles praising and glorifying God: "I will…sing to Your name" (Rom. 15:9b); "Rejoice, O Gentiles" (v. 10); "Praise the LORD, all you Gentiles" (v. 11); "in Him the Gentiles shall hope" (v. 12). The main thrust of Paul's point is that we have not been redeemed for squabbles over debatable matters but to praise our triune God. The weak and the strong have been redeemed to worship God. Paul's recipients allowed something as simple and ordinary as food to distract them from their God-designed goal—to glorify Him.

Paul desperately wanted his recipients to realize their God-given purpose, so he writes: "Now may the God of hope fill you with all joy and peace in believing, that you may abound in hope by the power of the Holy Spirit" (Rom. 5:13). Paul concludes this section, and even the material of the whole epistle of Romans, with a benediction to the Roman Christians that God would fill them with hope, joy, and peace. We should note the source of this hope, the Holy Spirit. We must not lose sight of Paul's overall argument, especially the eschatological context of everything he presents. Recall that we have identified, first, that everything in Romans 6–8 falls under the category of inaugurated eschatology—the fulfillment of the prophesies of Jeremiah and Ezekiel. Second, the driving forces of Paul's exhortations are Christ's (a) lordship over the church, (b) resurrection from the dead, and (c) sacrifice for both the strong and the weak.

The fact that he counsels the church to seek their hope through the power of the Holy Spirit indicates that Paul wanted them to be eschatologically minded. Even though they still lived in the midst of the present evil age, he wanted them transformed by the renewing of their minds—to remember that the new heavens and earth were dawning and thus to live accordingly. As they do this, Paul wanted them to place their hope in God as they awaited the consummation of the age. He wanted them to live in peace with God and one another. Peace, harmony, and love were supposed to be signs that Christ had unleashed the new heavens and earth and that the darkness of night was giving way to the light of day.

Seeking Our Chief End

How do we forget the chief end of the church, the worship of God? It is easy to recognize the wandering ways of many churches these days as they cater to the person in the pew rather than worship the living God. Paul had to remind the Roman Christians to be eschatologically minded—to pursue the chief end of the church: worship, life as a living sacrifice. The strong were not redeemed so that they could show contempt for the weak, and the weak were not redeemed so they could censoriously judge the strong. The testimony of Scripture is clear on this point—Jew and Gentile have been redeemed to glorify God, to worship Him. Yet it is easy to forget this truth, especially in our own circles. While it is true that we are not guilty of the foolishness of some churches, we nevertheless have a penchant to wander from our calling. Geerhardus Vos offers two ways by which we forget our chief calling.

First, he notes, "There is even such a thing as worshipping one's religion instead of one's God. How easily the mind falls into the habit of merely enlisting God as an ally in the fight for creature-betterment, almost oblivious to the fact that he is the King of glory for whose sake the whole world exists and the entire battle is waged."[1] He continues, "Our outgoing activities, our good works of service, our concern with the externals of religion, all this, unless kept in the closest, most vital contact with God himself, will inevitably tend to acquire a degree of detachment and independence in which it may easily withdraw from God and the consecration that ought to go to the satisfaction that ought to come from him alone."[2] This certainly

1. Vos, *Grace and Glory*, 16–17.
2. Vos, *Grace and Glory*, 16.

happened to the strong in Rome—they pursued what they believed was the truth and forgot to love their weaker brethren. Our theology can be as straight as an arrow, but if we forget to love others, we fail at our calling to be living sacrifices and fail to worship God truly.

Second, Vos makes another observation: "The true disciple does not seek to be made better for his own glory but in the interest and for the glory of God. He feels with Paul that he must apprehend, because he was apprehended for that very purpose."[3] It is very easy to think we must pursue obedience to God's law merely for the sake of obedience—so that we feel a sense of accomplishment or so guilt does not burden our consciences. While it is true that a motivation for obedience can be the freedom from guilt, it should not be the main reason we obey. It appears that the weak pursued obedience in this vein. Their consciences were unnecessarily wounded over the consumption of meat and drink. They did not pursue obedience for the sake of God's glory; had they done this, they would have recognized they were holding their stronger brothers to a higher standard than Scripture itself sets. They were trying to make their own convictions the standard of the community rather than those of God. They were indirectly pursuing their own glory rather than God's glory, however well-intentioned they were.

Conclusion

What is the chief end of the church? The answer, of course, is to glorify God. This is Paul's point to the strong and weak at the congregation at Rome. Christ was obedient to His Father's will, redeeming His people from sin and death, all for the glory of His Father. We have been redeemed for the very same purpose—that we would live obediently, as living sacrifices, not for our own glory but for the glory of our triune God. Pursue, therefore, your calling with an eschatological mind-set—not according to your own abilities but according to the power of the Holy Spirit. If you are strong, bear with your weaker brothers and sisters to the glory of

3. Vos, *Grace and Glory*, 39.

God. If you are weak, do not judge your brothers and sisters but instead draw near to God so that He would strengthen your faith. Pursue truth with a love and zeal for our Lord. Pursue your calling of obedience as living sacrifices, not for the sake of obedience or for conscience alone but for God's glory.

47

The Royal Priesthood

ROMANS 15:14–21

Now I myself am confident concerning you, my brethren, that you also are full of goodness, filled with all knowledge, able also to admonish one another. Nevertheless, brethren, I have written more boldly to you on some points, as reminding you, because of the grace given to me by God, that I might be a minister of Jesus Christ to the Gentiles, ministering the gospel of God, that the offering of the Gentiles might be acceptable, sanctified by the Holy Spirit. Therefore I have reason to glory in Christ Jesus in the things which pertain to God. For I will not dare to speak of any of those things which Christ has not accomplished through me, in word and deed, to make the Gentiles obedient—in mighty signs and wonders, by the power of the Spirit of God, so that from Jerusalem and round about to Illyricum I have fully preached the gospel of Christ. And so I have made it my aim to preach the gospel, not where Christ was named, lest I should build on another man's foundation, but as it is written: "To whom He was not announced, they shall see; And those who have not heard shall understand."

We all know that the Old Testament economy of redemptive history has passed us by. We no longer worship God through shadows and types. We no longer worship God according to the Levitical code. We no longer bring animals for sacrifice in a temple made of stone. Christ, our Passover Lamb, offered Himself as the supreme sacrifice (Heb. 13:11–12). We no longer require a high priest from the line of Aaron, from the tribe of Levi, to enter the Holy of holies on our behalf once a year on the Day of Atonement. Our High Priest, Jesus

Christ, entered the heavenly Holy of holies once, on our behalf, and intercedes for us at this very moment (Heb. 6:19–20). Now, we should recognize that though Christ is our High Priest, and though He has offered the one and only sacrifice to make satisfaction for our sins, this does not mean that the priestly service of God's people has ended, nor that we no longer offer God sacrifices, nor that we no longer worship God in His temple. Rather, there is a priestly order in the redemptive economy of the New Testament, we still offer sacrifices to God, and we still worship God in His temple. Paul explains how these things are true here in Romans 15:14–21.

Paul's Confidence

Unlike many parents and authority figures who deliver instructions and then wonder whether they will be followed, Paul had a confidence that his recipients would heed his counsel. Paul writes: "Now I myself am confident concerning you, my brethren, that you also are full of goodness, filled with all knowledge, able also to admonish one another" (Rom. 15:14). However, Paul's confidence in the church at Rome did not ultimately rest on them but on God Himself. Recall Paul's prayer for the church at Rome: "Now may the God of patience and comfort grant you to be like-minded toward one another, according to Christ Jesus, that you may with one mind and one mouth glorify the God and Father of our Lord Jesus Christ" (Rom. 15:5–6; cf. 15:13). Unlike many pastors who rely on persuading, cajoling, berating, and threatening their congregations, Paul rested firmly on the power of God to transform lives through Christ's gospel and the Holy Spirit. For this reason, Paul was confident that God would work in their midst.

At the same time, Paul did not let his confidence in God's grace keep him from giving pointed counsel to the church: "Nevertheless, brethren, I have written more boldly to you on some points, as reminding you, because of the grace given to me by God" (Rom. 15:15). True, God changes lives by making sinners into saints, but He does so through the preaching of His Word and, in this case, through the ministry of His chosen servants. Paul's confidence and boldness did not rest in a persecution complex, an inferiority complex, or an egotistical megalomania but in his divine calling—his apostolic office (Eph. 3:7–9). Paul's divine call was the driving force in his life so that he "might be a minister of Jesus Christ to the Gentiles, ministering the gospel of God, that the offering of the Gentiles might be acceptable, sanctified by the Holy Spirit" (Rom. 15:16).

There are at least five things that we should briefly note here. First, Paul calls himself a *leitourgos*, a minister, a Greek word from which we get the word *liturgy*. In fact, this term designates Paul's service as priestly, such as we find among the Old Testament Levites. Calling himself a *leitourgos* means that he was set apart by God for the sacred task of leading others in the worship of God. Second, Paul was specifically set apart to minister "the gospel of God," to preach and teach the gospel. Third, Paul's sacred calling of ministry was not to an indefinite goal. His goal was to make the Gentiles an acceptable sacrifice to God. The Old Testament prophet Isaiah presents a parallel idea to Paul's ministry of making the Gentiles an acceptable sacrifice. The prophet writes: "'Then they shall bring all your brethren for an offering to the LORD out of all nations, on horses and in chariots and in litters, on mules and on camels, to My holy mountain Jerusalem,' says the LORD, 'as the children of Israel bring an offering in a clean vessel into the house of the LORD" (Isa. 66:20). In other words, God was fulfilling ancient prophecies through Paul's ministry—the apostle was making the Gentiles an acceptable sacrifice to God (cf. 1 Peter 2:5).

Fourth, Paul carries out his calling not in his own power but in the power of the age to come, the Holy Spirit. The Holy Spirit is the one who converts, sets apart, sanctifies, and makes the Gentiles acceptable living sacrifices. Fifth, Paul's calling was rooted in the will of the triune Lord, not his own. The stamp of the Trinity is all over Paul's ministry. Paul was a minister of Jesus Christ, he preached the gospel of God, and he called on the sanctifying power of the Holy Spirit (Rom. 15:16). The triune Lord, therefore, was thoroughly intertwined in Paul's calling, ministerial labor, exhortations, love, service, and worship.

Paul's Boast

As much as Paul had reason to boast in his accomplishments, calling, authority, and office, he demurred such worldly conduct. Instead, Paul boasted in Christ: "Therefore I have reason to glory in Christ Jesus in the things which pertain to God. For I will not dare to speak of any of those things which Christ has not accomplished through me, in word and deed, to make the Gentiles obedient—in mighty signs and wonders, by the power of the Spirit of God" (Rom. 15:17–19a). Paul was concerned with boasting only of those things that Christ had done through him, whether in word or in deed. All who Paul was, all he did, and all he accomplished was on account of Christ. Like a merry-go-round, the themes of proclaiming the glory of Christ, living as sacrifices, obeying his calling, and boasting in Christ go round and round. Like a child who delights in singing the same song over and over again, Paul takes great pleasure in repeating the chorus of Christ's glorious works. These are the only things that drive Paul and give him a zeal and boldness in his calling. The fact that Paul performed "signs and wonders" might give him the occasion to take credit for these mighty acts, but Paul was doggedly determined to boast solely in Christ. Paul was content to take the gospel throughout the known world (Rom. 15:19b). His desire was to plow deeply into uncharted and untilled Gentile territory, from the biblical center of the world in Jerusalem (Ezek. 5:5) to the outer regions of what is now Albania. Paul moved far beyond Israel's borders so that he might take the gospel to where people had never heard the name of Christ (Rom. 15:20).

Because of his divine calling by Christ on the road to Damascus, Paul realized his mission was to take the gospel among the pagan Gentiles to fulfill Old Testament prophecy: "As it is written: 'To whom He was not announced, they shall see; And those who have not heard shall understand'" (Rom. 15:21). Paul quotes Isaiah 52:15 in support of his practice of not building on another man's foundation: "So shall He sprinkle many nations. Kings shall shut their mouths at Him; For what had not been told them they shall see, And what they had not heard they shall consider." The context of this prophecy is one where God would bring the Gentiles into His kingdom. So, then, Paul saw his own ministry as a fulfillment of this prophecy—namely, that the saving knowledge of God would go forth into the nations. This is why Paul was so adamant about going beyond the apostolic church-planting regions. His desire was to see the message of the gospel taken to the ends of the earth.

Paul's Goals

Everything Paul has written demonstrates that there is a priestly order in the New Testament, that these priests offer sacrifices to God, and that they worship God in His temple. First, Paul stated that he participated in the creation of a priestly order. Yes, the Aaronic line of Levi has passed away with the shadows and types of the Old Testament. They have been fulfilled in the person and work of Christ, our High Priest. Yet just as Aaron the high priest had assistant priests to aid him in bringing sacrifices, so too Christ has servant priests to assist Him. This particular pattern appears in Paul's own ministry. Along these lines Calvin writes: "The one who offers in sacrifice the people whom he obtains for God makes himself a priest or celebrant in the ministry of the gospel. It is in this way that he performs the sacred mysteries of the gospel. The priesthood of the Christian pastor is, as it were, to offer men in sacrifice to God, by bringing them to the obedience of the Gospel."[1]

Paul saw his own activity as priestly—he assisted the High Priest, Jesus Christ, by bringing more sacrifices to God the Father. As New Testament priests, do we assist pastors in their priestly labors or are we a hindrance to them? How do we advance and assist His ministers in their callings to preach and teach? Are we content to let our leaders and others do all the work, and maybe even criticize them, or do we look for ways to help? If we remember that we are all a part of the royal priesthood, then there is no person too small or insignificant, and no task too small. All things

1. Calvin, *Romans and Thessalonians*, 310.

in the church must work together for the preaching of the gospel—enabling pastors, like Paul, to bring more sacrifices to God.

Second, we must therefore realize that we still offer sacrifices. Yes, there is only one sacrifice for the propitiation and expiation of sin—the sacrifice of Jesus Christ. There is *nothing* we can do to expiate and propitiate our sin—only Christ can do this, and we can receive His work on our behalf only by faith alone. Yet how did Paul bring sacrifices to God? Paul brought converted Gentiles to faith in Christ by the preaching of the Word. These Gentiles were not converted by his powers of persuasion but by the regenerative and sanctifying power of the Holy Spirit. Again, Calvin writes:

> Now as ancient sacrifices were dedicated to God by outward sanctifications and washings, so these "sacrifices" are consecrated to the Lord by the Spirit of holiness, through the inward working of whose power they are separated from this world. Although purity of the soul arises from faith in the Word, yet because the voice of man can of itself accomplish nothing and is lifeless, the function of cleansing truly and properly belongs to the Spirit.[2]

We must not forget that Paul exhorted the Christians at Rome to be living sacrifices. Moreover, throughout the New Testament there are similar exhortations for Christians to offer sacrifices. Paul told the Ephesians, for example, to walk in love, and that such conduct was an offering, a sacrifice, and sweet-smelling aroma (Eph. 5:2). When the Philippian church sent needed supplies to Paul, he characterized their kind gift as a sweet-smelling sacrifice, something that was pleasing to God (Phil. 4:18). The author of Hebrews instructed his recipients to worship God and offer the sacrifice of praise—to give thanks to the Lord for all He has done (Heb. 13:15). All these passages, as well as Paul's words here, should cause us to ask, What types of sacrifices do we bring to God? Are they sweet-smelling aromas to our Lord? Do we offer up the praise of

2. Calvin, *Romans and Thessalonians*, 311.

our lips as sacrifices? Do we offer up our bodies and members as instruments of righteousness as living sacrifices? What do we bring to the temple to sacrifice to our Lord?

Third, we, the people of God, are the new temple. Paul saw his role as building the final temple. He sought to spread the knowledge of the gospel and the saving work of Christ throughout the nations. Paul was indefatigable in his efforts to build the new temple. In what ways do we contribute to the construction of the eschatological temple? Do we, with Paul, desire to see the nations flow to God's final dwelling place? Do we pray for the church's missionaries? Do we give sacrificially so that the gospel goes forth into the nations?

Conclusion

All these things show us that, though the shadows of the Old Testament have passed away with the first advent of Christ, many of the same patterns still exist in the redemptive economy of the New Testament. Under the lordship of Jesus Christ we, His people, are a royal priesthood charged with bringing sacrifices to our heavenly Father. We are charged with seeing others come to Christ through the ministry of the preaching and teaching of the Word, and with offering ourselves as living sacrifices. Fervor drove Paul to advance the kingdom of God and bring glory to Him. Our prayer should be that God would grant to us the same Spirit-wrought zeal for propagating His gospel, giving ourselves as living sacrifices, and building His temple.

48

To the Ends of the Earth

ROMANS 15:22–33

For this reason I also have been much hindered from coming to you. But now no longer having a place in these parts, and having a great desire these many years to come to you, whenever I journey to Spain, I shall come to you. For I hope to see you on my journey, and to be helped on my way there by you, if first I may enjoy your company for a while. But now I am going to Jerusalem to minister to the saints. For it pleased those from Macedonia and Achaia to make a certain contribution for the poor among the saints who are in Jerusalem. It pleased them indeed, and they are their debtors. For if the Gentiles have been partakers of their spiritual things, their duty is also to minister to them in material things. Therefore, when I have performed this and have sealed to them this fruit, I shall go by way of you to Spain. But I know that when I come to you, I shall come in the fullness of the blessing of the gospel of Christ. Now I beg you, brethren, through the Lord Jesus Christ, and through the love of the Spirit, that you strive together with me in prayers to God for me, that I may be delivered from those in Judea who do not believe, and that my service for Jerusalem may be acceptable to the saints, that I may come to you with joy by the will of God, and may be refreshed together with you. Now the God of peace be with you all. Amen.

Have you ever run across a story in the news about someone who purchased a seemingly ordinary painting only later to discover that it was actually a priceless object of art? To the original owner, the painting was common, worth a few dollars, but nothing more. But once a person began to study the painting closely, he soon realized that there was great skill in the brush strokes, carefully selected paints, and a specialized signature to the work that clued him in to the fact that his garage-sale bargain was far more than ordinary. I think we can approach the closing portions of Paul's letter in a similar fashion. When we read this portion of Romans we might be lulled into a sense of complacency. We have seen the spectacular fireworks in the earlier portions of Romans—the thunderous roar of revelation, man's depravity, justification by faith, sanctification, election, the preaching of the gospel, salvation of the fullness of Israel, and the imperatives to be living sacrifices. So now, as we wind our way to the end of the epistle, we might think that Paul has only routine details to report. He talks about his travel plans. Is this merely his travel itinerary? Or do we see the lifeblood of the kingdom flow through these verses? Do we actually see how God builds and advances His kingdom? Simply stated, this portion of Romans is not the mundane itinerary of the apostle. Rather, the lifeblood of the kingdom flows through these words as Paul discusses his desire to carry the gospel to the ends of the earth.

Paul's Travel Plans

As Paul closes out his epistle, he explains the reasons why he has not visited Rome. Recall that Paul said at the beginning of the epistle that he planned to visit them, but up to this point he was hindered (Rom. 1:13). Why was he hindered? Paul writes: "For this reason I also have been much hindered from coming to you. But now no longer having a place in these parts, and having a great desire these many years to come to you, whenever I journey to Spain, I shall come to you. For I hope to see you on my journey, and to be helped on my way there by you, if first I may enjoy your company for a while" (Rom. 15:22–24). Paul was hindered from coming to Rome because he was busy preaching the gospel and planting churches from Jerusalem to Illyricum. But now that his work was complete, he wanted to visit Rome and seek the church's help for his missionary journey to Spain. Once again, Paul's indefatigable efforts to spread the gospel leap off the page. Discontent with his efforts thus far, he wanted to take the gospel to the ends of the known world.

But before he could go to Rome and then eventually to Spain, Paul had other pressing plans: "But now I am going to Jerusalem to minister to the saints. For it pleased those from Macedonia and Achaia to make a certain contribution for the poor among the saints who are in Jerusalem" (Rom. 15:25–26). Paul wanted to bring an offering for the poor at the church in Jerusalem. In a sense, Paul revisits ideas he presented in Romans 11:16–17: The Jewish Christians constituted the olive tree to which Gentile wild olive branches were grafted on. Largely ministering among Gentile Christians from Jerusalem to Illyricum, Paul wanted to bring a material offering to the Jewish Christians in Jerusalem. His reasoning was that the Gentile Christians benefited from the spiritual treasures (the gospel) of the Jews, so the least the Gentiles could do was to share of their material wealth with their poor and suffering Jewish brothers and sisters (Rom. 15:27).

It may not be immediately evident, but Paul's offering-laden journey represents the inauguration of ancient prophecies. Isaiah foretold of a day when the nations would say, "Come, and let us go up to the mountain of the LORD, To the house of the God of Jacob; He will teach us His ways, And we shall walk in His paths." Isaiah says, therefore, "For out of Zion shall go forth the law, And the word of the LORD from Jerusalem" (Isa. 2:3). The gospel went forth from Jerusalem, and now the Gentiles were flocking to Zion and bringing their treasures to the Lord. This offering may look mundane, but closer examination reveals the gold of fulfilled prophecy and God's continued faithfulness to His Word. Once Paul delivered this offering to the Jerusalem church, he would then head back to visit Rome and make his way to Spain. Paul would not, however, arrive empty-handed but would bring with him the full blessings of the gospel of Christ (Rom. 15:28–29).

While seemingly ordinary, Paul's travel plans reveal the global extent of the church. This echoes a theme that runs throughout the Scriptures. God promised Abraham that he would be the father of many nations (Gen. 17:4). And Isaiah prophesied of a day when the nations would flow into Zion (Isa. 2:2). In Paul's own day, Christ gave His disciples a commission to carry the gospel into the nations (Matt. 28:19). And Paul's own missionary activity expanded along global lines—from Jerusalem, to Illyricum, and then to Spain. We should, as the famous hymn "How Sweet and Awesome Is the Place" states, long for the nations to know Christ: "Pity the nations, O our God, Constrain the earth to come; Send your victorious Word abroad, And bring the strangers home." As technologically advanced as our age is, we should not forget the simplicity of the church's task in advancing the kingdom. Too often we are perhaps distracted by multimedia and technology—if only we can spread the Christian faith through television, print media, radio, and the internet, then we can truly get the message of the gospel out. Yet while all these things assist in advancing the kingdom of God, we must not forget the simplicity of the preacher's task.

God ordained His kingdom's advancement through the preaching of the gospel. What ultimately fueled the sixteenth-century Reformation? Was it when Martin Luther nailed the Ninety-Five Theses to the castle door at Wittenberg? While that is certainly a watershed event, the Reformation would have died out with a whimper had it not been for the preaching of God's Word. The Reformers stopped preaching from the Roman Catholic lectionary (readings and prepared messages) and started preaching from the Scriptures. Preachers throughout Europe returned to the Word of God—this is ultimately one of the key elements that fueled the Reformation. Preaching was undoubtedly a foundational element in Paul's work to advance the kingdom. This, however, is not the only thing that propelled the kingdom.

When preachers herald God's Word, Jesus ultimately wields His sword against the nations. He breaks them with a rod of iron and dashes them like a potter's vessel (Ps. 2:9). As the book of Revelation tells us, a sharp, two-edged sword proceeds from Christ's mouth—the means by which He strikes the nations (Rev. 19:15). This is why the Reformation put such a high premium on preaching the Word. The Second Helvetic Confession (1566), for example, states:

> Wherefore when this Word of God is now preached in the church by preachers lawfully called, we believe that the very Word of God is preached, and received of the faithful; and that neither any other Word of God is to be feigned, nor to be expected from heaven: and that now the Word itself which is preached is to be regarded, not the minister that preaches; who, although he be evil and a sinner, nevertheless the Word of God abides true and good. (1.4)

No matter how slick, technical, and well marketed the presentation, *nothing* can replace the need for preachers proclaiming the gospel. Through the preaching of called men, Christ wields the sword of His mouth and advances His kingdom—He brings the *nations* into submission. Does your church, therefore, preach the gospel? And since Christ called the church to preach the gospel, does it preach it to the ends of the earth? Preaching the gospel and reaching the nations go hand in hand. They should never be separated.

Paul's Request

With the disclosure of his travel plans, Paul revealed a request to the church in Rome: "Now I beg you, brethren, through the Lord Jesus Christ, and through the love of the Spirit, that you strive together with me in prayers to God for me, that I may be delivered from those in Judea who do not believe, and that my service for Jerusalem may be acceptable to the saints, that I may come to you with joy by the will of God, and may be refreshed together with you" (Rom. 15:30–32). Periodically throughout his epistles Paul tells the churches of his prayers for them. Think, for example, of Paul's prayer in Romans 15:13, "Now may the God of hope fill you with all joy and peace in believing, that you may abound in hope by the power of the Holy Spirit." But Paul hoped and asked that his recipients would lift him up in their own prayers. Paul pleaded with the church to strive with him in prayer so that his ministry would be effective. Paul faced real enemies, trials, and even the possibility of death in Jerusalem. If Jerusalem were the Wild West, then there would have been posters with Paul's face plastered all over town, "Wanted, dead or alive." Paul's fellow countrymen sought his death, as the book of Acts well attests. He therefore earnestly sought the prayers of the church in Rome for his safety and eventual arrival in Rome. Paul closes this portion of his letter with a brief benediction: "Now the God of peace be with you all. Amen" (Rom. 15:33).

God has ordained prayer as one of the means by which He undergirds the evangelization of the nations. Paul definitely knew this and therefore coveted the prayers of the church in Rome. This was also nothing new, in that it comes from the very lips of Christ Himself in the Lord's Prayer. In Christ's model prayer we ask the Lord that His kingdom would come (Matt. 6:10). Again, this is why the Reformation placed a premium on prayer. The Westminster Shorter Catechism, for example, states: "What do we pray for in the second petition [of the Lord's Prayer]?" answering, "In the second petition (which is, *Thy kingdom come*) we pray, that Satan's kingdom may be destroyed; and that the kingdom of grace may be advanced, ourselves and others brought into it, and kept in it; and that the kingdom of glory may be hastened" (Q. 102). Do we place a high premium on prayer? Paul's words, though spoken some two thousand years ago, should echo in our minds today. We should pray that the kingdom of God would come and that God's will would be done here on earth, as it is in heaven. Moreover, if we understand the previous point—namely, that the kingdom advances among the nations through the preaching of the gospel by men called of God—then we must also lift these men up in prayer.

Do you pray for your pastor? Your pastor needs your prayers as much as Paul did, because he wields the very same sword of the Spirit. Lift your pastor and other men in the sacred office up in prayer that God would prosper their ministries—that through their preaching Christ would advance His kingdom. Dedicate a part of your week to pray for your pastor and other ministers. Set aside a time on Saturday evening and even Sunday morning to lift up your pastor in prayer. Pray for seminary students preparing to preach the gospel, and pray for the professors and institutions that teach them. As ordinary as Paul's request might be, his call for the church's prayers includes you!

God will indeed answer our prayers—He will advance His kingdom. We must recognize, however, that He will often answer our prayers in unanticipated ways. Take, for example, Paul's prayers and desires to advance the kingdom. He told the congregation at Rome that he wanted to visit them, yet his ministry kept him away. He now had plans to first visit Jerusalem to accompany the offering from the Gentiles to the Jewish Christians and then to visit Rome (Rom. 15:32). Did Paul ever get to Rome? Did God answer the Roman church's prayers? Yes, they were, though not in ways they expected. Paul visited Rome, though he did so in chains. Recall what happened to Paul in the lead-up to his visit to Rome. He was nearly killed in the temple (Acts 21:26–36), almost assassinated by his fellow Jews (Acts 23:12–35), and arrived at Rome by appealing to Caesar (Acts 25:10–12). God answered Paul's prayers and those of the church at Rome, though most likely in an unexpected manner. Yet how does the book of Acts end? Paul lived in Rome in a rented house and preached the kingdom of God with all confidence (Acts 28:30–31).

From a worldly perspective, the kingdom was stalled. Paul was a prisoner—people might even have speculated that God had not answered Paul's prayers and had not blessed his ministry. Yet we know this is not the case. The kingdom does not advance according to man's ways. The progress of the kingdom is not measured in terms of the number of people that are converted nor in the cultural and societal institutions that Christians may control. Rather, success is measured in terms of obedience to our calling and conformation to the image of Christ. Paul was one hundred percent successful despite his imprisonment because he followed in the footsteps of Christ—he was being conformed to Christ's image. Yet, as Luke notes, despite the apparent lack of success in Paul's ministry, God answered his prayers and he advanced the kingdom through the preaching of the Word.

Conclusion

This passage of Scripture, though seemingly mundane, pulsates with the vital lifeblood of the kingdom of God. Paul was building the kingdom of God by taking the gospel into the nations, preaching the Word, advancing the kingdom through prayer, and carrying out his ministry with a firm hope that God would answer his prayers. Are these truths that course through our veins? Do we seek to build the kingdom of God through His ordained means? Do we desire the salvation of the nations? Do we support the preaching of the Word through personal attendance, our offerings, and prayer for God's preachers? Like Paul, do we have the firm hope that God will answer our prayers? Our hope and prayer should be to build the kingdom and see God's glory extend throughout the world, that the gospel would spread to the ends of the earth.

49

Edification of the Body

ROMANS 16:1–20

I commend to you Phoebe our sister, who is a servant of the church in Cenchrea, that you may receive her in the Lord in a manner worthy of the saints, and assist her in whatever business she has need of you; for indeed she has been a helper of many and of myself also. Greet Priscilla and Aquila, my fellow workers in Christ Jesus, who risked their own necks for my life, to whom not only I give thanks, but also all the churches of the Gentiles. Likewise greet the church that is in their house. Greet my beloved Epaenetus, who is the firstfruits of Achaia to Christ. Greet Mary, who labored much for us. Greet Andronicus and Junia, my countrymen and my fellow prisoners, who are of note among the apostles, who also were in Christ before me. Greet Amplias, my beloved in the Lord. Greet Urbanus, our fellow worker in Christ, and Stachys, my beloved. Greet Apelles, approved in Christ. Greet those who are of the household of Aristobulus. Greet Herodion, my countryman. Greet those who are of the household of Narcissus who are in the Lord. Greet Tryphena and Tryphosa, who have labored in the Lord. Greet the beloved Persis, who labored much in the Lord. Greet Rufus, chosen in the Lord, and his mother and mine. Greet Asyncritus, Phlegon, Hermas, Patrobas, Hermes, and the brethren who are with them. Greet Philologus and Julia, Nereus and his sister, and Olympas, and all the saints who are with them. Greet one another with a holy kiss. The churches of Christ greet you. Now I urge you, brethren, note those who cause divisions and offenses, contrary to the doctrine which you learned, and avoid them. For those who are such do not serve our Lord Jesus Christ, but their own belly, and by smooth words and flattering speech deceive the hearts of the simple.

For your obedience has become known to all. Therefore I am glad on your behalf; but I want you to be wise in what is good, and simple concerning evil. And the God of peace will crush Satan under your feet shortly. The grace of our Lord Jesus Christ be with you. Amen.

I remember stumbling to the breakfast table at six o'clock in the morning to have our family devotions. My parents decided that we would read through the Bible in a year, so we sat down every morning to read. I must admit that many mornings I struggled to stay awake and I frequently did not understand the passages we were reading. The Old Testament genealogies were especially challenging: These chapters had long lists of names, which made me feel a bit like I was reading someone else's mail. I was sure that these names meant something to someone, but at the time they were largely lost on me. The more I matured and studied the Bible the more I began to realize how precious these genealogies are. As seemingly mundane as they might be, they trace a scarlet thread through redemptive history that begins with Adam and Eve and runs all the way to Christ. Under divine inspiration, Old Testament saints recorded the genealogy of Christ—they looked back to God's initial promise that the seed of the woman would crush the head of the serpent and deliver God's people from the tyranny of Satan, sin, and death. But a funny thing happened along the way. Once the bloodline reached Christ, the line of the woman began to spread in unanticipated ways—it began to spread among the Gentiles, strangers and aliens to the covenants and commonwealth of Israel. Paul's list of names here is not a perfunctory "thank you" list. This closing portion of Paul's letter constitutes a new covenant genealogy, one that has its roots in the promise God gave to Adam and Eve—that the seed of the woman would crush the head of the serpent.

A New Covenant Genealogy

As Paul closes his letter, he offers a list of names, one that bears a striking contrast with what he states in Romans 16:17–19. Note that in verses 17–19 Paul warns the church in Rome about those who cause divisions. Some create obstacles contrary to the doctrine they learned, they do not serve Christ, and they ambulate in the church, deceiving the naïve. By contrast, Paul commends and lists a number of people who have helped him in the work of the kingdom. Recall that Paul asked the church at Rome to pray for him (Rom. 15:30). The names he provides here are likely some of the very saints who prayed for Paul. We see, for example, Phoebe, who was entrusted with the task of bringing Paul's letter to Rome (Rom. 16:1). Priscilla and Aquila were a husband-and-wife missionary team who instructed Apollos in the faith (Rom. 16:3–5; cf. Acts 18:26). Epaenetus was a foundation stone for the church in Asia (Rom. 16:5). Andronicus and Junia, another husband-and-wife missionary team, and most likely Jews, were engaged in the work of the kingdom (Rom. 16:7). Amplias, Urbanus, and Stachys are all common Gentile slave names (Rom. 16:8–9). Aristobulus is possibly the grandson of Herod the Great and friend of Emperor Claudius (Rom. 16:10). Herodian was most likely a Jewish freedman in Herod's household since freedmen took the names of their patron (Rom. 16:11). And Tryphena and Tryphosa were two women with names that mean *gentle* and *delicate*, which indicates that they were most likely sisters (Rom. 16:12).[1]

These names read like an Old Testament genealogy but with one significant difference. These people were not related by blood as in the Old Testament. Rather, they were related by their faith in Christ. They were related by the blood of Christ and shared in common the same desire to see the gospel spread throughout the nations. All these names also demonstrate that the kingdom of God advanced not through the work of Paul alone but through the hands of many laborers. This is materially what Paul elsewhere explained formally—namely, that though there are many in the body of Christ, they are nonetheless individually members of one another, and they each use their different gifts for the church's edification (Rom. 12:5–6). Moreover, this list shows us that God's saving grace extends into all walks of life and that the body of Christ is diverse.

1. On the significance of these names, see Schreiner, *Romans*, 789–99.

There are men, women, Jews, Gentiles, married couples, the unmarried, slaves, freedmen, those commissioned by Christ, laymen, those in high government position, and commoners. All these people were called by God to directly minister or to undergird the church's ministry. The church at Rome labored to edify the body of Christ, to advance the kingdom of God.

Satan Crushed

Recall that in the opening chapters of the Bible God promised that the seed of the woman would crush Satan: "And I will put enmity Between you and the woman, And between your seed and her Seed; He shall bruise your head, And you shall bruise His heel" (Gen. 3:15). The seed of whom God spoke is Christ, but as Paul indicates, the genealogical line of the woman had now spread out into the nations. The line of righteous Abel now reached to the sons of Abraham, whether Jew or Gentile, slave or free, male or female (Gal. 3:28). Because of their union with the crucified, risen, and ascended Messiah, these sons of Abraham now saw the fulfillment of the long-awaited promise that was first uttered to Adam and Eve as they stood trembling before their covenant Lord. Paul writes: "For your obedience has become known to all. Therefore I am glad on your behalf; but I want you to be wise in what is good, and simple concerning evil. And the God of peace will crush Satan under your feet shortly. The grace of our Lord Jesus Christ be with you. Amen" (Rom. 16:19–20). The identity of the Roman Christians was known to all because of their obedience, the fruit of their union with Christ. But because they were united to Christ these saints would also soon see the ultimate destruction of Satan.

Satan's destruction was one of the main goals of Christ's work. As John tells us, "He who sins is of the devil, for the devil has sinned from the beginning. For this purpose the Son of God was manifested, that He might destroy the works of the devil" (1 John 3:8). In His first advent, Christ conquered sin and death, which we can classify under the category of the "already." That is, these are things that Christ has already accomplished. At Christ's return, He will completely destroy the forces allied with Satan. As Paul elsewhere explains, "For He must reign till He has put all enemies under His feet. The last enemy that will be destroyed is death" (1 Cor. 15:25–26). We can place this aspect of Christ's work under the category of the "not yet." These are things that Christ has not yet accomplished. Paul consoles and comforts this list of coworkers with the hope of the imminent, final, and utter destruction of Satan. That he lists these people as fellow Christians means they will be beneficiaries of Christ's victory.

Even though these blessings are part of the "not yet" aspect of Christ's work, we should connect this promise to Paul's warning against the deceivers he mentions in Romans 16:17–19. Why does Paul state the final defeat of Satan on the heels of his instruction regarding false teachers? Because Satan will always try to destroy the church as long as we dwell in this present evil age. Nevertheless, we press on knowing that Christ Himself will return at the end of the age and secure the victory over Satan. Christ will crush him under His feet.

Conclusion

Paul's words are testimony of God's grace. Paul names these saints in his gospel genealogy and reminds them of Christ's accomplished work and the hope of the conclusion of all things. Paul's message is simple—Christ is victorious, and you have begun to reap the benefits of His victory. But even then, greater days of glory and peace await the saints. The famous hymn "The Church's One Foundation" aptly captures the tension between the already and the not yet that Paul presents here in these closing verses:

> Though with a scornful wonder
> Men see her sore oppressed,
> By schisms rent asunder,
> By heresies distressed,
> Yet saints their watch are keeping,
> Their cry goes up, "How long?"
> And soon the night of weeping
> Shall be the morn of song.

'Mid toil and tribulation,
And tumult of her war,
She waits the consummation
Of peace forevermore;
Till with the vision glorious
Her longing eyes are blest,
And the great church victorious
Shall be the church at rest.

Rejoice at the inaugurated reign of Christ and the daily progress that the church makes. But remember that Christ will secure our final victory when He returns on the last day.

50

How Then Shall We Live?

ROMANS 16:21–27

Timothy, my fellow worker, and Lucius, Jason, and Sosipater, my countrymen, greet you. I, Tertius, who wrote this epistle, greet you in the Lord. Gaius, my host and the host of the whole church, greets you. Erastus, the treasurer of the city, greets you, and Quartus, a brother. The grace of our Lord Jesus Christ be with you all. Amen. Now to Him who is able to establish you according to my gospel and the preaching of Jesus Christ, according to the revelation of the mystery kept secret since the world began but now made manifest, and by the prophetic Scriptures made known to all nations, according to the commandment of the everlasting God, for obedience to the faith—to God, alone wise, be glory through Jesus Christ forever. Amen.

We finally come to the end of a long journey as we stand on the other side of one of the grandest peaks in all of Scripture—the epistle to the Romans. We started to climb this great peak with Paul's declaration that the gospel was the power of God unto salvation for all who believe and that in it God reveals His righteousness from faith to faith (Rom. 1:17). From this initial point we began our ascent and saw all of redemptive history, from beginning to end, unfolded for us. Now, as we make our way down the other side of this majestic mountain, what parting words does Paul have for the church at Rome and for us? Paul has important words to conclude this epistle. But we would be remiss if, after reading his grand epistle, we did not ask ourselves, How then shall we live? What difference does Paul's letter make? Have we simply mused before Romans, admiring its beauty and majesty only to walk away unaffected? Or do we recognize that Paul made a declaration to the congregation at Rome—a declaration about the very essence of life and history, the very reason for the world's existence, about incarnation, our salvation, and the whole scope of history? Paul has indeed made an important statement that tells us about the very axis on which all of life rotates. Identifying this axis will answer our question: How then shall we live?

Final Greetings and Doxology

Paul gives his last words of greeting to those who are in Rome and does so through the hand of an amanuensis, or a secretary. To all his colaborers—Lucius, Jason, Sosipater, Erastus, and Quartus—Paul pronounces a christological benediction (Rom. 16:21–24). After this greeting and benediction Paul offers the last words of his epistle:

> Now to Him who is able to establish you according to my gospel and the preaching of Jesus Christ, according to the revelation of the mystery kept secret since the world began but now made manifest, and by the prophetic Scriptures made known to all nations, according to the commandment of the everlasting God, for obedience to the faith—to God, alone wise, be glory through Jesus Christ forever. Amen. (Rom. 16:25–27)

Paul closes his epistle with the longest doxology that appears in any of his epistles. He first reminds his recipients that God alone establishes and confirms the saints at Rome. This doxological reminder comes on the heels of Paul's warnings about false teachers (Rom. 16:17–18). Therefore, Paul imbeds a reminder in his doxology that, ultimately, only God Himself protects, upholds, and establishes the church at Rome over and against the attempts of the false teachers to tear them down.

To what end, however, does Paul bless them? It is, of course, to the gospel of Jesus Christ. Paul wants the church at Rome centered on Christ and Him crucified (1 Cor. 2:2). Paul then explains the progressive march of the gospel through redemptive history. The gospel of Jesus Christ was a mystery in the Old Testament. But what is a *mystery*? Briefly, a mystery is something that was once hidden but is now revealed. Think of a classic Sherlock Holmes story, where someone commits a crime and Sherlock uncovers the criminal's identity only at the very end of the story. God formerly hid the specifics and the grandeur of the gospel of Christ. God's people knew its overall scope through various Old Testament passages, such as God's promise that Christ would crush the head of the serpent (Gen. 3:15), that His promise would come through Abraham (Gen. 12:3) and reach all the nations (Gen. 22:18), that it would come through King David (Ps. 2:7–8), and that it would eventually envelop the nations (Isa. 2:2). *Now*, with the revelation and incarnation of the Son—the second person of the Trinity, Jesus Christ, the Messiah, the God-man—we know the means by which God fulfilled these great promises.

Now, God has revealed the mystery. The Old Testament Scriptures were not the property of the nations but of one nation—namely, Israel. But through the propagation of the Word, the nations now possess the prophetic Scriptures and know of the revealed mystery of the gospel. Now the light of the gospel has burst forth on the nations. Recall that prior to the ministry of Christ the nations were enveloped in darkness and under the thumb of Satan. But now, as a result of Christ's ministry, He has poured out revelatory light on the nations. The Gospel of Matthew, for example, describes Israel sitting in the darkness and Christ's advent as the dawning of light (Matt. 4:15–16). Once Christ arrived, He entered the house of the strong man, bound him, and plundered his house (Matt. 12:29; cf. Luke 10:18; Rev. 20:2–3). By binding Satan, Christ shed the light of revelation on the world. What was once restricted to Israel now cascades throughout the world. Indeed, "the doctrines unfolded in this Epistle reveal to us the mighty plan of redemption, by which our powerful spiritual enemies are overcome, and all the strong and deeply-rooted evils lodged within our bosoms shall finally be subdued."[1]

1. Haldane, *Romans*, 710.

The Purpose of the Gospel

We must recognize the twin ends to which God revealed the mystery of the gospel of Christ. First, "the obedience of faith." Whenever ministers preach the gospel, God calls His people to obedience and repentance. Yes, God invites the world, as in the parable of the great wedding feast, but behind the invitation lies a command that requires our obedience. As Paul announced to the Athenians, God formerly overlooked the sins of man, but in the wake of the revelation of Christ He now commands everyone to repent (Acts 17:30). The same idea appears in the Great Commission in which Christ instructs the church to make disciples of all the nations (Matt. 28:19). The full and unfettered revelation of the gospel produces obedience, which in terms of the prophecies of Ezekiel and Jeremiah means that God places new hearts in His people and causes them to walk in His statutes (Ezek. 36:26–27; Jer. 31:33). This brings us to the second reason why God reveals the mystery of the gospel: so that their conduct brings glory to God. This is why Paul concludes his doxology with the words, "To God, alone wise, be glory through Jesus Christ forever. Amen" (Rom. 16:27).

How Shall We Live?

Paul concludes his epistle in the same way he began it. Paul is the herald for the inaugurated King, Jesus, and proclaims the gospel to the nations (Rom. 1:16–17). Everything Paul has written points to Christ. Christ is the culmination of all history—the revelation of the mystery of the gospel of Jesus Christ and the manifestation of God's glory, demonstrated in the salvation of Christ's bride, which is a display of God's love and mercy. The gospel is the means by which God causes His people to walk in His statutes—God's people obey His law. But when people do not repent and instead rebel, God still manifests His glory in His righteous judgment of the wicked. His judgment is a demonstration of his holiness and justice. All of history has been unfolding "according to the commandment of the everlasting God" (Rom. 16:26) for the supreme end of His glory: the revelation of the mystery of the gospel, the salvation of His people, and the judgment of the wicked. The revelation of the mystery, salvation, and judgment all rotate on the axis of God's glory. When we contemplate our lives, our actions, our thoughts, on what axis do they rotate? Do we listen to man and believe that our lives, actions, and thoughts rotate on the axis of self? Or do we believe that all life must rotate on the axis of God's glory? We must, of course, resoundingly affirm the latter, and only the gospel teaches us what we must believe and how we must act so we can glorify our triune Lord. God has redeemed us for obedience so that we can present our lives as living sacrifices. If we fail to do this, then we must ask the sobering question of whether we have truly understood the gospel of Jesus Christ.

Conclusion

God has brought us out from the kingdom of darkness into the kingdom of light. He has raised us from death to life. And God now conforms us to the image of His Son, Jesus Christ. The Holy Spirit enables us to walk in the paths of righteousness for the sake of Christ's name. Our triune God has given us all these blessings for one big reason—to glorify God and enjoy Him forever. How, then, shall we live? *Soli Deo gloria*, to the glory of God alone.